TIMED EXPOSURE

Mike Bugsgang

Best wishes
Mike Bugsgang
2015

ISBN 978-1-0685100-1-4

This book is dedicated to the memory of
Auntie Gertie:
Turned out nice again.

CONTENTS

PROLOGUE

3rd August 1970. It was a sweltering 94 degrees Fahrenheit afternoon in central London. With some trepidation, he crossed the grimy lino threshold of the short passageway adjacent to the entrance to the electrical shop that led to her flat's door. An overpowering smell of disinfectant pervaded, probably used by the shop staff to dispel the rank odours left compliments of the rough sleepers who used the passage as overnight accommodation. He stared at the buzzers on the wall and hesitated for a moment thinking back some twenty-four years since he had stood in this very spot. On that occasion, he was having a blazing row with the person whose name was displayed on one of the buzzers.

He had looked at himself in the shop windows on his approach to the flat. His appearance was a far cry from the stylish photographs he had taken in the past which had led to him being lauded in the media as the King of the Camera. A slight stoop made him look shorter than his six-foot height. His shirt with a worn and dirty collar was sticking to him from the heat. Ill-fitting baggy jeans looked as though they had just been rescued from a charity shop.

His tatty open toe sandals barely covered odd socks, one of which had a hole in it with a big toe protruding. His face was pale and gaunt exaggerating his large blue eyes with dark bags below them. The lenses of his trademark thick black glasses were scratched. His once sleek jet-black hair was, like his beard, grey and matted. And his breath reeked of alcohol consumed at the Valiant Trooper pub across Goodge Street. The publican had been eyeing him with disdain as he felt that this customer, although having paid for his drinks, was likely to turn off some of his regulars during the busy lunchtime period. Feeling the publican's vibe, he decided to depart.

Earlier, he dared not have attempted to visit the Fitzroy Tavern round the corner in Charlotte Street as somebody may have recognised him from the old days and demanded that his huge unpaid bar bill be settled. He had spent the past couple of hours drinking whisky until his money had run out. Dutch courage was the aim, but he was now questioning whether it had had the desired effect.

By a strange quirk of fate, the woman he was debating whether to call on, had earlier that lunchtime been dining with her nephew in the Spaghetti House on the opposite corner of Goodge Street to the Valiant Trooper. The nephew, the son of her elder brother, worked locally in Soho and regularly took his aunt out for a 'pasta treat' as she referred to it.

She was one of life's characters, a bubbly, diminutive powerhouse. Her pink plastic Alice band kept her blond highlighted perm in place. Her elfin shaped face was tanned from time spent in the sunshine on a bench in the public garden just behind the flat in Colville Place. Her modern, turquoise-coloured glasses perched neatly on the bridge of her tiny nose complemented her piercing blue eyes. Her jewellery consisted of a pair of small gold hoop earrings and a tiny gold Star of David pendant and chain necklace. Her white cotton blouse and navy slacks hung nicely on her petite frame.

She had lived in the area her entire life, all the local restaurateurs, shopkeepers and residents were extremely fond of her. The owners of the Spaghetti House were no exception. Mr and Mrs Lavarini, who had popped in that day, had come to her table, and made a great fuss of her. They recalled the fact that fifteen years previously, on the day the restaurant opened, she had been one of their very first customers. The couple insisted that she and her nephew's lunch would be on the house and instructed the restaurant manager accordingly.

His aunt had lots of Yiddish sayings that she

would whisper to him during lunch about other people in the restaurant. Inevitably, this would make him giggle. One of his favourites was 'look at the *fresser* over there.' This alluded to somebody who was gobbling their food down at a rate of knots. Another was when the waiters were moving around aimlessly. '*fershers*,' she'd say. In other words, they were wandering around without any real purpose. Two less than complimentary terms she used frequently were *putz* and *fershtinkiner*, the former meant a fool, also men's private parts, and the latter a louse or stinker.

Having finished lunch, she shared a joke with her nephew as they descended in the restaurant's old metal gated lift from her favoured third floor. As they walked out of the restaurant's main door to the sounds of *Arrivederci* and *Grazie* from the waiters and chefs, she gave them a regal wave. She took her nephew's arm as they were met by the summer heat and the unpleasant smell from the rubbish bins dotted along the pavement and exhaust fumes from the continuous flow of traffic along Goodge Street.

Her nephew always enjoyed the short walk back to the entrance of his aunt's flat as inevitably, shopkeepers would come out and chat to his aunt. The most amusing of these encounters was when the manager of the betting shop emerged and started to talk about the form for horse races that week and whether she would be coming in to place a bet on her favourite jockey Lester Piggott's mounts. This walk conjured up a scene towards the end of the recently released film *The Italian Job* when Noel Coward as Mr Bridger walked down a metal staircase in the prison to the cheers of the inmates and he casually acknowledged the applause with queen-like waves.

Part of the reason for this affection towards his aunt was that she had, for the past couple of years, been Camden Council's voluntary community officer for the area. Her sterling work had been recognised by the local press on numerous occasions and as a result, she was referred to in these articles as the Queen of Fitzrovia. She was extremely proud of her achievements and was quick to point one of these out to her nephew which was the placement of a new wooden bench seat on the corner of Goodge and Charlotte Streets. However, she was less pleased to see that local dogs had wasted no time in using the legs of the new installation as a urinal. 'That's really taking the piss,' she blurted out then immediately saw the funny side of what she had said and in unison with her nephew started to laugh.

Arriving at the entrance passage to her flat,

her nephew gave her a kiss on the cheek and headed off round the corner on the way back to his office. She pulled out her keys, opened the door and went up the stairs to her flat.

Shortly after, her tentative caller hovered in the same passageway, if he pressed the buzzer, the 'King' would be meeting the 'Queen.'

CHAPTER 1 – THE DAGO BANDITS

The saying: "Thick as thieves," could have been created specifically for the Levi family. The family's origin dated back to the 1700s when they went under the name of Levini. They were from the Sephardi sector of Jewry in Italy and were brigands who terrorised the inhabitants of villages around Naples.

This was a particularly turbulent period in Italian history. In 1701 the Conspiracy of Macchia took place which saw the nobles of Naples revolting against swearing allegiance to the new Bourbon King, Philip V of Spain. Presumably, with the aim of gaining more power for themselves, they favoured a new regime under the Austrian monarch, Leopold I. Although far from being considered nobles, quite the opposite, the Levini family decided to back the uprising. However, once the leader of the revolt, the Prince of Macchia, prohibited the looting of private houses, the lower classes of the Naples region, like the Levinis, had no appetite for the uprising and it petered out after just three days.

The Prince of Macchia fled to Vienna but the Levinis and others who had joined the conspiracy, had a ransom placed on their heads by the Spanish authorities. The Levinis were tipped off that a squad of soldiers was making its way to arrest the family at their extensive villa in Mercato, a suburb of Naples. With the prospect of execution, the only likely outcome, the Levinis, all twenty-nine of them, including women and children, gathered up their valuable ill-gotten gains and sped north on horseback and in carts. Their arduous journey took them through the various states of Italy, the Swiss Confederation and finally, France. From Dunkirk, they crossed the English Channel arriving at the port of Colchester in Essex. Italy's loss was certainly not England's gain.

The family established a base near Chelmsford and changed its name to Levi. The gold and jewels they had brought with them helped to ensure a seamless integration into the local community. This included the purchase of a large farm and livestock in a suitably remote area. Despite initial difficulties with the English language, the family gradually learned to converse with the locals and even picked up an Essex accent. But farming was never the intended source for the Levi family's future income.

Frequenting brewhouses in the region, the Levi menfolk heard stories about the lucrative rewards of highwaymen. This appeared to be an ideal opportunity to carry on where they had left off back in Naples, robbing. To avoid suspicion, the Levi men purchased pistols and ammunition from different locations far away from Chelmsford. They were all expert horsemen and with cloaks, masks and tricorn hats made by the women of the family, it was not long before they were fully equipped to begin a new reign of terror in the English countryside.

The Levis first forays into hold-ups verged on the hilarious. Having managed to halt the stagecoach, getting the driver and passengers to understand their Italian-Essex accented demands proved problematic. Despite the accompanying hand waving gestures by the Levis, the robberies were protracted. This together with the Levis, in typical Italian style, flirting with attractive female passengers, added to the danger of the Queen's soldiers, who were becoming increasingly adept at capturing highwaymen, arriving during the hold-up.

Following a couple of close calls with soldiers turning up literally a few minutes after the robbers had departed, to make their hold-ups more expedient, the Levis decided to rehearse a typical scenario on their farm. They even went to the extent of borrowing a stagecoach from the local stables. What they did not legislate for was the reaction of the ageing matriarch of the family who was posing as a passenger. In full highwayman regalia, two of the Levi men, the brothers, Giuseppe and Franco, halted the coach as it made its way through one of the more enclosed fields on the farm, far from any prying eyes.

'Hold hands this is an up-stick,' Franco cried. 'No, no said Giuseppe, you're saying it all wrong. You should point your pistol at the driver and shout, stick 'em-up, this is a hold-up.' '*Si, si,*' Franco replied in an exasperated manner. He then dismounted, flung open the stagecoach door and yelled at the role-playing family members inside: '*In piedi*, money or your liver!' 'Non, non,' said Giuseppe still on horseback, slapping his head, 'too much Italian, and wrong English words. Stand and deliver, money or your life, is the correct way to say it.'

Franco turned to his brother and was about to reply when he received a crashing blow to the head with a handbag that sent his tricorn hat flying. The matriarch who had leant out of the coach screamed: 'Franco, '*stupido*, can't you see it's your *nonna* you are robbing?' '*Mamma mia,*' Franco exclaimed, retrieving his hat from a cow pat, 'has nobody explained to *nonna* that we are rehearsing a robbery, not carrying out one?'

Eventually, Franco and Giuseppe mastered the art of the highwayman and made the London Road running through Epping Forest their hunting ground. Despite their efforts to disguise the Italian inflection in their speech, it still existed during their hold-ups. Consequently, they gained a reputation from the authorities, victims, and rivals, earning them the nickname, *The Dago Bandits.*

Highway robbery proved a lucrative business for the Levis and as the 1700s rolled on towards the beginning of the 19th century, other male and female members of the family succeeded Franco and Giuseppe in this line of work. Although not deeply religious, during these years, members of the Levi family married other Essex based Jews. The ceremonies took place in Synagogue Yard, Angel Lane in Colchester. In line with tradition, on these occasions, the bridegroom led by the bride's father, preceded by the Rabbi and friends with a band, were followed by the bride clad in white and veiled, with her mother and grandmother. Under a canopy supported by four men, the form of solemnisation in Hebrew was read out. At the conclusion, after the bride and groom had each drunk part of a glass of wine, it was thrown to the ground to denote that as the glass could never be made again, so difficult would it be for them to be separated in life. A public feast followed, and the day concluded with festivities. However, prior to any betrothals, it was made clear that newcomers to the Levi clan would have to enter the family business.

The spoils from their crimes enabled the Levis to purchase further properties in the Essex region. But as the new century dawned, it became apparent that the family would need to seek alternative income streams. In 1772 legislation was brought in that stated anyone caught perpetrating armed robbery in disguise on the roads would receive the death sentence. In addition, more mounted patrols were established around London and big rewards were granted to informers disclosing the whereabouts of highwaymen. The final straw came in 1802 when one of the Levi gang's close associates, Robert *Robber* Snook, became the last highwayman to be hanged. Some of the Levis travelled to Hemel Hempstead in Hertfordshire, the county adjacent to the family's farm in Essex, to witness the execution. Snook was a jovial fellow to the last. He quipped from the gantry as some of the crowd ran to see his demise that they should not hurry as nothing would happen until the hangman had secured the noose.

In the days that followed the hanging, the family started to plan new forms of crime that would keep them in the manner to which they had become accustomed since their arrival in England from Italy a century earlier. Profiting from burglary, drug dealing, extortion, prostitution and shoplifting in the 1800s would more than compensate for the good old days of highway robbery. And all this using the ever-popular music hall as a smokescreen. Intriguing? It would certainly prove to be just that.

CHAPTER 2 – THAT'S ENTERTAINMENT

The early years of the 19th century were highly lucrative for the Levis as their meticulous planning and execution of burglaries of wealthy people's homes in Essex netted huge quantities of gold, silver, jewellery and cash. Added to these hauls, the family were enjoying regular income from a protection racket extracting payments from innkeepers, acting as pimps for prostitutes that operated from Levi family-owned brothels near the inns and making laudanum available for clients in the brothels. But as the years passed, it became evident to the Levis that restricting their activities to the Essex region was becoming prohibitive. For example, the wealthy homeowners whose properties had been Levi targets bandied together to hire teams of vigilantes to prevent further break-ins. The innkeepers took similar action by contracting muscle from the docks at Colchester to be present when Levi family members called to collect their payments. The final straw came when the prostitutes upped skirts but not for the normal reason; they realised that plying their trade was considerably more profitable in the East End of London and departed.

A Levi council of war was convened to

discuss the situation and it was decided that moving their operations to London was essential. The capital now governed over a quarter of the world's population. And with its own exploding population, its inhabitants had an insatiable appetite for every conceivable pleasure known to man which provided an irresistible opportunity. The Levis had become highly skilled in the various forms of crime they had perpetrated in Essex, and this would serve them well in their new base. Arrangements were rapidly put in place to sell the properties they had acquired around Essex, but the existing *head office* farmstead would be retained as a countryside location to stash the proceeds of future heists guarded over by several Levi families. The priority then was to source a suitable property in London large enough to house the remainder of the clan.

The Levi patriarch in the mid 1800s was Alfonso, a short sixty-year-old muscular man with bowlegs, a barrel chest, powerful arms covered in gorilla-like black hair matching that surrounding his head below a bald pate. His eyes were dark brown on either side of a broken nose. His olive visage sported a small vertical scar on the left cheek. This was not the type of man you would want to argue with.

Alfonso had London based contacts in the Clerkenwell area where a community of Italian immigrants had been established. Through these contacts, he had heard about plans to build Italianate style villas as part of a redevelopment of parkland known as The Regent's Park on the outskirts of the capital. The architect was John Nash. Through an intermediary, Alfonso set-up a meeting with Nash at the site where the first villa was nearing completion. On seeing the property, Alfonso knew instantly that it was the ideal location for the Levis to be based, especially as it abutted a canal network along which "goods" could be transported under the cover of night. The three-story house had a stucco finish with Palladian pillars at the entrance and was surrounded in mature greenery. It had a raised ground floor providing elevated views of the grounds from its reception rooms. There were 14 bedrooms, one with a balcony that Alfonso mentally noted would be his, three dressing rooms, a library, kitchen, drawing room, garden room, two large reception rooms, and a second kitchen with a larder and cellar. It had about three quarters of an acre of grounds.

Despite his inner enthusiasm for the property, as a shrewd businessman, outwardly, Alfonso gave nothing away during the negotiations with Nash. In fact, he feigned indifference towards the place. 'This house is nice, but it is not as stylish as I would like. I want something that will really impress my business associates when they visit,' Alfonso explained. Nash was a distinguished man, taller than Alfonso and more articulate than the would-be purchaser but failed to use these attributes to his advantage during their exchanges. Desperate for a sale, Nash responded, 'I am sure that I could make adjustments to meet your requirements.' Alfonso's tactics worked. Nash was not well versed in matters of business, in fact, his company had gone into bankruptcy earlier in his career, the outcome was a price considerably lower than the architect's original estimation was agreed.

Part one of Alfonso's master plan was now in place. Part two, which entailed the construction of a plausible cover or front for the Levi's activities, would demand a great deal more thought. As a boy in the late 1700s, Alfonso had been taken on a trip to London by his parents during which the family visited the Vauxhall Pleasure Gardens. The experience of the visit lived on into his adulthood. The Gardens, originally opened on a sixteen acres site in 1660, had become popular with Londoners who, a century later, had tired of public hangings, cock fights and bear baiting as forms of entertainment. They wanted a more relaxed way to spend their weekends. Vauxhall offered a mix of concerts, dining, drinking, firework displays and walks in pleasant surroundings punctuated with fake gothic ruins. Initially, admission was free with revenues derived from food and drink, however, as time moved on, more activities were added such as gambling and an entrance charge was made.

The prospect of a single location that had thousands of people visiting eager to spend their hard-earned cash opened up all sorts of criminal opportunities in the mind of the adult Alfonso. But by the 1800s, the pleasure gardens concept was in decline. Londoners tastes in entertainment had changed again. In the cellars and basements of hotels around Covent Garden, Holborn and Marylebone, a new type of amusement was emerging, music hall. Following the conclusion of his successful negotiations to purchase the villa in The Regent's Park, Alfonso decided to extend his stay in London to carry out some research into this new pastime. His forays included visits to The Cole Hole in The Strand, Evans' Late Joy's in Covent Garden, and The Cyder Cellars in The Rose of Normandy Concert Hall in Marylebone.

It was at the latter he met an aspiring actor by the name of Charles Dickens, a handsome fellow with an oval face, beautiful eyes, and an abundance of thick brown hair. Although over thirty years Alfonso's junior, the older man was greatly impressed by the young man's confidence as he performed at an audition despite the encumbrance of a heavy cold. Following Dickens audition in which he mimicked the popular comedian, George Matthews, the two men sat and chatted with The Rose of Normandy's owner, Sam Collins.

Dickens admitted that his love of the theatre had started at an early age. 'As a child, I was taken to see the famous clown, Joseph Grimaldi in Kent. From that moment on, I knew that I was destined to become a performer. However, I am now torn between whether to pursue my dream or settle for a career in journalism which would provide a more secure regular income.' He went on to outline his awful experience in the boot blacking factory near Charing Cross where he had been forced to work as a child owing to his father's incarceration in the debtor's prison, The Marshalsea. 'This situation arose because of a lack of sufficient income for my father to support his family. It brought home to me the plight of London's poor, particularly in the Clerkenwell area, including the Italian community. Articles that I write could highlight this dilemma and help these folk.'

Quick to latch on to a potential opportunity, Alfonso thought that this earnest young man could be useful to him in the future. He made a note of Dickens' address in Camden Town and explained that he was in the process of moving his family to a location nearby and that he would be in contact to continue their discussion when convenient. Dickens left but Alfonso stayed to talk to Collins, an affable man who had made a name for himself treading the boards before purchasing The Rose. During the conversation, out of the blue, Alfonso stated that he would be interested in buying the concert hall. Naturally, Collins was taken aback by this suggestion but as he had been suffering ill health of late, said that he might be interested in such a proposal providing the price was right. The two men shook hands and agreed to meet the following week to discuss the matter together with their legal representatives present.

Unlike the architect John Nash, Collins was an accomplished businessman. He was over six feet tall with a chubby face and curly black hair. Born of Irish parents in Marylebone, he started life as a chimney sweep. Later he spent many years as one of the highest paid entertainers of the period performing at venues around Britain. His act combined bawdy Irish songs and jokes that audiences loved. In direct contrast to most of his contemporaries, Collins did not fritter away his earnings on drink and gambling but invested his money. This prudence enabled him to purchase the 800-seat Rose of Normandy Concert Hall in Marylebone which attracted sell-out performances virtually every night. Therefore, when the parties met, Collins was in a strong position to hold on for the price he was seeking, £8000, a not inconsiderable sum for the time. Indeed, Collins was already planning the acquisition of another concert hall, The Lansdowne in Islington, with the proceeds of the sale of The Rose.

'I was thinking that £5000 would be a fair price,' Alfonso said as his opening gambit in the negotiations. During the discussion that ensued, Alfonso gradually increased his offer but despite the haggling, Collins would not budge. 'What you are failing to recognise is the important fact that the price includes the contracts of the top-class acts that are booked for the year ahead,' Collins stated. 'This will inevitably result in full houses to be achieved during this period,' he added. Somewhat frustrated, Alfonso requested a week to discuss the deal with his advisors and family but assured Collins that it would almost certainly go ahead. The two men shook hands and parted amicably having agreed a time to reconvene the following week at The Rose. Although a relatively young man in his late thirties, Collins had not been in the best of health for some time. However, it seemed something of a coincidence that a few days after the meeting, he was found drowned in the canal to the north of The Regent's Park. The assumption was that he had been out walking alone and fallen in after suffering a seizure and the dent in the back of his skull had occurred by hitting the brick embankment as he entered the canal. Collins' widow who was a co-director of the business was still in shock when she hurriedly agreed to the sale to Alfonso Levi a short time after the funeral of her husband. Another coincidence was that one of the Collins' legal advisors hailed from the Italian community in Clerkenwell.

Having moved with a good proportion of the Levi family into the new mansion in The Regent's Park, Alfonso began to establish himself as an impresario at the nearby Rose. Unusually for him though, his entry to the world of entertainment was not properly thought through. Alfonso's intention from the outset was to use the concert hall as a cover for his family's illicit activities. But instead of going about this in a discreet manner, he unwittingly drew unwelcome attention to his plans for two reasons. Firstly, he decided The Rose needed some refurbishment. A small amount of work would have sufficed but Alfonso contracted John Nash to undertake the project. Consequently, the cost spiralled with the introduction of Italianate features including twenty huge crystal chandeliers. These luxurious enhancements naturally attracted the attention of the press and articles began to appear in newspapers and magazines accompanied by pictures of Alfonso. Realising the error of his ways, true to his business instincts, Alfonso considered ways to recoup the outlay for the refurbishment work. Additional matinee performances and a minimal increase in entry fees would be necessary whilst cost savings could be made by reducing payments to artistes and staff. However, the problem with the latter was that contracts were in place with these performers for at least the next twelve months.

Oblivious to the potential downside to this approach, Alfonso, flanked by two of his heavy-set sons, started to summon the contracted artistes and stagehands in to advise that they would have to carry out additional work and take a cut in their already low wages (between thirty shillings and £3 a week). Predictably, this action resulted in a rebuttal by the workers who immediately called a strike. Within a short space of time, Alfonso had once again accidentally managed to prompt journalists to write stories about The Rose. But this time, the articles were not flattering.

A picket line was formed outside the concert hall in Marylebone and was joined by leading artistes of the day. This provided great copy for the newspapers some of which depicted caricatures of Alfonso Levi as the Merchant of Venice. Other concert hall owners saw Alfonso's plan as an opportunity to increase their profits and started to take the same action. Almost immediately, the strike spread around all the London concert halls. Desperate to book artistes, the owners started to call upon retired performers, lesser-known acts, and youngsters keen to become entertainers, all of whom would be prepared to cross the picket lines. On one occasion an aged female singer was seen entering The Rose and the pickets shouted, 'let her through, she'll close the hall quicker than we can!'

The leader of the pickets outside The Rose was a burly loud-mouthed man named Mick Rafferty who had worked as a stagehand at the concert hall for the past four years. Not surprisingly, his militant style and ability to influence the other staff and performers' thinking irked Alfonso and his sons. Rafferty hailed from the growing Irish immigrant quarter in nearby Paddington and was noted for his boxing prowess in pub brawls that were a regular occurrence in the area. At first his fellow pickets were concerned about

Mick's failure to turn up for duty on the line assuming he had been involved in another of his bar room altercations. Then after a week, nobody thought anymore about his sudden disappearance simply believing that he had moved on to pastures new. These same pickets made no connection to the cuts and bruises that Alfonso's sons displayed during their appearances at The Rose in this period.

The dispute dragged on for a couple of weeks but as audiences started to dwindle, the owners ultimately had to climb down and withdraw their demands. The workers had won and formed a union to support them in the future should similar issues arise.

This outcome created a further quandary for Alfonso. Not only would he have to honour the contracts of the artistes and Rose permanent staff but would now have to find work for the lesser-known acts he had booked for the coming weeks as he had assumed the strike would be more protracted. Many of these performers were on the bread line and were desperate for money. As he had done many times in the past when faced with a problem, Alfonso's thoughts turned to his ancestors and the way they would have tackled an issue back in Naples in the 1700s. During this era, a special force of 12 regiments comprising Neapolitan men had been constituted to fight the Austrian army. In between battles, the soldiers who were paid a pittance, sought other forms of income and some had been co-opted by the Levinis to assist them in various criminal activities. This of course took place prior to the family's hurried departure from Naples ironically pursued by soldiers from the very same regiments.

Suddenly, the solution came to Alfonso. He would coerce these unfortunate impoverished souls into becoming his *Irregulars* and with the help of his family, train them to commit crimes that would provide a good source of supplementary income for the firm. It is speculated that many years later, the famous author, Arthur Conan Doyle, obtained the idea for the gang of street urchins named *The Irregulars*, in his Sherlock Holmes books from hearing about the Levis' criminals. The spoils from the Levis' group work could be brought to The Rose via the secluded back entrance and stored in a private area of the cellars before being transported in bulk by a trusted family member to a waiting barge on the Regent's Canal for its onward journey to the farm in Essex. Thereafter, the merchandise would be "fenced" by a network of shady dealers around England.

Following some initial teething problems which involved the younger and older artists failing to see eye to eye when carrying out robberies (on some occasions the oldies fell asleep whilst acting as look-outs when the youngsters were breaking into houses), Alfonso's plan began to pay-off. Despite the establishment of a police force in 1829 because of the Home Secretary, Robert Peel's Metropolitan Police Act, crimes in and around the London area were still widespread. Consequently, the Levi family's Irregulars were extremely successful in their exploits with hardly any arrests. The few that were caught obviously made no mention of their connection to the Levis for fear of retribution from the family whose tentacles extended even into prisons. With substantial hauls of cash, jewellery and expensive antiques pouring in via the back door of The Rose, Alfonso decided that the Irregulars activities should be expanded to include protection rackets, prostitution, and drug dealing, all of which had proved profitable when operated by the family in Essex.

Alfonso died of natural causes in 1846 at the age of eighty-one. He was succeeded as the head of the Levi family by his son, Lorenzo who seamlessly carried on the running of the "business" which continued to include the lawful concert hall enterprise as well as the unlawful activities. However, when Lorenzo was killed in a gangland knife fight on the steps of the Italian church in Clerkenwell in 1870, the baton passed to his twin brother Tommaso. After his sudden death just two years later, the reins were handed to his younger brother Davide. There was a fourth brother, Leonardo, but he was estranged from his father and siblings. The reason for this separation was Leonardo disagreed with his family's nefarious dealings and wanted no part of them. Instead, in 1860, he opened the first fish & chip shop in London, in the East End. This new cheap meal concept caught on fast and during the following years, he expanded the business with outlets across the capital including Soho.

Except for his swarthy complexion, Davide was physically quite different from his father and siblings. He was tall and lean at six feet with long black hair, brown eyes, high cheek bones, an aquiline nose and a pointy dimpled chin. Davide also spoke perfect English with no hint of Italian heritage in his accent thanks to his private education at Harrow School. This education had differentiated him in other ways too. He was much more of a thinker than a thug. A good description of his character would be brains rather than brawn. At the age of 22, he married his childhood sweetheart, a pretty petite local Jewish girl of Italian lineage, Rebecca Sandleman, at the synagogue in Great

Portland Street, London, shortly after it opened in 1869. A year later, the couple became proud parents to a daughter, Ruth.

CHAPTER 3 – BY ROYAL APPOINTMENT

The arrival of the 20th century saw the Levis' legal business empire expand further under the astute guidance of Davide Levi with the acquisition of two more concert halls, one in Holborn and the other in Hackney. This expansion also enabled the illegal side of the enterprise to increase by infiltrating areas around the new venues. In line with these moves, the Levis' army of Irregulars grew as performers and staff were keen to top up their meagre wages which were, despite strikes, still well below average for the period.

The death of Queen Victoria in 1901 heralded the coronation of her son King Edward VII. "Bertie" as he was known, owing to his appetite for the fair sex, was nicknamed "Edward the Caresser," or less flatteringly," Dirty Bertie," during his long wait to accede to the throne. Nevertheless, he was regarded as much more fun than his mother who in the latter years of her reign had become something of a recluse following the death of her beloved consort, Prince Albert. Both as a Prince and then King, Bertie was a great fan of music hall and regularly attended shows at theatres as well as requesting private performances at royal venues.

On one such occasion during his time as the Prince of Wales, Bertie went to see a play, the comedy, *She Stoops to Conquer* starring the socialite Lillie Langtry in her debut stage role at The Rose. The Prince was smitten by Langtry who had already achieved a degree of fame by becoming the first socialite to appear on an advertising poster for Pears Soap. Taking Davide Levi aside, the Prince asked if he could be introduced to the attractive actress. Only too delighted to assist with this request that could only benefit the Levis in the long run, Davide made the necessary arrangements but was then surprised to be asked by his royal highness to make a room available above the concert hall for subsequent meetings between the Prince and Mrs Langtry. The request included various ingredients for a cocktail created by the Prince should be placed in the room. The contents of a "Prince of Wales" cocktail were champagne, angostura bitters, sugar syrup, rye whiskey, maraschino liqueur, squares of pineapple and crushed ice.

This discreet arrangement continued into August 1888 when the Prince summoned Davide for a private word. 'Doubtless you will have read about these awful murders in the East End being perpetrated by a man referred to as Jack the Ripper in the newspapers,' the

Prince confided.' 'I most certainly have your Royal Highness, it's the talk of our customers on a nightly basis,' Davide replied. 'Well, this has presented me with something of a problem,' the Prince continued. 'You see, there is speculation in certain quarters that my younger brother Eddy, is somehow involved with these murders. Complete nonsense you understand but it's something I need to quash urgently as slurs on the Royal Family are unacceptable.' Davide thought for a moment before responding then said: 'I have the utmost sympathy your Royal Highness, family integrity is paramount in life, but how can I be of assistance?'

Although the two men were alone in the room, the Prince drew Davide closer and whispered, 'Obviously, I cannot disclose the reason for my regular visits to your establishment, but I need to provide an alibi for Eddy as the police inspector assigned to the case, a Mr Frederick Abberline, has requested permission to interview Eddy at the earliest opportunity.' Being aware of the Prince's younger brother's predilection for company of the same sex, Davide whispered back: 'Presumably, Prince Albert Victor does not have a suitable alibi for the nights in question?' 'Absolutely correct,' the Prince muttered whilst clearing his throat in a nervous manner. 'What I propose is that when he meets Abberline, he tells him that he was here with me on the dates in question enjoying drinks in a private room after the show. The Inspector is sure to want to verify Eddy's account of his whereabouts and will visit you to confirm these facts.'

'To quote the famous line from *She Stoops to Conquer* your Royal Highness, "Ask me no questions and I'll tell you no lies," Davide whispered under his breath, winking at the same time. 'You have my assurance that your request will be carried out when the Inspector calls. And have no worries about my staff, they will be suitably rewarded to collaborate the story if requested by the police.' The portly Prince gave a sigh of relief and thanked Davide profusely, suggesting that if he required any favours in the future, he should just ask. As the Prince departed, Davide's mind was already racing as to how this offer could be used to best effect in the development of the family business.

As correctly predicted by the Prince, the Inspector turned up without warning at The Rose a few days later and demanded to see Davide. Beneath his bowler hat, the policeman sported impressive bushy sideburns that wrapped around to form a beard and moustache. By the aggressive tone adopted by Abberline, it was apparent that he was under immense pressure to apprehend the murderer as large sections of London's soaring population, especially around the Whitechapel area, were living in fear. The streets of the East End were crammed with immigrants, Chinese, Malays, Irish, all competing for space with Jewish refugees from Russia. Before Davide could offer his guest refreshments the Inspector blurted out in a broad Cockney beer-soaked breath accent: 'Now look 'ere Levi, I've heard on the grapevine about yer little non-theatrical side-line, but I'm not interested in that, I've got bigger fish to fry right now. The sodding newspapers are printing sensationalist articles every day regarding vigilante groups being formed to patrol the East End streets because the police are failing to make an arrest.' Davide, as always, immaculately attired, remained cool during the interview and reassured the detective that the Prince and his younger brother were drinking at The Rose on the nights in question. In the light of yet another lead on the murders disintegrating, the Inspector stormed out of the concert hall without bothering to question any of the staff. As the door slammed behind him Davide grinned and murmured to himself: 'Enjoy your fish and chips Inspector.'

The early years of the Edwardian era saw another explosion in the popularity of music hall entertainment. Bigger and better theatres were being built in London, notably the Coliseum financed by Oswald Stoll. Whilst both sides of the Levi family business continued to thrive, Davide realised that the market for music hall audiences was becoming increasingly competitive. He had to find a way of differentiating his concert halls from others. Although several years had elapsed since Davide had "assisted" the Prince of Wales by providing an alibi for his younger brother, the time had come to call in the favour offered by the then Prince who was now King Edward VII. Whilst recently purchasing a pair of hand-made boots from John Lobb in Jermyn Street, Davide noticed a large sign on the shop's façade displaying the Royal Coat of Arms. Before leaving, he asked to see the shop's manager. The gentleman in question appeared with a flourish through a pair of thick velvet purple drapes at the back of the establishment and presented Davide with his card. It read R. Sole Esquire, Manager, John Lobb Limited, Bootmaker and bore the Royal Coat of Arms. Supressing his laughter about the man's apt but also humorous name, Davide was intrigued to learn that the sign on the shop's exterior and the card signified a Royal Warrant awarded by the monarch to businesses providing the highest standards of products and services. Subsequent enquiries by Davide revealed that no theatres had been issued a Royal Warrant to date. He reasoned that with the public's admiration for the monarchy running at an all-time high, it would be a coup to be able to display huge signs on the exterior of the Levi concert halls stating they had been granted a Royal Warrant by Appointment to His Majesty the King.

It was no surprise that Davide's application for a Royal Warrant was met with disdain by the King's advisors. Mutterings of "Dago Upstart" were heard in the corridors of power both in Parliament and at Buckingham Palace. But the King remained true to his word remembering the much-needed help Levi had provided and further stunned his entourage by suggesting that he would unveil the plaque at The Rose. Naturally, Davide was delighted with the King's response and immediately started to plan the event that would go under the title of a Royal Variety Performance. The biggest music hall stars of the day were duly booked including Marie Lloyd, Vesta Tilley, George Robey and Harry Lauder. Invitations were issued to the country's elite and the acceptances poured in by return. Before entering the concert hall for the show, the assembled nobility gathered outside to witness the King assisted by Davide unveil the gold embossed plaque that sparkled in the sunshine. A very proud moment for the Levi family members who had joined the throng. Everyone then filed inside for a champagne and caviar reception. Marie Lloyd opened the show with a rousing rendition of the song that had become her signature tune, "My Old Man Said Follow the Van," which even saw the King singing along in the Royal Box. During the interval, several of the guests fumbled for their wallets only to find that they had been mislaid. The Levi Irregulars obviously had a bumper day outside earlier.

It was not many years after this joyful event that things started to turn sour for the Levis. King Edward VII's short reign came to an abrupt end. His life as a bon viveur finally took its toll. Having returned from a holiday in Biarritz in France where he had become ill, he went to Buckingham Palace. His son, George, shortly to become King George V, told him his horse, "Witch of the Air" had won its race at Kempton Park. The King said: 'Yes, I have heard of it, I am glad.' These were his last words. Davide Levi was amongst the invited dignitaries to attend the King's funeral. As the gun carriage bearing the dead monarch's body passed, Davide thought back to a recent private audience he had had with the King a few months ago just before Christmas 1909. At this meeting, the King had expressed his concerns about his nephew, the German Emperor,

Wilhelm II. He predicted that Wilhelm would ultimately tip Europe into war.

The death of the monarch coincided with increasing competition in the Levis' music hall and criminal enterprises. Many of the new concert halls were considerably larger than the Levis' establishments and had expanded their gambling operations which delivered even greater profits. On the criminal front it had become apparent to Davide that the family needed to have a presence in the very centre of London's West End, Soho. It was here that the real money was to be made rather than in the peripheral areas of Marylebone, Holborn and Hackney, the locations of the Levis' venues. The trouble was that the Maltese and Chinese factions had already gained a foothold in Soho and would not take kindly to an interloper on their territory.

Around this time Davide received news from some of his cousins who had left Britain to set-up home in New York. They reported that the city was booming economically and if he was prepared to back them financially, they would be keen to start a branch of the family business in the city. In the circumstances, Davide thought it wise to explore the opportunity in America first before entering a turf war in Soho. An immediate problem that occurred to him in this connection was how could he get the considerable sums of money that would be required to start a New York company to his cousins without attracting the attention of the tax and customs inspectors on both sides of the Atlantic? Through the ages gold had always been the international currency. The Levis had plenty of the commodity stashed in their Essex farmstead awaiting the next round of deliveries to fences around the country. Now Davide thought was the time to put it to better use. Firstly, it would need to be smelted into bars then hidden in the chassis of a specially built car to carry it onto an ocean liner for the crossing to New York. Davide travelled to the Rolls Royce factory in Derby and discussed his requirements with the designers of the company's Silver Ghost model. Naturally, he did not disclose what the deeper footplates and extended boot compartment with a disguised second shelf was for. The cost of the car with the specially added features would be just under £5000. Davide confirmed the purchase and wrote a cheque for a fifty percent deposit. His next task would be to make the travel arrangements.

In early 1912 the newspapers were full of articles about the White Star Line's newest vessel, RMS Titanic. The liner was nearing completion at the Harland and Wolff Shipyard in Belfast in readiness for its maiden voyage across the Atlantic to New York. Davide Levi had read the coverage in the press about the "unsinkable" ship with its opulent cabins and decided that this would be the ideal way to accompany his new car with its special cargo to visit his relatives in America. He booked first class tickets at a cost of £30 each for himself and his wife and daughter. Before boarding, the Levis stood on the dockside at Southampton and watched the Silver Ghost with it secreted gold bars hoisted by a crane on to the Titanic and lowered into the cargo hold.

On the fateful night of 14th April 1912, the Titanic hit an iceberg just four days into its voyage. Earlier that evening Davide dined with Rebecca and Ruth. The ladies had retired to their cabins whilst Davide stayed in the first-class lounge drinking brandy discussing America's economic prospects with two New York based businessmen he had become acquainted with during the past few days at sea. Not long after the impact of hitting the iceberg, Davide noticed that the stewards were being briefed by a ship's officer. Davide strode over to the impromptu meeting and demanded to know what was happening. On hearing the severity of the news, he ran back to awaken Rebecca and Ruth, urging them to put on as much warm clothing as they possibly could and to follow him up on deck. Preparations had already commenced in uncovering the lifeboats with stewards calling for woman and children from first-class cabins to put on lifejackets and step forward. Davide kissed his wife and daughter and despite their reluctance to leave him, shepherded them onboard a lifeboat. As the craft was lowered to the sound of loud creaking, Davide waved to his beloved family who sat huddled together for warmth in the half empty boat and shouted 'Shalom.' It was the last time he would see them.

Instead of rowing away from the sinking ship, the two oarsmen on the lifeboat thought they should try to fill the boat to capacity. Therefore, they drifted near the ship to pick up people who were jumping into the freezing sea. This proved a fatal error of judgement. Literally within minutes, swarms of desperate passengers swam to the lifeboat and began to haul themselves onboard. The weight of this influx caused the boat to capsize, and Rebecca and Rachel Levi were trapped underneath and drowned in the icy water. Mercifully, Davide did not witness this tragic episode. Still onboard Titanic, he was told incorrectly by an officer that as all women and children had been safely evacuated, first-class male passengers should board a lifeboat on the other side of the ship. Davide followed these instructions without hesitation only stopping to grab a couple of bottles of brandy from the unattended top deck bar. He boarded a lifeboat that was also only partially occupied, and it was lowered into the sea. But unlike his wife and daughter's ill-fated journey, the oarsmen rowed as fast as they could to escape the final downward surge of the Titanic that was now three quarters submerged.

Swigging from the brandy bottle to keep warm, Davide passed it around the other men and oarsmen. The stern of Titanic disappeared into the black sea just two hours and forty minutes after it had hit the iceberg. The eerie silence was punctuated occasionally by screams for help from passengers drowning, then there was no sound at all until about an hour later. Through the darkness, lights from RMS Carpathia appeared. The rescue of passengers from the Titanic's lifeboats was carried out most efficiently by the Carpathia's crew but took several hours. Fit enough to climb a rope ladder, Davide was one of the first male survivors aboard. With a blanket wrapped around him, he scoured the ship's decks over the next few hours seeking his wife and daughter. To no avail. It was only when Carpathia set sail later that morning Davide finally realised that his dear Rebecca and Ruth were lost forever. As the ship slowly manoeuvred through the floating ice packs bound for New York, he leant against the rail shivering in the cold trying to hold back the tears. But the Levi resolve in him remained strong. Of course, he would grieve but ultimately continue with his plans for the business. However, the creation of an American branch would have to be shelved for the time being as the means to fund it now lay at the bottom of the Atlantic Ocean.

When the Carpathia arrived in New York the dockside was packed with thousands of people. Davide's relatives greeted him but were devasted to learn of Rebecca and Ruth's fate. They immediately arranged for him to attend the B'nai Jeshurun Synagogue in Manhattan where, the following day, joined by his US family members and their friends, they recited the Kaddish, the Jewish prayer for the dead, in memory of their relatives who had perished at sea just five days earlier.

Davide saw little point in staying longer in New York. After explaining to his cousins that the US Levi business would have to be temporarily put on hold, he booked a passage on the Carpathia which was due to sail for Europe, it's original destination before it was forced to return to New York with the Titanic's survivors. During the crossing he met a charming lady who had lost her husband on the Titanic. Joined in common grief, Sara

Strauss, a Jewess whose husband had been a wealthy textile manufacturer in Manchester, was 18 years Davide's junior, but they found comfort in discussing their deceased spouses over dinner most nights of the voyage. On disembarkation at Southampton, they agreed to stay in touch and went their separate ways.

Back at his home in London, Davide received an invitation to sit on the inquiry panel charged with investigating the Titanic disaster, but he declined. Nothing would bring back his beloved wife and daughter, so why bother? He needed to sharpen his focus on the Levi businesses now urgently requiring impetus.

CHAPTER 4 – OH WHAT A LOVELY WAR!

Just one year later in 1913, it became apparent that King Edward's prediction about his nephew, Wilhelm II of Germany, sowing the seeds of war in Europe, was coming to fruition. During the early years of the 20th Century, Wilhelm, nicknamed Kaiser Bill, revelled in the title the press had given to him of Supreme War Lord. He actively espoused militarist policies and ensured Germany was leading the arms race that had developed amongst the major powers in Europe. The establishment of the "Entente Cordiale," a treaty between Britain, France and Russia, had irked Wilhelm and together with his generals, he was planning for a conflict that seemed inevitable between Germany and these nations. It was therefore perhaps not surprising that the assassination of Austrian Archduke Ferdinand in Sarajevo, in June 1914, precipitated a war that would last until 1918 and account for the loss of millions of lives. The outbreak of the hostilities began in August 1914 and Davide Levi waited anxiously to see who Italy would align with in the conflict. His worry was that if Italy joined Germany and Austria through its membership with these countries in the "Triple Alliance," there would be a backlash in Britain with people of Italian heritage rounded-up and interred in camps. Such a move would have a disastrous effect on his family's businesses.

Another thing that Davide was grateful to King Edward VII for was that during their relationship, he had facilitated Davide joining the Freemasons. The King had become the Grand Master of the United Grand Lodge of England during his time as Prince of Wales. Joining "The Craft," as Freemasonry was referred to, had proved highly beneficial for Davide in respect of both Levi enterprises. On the legitimate side, it had enabled Davide to mix with influential businessmen who could assist with planning consents and bookings for upscale social events at his concert halls. And on the shadier side, Freemason senior police officer acquaintances, could bend the rules on arrests and alcohol and gambling license applications. In the context of the war, being a Freemason would now have the additional benefit of having access to powerful members of the organisation in Italy, some of whom were distant relatives of Davide. Freemasonry had a strong presence in Italy with some 25,000 members, the vast majority of whom were leaders in parliament, public administration, the army, and the press. Based on confidential information he received from his English Freemason Brethren, Davide commenced a series of detailed communications to his Italian Freemason contacts promulgating reasons why Italy should align with Britain and its allies in the war. Key amongst these messages was the yet to be announced news that America, with its large Italian migrant community, would be entering the war on the British side and how post war, this would be of substantial advantage to Italy in trade agreements. A campaign was subsequently launched by the Italian Freemasons, but under a separate guise, to sway public opinion towards their country joining the war on the side of Britain. As the deal included reclamation of Italian land now occupied by the Austrians, it was embraced, and the London Pact was duly signed in April 1915.

When the war began in 1914, Davide was too old to enlist which he had no intention of doing anyway. Conscription was not in place in Britain and the army which estimated it needed a further half a million more recruits started a poster advertising campaign featuring Lord Kitchener encouraging young men to enlist. Davide immediately issued a family edict that none of the male members should take this course of action. He then used his contacts within Freemasonry and the upper echelons of the British establishment to obtain waivers for these youngsters on the basis that they were "special cases" in aiding the war effort. This effectively meant that it was business as usual for the Levis and handled in the correct manner, the war could prove to be highly profitable for the family.

Firstly, Davide turned his attention to the concert halls. Music hall was still extremely popular with the public but the war, combined with the growing emergence of cinemas and the fact that large numbers of their audiences were enlisting, would undoubtedly present challenges to its successful continuation. The biggest stars of the day were still being booked to perform at Levi venues. These included George Robey, Ella Shields, Little Tich, Marie Lloyd and Harry Champion. These artistes were keen to play their part in maintaining audiences' patriotic groundswell singing songs such as "It's a Long Way to Tipperary," Pack Up your Troubles in Your Old Kit Bag," and "If You Were the Only Girl in the World." But of concern to Davide was some of the acts that had been booked had German sounding stage names such as George Mozart and Karl Hertz. Patriotism was prevalent within the public, even the Royal Family changed its name from Saxe-Coburg to Windsor. At Davide's insistence, these acts rapidly changed their names with many truthfully stating that their stage titles were fictitious, and they were actually British subjects with real names such as Smith and Jones.

Furthering his quest to satisfy public opinion, Davide went to great lengths to ensure that his music hall programmes demonstrated that his company was totally supportive of the war effort. This not only involved the cancelling of Wagner concerts scheduled but also went through to the back-of-house operations. A particularly amusing example of this was when Davide summoned the British based German Leopold Loewen to his office. Loewen, a former opera singer, had set-up a factory near London producing theatrical makeup for performers and supplied practically all the theatres around the country with his products. 'If you don't change the name of your products to a British name, I will cancel my orders and ensure that my fellow impresarios take the same action,' Davide said sternly. 'But I have invested heavily in promoting my wares and already have thousands of tins in my warehouse bearing the Loewen name waiting to be filled with makeup. Your proposal would ruin me financially,' poor Loewen blurted out in broken English. Never slow to seize a business opportunity and knowing that Loewen's company registered eye-watering profits, Davide calmly stated: 'Not a problem, I will loan you the money required to effect the changes but in return, I will choose the new brand name and be granted a thirty percent share in your business.' In tears, Loewen reluctantly agreed to Davide's terms. 'I will have the documents drawn up immediately and get them delivered to you for signature,' Davide added. Timidly, Loewen enquired what the new name for his products would be. 'The tins will bear the name "Great British Slap" across the centre of a Union Jack,' Davide replied as a downcast Loewen left the office.

Whilst famous music hall performers like Harry Lauder and George Robey went above and beyond in their support for the war by establishing funds for maimed soldiers, and the theatrical impresario, Oswald Stoll created a foundation to build flats for injured servicemen, Davide Levi kept a much lower profile, anxious not to draw attention to the non-music hall part of his empire. He had already started to formulate criminal plans to motivate his own army of Irregulars that would guarantee the Levi clan would not suffer the depravations that large swathes of the population were having to cope with.

The war was now in full flow, and it was generally assumed that with most of Britain's young men enlisting for service, women working in munitions factories and many families grieving the loss of loved ones in the trenches, that crime in London would have fallen to a new low. In fact, The Times reported that this was indeed the case. Sadly, this was far from the truth, London was still the crime capital of the country, particularly violent crime. Soldiers passing through the city on their way to the Western Front were easy prey for the bottom of the music hall bill Levi Irregulars' robbers and conmen. Their burglars and prostitutes were also making vast sums of money for the Levi coffers. Illegal drinking and gambling dens had become yet another string to the family's criminal bow.

The newly acquired share of the Loewen company had given Davide another income generating idea. Venereal disease transmitted by prostitutes was spreading like wildfire through London and there was consternation in the press about how this scourge was having a serious effect on "our brave boys", soldiers, fighting for the nation. Davide issued orders to the prostitutes in his Irregulars to start selling tins of the "Great British Slap" to their clients as part of the transaction, advising the clients that by applying the slap to their penis it would prevent them contracting VD. This led to the saying, "apply the slap and stop the clap" resulting in battalions of soldiers sporting patriotic red, white and blue willies beneath their uniforms.

Not content with this money spinner, Davide quickly latched onto a change in government legislation that would provide even more income. Initially, enlisting for military service was on a voluntary basis, but from 1916, conscription was introduced which meant that any male of military age could be called up. With news of the horrendous casualties incurred on the battle front filtering back to England, it was not surprising that many men were trying to get exemption from serving. However, to achieve this aim, it was necessary to obtain an exemption certificate. Almost 2 million men held these certificates because they worked in protected industries, primarily, government offices and factories. Davide Levi identified methods to obtain these certificates from his various contacts in government, the police and Freemasonry. Once in his possession, he had the details filled in with forged signatures of authority and sold them through third parties to the highest bidders.

Due to the huge amounts of cash pouring in from its concert halls and underworld activities, the Levi bank accounts were at an all-time high. The loss of the gold in the Titanic sinking had been more than compensated for and Davide decided that expansion on both business fronts was now a priority. While London remained the undisputed epicentre of music hall, he felt that opportunity existed in the provinces for more venues. The Levis had good contacts in the Jewish Italian community in Manchester so it was only natural that Davide should begin his research there. He could combine his visit to the city with seeing Sara Strauss who he had kept in contact with via letters since their return from the US a couple of years earlier.

Davide's train journey to Manchester was not what he was used to. Ordinarily, he would travel in the comfort of a first-class carriage with his assistant (bodyguard) Enrico Monza alongside to organise the luggage and take care of his master's every wish. But there was a war on, and trains were mainly used for the transportation of troops. Hence the carriages on this journey were packed with servicemen smoking and shouting obscenities at one and other. Davide was therefore relieved to disembark from the train at Manchester to the waiting cab that Enrico had prearranged. Sara Strauss had kindly offered to accommodate Davide and Enrico at her home at Plymouth Grove, in the city.

On the approach to the house, Davide was struck by the similarities with his own in London. Although a little smaller, the villa was designed in the Regency style having been built in the mid 1800s with a stucco facade. It was located in a middle-class area of Manchester, but Davide noted that the development of housing estates nearby would doubtless have a derogatory effect on the value of the property in years to come. Sara's late husband had purchased the house just prior to his demise on Titanic from the family of the famous Victorian author, Elizabeth Gaskell who wrote the novel "Cranford," and lived there until her death in 1865.

Sara was waiting on the steps to welcome Davide as his cab drew to a halt outside. Clearly delighted to see him, Sara greeted him warmly, took his arm and led Davide inside while Enrico and her staff unloaded the luggage. Having washed and changed into clean clothes, Davide sat down with Sara to take tea in the library. The room was impressive with a distinct smell of leather from the packed shelves of books acquired over many years by Sara's husband who was a bibliophile. Sara was an attractive petite woman with a pale blemish-free complexion, blue eyes, and light brown hair. Her outfit looked like something straight out of the pages of the fashion magazine Vogue, the first British edition of which had appeared that year. It was a tailored navy silk two-piece suit with a Basque style tunic top and pleated long skirt. A limited edition made in Paris; its expensiveness reflected Sara's status in local society. Her hand-made pointed shoes were in the same material as the suit.

'I was excited to read in your last letter that you are interested in expanding your entertainment business in Manchester,' Sara said as they sipped their Earl Grey tea from the finest bone China cups. 'I am sure that my local knowledge and contacts could be helpful to you,' she added. 'I would be most grateful for any assistance you can provide,' Davide replied. 'I do have some family connections in the region but none of them would know the sort of people who might be interested in investing in my business operations,' he lied. As their conversation continued, Davide became aware of feelings he had not experienced since he first met Rachel, his late wife. He was becoming attracted to the woman sitting opposite him and hoped that he might develop their friendship to a more intimate level. Unbeknown to him, Sara was experiencing the very same feelings about Davide but as a well-bred lady, was reluctant to show this emotion at present.

Over dinner that evening they swapped stories about their respective families and businesses. Sara's recollections were detailed and truthful, but Davide's were less so and purposely sanitized to omit information relating to the "dark" side of his business. Sara was a fan of music hall and regularly attended shows at Manchester's venues. She was therefore fascinated to hear about Davide's dealings with the famous music hall stars of the day and quizzed him intently on what these people were really like away from their stage persona. She expressed surprise that Marie Lloyd had a foul mouth even though this was well documented in press articles. However, she was pleased to learn that most of these stars were making considerable contributions to the war effort.

At a war fundraising event she was scheduled to attend the following day, Sara was certain that members of the consortium that owned the Palace Theatre in Oxford Street, Manchester would be attending as the meeting was taking place at the venue. On hearing this Davide's opportunity antennae pricked up and he was quick to accept Sara's invitation to join her at the gathering. It was now his turn to go into interrogation mode and he fired off several questions about the theatre. Fortunately, Sara was well informed on the subject owing to her husband's dealings with an architect, Arthur Darbyshire, who had designed factories for her late spouse. It was Darbyshire who also designed the Palace Theatre that opened in

1891 at the huge cost of £40,500 and seated almost 4,000 people. But from the outset, the emporium was plagued with financial difficulties, the principal one being that it was not granted a liquor license for the first five years of its existence. Although it did obtain a license subsequently, it had struggled to contract the big music hall stars. It was hoped that a major renovation programme in 1913 would increase the theatre's appeal but three years later, this had not occurred and its competitors in the city continued to thrive at its expense. Davide's interest was further heightened when Sara advised she had heard on the gossip grapevine that directors of the consortium were keen to talk to prospective investors.

Waiting in the hall the following morning, Davide turned to see Sara descending the central staircase. She was a vision of elegance dressed in another French couture outfit, this time crimson with lace trim. Her hat, gloves, shoes and parasol were a slightly lighter shade of crimson. Enrico was outside with a cab in readiness to escort the couple to the Palace Theatre a short distance away. On arrival at the theatre, Enrico opened the door of the cab and helped Sara out. He then took a position by the entrance and said to Davide that he would stay there until they were ready to return to the house.

Looking up at the theatre's façade with round arched windows and a balcony above the entrance, it was certainly imposing but somewhat grimy, presumably Davide thought from the smoke emitted by the factories in the area. Once inside Sara introduced Davide to the great and the good of Manchester. Whilst politely feigning interest in these individuals, Davide was concealing his impatience well as really the only people he wanted to meet was the directors of the Palace. He did not have to wait too long as Sara spotted them in a group just below the stage that was dressed in red, white and blue drapes in readiness for the fundraising speeches.

'Good afternoon gentleman,' Sara said to the three men, 'I am sorry to disturb your conversation, but I have someone with me who would very much like to meet you. This is Davide Levi, a close friend of mine who runs a number of successful theatres in London.' Davide particularly liked the words "close friend" and "successful" that Sara had used in her introduction. Messrs Freeman, Hardy and Willis knew Sara well through her late husband. They had made their fortunes as partners in a shoe manufacturing company that they started in 1875 before selling it at a substantial profit a few years later. In fact, they had been considering an approach to Sara to become an investor in the Palace. Therefore, they were pleased to see her and smiled broadly as Davide shook hands with them. All three were considerably older than Davide and judging by the size of their waists, had enjoyed a good life since disposing of their shoe business. Introductions complete, Davide asked: 'I wonder whether it would be possible to have a private word with you after the speeches to discuss my interest in the development of my business operations in Manchester?' Without hesitation, in unison, the three men agreed and suggested they reconvene later in an office behind the stage.

The series of speeches by seasoned orators achieved the desired effect with the assembled dignitaries vying to outdo one another with pledges of large sums of money and goods to support the brave boys fighting against a dastardly enemy. To Davide's surprise, Sara was one of these with a commitment to supply thousands of pounds of textile material for the manufacture of uniforms for the troops. Not wishing to be left out and moreover, to ensure that he was recognised as a wealthy businessman by the audience, Davide pledged hundreds of free tickets to be made available at his theatres for troops on leave in London from the front. This generous gesture was widely applauded and duly noted by a reporter from the Manchester Evening News, who arranged for a photograph to be taken of him immediately the formal proceedings ended.

Although at first Sara was reluctant to accompany Davide at the meeting with the Palace directors, he coaxed her to do so explaining that her local knowledge would prove invaluable. The three directors were already seated around an expensive oval oak table when the couple entered the office. The air was thick with cigar smoke and the directors were drinking port, glasses of which were offered to Sara and Davide but declined. It was not long into the discussion that it became clear to Davide that the theatre's finances were in a far more perilous position than at first envisaged. Indeed, it was on the verge of bankruptcy. Bearing in mind the severity of the situation, Davide was amazed at the jolly Mr Micawber type stance the directors were taking. 'When we have won this wretched war in the next few months, we are convinced the theatre will quickly start to make money,' one of them stressed. Another added: 'If you, or perhaps both of you, were interested in investing in the business, we are sure that you would see a return within a couple of years.' Maintaining a poker face, Davide expressed interest in the proposition but stated he would need to see detailed accounts. Unwittingly showing their desperation, the directors said that this could be rapidly arranged if Davide and Sara could return the following day to continue the discussion. The couple looked at each other, nodded and agreed that this would be possible.

Over dinner that evening, Sara and Davide talked about the prospect of investing in the Palace Theatre. Davide explained that he had been in contact with his relatives in the region and they had told him that the theatre was poorly managed. This was reflected in its insistence to stage mainly classical music concerts for which there was no public appetite. Furthermore, it had swallowed up vast amounts of money in recent years without any significant upsurge in takings. Sara concurred, saying that in her opinion the competitor theatres in the city were much more successful than the Palace in that they were closely in touch with the public's preferences in entertainment.

Shortly after Sara had retired to bed, Davide summoned Enrico. 'I have a little job for you,' he began. 'Select a couple of the most trustworthy of my local cousins and in the middle of the night, break into the Palace Theatre. Once inside, paint in large letters on the walls in the stalls area: "This is just the beginning," then light a tiny fire in the centre of the stage. When your team has exited, telephone the fire station and tell them the theatre is on fire. Then phone the Manchester Evening News and give them the same message.' Enrico carried out his master's orders to the letter.

An acrid smell of smoke was in the air when Sara and Davide arrived at the Palace the following day. Clearly shaken, one of the theatre's directors, Mr Freeman, was shouting instructions to a group of workmen in the auditorium who were scrubbing furiously to remove the messages emblazoned around the walls. The same journalist who had interviewed Davide was present with a photographer, and another of the theatre's directors, Mr Hardy, was attempting to shepherd them off the premises. 'Terrible business,' the journalist remarked to Davide as he passed by. 'Somebody's obviously got it in for the dear old Palace.' Davide nodded but made no comment.

The third theatre director, Mr Willis, now appeared and seeing that his two colleagues were otherwise occupied, beckoned Sara and Davide over to the door of the office where they had met previously. He too was visibly shaken and much less composed than the day before. 'What's happened?' Davide enquired.

'Some vandals broke in last night and started a fire,' the director replied. 'The message on the walls appears to be some sort of threat,' Davide said. 'We're not entirely sure what the meaning is, nothing like this has ever happened in the past,' the director responded, desperately trying to give the impression that he was unfazed by the event. 'It was only a small fire so it's business as usual, 'he added.

'If somebody has a grudge against the Palace, it must be taken seriously. Have you contacted the police?' Sara asked. 'They were here earlier this morning and are investigating the matter,' the director hesitantly replied. Turning to Sara, Davide said, 'In the light of what has taken place, I think we need to talk privately about whether to continue considering investing in the theatre.' Sara agreed and they started to make their way towards the exit when Mr Willis pleaded with them to at least examine the accounts documents. But Davide was adamant, taking Sara's arm he led her up the central aisle leaving a crestfallen Mr Willis almost in tears.

Prior to dinner that evening Davide and Enrico went out for a walk. Davide congratulated Enrico on a job well done at the theatre. He then outlined phase two of his plan. The business cards handed to Davide by Messrs Freeman, Hardy and Willis included their home addresses. 'In the early hours of tomorrow morning, before daylight, at exactly the same time, your team will pay a visit to these three houses. On the outside walls they will paint in big letters, "We are coming for you." When the task is completed, phone the Manchester Evening News and say you have been informed that criminals have been at work at the houses. As previously, you will not give your name.' Davide instructed. Enrico smiled and said, 'Sure boss, no problem, just like the three little pigs story.' 'Yes, but don't blow the houses up, just tell them to paint on the walls,' Davide chortled.

Amusingly, Enrico's three little pigs analogy was not far from the truth when it came to carrying out Davide's orders. Painting the message on Messrs Freeman and Hardy's houses went without a hitch. But Mr Willis's house proved a different proposition. The cousin allocated this property was on the short side so arriving at the house, he was surprised to see that it was surrounded by a high fence covered in brambles. He clambered over with some difficulty whilst trying not to spill the paint. Stealthily he crept over to the white wall and had just painted the word "We" when he heard a low-pitched growl behind him. Turning around slowly, to his horror, he saw a huge Doberman eyeing him up as if he was the first course of the dog's dinner. He dropped the paint pot and brush and sprinted towards the fence. Barking loudly, the dog gave chase and just as the cousin leapt onto the fence, the dog flew through the air and sunk its teeth into the vandal's right buttock. At this moment, Mr Willis appeared in his dressing gown brandishing a revolver. He took aim at the bloodied moon-like shape on the top of the fence but as he went to squeeze the trigger, it disappeared down the other side emitting screams of *fanculo, fanculo, fanculo* in a distinctly Italian accent. Seeing the word "We" on the wall, Mr Willis scratched his head and was perplexed by the whole incident. Was this the work of some semi-literate lunatic hell bent on urinating on his wall and then leaving a message to prove it? Stroking his dog, he praised him for his work and went back inside the house to return to his bed. It was not until later that morning when he received calls from Freeman and Hardy advising what had happened at their houses that Willis realised the purpose of the mission he had thwarted.

While all these clandestine activities had been taking place, Davide and Sara had consummated their friendship with a night of unbridled passion. Both had been sexually abstemious since the loss of their partners and were anxious to make up for lost time. And this they certainly did to the point of exhaustion. Just after 7am, as Sara slept soundly, Davide slid out of the bed and quietly returned to his own room, bathed, and dressed. He then went in search of Enrico. He found him alone in the kitchen devouring a large chunk of bread with cheese. Enrico explained that the task he had been set by Davide had been mainly successful. 'Two of the houses now have a new paint job but we did not legislate for the fact that Mr Willis would be more security conscious than his fellow directors. As a result, one of your cousins now has a set of dog's teeth marks adorning his arse,' he said. Davide laughed out loud. 'No matter, the main thing is that the message has reached the three of them. It won't be long before they are begging me to take the Palace off their hands,' he added.

Meantime, over at the Palace Theatre, it appeared that Davide's prediction was already starting to become a reality. Freeman, Hardy and Willis were seated around a table in the office listening with anguish at the comments of the head of the Manchester Constabulary, Chief Inspector Duggan, who they had invited in to discuss the unnerving events they were experiencing. 'I'll be honest with you, this has all the signs of a crime syndicate muscling in on the entertainment business in our city,' Duggan stated. 'Of course, we will do everything we can to stop them, but we are currently short of manpower, and I cannot make any guarantees that things will improve in the immediate future,' he told the directors. 'With respect, if I were you, I would ask the question, do you want this kind of hassle at this stage in your career? Even by hiring in heavies, engaging in gang warfare could have serious consequences for you and your families,' the Chief Inspector stressed.

After Duggan departed, the three directors decided that instead of seeking investors, they would sell the Palace and let the new owners deal with the gangsters. They had worked hard throughout their lives and wanted to enjoy retirement.

By ensuring the Manchester Evening News would run stories on both the arson and graffiti attacks, Davide knew that potential investors in the Palace would be deterred. And so it came to pass. Having publicised that offers for the theatre would be welcome, there was no interest registered. Not wishing to wait any longer than necessary for fear of more intimidation, Freeman, Hardy and Willis agreed that contact should be re-established with Sara and Davide. On receiving the telephone call from the solicitors acting on behalf of the Palace's directors, Sara was keen to set up a meeting. But Davide said: 'Let them stew for a while, that way, we will be able to negotiate a better price.' Once again, he was proved right. Having discussed their tactics in detail, at a meeting some weeks later, Sara and Davide put forward a strong argument why the asking price of £75,000 was far too high. The points they raised were valid. The war had drained the economy as well as the good folk of Manchester's available disposable income. There was still a risk of bomb damage from German air raids. And even if the war ended soon, it would be years before things returned to normality. Furthermore, the cost of contracting performers had increased as had goods such as food and drink to sell at the venue. With these factors in mind, Sara and Davide made it clear that their final offer was £40,500. The directors pleaded that this was the price that they paid to build the Palace over 20 years ago and that it must be worth more as a going concern. Sara and Davide politely disagreed and left the meeting.

Just 24 hours later, Sara's phone rang and the solicitors acting for the directors advised that they were reluctantly prepared to accept the offer. Sara put down the phone and rushed into Davide who was sitting in the drawing room. She kissed him exclaiming, 'It's ours, they've accepted our offer.' They immediately retired to Sara's bedroom with a bottle of champagne and two glasses to celebrate their acquisition.

Whilst Davide's solicitors in London drew up documents to formalise his partnership with Sara in the new business venture, the couple sat down to consider their plans for the Palace. Based on the theatre's miserable track record, simply maintaining the status quo was not an option. The place needed to offer something different to its competitors that would appeal to the public. Davide told Sara that back in 1895, he was invited to Paris to attend the demonstration of a piece of equipment that he believed would revolutionise the worldwide entertainment business in the 20th century. It was therefore ironic that its inventors thought the total opposite. The Lumiere Brothers, Auguste and Louis, were Frenchmen who had developed the Cinematographe motion picture system. At the demonstration, 10 short films lasting around fifty seconds each were screened. The films were in documentary format, mainly depicting scenes such as workers leaving the Lumiere factory in Lyon, a blacksmith at work and seascapes. As he watched in awe, Davide instantly saw the way this new-fangled system could be used to film music hall acts and plays to show to paying customers at theatres.

In 1896, Davide arranged to meet the Lumiere Brothers in London where they were visiting as part of a world tour to demonstrate their invention. To his astonishment, they told him they could see no future in the equipment. They had no interest in selling the system and on their return to their native France, would discontinue its development to concentrate on the production of colour photographic processes. This they did successfully and in 1907, commercially launched their Autochrome Lumiere process. During the early 1900s, it was no surprise that others, such as the Brighton, England based photographers George Smith and James Williamson, developed motion picture cameras for sale. And by the beginning of the First World War, more and more people were paying to visit cinemas, many of which were previously concert halls, to watch films, albeit mainly in the south of England.

Davide was fascinated by the whole subject of filmmaking and photography. He told Sara that he firmly believed that by incorporating a screen and projection equipment at the Palace, they could not only put on music hall performances but also show films. To date, none of their competitors in Manchester could offer this facility and through his London contacts, he would ensure that only the Palace would have access to the most popular films available.

As an intelligent lady, Sara did think it odd how business deals seemed to fall neatly into place with Davide's handling. But she was smitten with him and in her eyes, he could do nothing wrong. It therefore did not come as a shock to their contacts when, following the successful introduction of film shows at the Palace, Sara accepted Davide's marriage proposal. The couple travelled to London and the wedding ceremony took place soon after at Marylebone Town Hall. Davide had decided against holding the event at the synagogue in Great Portland Street as this would bring back painful memories of his marriage to Rachel, and it would not be appropriate for Sara either. However, the wedding reception, held at The Langham Hotel in Regent Street, followed the Jewish traditions enacted on such occasions. The Hora, the celebratory dance where the guests dance in a circle around the bride and groom was carried out with vigour, and after Davide broke a glass under his shoe, the assembled throng excitedly yelled, *"Mazeltov!"*

Sara quickly adapted to the faster pace of life in London. Business at the Palace Theatre in Manchester had gone from strength to strength and needed minimal input from her since Davide's cousins had been installed to run the place. She loved the house in Regent's Park and in a short period of time, had integrated herself into some prestigious social circles. One of the people included in these circles was Emmeline Pankhurst. Sara was delighted to renew her acquaintance with Emmeline as she had known her through her friendship with her daughter, Christabel, when they all lived in Manchester. Of course, Emmeline and Christabel, had gained notoriety prior to the war with the much-publicised activities of the Woman's Social and Political Union they founded. The WSPU advocated women's suffrage and its members, the Suffragettes, engaged in violent protests to demand the right for women to gain the vote. Both Emmeline and Christabel had received prison sentences during which they went on hunger strike and were force-fed. At the outbreak of war, the WSPU called off its protests in support of the country's fight against Germany. When the First World War ended in 1918, women over 30 years were granted the vote.

Over tea with Sara at the Regent's Park house, Emmeline outlined her next political move. Her trim figure, thick black glossy hair, high cheekbones, and slightly rouged complexion belied her 59 years. Clearly, she was in no mood to give up on her work to achieve more recognition for women in society. She fixed Sara with her violet colour eyes. 'This is not the end of the fight you know,' Emmeline said. 'I am using the WSPU's extensive network around Britain to form the Woman's Party. Christabel will lead the Party. The principal aim of this new organisation will be to promote equality for women in public life. It will advocate feminist policies, including equal pay for equal work, equal marriage and divorce laws, equality of parental rights and raising the age of consent. The Party will also campaign for maternity and infant care, which will be subsidised by parents according to their income,' she continued.

'Fascinating, but to achieve those goals, it is going to require a huge amount of work,' Sara replied. 'That's where you come in Sara my dear. I want you to work alongside Christabel to establish a public profile for the Woman's Party. Your husband's influence amongst high-ranking government officials and business leaders would be invaluable to the cause,' Emmeline stated. 'Hmm, I am not sure such an approach would be welcome at present. Whilst he is totally liberal in his views about women's emancipation, he is currently totally focused on expanding his various entertainment enterprises. But leave it with me, I will certainly try,' Sara explained.

True to her word, Sara broached the subject with Davide over dinner that evening. His response was as she had predicted. 'Look darling, I think it's a great idea for you to assist the Pankhursts with their plans. But I'm afraid I cannot help just now. I am using up all the political favours owed to me to press for amendments to the licensing laws that are restricting the growth of our businesses. It would be a folly to muddy the waters by adding another quite separate issue for consideration.'

Undeterred, Sara contacted Emmeline and arranged a meeting with her and Christabel for later that week. The three women duly met and began plotting their strategy to reform the laws relating to women's lives in Britain. They agreed that the first step should be to put forward a female candidate to gain a seat in the House of Commons in the forthcoming General Election scheduled for the end of 1918. The funding of such an exercise would obviously prove costly but Sara said that subject to seeing detailed budgets, she should be able to provide financing for part, if not, the entire campaign. 'Depending on the location of the constituency, I will also help by circulating election pamphlets and displaying posters for our candidates at my husband's entertainment venues. With the large numbers of customers the venues attract, we will get our message to the very people from whom we are seeking support,' Sara suggested.

Despite Sara and Christabel's efforts to get

Emmeline to be the candidate, she insisted that Christabel, as leader of the Women's Party, with her youthful energy, was the obvious choice. Emmeline added: 'The Party has a conference booked at the Queen's Hall in Langham Place in London shortly. During my address, I will announce that Christabel shall be the first ever female candidate to fight for a seat in Parliament. But first, I must lobby my good friend the Prime Minister, David Lloyd George, to ensure that Christabel's candidature is endorsed by the Liberal and Conservative coalition. The PM has quite a reputation as a ladies' man, so I do not envisage any problems.'

Soon after the meeting, Sara was delighted to receive a call from Christabel confirming that her candidature had been ratified by the coalition. However, Sara became less optimistic when Christabel confided that she and Emmeline had changed their mind about the constituency seat for which the Women's Party would contend. 'Our original target was Westbury in Wiltshire,' Christabel explained. 'But we have now switched our attention to Smethwick on the outskirts of Birmingham,' she continued. Hearing this news, Sara felt it was a bad decision. Westbury was in a rural area of the country where voters were likely to be more sympathetic to the Women's Party manifesto. Conversely, Smethwick was in the industrial "Black Country" with a majority of male, Labour Party orientated voters.

Sara related this news to Davide, and he said he would give some thought as to how he could help to persuade the constituents of Smethwick to vote for Christabel. Their conversation started Davide thinking about ways he could scupper the Pankhurst's' plan. Although he feigned liberal views about equal rights for women, deep down, he was a chauvinist. The previous Sunday he had seen a sensationalist headline in the News of the World newspaper which read, "In Female Attire/Masqueraded As Girl To Have Fun With Soldiers." The article stated that Victor Wilson, a Labour Exchange official, had been arrested in Peckham, London, masquerading dressed as a young woman to pick up soldiers. His case was due to be heard at Camberwell Green Magistrates' Court very shortly. Davide spoke to his bodyguard, Enrico, and gave him instructions. 'Make sure you arrange a top lawyer for this Wilson. That should result in just a fine. When Wilson is released, take him for a drink and pump him for information. I guarantee he will know lots of blokes of a similar persuasion to him. I want him to contact them and arrange a charabanc outing for them all dressed in their best female finery. They will be going to Smethwick in the

Midlands for a few days to knock on the doors of the locals to hand out pamphlets telling them to vote for Christabel Pankhurst of the Women's Party in the General Election. We will pay for Wilson's fine and the brief. Also, the charabanc, accommodation, and expenses for the nonce's trip. As usual, absolutely no connection to me whatsoever.'

Davide's plan to damage Christabel Pankhurst's campaign worked even better than he could have expected. On the first night of their arrival in Smethwick, the transvestites, all dressed to the nines, led by Victor Wilson, decided it would be a good idea to attend an election husting by the Labour candidate, John Davidson, in the town's Baptist church hall. The transvestites began handing out the Christabel Pankhurst leaflets to the audience who initially could not believe their eyes as the "ladies", in their lace dresses, handbags, veiled hats, high heels and cheap perfume moved amongst them smiling. It was not long though before the muscular men in the audience wiped the smile from the thickly made-up faces of the transvestites. Within minutes, a full-scale riot had erupted with fists and wooden chairs flying in all directions. The piercing blasts of police whistles failed to stop the fracas and the local constables were hard pressed to contain their laughter at the sight of men dressed as women fighting men dressed as men. Fortuitously from Davide's point of view, a journalist from the Smethwick Telephone newspaper witnessed the brawl. His report, that appeared the following day, was quickly syndicated to other Midlands and national newspapers accompanied by photographs of the battered transvestites behind bars in Smethwick's police station.

Unsurprisingly, the combination of Sara's concern about the switching of the choice of constituency and Davide's clandestine transvestite intervention, proved the undoing of Christabel's campaign. Sara was standing in Smethwick Town Hall with Christabel and Emmeline as the results of the count were announced. Christabel was defeated by the Labour candidate by just 775 votes, a narrow margin. Naturally, Christabel was disappointed, but the drama of the evening was about to take another turn when Sara fainted. She had been nauseous in the morning during the previous few weeks and on visiting her doctor when she returned to London, was told that she was pregnant.

CHAPTER 5 – ALL THAT JAZZ

Davide was overjoyed to hear the news from Sara that he was to be a father once again. However, his happiness soon turned to concern about this development. It was December 1918, the result of the General Election was a landslide victory for the Liberal/Conservative coalition led by Prime Minister, David Lloyd George, but Britain had been hit by the Spanish Flu pandemic. Thousands of lives had already been lost in this worldwide epidemic; indeed, the Prime Minister had contracted the virus a few months before the election, but the details had been kept under wraps, and he survived. Davide was rightly worried that Sara's exposure to large groups of people at social events, concerts, and political meetings in London, could prove fateful as the death toll continued to rise. He decided that Sara should move to the Levi family base in Essex for the remainder of her pregnancy. Arrangements would be made for the best doctor in the area to be available at a minute's notice should Sara require attention. Reluctantly, Sara agreed. Davide would visit her regularly during the coming months but only after ensuring that he had not contracted Spanish Flu. Likewise, the family members in Essex would be instructed to observe similar precautions and stay away from large gatherings in nearby towns and villages.

Harry Alfonso Levi was born on Tuesday 29th July 1919 at the Levi Essex homestead. Nothing of particular significance took place on that day although the Treaty of Versailles, the peace treaty that formally ended hostilities between Germany and the Allied Powers, was signed twenty-four hours before in Paris. Davide entered the bedroom just in time for his son's arrival after a frantic drive from London with Enrico breaking the speed limits throughout the journey. The proud father cradled his son in his arms and softly sang *Numi, Numi*, a traditional Jewish lullaby. Davide gently kissed Sara and they both sat mesmerised looking at their tiny offspring. Harry was a Leo who would inherit many of the star sign's associated characteristics such as being the centre of attention, confident, drama-loving, ambitious and a desire for luxury living.

In accordance with Jewish religious tradition, Harry was scheduled to be circumcised at a ceremony conducted by a Rabbi from Chelmsford 8 days after his birth. On the agreed day, Rabbi Rabinowitz arrived at the Levi Essex home. He was rather scruffy looking, short with long grey hair and a stubbly beard. Davide was horrified to see that the Rabbi was wearing pebble lenses spectacles and bumped into two pieces of furniture as he entered the house. The final straw came when the Rabbi dropped his implements while extracting them from his bag and spat on them to remove some dust. Davide politely thanked the Rabbi and advised him that there had been a change of plans. Taking his arm, he gave the Rabbi a donation to Chelmsford's Jewish community and shepherded him off the premises. As the bemused Rabbi made his way along the path from the house, behind the closed door, Sara and Davide broke down in fits of laughter. 'Of all the Rabbis, in all the world, we get the one with impaired sight,' they blurted out.

Following over 200,000 deaths from the Spanish Flu pandemic in Britain, the virus was now finally in retreat. Consequently, Davide felt that it was safe for him, Sara, and baby Harry to move back to their London home in Regent's Park. Harry's circumcision was carried out by a charming Rabbi from the Great Portland Street schul who, thankfully, especially in relation to Harry's life to come, had perfect vision.

Still blissfully unaware of her husband's criminal activities, Sara slipped seamlessly into motherhood. Harry was a beautiful baby who was fortunate to inherit the best of both his parents' features. That said, his resemblance was closer to Davide with jet black hair, a swarthy complexion, and a dimpled chin. But he did have his mother's blue eyes. The Levi household staff adored baby Harry, particularly his newly appointed full-time live-in nanny, Mary Brogan. She was a buxom young Irish lass who was recruited based on having helped her mother to raise a family of eight siblings in the crammed upstairs of a house in nearby Chalk Farm.

Whilst delighted with the way his domestic life had stabilised since the end of the Great War and the arrival of his son, Davide was less enthused with the progress of his business empire. The war years, 1914-1918, had witnessed a massive increase in the Levi fortunes because of the high demand for the services of prostitutes in London by soldiers. But post 1918, this demand had tailed off. This was due to the fact there were fewer men around, a consequence of the death toll incurred in the trenches, and those that had survived, returned to their hometowns around the country and overseas. The spoils from robberies undertaken by the Levi Irregulars had also declined. Many of the male Irregulars had been killed during the war and rich people had upgraded security measures at their houses to prevent looting. This combined with the expansion of the police force in London had proved another blow for Davide's profits.

As experienced by past generations of the Levi family, the public's taste in entertainment was changing yet again. Davide had replicated his introduction of cinema at the Palace Theatre in Manchester to his other venues in the London area, but the lucrative side-lines of gambling and prostitution associated with the music halls previously, were now absent. An additional downside was the level of competition in London to attract cinemagoers was considerably higher than in Manchester. The music hall stars such Marie Lloyd, Harry Champion, Vesta Tilley and George Robey, who had served Davide so well over many years, were still drawing large audiences at Levi venues, but new forms of entertainment were starting to emerge. Cinema had already established a strong foothold in the market. Hot on its heels was the arrival of the jazz age in Britain and the first radio broadcast.

Following in the family tradition, Davide had always prided himself on being ahead of the curve in predicting trends in popular entertainment but on this occasion, he had been caught somewhat unawares. Drastic action was required to address the situation. Like any businessman worth his salt, Davide firstly examined the overheads in the least profitable parts of his operations. The numerous properties he owned in and around Soho that were run as brothels, would have to be reduced and at the same time, the "ladies" and their pimps, told to ply their trade elsewhere. The remaining Levi Irregulars would be told their services were no longer needed but firmly reminded by Enrico and his elite group of henchmen that they should keep their lips tightly sealed about this move or suffer an unfortunate "accident" whilst passing through one of London's many dark alleyways.

Turning to the areas of the business offering growth potential, Davide would take a close look at the jazz phenomenon that was about to sweep Britain. He thought about how this might be developed on the American speakeasy bar model with the opening of night clubs financed by the sale of some of his brothels. For the time being, he would stay loyal to his music hall stars but see if he could mould their talents to records and performing on the new invention of radio. He was reasonably happy with the cinema network he owned but would now seek to expand it. The rapidly increasing number of shops, bars and restaurants in Soho and the surrounding areas were ripe for extracting protection monies by Enrico and his thugs. The Levis previous dabbling in drugs trafficking had proved profitable and therefore, Davide decided that this should also be added to the list of his empire's future activities.

In late 1919, Davide and Sara sat in a box at the Hippodrome Theatre for a performance of "Joy Bells," a revue starring one of Davide's stable of music hall artistes, George Robey. Making their London debut as part of the show was The Original Dixieland Jazz Band, who had been formed by a trumpeter, Nick La Rocca, in New Orleans and subsequently made the big time in Chicago, then New York before coming over to England. The audience gave them a rapturous reception and Davide could instantly see that this type of music was going to be a huge hit with the British public. His instincts were confirmed when a review of their performance in the Daily Mail described the band's music as "wild, savage and of the jungle." Davide immediately contacted his family members in the States to check out the band's credentials and was impressed to hear that they had had no qualms in playing in clubs operated by the mafia.

Davide set-up a meeting with La Rocca and over large tumblers of bourbon immediately started to exaggerate the size of his business. 'We are the largest entertainment organisation in the country with all the biggest show biz stars signed up to us. Confidentially, we are in the final stages of agreeing a deal with Guglielmo Marconi, an old friend of mine from Chelmsford, that our stars will be the first to record for his new British record label and his initial radio broadcasts.' Davide lied. 'Well Mr Levi, that's very interesting because my band has been bowled over by the reaction to our music by you Brits. We are certainly keen to maximise that popularity and we have a song I've just written that would be ideal for Mr Marconi's record label, it's called "Tiger Rag," how soon could we start?' La Rocca asked. Pouring La Rocca another large measure of bourbon, Davide sat back in his Chesterfield leather chair and continued the schmooze offensive by saying: 'Please call me Davide. You know Nick that both our families have Italian origins. Mine were from the Naples area and yours were not that much further south in Sicily.' 'Wow, you've certainly done your homework Davide, that's absolutely correct. We were immigrants to the United States in the same way I guess as yours were to Britain a long way back?' La Rocca replied.

The Italian reminiscences went back and forth as La Rocca's glass was continuously topped up by Davide. As La Rocca, a short man with black hair parted in the middle became sleepy, Davide took a document out of the top drawer of his desk and placed it in front of the trumpeter. 'Cast your eyes over this Nick, it's a standard contract that my people have drawn up that all our artistes have. You won't get a better deal anywhere in this country.' La Rocca gave it a cursory glance through without reading any of the clauses in detail and signed alongside Davide's signature on the last of the six pages. The two men shook hands and Davide escorted La Rocca to the reception of his office and arranged for a taxi to take the musician back to his hotel.

Having achieved his objective of getting La Rocca to sign an exclusive contract for The Original Dixieland Jazz Band's performances and recording in Britain, Davide now had to move quickly to follow up on some of the lies he had told. In truth, he had met Guglielmo Marconi several years ago in 1912. But the inventor could hardly be described as an old friend. At the time, Marconi was in the process of opening a factory in Chelmsford for the manufacture of his communications products. Just before departing on his fateful voyage on the Titanic, as a local dignitary, Davide was invited to the opening ceremony of the factory in New Street. At the event, the two men chatted briefly about the potential of radio transmissions for the entertainment business and agreed to continue the discussion in the future. However, no further meeting took place. It was nevertheless a coincidence that one of Marconi's inventions had been responsible for saving Davide's life. Marconi's SOS equipment played a vital role in ensuring the rescue of survivors from the Titanic.

Davide decided that this fact would be the ideal way to re-establish contact with Marconi so that he could, albeit belatedly, thank him personally for the role he had played in saving him from death in the Atlantic. Meantime, Davide would, set about digging up any information about Marconi that would be to his advantage when they met. Although the two men were of Italian heritage, they were poles apart in terms of their background. Marconi was descended from Italian nobility whilst Davide's ancestors were rogues. Therefore, on this occasion, Davide would not be able to generate bonhomie based on the shared Italian link that he had deployed so successfully with targets in the past. But, typical of Davide's uncanny knack of coming up trumps, it was only a matter of days before he received some very juicy gossip about Marconi from one of his underworld contacts. Apparently, the inventor was, unknown to his wife of fourteen years, Beatrice, in a relationship with Maria Cristina Bezzi-Scali, the only daughter of Count Bezzi-Scali. Maria was twenty-six years Marconi's junior. If news of this liaison reached the press, it could prove extremely damaging to Marconi's imminent launch of radio transmissions.

On arrival at the factory in Chelmsford for the meeting, Davide could not help but notice the massive aerial masts that had been erected on the building's roof. Evidently, the first ever commercial radio broadcast that had been speculated in the newspapers, was imminent. Armed with the precious information from his contact, Davide was shown into Marconi's office. Marconi was a handsome man of average height with neat dark hair held in place with Macassar oil. He was smartly dressed in a brown pinstripe three-piece suit with a heavy gold Albert chain protruding from his waistcoat pocket. Noted for his charming personality and ability as a self-publicist, he welcomed Davide warmly with a firm handshake. 'How nice to see you again, it must be seven years since we last met,' he said. Directing Davide to a chair, Marconi asked, 'Can I interest you in a glass of whiskey?' 'Most kind,' Davide replied, noting the brand name on the bottle. Following the initial pleasantries about the relieve of the ending of the Great War and Marconi's hugely influential work with wireless that had saved Davide's as well as many others lives, the meeting entered the business phase.

Taking a sip of his drink Davide cut straight to the chase. 'You will be aware of the public's current enthusiasm for jazz music. Broadcasting a new song performed live by the genre's leading exponents as part of the launch of your new radio invention would prove popular to listeners. Furthermore, if the song was available for purchase on your Marconi record label, money could be made for both of us from sales of the record.' Marconi smiled and responded: 'I like your idea, but we have already contracted the famous Australian soprano, Dame Nellie Melba, to sing some arias in our historical first broadcast. We feel that the sound of a woman's voice would be much more impactful than band music.' Undeterred, Davide countered with: 'I appreciate that the Dame is revered by opera lovers, but they represent a small percentage of Britain's population. Jazz band music would appeal to a mass audience and additionally, be a money spinner for us.' Marconi thought for a moment but stuck to his guns: 'I'm sorry but I must honour our contract with Dame Nellie. Perhaps we could feature your jazz band at a later date? Marconi remained resolute so Davide decided it was time to adopt a different tact. 'I see that the whiskey is Jamieson's, the company owned by your mother's family. The brand has a great reputation, as of course has your entire family. It would be a pity if that reputation was sullied, especially in the run up to the launch of the first radio broadcast.' Hearing this Marconi stiffened in his chair. 'What exactly are you implying by that remark?' Davide leant across the desk and whispered: 'Well I have it on good authority that your close relationship with Maria Cristina Bezzi-Scali would be of interest to the press, particularly as they see the development of radio as a major threat to their business.' Marconi's face turned ashen. 'That is outright blackmail,' he complained. 'Spot on, but a small price for keeping schtum eh?' Davide suggested. 'I will have the contract sent round for your signature in the next few days. It will state that The Original Dixieland Jazz Band will open the broadcast followed by Dame Nellie's piercing trills. There will be a separate contract for the record label deal. Pleasure doing business with you. I'll show myself out,' he concluded. Marconi was left staring out of his office window in a state of shock.

CHAPTER 6 – QUEEN OF CLUBS

"Too-Ra-Loo-Ra-Loo-Rai," Mary repeatedly softy sang the verse from the Irish lullaby as she gently rocked Harry in his cot. The baby finally fell asleep, and Mary sat in the beautifully decorated creche taking in her surroundings. A mural depicting the verses of another lullaby, "Twinkle, Twinkle, Little Star," ran around the walls. It was a far cry from the room in her own house where, over several years, she had carried out a similar duty for her infant brothers and sisters. She counted herself lucky that her employment by the Levis had provided an escape from the domestic incarceration in the dank prison she had called home. This upbringing had meant her childhood was virtually non-existent. Most of it had been spent helping her mother with the washing, mending and cooking for the annually expanding family. Mary had received hardly any schooling and as a result, was a little slow in understanding the ways of the world. She had basic reading and writing skills though, and one story that resonated from her limited attendance at school was Cinderella. But her major asset was her caring nature and her love for baby Harry. Still humming the lullaby, Mary quietly stood up and slipped out of the room, gently closing the door behind her. She took a few steps and entered her room which was adjacent to Harry's, but much smaller.

Mary undressed and went over to the mirror and breathed in. She was just over five feet tall, broad-beamed with large breasts. Her black hair was cropped short with a fringe. Bushy eyebrows, a squat nose, podgy freckled rosy cheeks, and the beginnings of a double chin, completed her facial features. Mary pulled on her night gown, laid down on the bed, and quickly fell asleep. Like Cinderella, she dreamt that one day her Prince would come.

From first meeting Mary at her interview for the post of nanny, Sara knew she was the perfect person to look after Harry. Although she was a little rough round the edges, with the right training, Sara believed Mary could be moulded to become a credit to the Levi household. As a staunch supporter of the Suffragette principal of equality for women, Sara was determined to give Mary every opportunity to carry out her duties with aplomb. On her daily walks through Regent's Park, Sara had seen the smartly uniformed nannies perambulating their charges in prams. Speaking to some of her friends with young children, Sara ascertained that there was a place not far from her home that ran training courses for nannies. She duly made an appointment to meet Emily Ward, the founder of The Norland Institute in Norland Place, Shepherd's Bush, London. Having been shown round by Ms Ward, the two women returned to her office. 'I must say I am very impressed with the Norland's work. Some of the sessions we sat in on demonstrated exactly the type of direction young children should receive,' Sara enthused. 'For obvious reasons, we do not shout about it too loudly at the present time, but our training is based on the principles of Frobel, the German educationalist who set-up the kindergarten system. I founded Norland back in 1892 and I am proud that we were the first educational establishment in Britain to offer any form of childcare training. Prior to our arrival, children from elite families would be cared for by untutored housemaids before going to school,' Emily Ward explained.

'I have recently recruited a young lady, Mary Brogan, as nanny for my son Harry. Mary has had some basic education and considerable experience in bringing up her siblings, but she could benefit from the courses that Norland provides,' Sara stated. 'Well, I will need to meet Miss Brogan but from what you have told me, I see no problem in her becoming one of our students. We currently have limited spaces available so to speed things up, may I suggest that you complete the enrolment forms while you are here,' Ms Ward replied.

Shortly after the meeting, Mary began attending the Norland Institute courses each evening. There were 20 girls in her "set" as it was known. The courses were conducted by Miss Simpkins and her assistant, Miss Rutherford. Both women terrified Mary and her fellow classmates as they barked out instructions on how to polish and clean to perfection shoes, prams, toys, and lavatories. Beds had to be made just so, with corners neatly tucked in and the crease of the sheet running perfectly down the middle. The last thing every day was "pram parade" at which the student nannies gathered on the lawn with their polished Silver Cross perambulators so Miss Rutherford could inspect them. Woe betide the girl who had failed to wax the high black sides to less than a mirror shine or purged the wheels of dirt.

Despite receiving a lower level of schooling than the other students had achieved, Mary's practical experience of caring for young children compensated and she was well regarded by the tyrant teachers although they did not express it. Norland nannies were instantly recognisable by their fawn uniforms with stiff detachable white cuffs and collars, which they wore with gloves and hat to ensure that they wouldn't be mistaken for a house maid. Mary was overjoyed to have two sets of this uniform which she proudly wore on all possible occasions. Unlike other wealthy mothers who had little contact with their children and regarded it as the nanny's job to look after them most of the time, Sara was the complete opposite. She tried to create time for baby Harry whenever possible between her social engagements.

In similar vein, Davide, quite contrary to the position adopted by other upper-class fathers during this era, also made a point of spending time with his son. Harry provided the ideal excuse for Davide to consume his passion for photography. Photojournalists' coverage of the Great War had helped to increase the public's awareness of the art form and as a result, its popularity grew rapidly. However, purchases of equipment were restricted to the middle to upper classes. The introduction of single lens reflex technology meant that photographers could view an image as it would appear on film before a shot was taken. Cameras were now constructed with metal and Davide had already bought several models including Kodak's Vest Pocket Autographic. With no expense spared, Davide had converted a room in the cellar of the Regent's Park house to develop his photographs. His darkroom included all the necessary equipment such as a red light, film holder and developing tank, an enlarger, photographic paper, developer and fixer chemicals. This was Davide's private domain and he loved spending time here processing the photos he had taken of baby Harry and Sara, which now, expertly framed, adorned the walls around the house. He had gleaned his photographic skills by becoming a member of The Camera Club in London. Based in Covent Garden, the club, established in 1895, boasted some of the most notable photographers of the time among its members.

Davide had gone to great lengths to become friendly with one such member. Bertram Meadows was extremely well connected within society circles. Born in Bloomsbury in London and funded by the Egyptologist, Lord Carnarvon, Meadows established studios in Dover Street with his wife Yvette, who was also a photographer. He was primarily a portrait photographer and had received several commissions from British and European royalty. Outside his photographic work, Bertram Meadows was a leading authority on roses and wrote several books on the subject which included his photographs. But it was Meadows' role as Commandant in the Metropolitan Special Constabulary, that Davide Levi was most interested in.

During his extensive research into opening nightclubs in London, Davide had noted the number of police raids on the establishments that had resulted in their closure. Before embarking on his business expansion plans, he needed someone senior within the police force to ensure that he was warned in advance if a Levi club was to be raided. Despite the drinking laws having been tightened throughout the First World War to prevent disasters involving drunk workers in munitions factories, they were not relaxed post war. In fact, in 1921, the laws were revised making them even more complicated. Different laws were introduced for different types of establishments, for example, private member clubs, pubs, restaurants and dance clubs. The key element though was the times during which alcohol could be served. The price of drink, food and cigarettes during legal licensing hours was normal but in illegal periods, it increased by three times. If you held a license, you had to comply with the law within these legal hours. However, many clubs did not bother obtaining a license. If they were raided by the police and closed down, they just opened somewhere else, incredibly, sometimes within the same building but on a different floor.

Anxious to become a closer acquaintance of Bertram Meadows, during a game of billiards between the two men at The Camera Club, Davide expressed his admiration for Meadows' knowledge of roses: 'Our gardener has tried to cultivate various types of roses at our home in Regent's Park but with limited degrees of success,' he said. As he completed a canon, re-chalking his cue, Park replied, 'Strange, we have no such problem at our place not far from you in Hampstead. Perhaps you and your wife would care to visit us for tea? I could show you round our garden and give you some tips to pass on to your gardener.' The invitation was just what Davide had been angling for and he gratefully accepted.

The visit to the Meadows' house took place shortly afterwards. Sara and Meadows' attractive wife, Yvette, struck up an immediate rapport and discussed the latest fashions over cups of tea while Bertram and Davide strolled around the large garden. Meadows was a tall slim well-groomed man with dark hair and a small moustache. He had a long-pointed nose on which sat a pair of round metal framed glasses. A pipe was clamped firmly between his lips but was rarely lit.

Davide opened the conversation by enthusiastically commenting: 'I have never seen such a magnificent display of roses anywhere. You must have every variety known to man growing here.'

‘Well, not quite, but a fair few,’ Meadows somewhat embarrassingly responded. ‘What was the type that your gardener is having difficulties with?’ Davide pointed at a red-purple coloured cluster. “Ah, the floribundas, a cross of hybrid tea and polyantha roses. They don’t have a scent but make up for that in looks,’ Meadows explained. ‘I will give you some cuttings for your gardener,’ he continued, taking a pair of secateurs from his pocket and carefully clipping some stems before placing them in a bag he had brought with him. He repeated the exercise on some other varieties that Davide identified, placing the cuttings in separate bags, and tagging them.

‘Thank you so much for the cuttings,’ Davide said but quickly moved on to the main objective for his visit. ‘While I’m here, I would appreciate a tour of your photographic studio, if that’s convenient?’

‘Of course, no problem, but as you are aware, my main studio is in central London, so I only do a certain amount of my work here in Hampstead.’

Similar to Davide’s studio, Bertram’s was in the basement of the house but was much smaller in size. Nevertheless, all the necessary equipment was present. It was not the equipment that Davide was interested in though, it was the framed photos that he had been tipped off about that were on the walls. Noting Davide's fixed gaze on the photos, Bertram coyly remarked: 'A little side-line of mine. I supply photos to naturist magazines of ladies who model for me. All above board of course. The nude female figure should be considered an art form as it has been by painters through the ages. But sadly, there still exists a hangover from the Victorian era where such pictures are considered lewd by some people. As a man of the world, I am sure you understand Davide?' Davide supressed a smirk and replied straight-faced, 'I do indeed Bertram, but as you say, there are others, for example, those connected with your position in the Special Constabulary, who might think otherwise about this little side-line?'

'You are absolutely correct, and that's why I restrict this information to people like you, who I can trust Davide.'

A couple of weeks after Sara and Davide's visit to the Meadows place, Enrico and two of his gang were stationed in a doorway opposite the entrance to Bertram Meadows' studio in Dover Street. It was early evening and Park's wife and the staff had all left the premises. Not long after, three young girls arrived at the studio and were admitted by Meadows. Fifteen minutes later, a hand appeared at one of the studios first floor windows in the form of a thumbs up sign. Enrico's plant had carried out the plan he had briefed her with precisely. 'Here we go,' he said to his colleagues. The three of them crossed the street and quietly opened the door with a master key that had been used for many such sorties elsewhere in the past. One of the men remained on the doorstep to act as a look-out while Enrico and the other entered. Once inside, they removed the cameras they were carrying, primed them ready to take photos, and stealthily climbed the staircase. Listening outside the studio door, they could hear Meadows telling the girls the pose he wanted them to strike for the pictures he was about to shoot. Seconds later, the intruders burst into the room and began taking photos of Meadows and the nude models who were now screaming and desperately trying to find an item of clothing to cover their modesty. In the mayhem that followed, Meadows tripped over his camera tripod and grabbed at the arm of one of the models as he fell. This caused her to topple over onto him creating the perfect photo for Enrico and his mate who turned and rapidly made their escape out of the studio and into a waiting car that was parked two streets away in Bond Steet.

Davide and Enrico laughed out loud as the images on the photographs the latter had taken started to appear in the water tank in the dark room in Regent's Park. 'These are brilliant, especially the one of poor Bertram being straddled by the nude girl. Was she your plant?' Davide enquired.

'Yes, she was, and the smile on her face makes the picture even more convincing, as though she's enjoying herself.'

'My dear friend, I think we have in our possession a license to make money in the nightclubs we will be opening and insurance that we can do so without any police interference.'

Property prices in central London had rocketed upwards since the end of the war. Although the Levi business bank accounts were looking extremely healthy, the outright purchase of premises for nightclubs might just stretch them too far. Davide was mulling over this conundrum as he was thumbing through the properties for sale listing in the Daily Mail, when an article on the opposite page headlined "Queen of the Night Clubs: Woman without scruples," caught his eye. The report covered the appearance of Kath Connell, the owner of The 40 Club and The Pigalle Club, in Gerrard Street and Newman Street respectively, at Marlborough Street Magistrates' Court. She was charged with serving intoxicating liquor after permitted hours following a raid on the establishments by the police. Davide had some knowledge of this lady as he had visited the 40 Club as a guest of a business associate. He recalled that the Club was popular with celebrities, theatricals and even royalty. Indeed, during his visit, he had spotted the famous actor, Rudolph Valentino, at a nearby table. Rather than starting nightclubs from scratch at great expense, and having to attract the clientele, why not forge a partnership with an existing, established business, Davide thought?

As was usual in such situations, Davide sat down with Enrico and asked him to find out as much information as he could about Kath Connell and her business operations. Enrico set to work immediately briefing his network of informants and corrupt police officers. Within a matter of days, he had compiled a dossier that he knew would make interesting reading for his boss.

Sitting in Davide's study, the two men went through the dossier. Kath Connell was Irish. She moved to London via Hampshire from Dublin during the war with her husband and had six children. The couple separated in 1918 at the end of the war and Kath was left to support the children with a limited income. Together with a man called Henry Daley, she opened Daley's, a dance club, in Leicester Square. The enterprise was short-lived as Connell and Daley were both fined at Bow Street Magistrates' Court. In the proceedings the club was described as a "dancing hell and a sink of iniquity." Undaunted, Connell then went on to open several clubs in and around the West End. Further police prosecutions and fines resulted but as one club was closed, she opened another.

'It seems that although Mrs Connell is a serial offender, the accounts you have purloined Enrico shows she is making vast amounts of money from her clubs. Certainly, enough to pay for her children's education at private schools and fund the purchase of a nice house close by Hampstead Heath. But what interests me most is that she does not appear to have any proper security arrangements in place at the clubs.'

'That's right boss, a couple of heavies on the door and barmen that would be useful in a ruck but nothing that we would call serious.'

'So, none of our competitors providing protection?'

'No, definitely not. My informants would have found that out if it existed.'

'Ok, this is the plan. You call up some of our Clerkenwell Italian boys and brief them. On the same night at the same time, they pay a visit to the two clubs, The 40 and Pigalle. They force their way in, fire a couple of shots in the air, smash a few tables and chairs, bottles and glasses, but not too much damage. Scare the shit out of the clients but nothing physical other than the doormen and barmen.'

'Consider it done boss.'

Two nights later, Davide's plan was executed with precision. The morning after he made a call to Kath Connell. 'Good morning, Mrs Connell, my name is Davide Levi, I was very sorry to hear about the problems you encountered at your clubs last night.' Clearly aggravated, Connell replied sharply: 'Look, I've had enough of *feckin'* reporters phoning me, no comment, now piss off.' Before she could hang up, Davide quickly stated: 'I am not a reporter Mrs Connell, I have a business proposition that will prevent a repetition of last night's events. Furthermore, and importantly from a profitability standpoint, it will ensure that you are no longer troubled by the police regarding the licensing laws at your establishments.' There was a moment's silence before Kath Connell answered: 'If this is some kind of wind-up, I warn you that if we meet, I will be accompanied by my two sons, and they are big lads.'

'Please Mrs Connell, I can assure you that things will not come to that. What I have to say really will be in your best interest.'

The meeting between the parties took place a few days after the telephone call. True to her word, Kath Connell was accompanied by her sons who sat on either side of her in the plush office at The 40 Club. They were huge muscular men that had obviously indulged in rugby in their youth as one sported a cauliflower ear, and the other, a broken nose in two places. Sitting alongside Davide, Enrico, eyeballed the men with menace. Stroking the stiletto in his pocket, he thought about how he would shred them like tagliatelle with pomodoro sauce. Then he would take the cauliflower ear and nose as prizes like the bullfighters in Spain after killing the bull.

Kath Connell was an attractive woman in her forties with black wavy hair and petite facial features. She did not wear make-up but was smartly dressed in a light grey flapper style dress with sequins. Strangely, as the meeting was taking place indoors, she was wearing a fashionable bell-shaped cloche hat. During the past few years, she had become something of a celebrity owing to her rapid rise to fame as a nightclub owner, and her numerous appearances in court. As a result, Mrs Connell had featured in newspaper and magazine articles including Tatler. A little impatiently, she opened the discussion, 'I have been doing some digging and found out that you are a big noise in the entertainment business Mr Levi. However, it's not star acts I require, it's quality protection from the sort of thugs who turned over my places last week. And I'm prepared to pay top dollar for it.'

'My organisation can provide that service without any problem under the direction of Enrico here. But I do not need to be paid for it.'

'So, you provide it free of charge, do you?' She enquired chortling at her sons who joined in the laughter.

'Not exactly. The protection comes as part of a package that includes your clubs not being raided by the police. Or if they are, you will receive advance warning so that you can ensure everything is kosher before they arrive.'

'Mr Levi, we too have policemen on our payroll, but they are not privy to that kind of information.'

'Ah ha, you see Mrs Connell, I guarantee I do have access to that level of information and that comes as part of the deal.'

'And what would that deal be?'

'We enter into a 50/50 partnership agreement.'

‘50/50, now, to be sure, I know you are taking the piss Mr Levi.’

The Connell brothers slowly drew themselves out of their chairs and Enrico followed suit with his hand in his pocket ready for action.

‘There’s no need for any unpleasantness, I would hate to see your beautiful carpet stained. Please consider my proposal and let me know,’ Davide said.

‘I can tell you now, get lost,’ Connell shouted defiantly as Davide and Enrico left the office.

That evening the clubs were placed under siege again but this time, more damage was sustained and a few of the male clients who had fancied their chances against the insurgents were injured in the fracas. Kath Connell telephoned Davide the following morning and agreed to his terms for the deal. Davide had gained rapid entry to London’s booming nightclubs business at minimal cost. Pure Levi chutzpah.

The news of Davide Levi’s audacious move within London’s underworld and police force travelled fast. Views on the subject were mixed. Criminal gangs behind some of the other London night spots were annoyed that the Levis had stolen a march on them by getting their hands on two of the jewels of the capital’s night-time scene. One in particular, who had been keen to take over Connell's clubs, was extremely irked and its ringleader was already contemplating reprisals. The police, although having had their suspicions about the Levi's business empire for many years, had never been able to prove that any crimes had been perpetrated. Therefore, they were generally happy that a well-known entertainment impresario had become involved with Kath Connell and hoped that it would lead to a change in her flagrant disregard of the law.

Initially, the Levi-Connell business marriage went smoothly. Both parties grudgingly pooled their considerable experience of ways to extract as much money as possible from clients visiting the clubs. The Levi's upgraded security cover at the clubs deterred rivals from undertaking any subversive action. And, as promised by Davide, there were no police raids. Furthermore, Davide's ability to secure top class entertainers and bands to perform at The 40 and Pigalle led to increased demand for tables. He even devised a plan to sell a range of perfumes and deodorants manufactured by the make-up factory he acquired during the war. The "Bright Young Things," as most of the customers at the clubs were referred to, sweated profusely during their lengthy Charleston and Black Bottom dances, and snapped up this Club branded over-priced merchandise. All these factors combined meant that profits started to soar. But fifty percent of these profits was not enough for Davide, he wanted a hundred per cent. Mrs Connell and her brood would have to go. Quite separately, Kath Connell was having the same thoughts, although hers were concentrated on removing the Levis from what she regarded as her company.

CHAPTER 7 – EVERYONE'S WILD ABOUT HARRY

'What a cute baby', said the good-looking young man who had sidled up alongside Mary as she pushed Harry in his pram on a secluded path flanked by high bushes in Regent's Park. He seemed to have appeared from nowhere and gave her quite a start. 'I love your uniform, are you one of those specially trained nannies that the posh people have?' he asked. Eyeing him up and down, Mary was immediately attracted to this swarthy chap with inky black hair. He stood at around six foot and was smartly dressed in a dark grey suit, white shirt and navy-blue tie. 'Name's Martin, Martin Zermatt, pleased to meet you,' he informed Mary, in a slightly foreign sounding accent, as he extended his hand. Mary politely took his hand and shook it.

'Mary Brogan, and yes, I am a Norland nanny. I work for a Mr and Mrs Levi, a lovely couple who live in a big house on the other side of the park. This is their son Harry.'

'I work as rep in my father's printing firm down the road at Camden Town. Weather permitting, I tend to pop up here to have my lunch each day. Gets me out of the office for a while.'

As the couple approached a bench, Martin suggested they stop for a chat. 'Care to share my lunch? My mum always makes too much.'

'That's very kind but are you sure?'

'Of course, I've even got a couple of small bottles of Tizer, and you are welcome to have one. Besides, it's not every day I get to eat my lunch with a pretty girl.'

Mary blushed and sat down next to Martin on the bench. She was always up for some food and Martin seemed a nice enough boy.

As they began eating the sandwiches, Mary sipped from the bottle of Tizer that Martin had given her. 'This tastes a bit sweeter than normal.'

'Mine tastes ok.'

'Oh, it's alright, it's probably the sweet I was sucking earlier. Zermatt, that's a funny sounding name, where's it from?' Mary asked taking another swig.

'My family is from Malta.'

'I've heard of the place, but where exactly is it?'

'It's an island in the Mediterranean Sea.'

Suddenly Mary started to feel sleepy, and her next sentence was slurred. She slumped against Martin and dropped the half-drunk bottle of pop. Martin looked around to make sure there was nobody else around then let out two whistles. At that moment, a well-dressed middle-aged lady appeared from behind some bushes and wheeled Harry's pram away. The baby had slept throughout the entire brief encounter. Martin propped Mary up against the back of the bench, picked up the remaining pack of sandwiches and walked off at a pace in the opposite direction. However, the bottle from which Mary had been drinking had rolled under the bench where she dropped it and he forgot to pick it up. As he made his way out of the park, he reflected on a job well done. Exactly to the orders he had been given. Naturally, he had given the girl a false name, but should he have been truthful about his Maltese heritage? Probably not.

The hammering on the front door woke Sara from her afternoon nap. As she opened the door, Mary slumped into her arms screaming "Harry, Harry," in a barely coherent voice. The girl was in a dishevelled and distraught state sobbing loudly with tears streaming down her face. Carefully laying Mary down in the hall, Sara called out for help and her house maid arrived to tend to Mary. Sara rushed outside but there was no sign of the baby or his pram. Re-entering the house, she knelt next to Mary and tried to find out what had happened.

‘Mary, Mary, calm down. Where is Harry?

‘Malta, Tizer, sandwiches, boy.’

Mary was making no sense. She merely kept repeating these words in between sobs. Sara was certain that Mary did not drink alcohol, but the girl’s breath smelt as though she had been imbibing. Now in a high state of anxiety, Sara rushed over to the telephone and called Davide at his office. She was put through immediately and recounted the chain of events. He told her to stay in the house and try to extract some sensible information from Mary. Meantime, he would head to the park with Enrico and some employees to conduct a thorough search of the area. Having occasionally accompanied Mary on her walks with Harry, Davide knew the routes she took. He reassured Sara that everything would be ok and that he would find Harry. He told her that Mary had probably had some sort of fit and that Harry was still in his pram somewhere in the park. However, deep down, he knew that there was something more sinister at play.

Ignoring Davide’s advice, Sara telephoned the police and reported that her baby son was missing under suspicious circumstances. The desk sergeant who took the call at Marylebone Lane Police Station was something of a music hall buff and, having taken down the details of the incident, quickly realised that he was speaking to the wife of the famous impresario, Davide Levi. Knowing that his egotistical superintendent would be keen to rub shoulders with celebrities, the sergeant informed his superior officer and as predicted, that was the case. The superintendent recalled that Davide Levi's name had come up at a meeting he had recently attended with his boss, William Horton. The inference was that Levi was connected to organised crime in London but to date, no evidence had been forthcoming. With this thought in mind, the superintendent summoned five constables who had been enjoying a cup of tea in the station canteen, and the group set off to the Levi's house. On arrival, they were shown into the kitchen by the house maid. Mary was now in much better shape. Seated at the table, she told the officers precisely what had happened and the location of where it occurred. The policemen then asked the maid the whereabouts of Mrs Levi, she informed them that having obtained the details from Mary, Sara, together with the gardener, had headed out into the park to the spot in question.

Not long afterwards, all three groups of searchers gathered around the bench that Mary had described. Davide was not best pleased to see that the police had become involved but held back his annoyance with Sara who had obviously contacted them. The superintendent bent down and retrieved the Tizer bottle from under the bench. A small amount of the drink was still inside. Sniffing the contents, he said: 'Just as I thought. This is the smell that was on your nanny's breath. Some sort of Mickey Finn has been added. Probably chloral hydrate.'

On hearing the words "Mickey Finn," Davide and Enrico exchanged knowing glances but remained silent. Never having heard the term before, Sara simply looked bemused.

'No doubt about it,' the superintendent continued, 'Your baby son has been kidnapped. Any idea why? We will check out the name the boy gave your nanny, but it's almost certainly a false one. Also, he was probably lying about coming from a Maltese background.'

'Maltese, eh?' Davide whispered to Enrico.

'No superintendent, I cannot think of any reason why somebody would want to take our son, but I know that I can rely on you and your officers to return him to us safely. Rest assured, I will pay a handsome reward into the police benevolent fund,' Davide added.

The superintendent despatched one of his constables to stand guard at the Levi's front door before setting off with the rest of his men for the police station. As soon as he was back in his office, the superintendent telephoned William Horton and updated him on what had happened. Sara, Davide, Enrico and the gardener, made their way back to the Levi house a short walk away. Once inside, Sara grabbed Davide's arm and pulled him into his study, slamming the door closed behind them. 'What in heaven's name is going on here Davide? Why would someone want to kidnap our son? I have long suspected that your business interests are not all what they seem, but I have kept schtum. Now though, now, this is different. Harry's life could be at risk because of your shady dealings. I am no longer prepared to be the good little wife at home that does as she is told. I saw the look you gave Enrico when the word Maltese came up during the meeting with the police. I demand to know what this is about.'

Davide was quite taken aback with this verbal assault by Sara. He had never seen her so angry. 'My darling, honestly, I do not know how this has come about. However, I have a strong suspicion that Mrs Connell is involved. She has close links with the Maltese community in London, hence my expression to Enrico. I am confident that Harry will not be harmed in anyway. To the people holding him, he is their only bargaining chip.'

'Bargaining chip? This is not some game of poker you play with your relatives on Sunday afternoons, this is your own flesh and blood, our baby boy.' Sara screamed. Davide was about to reply when there was a knock at the study door. The house maid entered and advised Davide there was an urgent telephone call. The foreign sounding caller insisted that this was a personal matter, and he would speak only to Mr Levi.

As Davide picked up the phone, he had no doubt what he was about to hear.

'Good afternoon Mr Levi. Please do not waste our time by asking who I am and issuing threats you cannot carry out. Just listen to what I have to say then do as I tell you. Providing you follow my instructions; your dear baby son will be returned unharmed. Immediately our conversation ends, you will call your solicitor and tell him to draft a letter to Mrs Connell confirming that the existing contract regarding joint ownership of The 40 Club and Pigalle Club is null and void. It will also state that you agree to sell your fifty per cent share in both clubs to Mrs Connell for two pennies. You will sign the letter and have it delivered to Mrs Connell's solicitor, Golding & Partners, 77 Great James Street, London,

WC1. On receipt of the signed letter, an acknowledgement confirming your wish will be delivered to your home with two pennies. You will then be telephoned and told the location of your son.'

Before Davide could say anything, the line went dead. His suspicion that the bitch woman Connell was at the heart of this affair was correct. He also knew she and her thick sons could not have come up with such a plan. No, she had obviously conspired with the Falcons, a Maltese gang run by the Messara brothers. Based in Curzon Street, they operated most of the vice in the West End and were desperate to expand their business into nightclubs.

Davide saw Enrico in the hall and beckoned him to join him in the garden. He recounted the details of the call he had just received. 'Maltese *bastardos*, I will cut their *testicolis* off and they will wear them as earrings,' Enrico exclaimed.

'All in good time my friend. But first we must get Harry back and safely house him together with Sara in Chelmsford under heavy protection. Then, and only then, we will deal with Mrs Connell and the Messara clan. I will now instruct my solicitor to carry out their wishes. In the meantime, Enrico, you will alert the troops including my relatives to be prepared for war. The Maltese scum and the

Irish whore have insulted the Levi name and they will be made to pay for it.'

Davide returned to Sara who was still in the study and explained that Harry would be back with them the following day. He said he would advise the police after Harry was safely home as he did not want them to mess up the arrangements he had made with the kidnappers. Despite Sara's plea for more information, he lied that it would be best for everyone if the details were kept with him alone. After all, Harry's safety was the priority. Sara was not happy but had no option than to agree.

The day after, the legal papers were duly signed and agreed by both parties. Davide received a telephone call advising that Harry was in his pram alongside the bench from where he had disappeared. Davide and Enrico raced to the spot and sure enough the baby boy was there giggling in his pram. Davide picked him up, hugged him and exclaimed: 'Boychick, my beautiful boychick. You little *fershtinkiner*, your nappy needs changing!' Enrico scanned the park for any sign of the kidnappers. There was none. Davide placed Harry back in his pram and wheeled him home. On entering, Sara and Mary rushed to greet them, both had tears streaming from their eyes. Davide called the police superintendent and lied that he had paid a ransom of £500 demanded for the return of his son to the unknown kidnappers. He made no reference to the business transaction that had been made to achieve this. Davide said he had posted a cheque for £100 as a donation to the police benevolent fund and would be sending batches of tickets to the station for West End shows to be distributed to the officers. The superintendent thanked him but said that he should have kept the police informed of developments as they may have been able to apprehend the culprits. However, he was delighted that the baby was unharmed.

Once Sara, Mary and Harry were, under heavy guard, at the Levi Chelmsford household, Davide started to plan retribution for his adversaries. To act immediately would be exactly what the Messaras would expect and be ready for. Naturally, Enrico was thirsty for revenge, but Davide said they should leave it for a while and lull them into a false sense of security. Thereafter would be the time to strike.

CHAPTER 8 – GOOD-BYE-EE! END OF AN ERA

'Divide and rule, that's how we are going to defeat them,' Davide explained to Enrico. 'Firstly, we get word out on the street that the Levis are planning to do serious damage to The 40 Club. On hearing this, the Messaras will deploy most of their Falcons gang at that location in readiness for our arrival. Then, through a friendly third party, strictly no mention of us, we set up a meet with the youngest Messara brother Milo. He's a hot head always out to impress his siblings. The bait will be a huge consignment of cocaine for sale. The venue will be the first-floor room at the Newman Arms pub, round the corner from The Pigalle Club. Make sure that landlord friend of yours is well paid to keep him and his regulars tight lipped about what happens. It is vital that Kath Connell is at the club the night the meeting with Milo takes place so you will need to do some digging to find out when that's the case. When you've finished off the Messara kid, come round and meet me at the back door of the Pigalle. You will then order our boys to storm in and completely smash the place to pieces. When Connell makes a bolt for the back door, our men inside will let her through but nobody else unless her thicko sons are with her, that will be a bonus. If the sons are not with her, ensure they are eliminated in the club. As in some of our past outings, I will plan for a journalist to be at the club to witness the mayhem. Connell, Messara and Falcon members killed will have a penny placed in their eye sockets before we leave.'

Enrico smiled broadly: 'Brilliant boss, I will get to work on it straightaway.'

It did not take Enrico long to find out when the Pigalle had a big event taking place. Kath Connell was intending to host some high-profile society types to an Independence Day party given by the American Ambassador to England, George Harvey. Enrico updated Davide and then briefed the Levi troops with detailed timings.

Enrico and one of his lieutenants waited silently in the adjacent room to where the meeting with Milo Messara was scheduled to take place. The cocky young man and his sidekick were led up the stairs through a door adjacent to the pub by the Newman Arms publican and shown into the meeting room. He closed the door behind them. Inside, the man they had come to meet said nothing by way of greeting, he produced a large packet from his pocket and tossed it to Milo. He in turn passed it to his companion who took out a knife and slit the package. The young man sniffed the contents, put a small amount of the powder on his wetted finger and tasted it. He nodded at Milo who enquired, 'How much of it is there and what is the price?' Before the supposed vendor could answer, the door burst open, and Enrico lunged at Milo with his stiletto. The blade glanced Milo's cheek but embedded itself in the raincoat he was wearing over his shoulders. At the same time Milo's colleague thrust at Enrico with the knife he was already holding but before contact was made, Enrico's lieutenant landed him a crashing blow in the face with his fist sending the man backward, hitting his head against the stone fire hearth. He did not get up; the fall had cracked his skull. Milo threw his coat over Enrico's head and shoved him aside before running down the stairs two at a time. Recovering instantly, Enrico picked up his weapon and gave chase. Milo was about to sprint up Newman Passage when the leather soles of his brand-new shoes slid on the wet cobblestones, and he fell over. Before he could rise, Enrico grabbed his hair, pulled back his head, and slit his throat. He dragged the body over to a dark corner of the alley and pulled a dirty tarpaulin he had arranged for the publican to leave there earlier, over it. He then bounded back up the stairs and with the help of his lieutenant, carried the other body down and put it alongside Milo's. Before leaving the scene, they placed pennies in the dead men's eye sockets.

Both men walked briskly up Newman Passage into Newman Street leaving the pub landlord to clear up the remains of any evidence in his upstairs room and staircase. As he carried out this task, he looked at the brass ornament of the three wise monkeys on the mantelpiece above the fire and said: 'Blimey, see no evil, hear no evil, speak no evil – how very true.'

The decoy drug dealer was long gone.

Enrico checked that Davide and two of their trusted team were located at the Pigalle's' back door. He then returned to the front and gave the signal for the twenty heavily built men carrying an assortment of weapons waiting in doorways along the street to proceed. This they did with alacrity stabbing the two Maltese doormen to death at the entrance. Once inside, they commenced breaking tables, chairs and heads as they went about their business. The ferocity of the onslaught deterred any clients from getting involved, including the reporter from the Daily Express who was cowering under one of the as yet, unbroken tables. They were even more petrified when guns were fired by the attackers at the club's security guards. Three were shot dead and another seriously wounded. On hearing the commotion, Kath Connell rushed downstairs from her office, took one look and made for the back door beckoning her sons who were at the centre of the brawl to follow. They ignored her and carried on trading punches with the insurgents. Arriving at the back door she was surprised to be let through by two thugs who were not letting anyone else make their escape.

'Good evening Mrs Connell,' Davide said. 'In for a penny, in for a pound, eh?'

'You fucking wop yid bastard,' she screamed.

'Big mistake starting a vendetta by kidnapping my son.'

Davide put the barrel of his .38 revolver on Kath Connell's forehead and pulled the trigger. The bullet passed through her skull, exited the other side, ricocheted off the wall close behind her and hit Davide in the chest. Horrified, Enrico caught hold of Davide as he was about to fall and gently lowered him to the ground beside Kath Connell's lifeless body. He pulled out the white silk handkerchief from Davide's top pocket and pushed it hard into the wound to try and stem the bleeding.

'Help me get him to the car,' Enrico shouted to the two Levi gang members standing nearby. As they picked him up, Davide grabbed Enrico's wrist.

'The pennies, don't forget the pennies.' As instructed, Enrico placed pennies in Kath Connell's eye sockets before following the men carrying Davide to the car parked close by in Berners Mews.

Back inside the Pigalle, hostilities were coming to an end. Both the Connell boys had been battered to death with baseball bats. Pennies were, with some difficulty because of the beating, placed over their swollen eyes. Prior to leaving the club, the Levi team carried out the same procedure on the dead Falcon gang members. Staggering towards the exit, the American Ambassador and his guests were numb with shock at what they had just witnessed. The noise of police car horns grew louder as they neared the club.

Laying on the back seat of the Lancia car, Davide was rapidly losing consciousness as it sped towards a Levi safe house in northeast London, just behind the Hackney Empire theatre. Enrico knew it would be a folly to take his boss to the house in Regent's Park in case the police came calling. Once well away from Newman Street, Enrico told the driver to stop the car so he could make a call from a telephone box, a relatively new addition to London's streets. It was vital to get a trusted doctor to be at the safe house when they arrived.

'He's lost a lot of blood,' the doctor, a tall man with a plummy English accent, inexplicably dressed in a three-piece tweed suit in summer, explained to Enrico. 'It's touch and go whether he will make it. He urgently needs to be in hospital. The bullet is lodged close to his heart. If it stays where it is, he will bleed to death. But if it's removed, the same thing may happen.'

Despite being only semi-conscious, Davide could hear the exchange. 'No hospital Enrico. Tell the doctor to get it out here.'

The doctor grimaced. Whispering to Enrico he said: 'Impossible, I don't have the instruments to carry out such an operation. It would have to be done in a proper operating theatre by a highly skilled surgeon with all the equipment to hand.'

Impulsive as ever, Enrico's immediately replied: 'Ok, so is there a surgeon you know who would be prepared to do this on a strictly private basis for a mega fee?'

'It's not that straightforward. As I said, even if I could find somebody, they would need to have all the facilities available, the operating theatre, an anaesthetist, surgical instruments and nurses. You cannot just roll up at a hospital and commandeer these things.'

Enrico was about to respond when Davide called him over. 'Listen carefully my dear friend. I can feel that I am not long for this world. Please tell Sara I am sorry. Tell her that I loved her and Harry more than anything. You must cover up the circumstances surrounding my death. As far as everyone is concerned, you and I were out on music hall business, and I became unwell. Before a doctor could be called, I collapsed. When the doctor here arrived, he pronounced me dead, probably from a heart attack. You will pay-off the pathologist and coroner to ensure that is recorded as the cause of death. Nobody will be allowed to examine me from the neck down. Not even Sara. In line with Jewish tradition, I should be buried within two sunsets. You will stay with my body prior to the burial at Golders Green Cemetery. There is a plot reserved there for the Levi family.'

'But padrone, you're tough, you're going to pull through.'

'Not this time Enrico, not this time, this is the final curtain call, no encore,' Davide said coughing up blood. 'You will take over the running of the business. When Harry comes of age, you will mentor him so that he can ultimately take control. Hold my hand Enrico, swear to me you will do everything in your power to make my wishes come to pass.'

Close to tears, Enrico took Davide's hand. 'I promise boss, I promise. Rest assured this will happen.

Davide smiled and gripped Enrico's hand more tightly. 'Thank you, my friend, thank you. Arrivederci.'

Enrico summoned the doctor as Davide's hand went limp. The doctor checked Davide. 'I am sorry, he has gone.'

Taking a wad of bank notes he had been carrying from his jacket, Enrico gave it to the doctor and briefed him on Davide's instructions regarding arrangements for the burial. He emphasised that the time of death on the official documentation should be recorded as 6pm the previous evening. The location should be shown as Manchester. This way, there could be no question of Davide's involvement in the Pigalle debacle.

'I will ensure that it is done. I will get on to my pathologist and coroner contacts immediately. I will then wait here with Mr Levi until you return. Nobody will be allowed to enter the room.'

'Thank you. I now must travel to Chelmsford to break the news to his wife and family,' Enrico said as he departed, stooped, holding back his tears. But before heading to Essex to see Sara, he had two important calls to make. Firstly, he had to make sure staff at the Levi's Regent's Park house were told to say that Mr Levi had not been in residence since leaving for a business trip in the North earlier in the week. They should also add that Mrs Levi had been staying with relatives in Essex with her son since the kidnapping. Secondly, he needed to put an alibi in place with his contacts in Manchester regarding Davide's demise.

Reading the report of the incident on the front page in the late edition of the following day's Daily Express, the Commissioner of the Metropolitan Police, William Horton, was apoplectic. He was already under tremendous pressure from the Home Secretary, Edward Long, to clean-up London's police force. The press had continuously run stories about corruption and misconduct in the force, and this article highlighted that fact within the introductory paragraphs. The headline read "11 killed in nightclub carnage - Chicago style gangsters now rule London's lawless streets."

As sure as night follows day, Horton knew that any moment, he would be receiving a call from Long. He was not wrong. Just as he finished reading the newspaper article, his secretary stuck her head round his office door and announced the Home Secretary was on the line.

‘I assume you have seen the morning papers. The Prime Minister is furious. He is already being pressed to explain how something like this could occur in our capital city with the American Ambassador present as a witness.’ Long bellowed down the phone.

Horton sheepishly replied: ‘Our initial investigations have shown that the Messara brothers are at the heart of the incident. The body of the youngest Messara, Milo, was found outside the Newman Arms pub just round the corner from the Pigalle Club in the early hours of this morning. There was another body alongside him. Both had been covered by a tarpaulin. We know the Messaras provide protection for the Connell woman’s clubs. But we have no idea about the identity of the other party involved in the fracas. Even more baffling is the reason why the dead bodies at the scene, including Mrs Connell, her sons and members of the Messara gang, and the bodies in Newman Passage, all had pennies placed in their eye sockets.’

‘Have you taken leave of your senses man? Are you suggesting the perpetrators were all Greek and Latin scholars keen to demonstrate it as a payment to Charon?’

‘I’m sorry Home Secretary but I don’t follow.’

‘God give me strength. Charon was the

ferryman who conveyed the souls of the dead across the river that divided the world of the living from the world of the dead.'

'Oh, I see,' Horton said somewhat unconvincingly.

'Look, I don't care a jot about pennies. I just want results. Get off your backside and galvanise your men to make some urgent arrests. I need to provide the PM with something to answer his critics.'

Fortuitously, Horton was holding the telephone receiver away from his ear as the caller slammed down the phone at the other end. 'Cunt,' he said out loud without realising his secretary had come into his office. The poor woman went bright red. 'I am so sorry Mrs Wainwright, my sincere apologies. I was not referring to you.' She placed his cup of tea and two digestive biscuits on his desk and hurriedly withdrew without uttering a word. Elbows on his desk, Horton stroked his curly greying sideburns with his thumbs in concentration. He knew that Davide Levi was in some way involved in this debacle, but he couldn't fathom out in what way. Furthermore, to date, there was no evidence to substantiate his suspicions. He would get that incompetent superintendent at Marylebone Police Station to call on the Levi's residence on the pretext of a follow-up to check that there had been no untoward issues since the kidnapping of the Levi baby boy. With any luck, he might obtain some worthwhile information regarding Mr Levi's activities.

Sara sensed that something was amiss as soon as she saw the look on Enrico's face when he came through the front door at Chelmsford. 'Where's Davide?' she asked as the two men were usually literally joined at the hip.

'Let's go into the study,' Enrico suggested.

Once inside, he asked Sara to sit down. She did so in the chair behind Davide's desk. Enrico remained standing.

'I have some terrible news.'

Alarmed, Sara said: 'What is it Enrico, what's happened?'

Barely able to get the words out, Enrico stuttered: 'I'm afraid, Davide is dead.'

With a look of disbelief Sara screamed: 'He can't be, he was perfectly well when he left here for his business trip.'

'You are right, he was. We had successfully concluded a series of meetings in Manchester about future music hall bookings when Davide collapsed off his chair. I attempted to pick him up but Davide seemed to know that he was seriously ill and instructed me to leave him where he lay. He told me to tell you that he loved you and Harry more than anything in the world. A doctor arrived within minutes, but Davide had died. The doctor said it was a heart attack.'

With tears streaming down her face, Sara sat in a state of shock, her head resting on the desk, for what seemed like an eternity before saying: 'I must see him Enrico. Take me to him now.'

'Of course, Sara, but it is not possible right now. It will not be allowed. The pathologist must carry out his examination and then there is the coroner. Davide's body will have to be brought down to London. You are aware of the procedures within Judaism, that these things must happen rapidly so the burial can take place before two sunsets. I understand there is a Levi family plot reserved at the Hoop Lane Jewish Cemetery at Golders Green. With your permission, I will contact them and a Rabbi at the Great Portland Street schul. Once I have finalised details, I will inform you so you can advise Davide's relatives and friends.'

Sara lifted her head from the desk momentarily and nodded her agreement. Her tears had created small pools on the green leather desktop.

That afternoon, the superintendent from Marylebone Police Station, called at the Levi's Regent's Park house. The maid relayed the information as per Enrico's brief and the inspector left. On arrival at his office, he telephoned Horton and advised that Davide Levi had been away on business in the North of England since earlier in the week. 'Curses, back to square one,' the Commissioner exclaimed.

News travels fast in the criminal underworld. It was still less than 24 hours since the attack on the Follies but the Messara brothers had already received word from their police informants that they were on the Met's most wanted list. The four remaining brothers had no intention to wait and see what British justice had in store for them. That evening they stood smoking staring back at the white cliffs of Dover on a cross-channel ferry bound for France. Their reign as the kingpins of London's vice industry was over for the time being. Although their departure was hurried, they had however, left instructions, together with a hefty payment, for the elimination of Davide Levi and Enrico Monza. Had they known that the former was already in a coffin in Hackney, they could have saved themselves a great deal of cash.

Enrico was then driven from Chelmsford back to Hackney. During the journey he slept on the back seat of the Lancia. The doctor confirmed that all the documentation had been secured so the funeral could proceed the following day. During his brief stop in Chelmsford, Enrico contacted the schul and the funeral parlour. Everything was in place for the burial the following day. He had advised Sara who had immediately commenced telephoning relatives and friends giving them the details for the funeral. But she was still insisting to Enrico that she wanted to see Davide after the *tahara*, the Jewish ritual of washing of the body, was completed before he was interred. Naturally, this presented a major problem for Enrico. He had been assured by the doctor that the pathologist had made a good job of cleaning up and disguising as much as possible the bullet wound in Davide's chest, but it was obviously still visible. According to religious tradition, after washing, the body would normally be dressed in a *tachrichim*, a simple linen garment through which the wound would be seen. The funeral parlour team carrying out the custom were not an issue as they were being paid handsomely to keep schtum about the wound. Enrico telephoned the manager of the long-established funeral parlour to seek his advice. The poor man was clearly nervous about the whole situation and responded to Enrico's questions in a staccato manner. Finally, after some thought, he replied.

'May I suggest Mr Monza that you provide us with a set of clothing for Mr Levi. We are finding that more families are choosing this option rather than the traditional tachrichim. This way, Mrs Levi will be able to see her beloved husband before the burial without seeing the hmm, you know what.'

'*Molto bene*. An excellent solution. Thank you so much. I will bring the clothes to your office later today,' Enrico said. He then set off for the Regent's Park house. Once there, he showered and changed into the clothes that he would wear at the funeral the following day. He then went into Sara and Davide's bedroom, opened Davide's wardrobe and selected a beautiful Savile Row tailored navy-blue suit that appeared to be brand new. He also took a white shirt, maroon tie, a vest, underpants, socks and highly polished pair of black brogue shoes. Before leaving the house, Enrico gathered the staff and told them the sad news about Mr Levi's heart attack and death in Manchester. Mary and the maid burst into tears and were consoled by the gardener.

'I know that this has come as a shock but it is important to Mrs Levi and the family that you carry on with your duties as normal. Any enquiries about Mr Levi's death or funeral arrangements should be directed to me. Just take a note of the caller, their telephone number, their company if applicable, and the information they require. Tell them that somebody will get back to them as soon as possible. I will telephone here to pick up the messages from time to time,' Enrico instructed.

By the time Enrico arrived at the undertakers, it was late at night. He dismissed his driver and took the case of clothing into the office where the staff were waiting. They relieved him of the case and proceeded with the *tahara* in an adjoining room. Enrico sat down and listened as they recited psalms and prayers in Hebrew while they carried out their task. Having completed their work, Enrico was ushered into the room and saw Davide's body looking resplendent in the outfit he had brought. He thanked the team who departed rapidly and locked the office behind them. In compliance with Davide's wish, Enrico pulled up a chair and sat next to the body before dropping off into a deep sleep. He awoke the following morning with a start. There was a loud banging on the front door of the undertakers. Rubbing the sleep from his eyes, he walked into the front office and saw Sara peering through the window with two of his men who had driven her down from Chelmsford. Enrico acknowledged them and indicated that he needed to find the keys. As he was going through the drawers of a desk, the manager of the funeral parlour arrived, opened the door and followed Sara in.

'Where is he Enrico?'

'Through here,' he replied, showing her the way.

The manager locked the office door and sat down at his desk. Sara's drivers remained outside.

'He looks so peaceful, please leave me Enrico, I want to sit here with Davide for a while.'

'As you wish Sara but please do not touch the body. It has been carefully prepared for the service.'

Sara looked puzzled but closed her eyes in agreement. She sat for a long time thinking back about the times she and Davide had been together. The meeting onboard the Titanic, the first time they made love, the purchase of the Palace Theatre in Manchester, the houses in Chelmsford and London, their attendance at society events, and last but by no means least, the birth of their lovely son, Harry. Why had Davide died? He was always fit and healthy, not like some of the obese businessmen he dealt with. Why had she admonished him for Harry's kidnapping? Was it really down to his questionable business dealings? Why had she not told him how much she loved him before he left for his business trip? She took her white lace handkerchief from her sleeve and dabbed her eyes. He would want her to be strong today. It was essential that she should show the Levi mettle at what was about to follow.

Sara must have been in the room for some considerable time when her train of thought was broken by a soft tapping on the door. She rose, kissed Davide on the forehead and went over to the door. The funeral parlour manager introduced the Rabbi.

Shaking her hand he said: 'My sincere condolences Mrs Levi, I am so sorry for your loss. It is good to see you again but obviously, I would have preferred it to be in different circumstances. You probably don't recall but I attended to your son shortly after his birth. Your husband was a great supporter of our synagogue.'

Sara was somewhat bemused by his comment about the schul as Davide had never demonstrated any great interest in religion.

The Rabbi continued: 'I had the pleasure of meeting your husband on many occasions over the years. This, together with what I have read in the newspapers about him, has enabled me to put prepare this eulogy for the service. I would be grateful if you could cast your eye over it to ensure I have not made any serious errors.'

Sara took the two sheets of foolscap paper and read the Rabbi's glowing words. How could a life be summed up on just two pieces of paper? It simply did not seem right. She was choked but could not think of anything to say other than to thank the Rabbi.

An overcast sky surrounded the spire of St Jude on the Hill Church close by Hoop Lane Cemetery, Golders Green. It was humid and rain was a distinct possibility.

The memorial hall at the Jewish cemetery was full to bursting. Standing room only in fact. The mourners list read like a who's who of British music hall. Everyone entering had been greeted and vetted by Enrico at the entrance. Like Enrico, all four of his men alongside him were smartly dressed in black. Others were stationed inside the hall in case of trouble.

The cortege pulled up outside the hall and the pallbearers stepped forward as the back door of the hearse was lifted open. They included Davide's estranged brother Leonardo or Lenny as he was known in the Levi family, Enrico and the Jewish actors Bud Flanagan and Leslie Howard.

Sara stepped out of the car behind the hearse accompanied by her dear friend, Christabel Pankhurst. Both were dressed in black, and Sara wore a black lace veil in the style of a Spanish mantilla. The five cars that followed disgorged an assortment of Davide's close and distant relatives. Watching the arrival through the cemetery railings a little way up Hoop Lane, in plain clothes, was Police Commissioner Horton and the superintendent from Marylebone Police Station. Horton was still convinced that the attack on the Pigalle was masterminded by Davide Levi. Suspicions were all well and good, but evidence was another thing. And, so far, he had been unable to uncover a link between the impresario and the Newman Street Massacre as it was now being referred to in the press. Seeing the coffin, the Commissioner realised that his task had just been made more difficult, if not pointless.

The policemen were not the only spectators. From another vantage point opposite the gates, two heavily built men were observing the proceedings. However, their focus was not the coffin, their eyes were fixed solely on Enrico Monza.

As Sara, Christabel and the family members made their way slowly into the memorial hall, an altercation arose at the gates of the cemetery. Enrico had spotted a photographer taking pictures. He alerted one of his men who strode over to the photographer and ripped the camera from his hands. Despite protestation, the thug opened the back of the camera and removed the film, placing it in his pocket. He then threw the camera on the ground and stamped on it several times before returning to Enrico's side. Witnessing the incident taking place, the police superintendent was about to intervene when Horton grabbed his arm and pulled him back.

'Leave it, we don't want to advertise our presence,' he hissed between gritted teeth.

Prior to taking their seats in the hall, the *Kriah* took place. Sara and Davide's family members had an item of their clothing torn. This Jewish tradition demonstrates that your heart is torn by the death, and you are formally in mourning.

The service conducted by the Rabbi was dignified, just as Sara had requested. Although some of Davide's entertainment friends had asked to speak, she declined for fear that the ceremony would turn into a frivolous music hall act. Davide's coffin was placed on a cart and wheeled to the graveside by Sara assisted by Lenny Levi. Once there, the pallbearers lowered the coffin into the grave. Sara was handed a shovel which she firstly turned upside down to show, in accordance with tradition, reluctance to bury a loved one. She then shovelled two lots of earth into the grave. Thereafter, this procedure was undertaken by all the mourners. Just as the Rabbi was about to recite the *Kaddish*, the Jewish prayer for the dead to conclude the ceremony, Florrie Forde, the music hall star whose rise to fame had been greatly assisted by Davide, started to sing the chorus of her popular song.

"Good-bye-ee, good-bye-ee
Wipe the tear, baby dear, from your eye-ee
Tho' its hard to part I know
I'll be tickled to death to go
Don' cry-ee, don't sigh-ee
There's a silver lining in the sky-ee
Bonsoir, old thing, cheerio chin chin,
Nah-poo, toodle-oo, good-bye-ee."

Following the reading of the *Kaddish*, the mourners filed away to the taps at the cemetery's entrance to cleanse their hands. Sara stood alone by the grave. A light rain began to fall.

The day after the funeral, Enrico convened a meeting of his troops in the Levi owned house behind the Hackney Empire. In the large downstairs room dense with cigarette smoke and a pungent smell of body odour, where Davide had died just three days earlier, Enrico addressed the men.

'Business as usual,' was his opening gambit. 'With the boss gone from now on, I'm running the show. It's what he wanted. We've got rid of the Connell woman and the Maltese bastidos. You could say the Falcons have flown.'

Hearty laughter from the men and a burst of applause greeted Enrico's quip.

'The music halls and cinemas are doing nicely, so no need for any radical changes. Besides, they are legit. The Messara's brasses business is up for grabs and we are going to do just that.'

Enrico then outlined how they should go about this task.

'The first thing we must get a across to these slappers is their Messara pimps are no longer around to protect them. They have to quickly understand that we are now taking that responsibility on, and they will have to pay for it just as they did to the Maltese scum. There's bound to be a few mouthy ones who object and say they can operate on their own. In those cases, I will leave it to you to convince them in the usual way that is not going to happen. Word will soon get around and any thoughts of a rebellion will be quashed.'

A knowing smile broke out on the men's faces except for one at the back of the room. He was a young new recruit to the Levi mob. Immediately after the meeting he would need to report back to his boss on Enrico's plans.

Following the gathering, Enrico with two of his cohorts, headed over to the Levi house in Regent's Park. Sara had opened the doors to friends and relatives to sit shiva, the Jewish form of mourning that would last for a week.

Meanwhile, things had fallen neatly into place for Police Commissioner Horton. The newspapers were reporting that the Messara brothers had been driven out of the country because of the swift action taken by the police. The articles went on to state that London's streets would now be much safer. The critical tone adopted previously had now been replaced by praise for the efforts of the Metropolitan Police Force. Naturally, Horton revelled in this newly acquired positive image. However, deep down he knew that this was not the end of gang warfare in the capital, it was merely a respite. And mercifully, there was no reference to the other party involved in the incident at the Pigalle Club which he was still sure was linked to the now deceased Davide Levi.

Later that week Enrico received word from one of his men that Anna Kowalski, a self-appointed spokeswoman for the biggest group of prostitutes formerly under the Messara's rule, was creating waves. She was protesting about the level of charges being demanded by the Levi mobsters. The charges were much higher than their previous "protectors." Furthermore, the strong-arm tactics being adopted were frankly stupid as girls who had been beaten up were now in no fit state to attract customers, thereby reducing income for everyone concerned. Begrudgingly, Enrico decided to take one of his men along with him and pay a surprise visit to Miss Kowalski's at her Shepherd's Market flat.

'This could prove amusing in more ways than one,' he joked to the lieutenant who had ably assisted him disposing of Milo Messara at the Newman Arms. 'We will go round there tomorrow. Firstly, I will get her to perform a trick for me as part of the negotiations, then I will tell her to fuck off,' he said.

The lieutenant was delighted that Enrico had once again chosen him to escort him on an important mission. Indeed, he couldn't wait to tell his news to some other members of the gang as they sat supping beers in the York Minister pub in Soho that evening. Amongst them was the new recruit.

As the two men climbed the stairs to Anna's flat, Enrico was surprised by the expensive décor. Flock wallpaper and deep pile carpeting everywhere.

'Not what you'd experienced when visiting a whore's place in Soho. Business is obviously good for the tart to afford this in Mayfair,' he muttered to the lieutenant.

Anna gave the appearance of being shocked as she opened her door. She knew who Enrico was having been shown a photo of him but made out she did not. She assumed the other man was one of his gang.

'Who are you?' she asked blocking the entrance to the flat. 'You don't have a booking and I definitely don't do threesomes,' she insisted.

Enrico pushed Anna aside and barged his way in.

'Wait outside,' he ordered his sidekick, slamming the door behind him.

'I'll call the police,' Anna shouted moving towards the telephone.

Slumping into a sumptuous chesterfield sofa, Enrico replied: 'Sit down and shut up. I am Enrico Monza of the Levi organisation and I'm here to listen to your concerns about the charges we are making to look after you and the other girls on the former Messara circuit.'

Regaining some of her composure, Anna said: 'Oh, I didn't realise. Of course, I've heard of you. You could have let me know you were going to come round here.'

'Ah, but that would have spoilt the surprise wouldn't it Anna?'

Enrico looked around the spacious flat. New furniture, classy light fittings, modern paintings and ornaments. The bedroom door was open revealing a large bed with a mirror above it on the ceiling.

'Drink?' Anna enquired.

'Judging by the surroundings, I guess champagne should be the call of the day,' he laughed. 'But a scotch on the rocks will be fine,' he added.

Anna poured two scotches from a cut glass decanter. She used an ice pick to break up two blocks and placed them into Enrico's glass. She handed it to him and sat down opposite. She was a very attractive lady in her early thirties with auburn hair and high cheek bones. As she crossed her long legs, her low-cut, short red sequined dress showed that she was not wearing stockings or panties.

'I am sure that we can reach an amicable agreement about our charges,' Enrico advised as he sipped his drink with his eyes fixed on

Anna's ample décolletage.

'Let's discuss the matter in more detail in there,' he said pointing to the bedroom.

'Christ, you don't hang about do you?' Anna replied, indicating the way for Enrico.

As she followed him in, she slipped the ice pick on the sideboard up her sleeve. Once in the bedroom, she pretended to plump up the pillows and as she did, put the pick underneath.

The pair of them quickly undressed and got into bed. Enrico's erect penis indicated to Anna that there was not going to be any foreplay. She passed him a condom which he hurriedly put on.

'As Enrico mounted Anna, she whispered in his ear: 'Easy tiger, what about the charges?'

In an obvious state of extreme excitement as he entered her Enrico stammered: 'Afterwards, afterwards.'

Meantime, outside the flat, Enrico's lieutenant was smoking and thinking about the fun his boss was having inside.

'Excuse me.'

The voice came from an elderly lady whose head was poking out of the door of a flat further along the corridor.

'I cannot seem to turn the gas knob to off on my oven and I'm afraid I'll blow the building up,' she pleaded.

Stubbing out his cigarette by squeezing the tip between his fingers, the lieutenant responded: 'No problem, I'm coming luv, didn't want to come in with a fag on if there's gas escaping.'

He followed the old lady into her flat towards the kitchenette area when a big man stepped out smiling from behind its sliding door. Before the Levi man could react, he felt a cord wrapped round his neck by another man who had been hiding behind the front door. The powerful arms pulled the cord tightly and did not release it until the victim's body crumpled lifeless to the floor. The two thugs who had been spying on Enrico at Hoop Lane Cemetery packed the body into one of the two large trunks they had brought with them.

Caressing Enrico's back as he slowly moved up and down on top of her, Anna feigned ecstasy. Carefully she reached under the pillow and removed the ice pick concealing it in her right hand whilst the fingers on her left hand located the precise location on Enrico's spine where she had been trained to ram the ice pick. As Enrico reached climax, summoning all her strength, Anna thrust the pick into his back.

He screamed a stream of Italian obscenities and grabbed Anna by the throat with both hands. But as he squeezed his grip loosened. He toppled sideways off Anna and the bed landing on the floor face up, causing the ice pick to go even further into his back. His body writhed in agony a couple of times then lay completely still. Enrico's penis remained erect with his semen in the nozzle of the condom hanging over one side. The reflection in the mirror above made it resemble a mini airfield windsock.

Anna stepped out of bed and pulled on a Liberty print silk dressing gown. She telephoned the number of the flat along the corridor, confirmed mission accomplished and waited. Minutes later there was a knock at the flat door. The two men came in and placed Enrico's body into the second trunk they had brought with them. Without saying a word to Anna, they placed a thick envelope on the sideboard. They then left the building assisted by two other men with both trunks and loaded them into a van outside. After she had closed the door behind them, she opened the envelope and counted out the wad of notes. More than enough for her to return to her native Warsaw, set up home and ply her trade there. She called for a taxi and went downstairs with the suitcases she had packed in readiness to await its arrival. Anna had no intention of sticking around to be on the receiving end of retribution from Enrico's colleagues.

The bodies were driven a short distance to Brook Street and, through a financial prearrangement with the site foreman, deposited in the foundations of an extension being built on Claridge's Hotel. On receiving the news in France, the Messara brothers raised a toast. Their cocktail of choice was "The Flapper" created by Claridge's barman, its ingredients included champagne, crème de cassis and strawberry puree.

'Santé to the late Enrico Monza, the only guest at Claridge's who will stay the longest without having to pay,' the eldest Messara roared.

Predictably, there was considerable consternation following the disappearance of Enrico and his lieutenant, amongst the Levi mob. Also, mysteriously, the whereabouts of the new gang recruit were not known. Shortly afterwards, the gang members who were present when drinking at the York Minster recalled their mate's comments about joining Enrico for a surprise visit to Anna Kowalski. A team of Levi men went round to Anna's flat to investigate but ascertained from a well-dressed elderly lady neighbour, wearing a great deal of jewellery, that she had moved out days ago.

A week came and went when two of the senior Levi gang members made a power play for leadership. The resulting razor fight, cheered on by gang members, in the cellar of the Hackney house, was a draw. Both contestants were left dead on the floor lying amongst various body parts and an ocean of blood. The aftermath followed a pattern similar to previous criminal dynasties that had existed in London. Another mob, the Cortesis, also of Italian heritage, stepped in to fill the void left by the Levis whose empire, in no time at all, unravelled. Levi gang members drifted away and joined the Cortesis or other outfits. Davide Levi's death had undoubtedly brought about the end of an era.

CHAPTER 9 – GROWING UP

Through reliable sources, Sara and her brother-in law Leonardo had heard that the family's connections to the underworld were now severed for good. Whilst devastated by Davide's passing, both were relieved that involvement in "questionable businesses" was now a thing of the past. The contents of her late husband's will made Sara an extremely rich woman. Huge amounts of properties, investments and cash meant that she and Harry were financially secure for the rest of their lives. Even so, Sara felt it was necessary to review what had been bequeathed to her and consolidate, particularly the properties. For a start, she had no real need to retain the Chelmsford farmstead, so she decided to pass the deeds to the Levis who lived there. She had no real understanding of the entertainment industry. This was Davide's province and she decided that it would be better to sell-off the music halls and cinemas. Sara instructed the Levi company solicitors accordingly and at the same time asked them to look at devesting from various businesses that Davide had accumulated either through outright or partial ownership over the years. Whilst at face value this was the logical thing to do, on reflection, perhaps she should have thought about it more deeply because this company had been party to all of Davide's nefarious dealings. In other words, they were far from whiter than white in the way they conducted their business. However, Sara believed the proceeds of these actions would further increase the cash available for the family in perpetuity. Sorting these things out together with Sara's women's rights and charity activities would consume a great deal of her time. She had always been an attentive mother but in the immediate future, Harry's upbringing would have to be left mainly to Mary. Sara also intended to ask Leonardo if he would lend a hand with Harry as a father figure in the boy's life.

Leonardo or Lenny as he preferred to be called was a Batchelor but loved children. He was physically quite different in appearance to his brother Davide. His stature was more in the mould of their father, Alfonso, short, dark-skinned, muscular and hairy. From an early age Lenny decided he wanted nothing to do with the "family business." He was the epitome of "poor boy makes good." He left his parents' home in his early teens and cut his teeth selling crockery from a stall in Ridley Road Market in Hackney. Lenny had all the spiel for flogging his goods performing juggling acts with cups, saucers, plates and tea pots to attract the punters to his stall. The demand for cheap homeware was high amongst poorer Londoners and Lenny's business went from strength to strength. Unlike the other stall holders, Lenny did not waste his money at the bookies or the pub. Instead, he saved his profits and very soon had the money to open a fish & chip shop in the market. The first shop of this kind had appeared in the mid 1800s in nearby Bow and had become a staple diet of Londoners. By pure hard graft, Lenny had expanded his outlets to five around the capital. The nearest to Davide and Sara's house was in Whitfield Street, Fitzrovia. Despite its proximity to Regent's Park, there was little contact between the brothers when Davide was alive.

Lenny and Sara sat in the white-tiled back room of the Whitfield Street chippie drinking tea with the smell of oil wafting through from the fryers in the shop.

'Look Sara, I am more than happy to keep an eye on Harry as he grows up and steer him in the right direction. But I don't want him to become a spoilt brat and shipped off to a private school at the earliest opportunity. He should have as near as possible, a normal upbringing. This will make him understand that to be successful in life, you must work hard by honest means.

'I hear what you say Lenny, but Davide would have wanted only the best for his boy. Eton or Harrow, then Oxford or Cambridge.'

'Sounds great but I'm sorry to say that is more likely to lead him down his father's career path.'

'That's a ridiculous notion. Like you, in the early days, Davide was brought up in a non-privileged manner. Surely, by giving Harry a better start in life with children from upper class backgrounds, he will develop into a nice young man?'

'You must be joking. Most of the *mushuganahs* that have come through that system are bent as hell, in more ways than one. Politicians, the police and the aristocracy, to name but a few. No, a local school with kids from all sorts of backgrounds and regular visits to Levi family gatherings is the answer.'

'Do you honestly believe that sitting watching you and your aunts and uncles spieling around the poker table for pennies on a Sunday afternoon will be of benefit to Harry?'

'Yes, I do, because it will give him a sense of belonging as part of a wider family. Besides, on occasion, some of his cousins will be there, so it's not just a bunch of *alte kakers*. Much better than being stuck here with the Irish Molly, night and day, doting on his every whim.'

'Her name is Mary, not Molly, but I suppose you may have a point.'

After a good deal of toing and froing, Sara finally relented.

'Alright Lenny, I am prepared to accept your approach. But if the plan goes awry, we will revert to my original thinking.'

'Excellent, now what do you fancy for supper, a nice bit of cod or plaice with your chips and a wally?'

'A wally? What for heaven's sake is that?'

'That's what they call a *haimisha* cucumber over in the East End.'

'Oh, I see, a pickled gherkin. I'll give it all a miss thanks Lenny. I'm putting on weight and that will certainly not help matters.'

Sara gave Lenny a peck on the cheek and bade him farewell as she glided down the steps of the chip shop. Her driver was waiting outside finishing off a bag of chips. Quickly disposing of the bag, he rubbed his hands and opened the door of the Lancia. The car pulled away for the short journey back to the house in Regent's Park.

During the following couple of years, Lenny

stayed true to his word. Despite the pressures of running his constantly expanding chip shop business, he made regular visits to see his nephew. Such visits usually comprised Lenny taking Harry out into Regent's Park to play. It seemed to him that the boy was continually cooped up indoors waited on hand and foot by Sara, Mary and the house maids. What he needed was more fresh air and exercise to toughen him up. Harry greatly enjoyed the time his uncle spent with him, particularly when they took a ball with them for a kick about. He loved to see the look of horror on his mother and Mary's faces when they returned, and he was covered in mud from his exertions diving around like a goalkeeper. On days when the weather was too inclement for playing in the park, Lenny would take Harry out in his van to call in at his shops. While Lenny was chatting to his employees at these locations, Harry would be given a bag of chips and a bottle of pop. In his eyes, preferable to the food he was fed at home.

Another trip that Harry was always keen to go on was when his uncle took him to Club Row Pets Market in the East End. Harry loved to walk amongst the stalls looking at the exotic birds in cages, tortoises, dogs, cats and just about every other animal imaginable. Far and away Harry's favourites were the dogs.

He quickly learnt all the different breeds and begged Lenny to buy him one to take home. Appealing as his eyes were, his uncle pointed out that it was more than his life was worth if he bought a dog without Harry's mother's permission.

'Perhaps when you are a bit older,' was the stock reply from Lenny.

One visit to Club Row in 1923 proved memorable for all the wrong reasons. As Lenny and Harry were wending their way around the stalls, with Lenny talking to some of the owners he knew from his crockery selling days, there was an explosion followed by hordes of screaming people stampeding down the street.

Yells of: 'Earthquake, runaway horses, men with guns,' rang out as the mob steamed by.

Lenny grabbed Harry and pulled him into the safety of a doorway behind one of the stalls.

In the panic that ensued, hundreds of birds, cats and dogs escaped from cages overturned by the marauding crowds. The scenes in the surrounding streets were reminiscent of a zookeeper's worst nightmare. The colourful birds in flight created a rainbow canopy above. Eleven people were seriously hurt in the crush and over a hundred injured. It transpired that the explosion had been caused by the tidal wave of humanity as a stall selling petrol had been knocked over. The police blamed the incident on a gambling game of crown and anchor that had got out of hand when rival gangs clashed. But the stallholders knew this was not the true reason. Although gangs existed in the area, they would never do anything that would harm children and animals. No doubt about it, the stampede was triggered by a brawl between honest and dishonest canary sellers.

'For gawd's sake, don't breathe a word of this to your mother,' Lenny instructed Harry before they started back to the relative calm of Regent's Park.

As anticipated, Sara continued to be supportive of her dear friend Christabel Pankhurst's women's suffrage activities. But she was finding it increasingly difficult to come to terms with the Women's Social and Political Union's more militant crusade to achieve its ends. Hunger strikes and damage to public property had become an integral part of the movement's plan to get the government to grant votes to women. So, when Christabel advised, she was moving to California, Sara breathed a sigh of relief. Sara maintained an interest in women's suffrage but focused more of her efforts on charitable organisations, especially those involving London's Jewish community.

Lenny's plans for Harry evolved just as he originally conceived. The boy was now four and would shortly be starting infant school. Accompanied by Lenny, his initiation into the Levi poker school on Sunday afternoons had already taken place. Sara rarely attended these sessions at Aunt Zelda's Rathbone Place flat but was happy for her son to go as it gave him the opportunity to meet other members of the Levi clan.

'Somebody's shy, it's ace pot and the kitty is short of two coppers, who's not put in?' The words came from a formidable looking woman dominating proceedings at the huge round table surrounded by seven Levi family members. Aunt Zelda was the archetypal Jewish matriarch. Every Jewish family had one and Zelda played the part perfectly. Dressed from head to toe in black, she was a rotund woman whose bottom spilt over the sides of the bentwood cane chair that creaked under the strain of her weight. Now in her eighties, Zelda's short grey hair although brushed had an unkempt appearance. Her spectacles, that could have done with a clean, were perched low on the end of her pointed nose allowing her to peer over them to scrutinise the other players. Her pudgy face sported a tuft of grey hair on the chin that was almost goat-like.

Lenny piped up: 'It wasn't me but to prevent further hold-ups, I'll put it in,' he said tossing a couple of pennies into the pile in the centre of the table.

'Mr *Gvir*, eh? Must have a good hand,' Aunt Zelda blurted out. Summoning Harry she said: '*Bubbleleh*, come over here to help your Aunt Zelda with her cards.'

Zelda was in fact, Harry's great aunt but everyone in the Levi brood referred to her as "Aunt" irrespective of whether that was correct in relation to them or not.

Harry had been sitting in the corner going through piles of black and white photographs, some in albums and some loose. He had been informed that they had been taken by his late father Davide, rest his soul. The photos were mainly of Levi family members including Harry when he was a babe in arms. But there were also many of people in theatrical costumes on stages. Deep in concentration, Harry was fascinated, especially with the ones depicting music hall artistes, and did not respond to his aunt until her second call. He had already learnt the basics of poker and standing behind Zelda, could see that she had a full house, three kings and two tens.

'Looks good he whispered in his Auntie's ear, worth a punt.'

‘I’ll chip sixpence,’ said Zelda.

Murmurs of: ‘Snow in the kitty,’ resounded around the table followed by everyone except Lenny, throwing in their cards.

Opening his hand of cards again to consider his next move, Lenny replied: ‘I will see you and raise you sixpence,’ putting the coin in.

‘What d’ya think *Bubbleleh*?’ Zelda asked Harry. ‘Is your uncle bluffing?’

Looking at Lenny across the table Harry thought for a moment then said: ‘Did he buy any cards?’

‘Yes, one,’ Zelda answered.

‘Then he could have the same as you or fours. Your call.’

‘Hmm, ok, I’ll see your sixpence,’ Zelda pronounced.

The Levi’s played their own version of poker, slightly different from the standard rules. Theirs did not permit ‘raises’ to go beyond two. After all, despite the inevitable Jewish competitiveness, the game was only for small change. Lenny laid his cards out on the table face up. Two aces and two Jacks.

‘Two lousy pair, you bluffing *mamzer*,’ exclaimed Zelda, scooping the pile of coins towards her.

'Well, it was worth a try,' Lenny laughed.

Giving the sixpences from the kitty and a sloppy kiss to Harry, Zelda whispered: 'You brought me luck *bubbleleh*, put this in your money box when you get home.'

Harry politely thanked his great aunt, pocketed the gelt and returned to sifting through the photographs. Reverting to the theatrical selection, he separated those that featured people with black faces which gave him an idea. He slipped out into the kitchen. Nobody noticed as the poker game was reaching a heated climax before the players broke for the traditional tea Zelda had produced. Once in the kitchen Harry searched for the box his Auntie kept under the sink containing shoe cleaning items. Harry removed the lid of the black polish, took a cloth and went over to a mirror and started to rub the polish onto his face and hands. Satisfied with the look he had achieved, he walked into the room where the adults were finishing their card game. He announced a song he was going to perform for them that he had learnt from playing gramophone records at home.

'Ladies and gentlemen, I give you a rendition of "Lily of Laguna" by the "Chocolate Coloured Coon."

'She's no girl

for sittin' down to dream

she's the only Queen

laguna knows

I know she likes me

I know she likes me

because she said so

she is my lily of laguna

she is my lily and my Rose'

On seeing and hearing this spectacle, the adults became hysterical with laughter shouting "Encore, Encore." Harry then sang the second verse:

'She's my lady love

she is my dove

my baby love

She's no girl

for sittin' down to dream

she's the only Queen

laguna knows

I know she likes me

I know she likes me'

He took a bow and cheekily went round the table with one of Aunt Zelda's hats. The adults, still in fits, readily poured their pennies into the hat. Lenny joined in the laughter but immediately started to worry how he would clean the polish off before taking Harry back to his mother.

Lenny dropped Harry off at Regent's Park later that evening and gingerly attempted to creep out quickly but on seeing her son's face, Sara shrieked for him to return.

'How did he get all this blacking over his face?' Sara demanded.

'Ah well, you see, Harry spent a good deal of time at Zelda's thumbing through lots of old photographs. I guess he saw some of Davide's photos of G.H. Elliott performing when he was blacked up.'

Desperately trying to change the subject, Lenny continued: 'Seems he may be interested in learning more about photography, just like his old man.'

Harry then interrupted: 'Can I go down to father's photographic studio?'

Both Sara and Lenny were surprised by this request as the lad had not expressed any interest in the room in the past.

Sara thought for a moment then replied: 'Very well but not for long Harry. It's getting late and it will soon be time for bed. Can you take him down Lenny? I have some last-minute changes I need to make to my speech for the opening of the *Hanukah* charity bazaar tomorrow at Woburn Square.'

Phew, saved by the bell Lenny thought to himself: 'Come on then Harry boy, let's go before your mama changes her mind.'

Lenny and Harry ran off along the corridor down the stairs as though in a race. Sara stood and laughed to herself before going into the library.

As they entered the studio, Harry's grip of Lenny's hand grew tighter. He vaguely remembered being taken into the room before, but he now had a strange feeling that made the hairs on the back of his neck stand up. Other than the occasional dust by the maids, the room had remained untouched since Davide was alive. Harry was overwhelmed by the amount of equipment that was dotted around. Of course, he knew what a camera looked like and there were plenty of those on shelves in the room but what were all the other contraptions, bottles and pots for, he wondered.

Lenny flicked a switch and suddenly, the room turned red. Harry's eyes widened as the framed pictures on the walls seemed to take on a more sinister complexion.

'It's alright Harry, nothing to be frightened about. The red light is just part of creating a dark room when you are developing photos,' Lenny explained. 'We will tell you more about all this stuff as you get older. Your father loved this studio. Photography was his passion. Perhaps one day you will take it up as a hobby like he did.'

Lenny turned the switch again and the studio's normal lighting resumed. Harry's barrage of questions was about to come out when Sara's voice could be heard from above.

'Come on Harry, bath and bedtime. You've had a long day. The scrubbing brush awaits for that polish.'

Lenny smiled at Harry and said: 'Better do as your mum says, if you are as interested as I think you are about photography, we can spend more time in here when I'm next over.'

The two of them slowly climbed the stairs. Lenny kissed Harry on the head and left. That night Harry lay in bed and dreamt about taking pictures with his father's cameras of a dog that his uncle had bought for him.

CHAPTER 10 – SCHOOL'S OUT

Finally, the big day had arrived. Just five years old, Harry was about to attend his first day at school. Sara was finding it difficult to hold back her tears of pride as she made the final adjustments to her son's school uniform. Kneeling in front of him outside the gate of the Westminster Jews' Free School in Hanway Place, she tugged down the slightly oversized four buttoned jacket so that it sat neatly on his shoulders. She plucked a small hair that had nestled on his large crisp white shirt collar and then gave a quick wipe to Harry's already well-polished shoes. Owing to her financial status, Sara had been able to pay for Harry's uniform. However, many of the boys and girls at the school came from poor Jewish families and had their uniforms provided from a charitable trust. In her mind, Sara was still questioning the validity of Lenny's insistence that Harry should attend a "normal" school like this one. But it was too late to turn back now so she would just have to go through with it.

The Westminster Jews' Free School was opened in 1883 and was mainly funded by wealthy Jews in the London area. It was founded on the principal that a good education should be available to all Jewish children, no matter what background they came from. A main aim was to anglicise pupils and patriotism was drilled into them. The significance of Empire Day and Shakespeare Day was emphasised. And, as many pupils heard only Yiddish at home, great attention was paid to their accents. An early 1920s admissions register revealed that 65 percent of the fathers of pupils were in tailoring or allied trades. The remainder consisted of shoemakers, tobacconists, hairdressers, small shopkeepers, and restaurateurs. The school achieved extremely high standards and pupils generally did very well, consistently winning scholarships.

The school had a striking red brick façade. It was located in Hanway Place, a narrow-cobbled thoroughfare off Hanway Street that ran in an arc shape connecting Tottenham Court Road at one end and Oxford Street at the other. The planning of the building had been dictated by the peculiar shape of the site. The rooms were built to such a height that the buildings opposite would not block the light and air. Moreover, the limited space made it necessary to allocate as much of the land as possible for playground purposes. Unlike similar structures of the Victorian period, the school staircases and corridors were fireproof, and all the drinking water passed through proper filters.

The building could accommodate 500 children.

The journey from the Levi's house in Regent's Park to the school was quite straightforward. No more than 20 minutes. Most journeys to and from Hanway Place would be made by car with somebody dropping off and picking Harry up. On other days, Mary would take Harry on the underground or by bus. And in the unlikely case that a family member was needed to attend the school urgently, Aunt Zelda lived just round the corner in Rathbone Place. Since Davide's death and with it, detachment from London's criminal fraternity, the possibility of Harry being kidnapped again was extremely unlikely. Therefore, Sara was quite relaxed about these arrangements.

Sara and Lenny had gone to great lengths to prepare Harry for his impending school days. For weeks they had talked positively to him about the new friends he would make and all the activities he could participate in. They had impressed upon him that he should always be courteous to his teachers and fellow pupils. But judging by the expression on Harry's face during these chats and the one he now had outside the school gate, he appeared less than convinced. Not wishing to prolong the agony for both of them, Sara kissed Harry on the cheek and waved to him as he walked slowly into the playground already packed with children and teachers. A final wave from Sara and she rapidly moved out of sight. Dabbing the tears from her eyes, she made her way back to the car that was waiting with its driver in Oxford Street.

Harry stood in the playground feeling sorry for himself. He was determined not to cry. The noise from the students running hither and thither was deafening. Lost in thoughts of photography and dogs, he jumped when he received a tap on the shoulder.

'Hello, my name's Sidney Solomon, I'm a new boy, are you?'

Somewhat taken by surprise, Harry hesitated before answering: 'Yes, I am. My name is Harry Levi.'

'Well, pleased to meet you,' Sidney said, taking Harry's hand and shaking it vigorously.

Sidney was a tad taller than Harry with a shock of black curly hair and blue eyes. His uniform was neat but not as pristine as Harry's. His shoes were scuffed as a result of a kickabout with a tennis ball that Sidney was engaged in with some boys before coming over to talk to Harry. His parents ran a tiny grocery shop in Dean Street, Soho, just on the other side of Oxford Street.

Plucking up a bit of courage, Harry asked

Sidney what class he had been allocated. The details, along with other information, had been sent in a letter to parents in advance of the new intake's arrival.

'1A, it's supposed to be the top class for our year,' Sidney replied in a boastful tone.

'Me too,' said Harry.

'Splendid, hopefully we can sit together,' Sidney responded.

As Harry nodded in agreement, a bell wielded by one of the teachers started to ring loudly summoning the pupils to enter the main school building.

Side by side, the two boys trotted over to the entrance and the beginning of a life-long friendship.

Once inside, they were directed along a corridor to Class 1A where the teacher, Miss Woolfson, welcomed the 25 children, a mix of boys and girls, individually at the door. Harry and Sidney achieved their objective of being seated next to each other at a desk at the back of the classroom.

Miss Woolfson was a petite woman in her mid-forties. She was going grey prematurely with brown eyes, a sallow face and a dimpled chin. She wore a cream-coloured blouse with four vertical thin pink lace strips down the front. Her black skirt was calf length topped by a wide red leather belt. Black patent shoes with small block heels completed her outfit.

Addressing the class Miss Woolfson said: 'Good morning children.'

The class replied as one: 'Good morning Miss Woolfson.'

The teacher then proceeded to outline the way that the school operated. The timings of breaks and lessons, particularly Hebrew, was communicated, and how it was essential for children to be punctual. She said that most of their lessons would be held in the classroom they were now sitting in but obviously, things like PE and Drama would take place in other parts of the school. Although Sidney hung on Miss Woolfson's every word, Harry became bored after the first ten minutes of her talk. The only word she had spoken that resonated with him was "Drama."

The sound of the bell notifying the morning break came as a relief to Harry in that it brought his teacher's droning to an end. As he walked briskly down the corridor towards the exit to the playground with Sidney, he confided to his newfound friend.

'I thought she was never going to stop talking.

Why do adults always have to talk at us rather than trying to ask for our opinion every now and again?'

'That's a good point, Harry, but I suppose she's only doing her job. After all, we do need to know how things works at the school,' Sidney replied.

'The only thing she's said so far that interests me is drama. That stuff about the school play, I'd love to be in it. Perhaps they'd let me sing my music hall songs.'

Stepping out of the door onto a raised concrete plinth surrounded by railings that had three steps down to the playground, Sidney asked Harry: 'How did you learn the songs?'

'My father was in showbusiness, so we have lots of gramophone records at home. Mother says he knew many of the stars that made the records.'

'What's your favourite song?' Sidney asked.

Without a moment's hesitation, Harry started to sing "Lily of Laguna" at the top of his voice. He imagined that the concrete plinth was his stage, dancing around it and making exaggerated gestures with his hands as he sang. Within seconds, in the playground below, a crowd of pupils gathered to watch Harry's performance. He was part way through the second verse of the song when a deep voice from behind spoke gruffly in his ear.

'Stop that at once boy, this is a school, not a music hall. There's a time and place for everything. Your name?' The voice belonged to Mr Silver, the school's headmaster.

Startled, Harry mouthed the word Levi, but nothing came out.

'Lost your tongue boy?' Mr Silver enquired. 'It's Levi isn't it? I met your mother recently at a charity event.'

Now somewhat recovered, Harry replied: 'Yes sir.'

'Well, I think we can find a suitable occasion for you to display your talents to a bigger audience than these,' Mr Silver remarked pointing at the pupils assembled below, at the same time waving them to disperse. 'I shall have a word with our drama and music teacher, Mrs Philpott, to give you a part in this term's school play, "Cinderella." Now run along.'

As Mr Silver turned and went back inside, Harry and Sidney looked at each other in amazement.

'What a stroke of luck, looks like you've got what you wanted, a part in the school play,' Sidney observed.

'Yes, but what part Sidney?' Harry asked.

It did not take long for him to find out.

'One of the mice pulling Cinderella's coach.' Harry exclaimed incredulously to the drama and music teacher, Mrs Philpott. 'I won't be able to sing one of my songs as that,'

'All in good time Levi, when you are in the third year, I'm sure there will be a starring role for you in the school play.'

Mrs Philpott was a well-rounded lady in her late fifties with permed mousey brown hair and a chubby face with a couple of chins. She wore thick rimmed glasses. Her shiny material dress was far too tight in relation to her size which only served to accentuate her large bust and bottom. However, she was a kindly soul and could see that Harry was not happy about the part he had been given. She asked him to stay behind at the end of the class for a chat.

'I admire your chutzpah Levi but as I've explained, the speaking parts in the play are allocated to the older boys and girls as they are more able to learn their lines.'

'But I can do that Miss. If I can remember the words of all the gramophone records, we have at home, learning the lines for a play would be easy for me.'

'I don't doubt that you can do that Levi, but lines and the way they integrate with those of others is a totally different proposition. Learning the words of a song that you and you alone, is going to perform, is much more straightforward.'

Harry did not really comprehend what the teacher was driving at but gave a nod indicating that he had.

'Alright Levi, I hope that clears things up. But rest assured, I will keep you in mind for future productions. And don't forget, you will be one of the mice pulling Cinderella's coach in this year's production. Now run along, it's still playtime.'

Harry trudged off far from happy and recounted the meeting with Mrs Philpott to Sidney.

The rest of Harry's first year at school did not run smoothly. He was not academically inclined. The "Three Rs,'reading, 'riting and, 'rithametic," the cornerstone of primary school education, were of no interest to Harry. Art, music, and drama were the only subjects that stimulated him. Disappointingly from Sara and Lenny's point of view, Harry was also proving to be a disruptive influence in his class. Sara was summoned to the school on several occasions to discuss the matter with the headmaster. However, despite the withdrawal of certain privileges at home and school, things did not improve.

The only positive development that occurred during that year was the friendship established between Harry and Sidney. The boys became inseparable both at school and outside it. Harry was spending more and more time at Sidney's home and his parent's grocery shop below. Playing with Sidney and other kids in the Soho streets around the shop were, in Lenny's opinion, good for Harry as it would toughen him up. Sara was less convinced though. She did not consider herself a snob but had doubts about the free rein that Sidney's mother and father gave their son, and Harry when he was in their charge. Most of the Solomon's time was taken up with the running of their shop to make a living. Consequently, discipline for Sidney and Harry took a back seat.

As the school year drew to a close, the evening of the annual play arrived. There was a buzz of expectation amongst the audience comprising the pupils' parents and relatives. Sara, Lenny and Aunt Zelda were seated in a prime location near the stage. Following a brief welcome and introduction by Mrs Philpott, the curtain rose and the story of Cinderella unfolded with generous intermittent applause and whisperings in the audience as their children appeared. After what seemed like an age, the Fairy Godmother, Ruthie, a girl from year three, took centre stage. She announced how she was about to turn a pumpkin and the three mice, one of which was Harry, into a coach and horses. There should have been a fourth mouse but the lad who was taking that part was sick just as he was about to emerge from the wings, preventing him from going on stage. Just as Ruthie was about to wave her wand, Harry stepped forward and began to sing "Three Blind Mice" at the top of his voice. Sensing this was not part of the script, as one, the audience instantly erupted in raucous laughter. Mrs Philpott screamed from the wings for Harry to stop but he continued regardless. As he completed the last line: *"Did you ever see such a sight in your life as three blind mice?"* Harry took a bow in response to the audience's standing ovation and strode over to the stunned Ruthie and kissed her firmly on the lips before returning to his role of one of the three mice.

The production ended and the cast bowed in unison to the rapturous applause. But Harry was not done yet. He walked between Cinderella and Prince Charming to the front of the stage and bowed and as he did so, the clapping intensified. Mrs Philpott and the Headmaster, Mr Silver, were not impressed.

However, they were reluctant to chastise Harry in front of the parents during the refreshments reception that followed in the adjoining hall. In the circumstances, Harry thought it prudent to stick close to his mother, Lenny and Aunt Zelda. Harry's uncle and aunt were naturally gushing about Harry's performance, but Sara was decidedly unenthusiastic. Her concern was justified almost immediately as Ruthie's parents with their daughter in tow approached. The couple had a stern look on their faces. Ruthie's mother launched the first barrage.

'How dare your son kiss Ruthie like that. She will be the laughingstock of the school and she's very upset.'

Sara had no alternative but to apologise: 'I'm so sorry, I simply don't know what prompted him to do it.'

'Well, it seems to me that it's a total lack of parental control where the problem lies,' Ruthie's father chipped in.

'Now hang on a minute,' Lenny countered. 'They're just kids,' let's ask Harry what he has to say.'

All eyes turned to Harry. 'I love Ruthie, that's why I kissed her,' he said. 'I'm really sorry if I've upset her but that was not my intention.'

‘There you are, the boy has apologised, surely that’s good enough?’ Lenny added.

Unconvinced, Ruthie’s parents stormed off with Ruthie. As they did so she stared back at Harry with a broad smile across her face.

The next morning, the last day of the school year, Harry was summoned to the headmaster’s office. Like Ruthie’s parents, he was equally unconvinced about Harry’s apology come explanation about his behaviour which he had received word of from Mrs Philpott.

‘Now listen Levi, you will have to change your attitude next term. Your marks in all but a few subjects are woeful. I, together with your teachers and your mother, are far from happy. Your antics during the school play were reprehensible. I would normally punish you with the cane but as it’s the final day, I am going to be lenient and set you some homework. Let me be clear about this. It will all have to be completed during the holidays. No excuses.’

Mr Silver then handed Harry some books and a letter containing instructions regarding the various work that needed to be undertaken.

‘I have advised your mother that you will be bringing this work home so don’t get any ideas about mislaying it. Now on your way and think about what I have said in the weeks ahead. I look forward to seeing you and the excellent work you have produced on your return in September.'

Harry placed the books and letter in his satchel, bowed his head and half-heartedly mumbled his thanks to the headmaster as he left the office. His immediate thoughts turned to how he could get out of having to do the considerable amount of homework he had been set. As he walked out into the playground Harry saw Sidney and a few of his other schoolmates huddled in a corner engaged in "swapsies." The solution to his problem instantly came to him. Cigarette card collecting had reached fanatical levels amongst kids. Achieving full sets of these "fag cards" depicting footballers, cricketers, film stars, cars, animals, and flowers, bestowed massive bragging rights to the holder. Harry had a distinct advantage over most other children because the members of his huge family all smoked liked troopers. At the weekly poker sessions at Aunt Zelda's, his relatives would dutifully bring along their cards for Harry who consistently pestered them, so they did not forget. This constant stream of supplies had enabled Harry to accumulate an enviable collection of full sets.

Harry knew that the class swat, Herbert

Steiner, was desperate to obtain more cards but his family were all non-smokers.

'Hiya Herbie, come over here a moment,' Harry called out.

Herbie broke away from the huddle and sidled up to Harry. He was a well-mannered chubby lad with red hair and glasses.

'I've got a proposition for you. How would you like two complete sets of fag cards?' Harry enquired.

Without hesitation, Herbie replied: 'Yes please, but what are they and what do you want for them?'

'Farm animals and flowers. All you would have to do is some homework that has been given to me.'

Now Herbie was a bright boy well versed in the art of negotiation, and thought for a minute before answering: 'Not keen on flowers and animals, what else have you got?'

Harry had anticipated this response so had offered his less favoured sets first. He was certain his second proposal would do the trick: 'Ok, how about cricketers and footballers?'

'You're on, cards first then I will do the work for you.' Herbie said.

'No, one set first, you give me the work in neat writing because I will need to copy it, then you get the second set, deal?'

'Deal.'

The boys spat on their hands and shook. This type of exchange had been introduced to the playground by Harry as he had seen it taking place between stallholders on his trips to Club Row. Harry passed the books and instructions to Herbie who put them in his satchel, and they parted.

CHAPTER 11 – THE JOKING SCHEMER

On this occasion, the ruse was successful and despite Mr Silver's suspicions when school re-started, he commended Harry for his work. However, Harry's flagrant disregard for schooling continued. The number of pranks he perpetrated increased and two in particular led to him being on the receiving end of the headmaster's cane.

The first involved Harry roping Sidney into his ploy. They gained entry to their classroom before anyone else and removed four empty ink wells from unused desks. Carefully they lifted Miss Woolfson's desk, placed an ink well under each leg and then crept outside. Making sure they were the last to enter the classroom when the bell rang, Harry and Sidney took their seats and waited. Miss Woolfson began to call out the register. When she had completed this task, she rose to start the lesson and in doing so, slightly nudged her desk which tipped over spilling everything onto the floor. The pupils thought this was hilarious and started to laugh at the same time looking knowingly at Harry and Sidney. It only took seconds for the poor teacher to deduce who was responsible for this practical joke. She ordered the culprits to stand outside the class. The headmaster duly meted out the punishment later that day.

Another incident that had the same result was when Harry, this time without Sidney's help, put empty milk bottles in Mrs Philpott's piano before assembly commenced. The teacher counted the children into a hymn but as she hit the instrument's keys, the only sound that emitted was a loud clanking noise. Once again, the class roared with laughter but gave the game away by staring at Harry. Six of the best followed.

Much to Sara and Lenny's despair, things carried on in this vein. Harry remained resolute in his stance that he was only interested in drama, music, and art. In his opinion, every other school subject was a waste of time. Away from school, playing at Sidney's and photography were the only activities that sparked any enthusiasm. Like most children of his age, Harry was also extremely reluctant to go to bed and would do anything to prolong staying up at night. In this respect, one incident occurred each week that enabled him to extend his waking hours.

Every Wednesday Sara attended her women's group meeting and Mary had the night off which meant that Elsie, the housemaid, was left alone with Harry to supervise his bath and then get him to bed. Elsie was a slim, dark skinned attractive girl with a jolly demeaner and a throaty cockney accent. Once Harry was tucked up in bed, Elsie would slip out of her clothes, put on one of Sara's silk dressing gowns, and come into his room. In front of the full-length mirror, she would strike some poses before removing the gown and sitting on Harry's bed. But instead of reading him a story as per Sara's instructions, Elsie would recount explicit details of her latest love affair. As she did so, she asked Harry to fondle her breasts. Obviously, he had no idea what the maid was talking about but as long as he could stay up, he was not bothered. The only thing that intrigued him was the way that Elsie's nipples hardened when he touched them.

Elsie repeatedly reminded Harry that these encounters were very much a secret between the pair of them and that he should never tell anybody about what happened. This secrecy appealed to Harry's child-like mind, and he maintained his part of the bargain. Elsie's Wednesday visits continued for several months but then ceased. Apparently, Elsie had left the employment of the Levi household. Harry overheard hushed comments amongst the adults such as "in the family way" and "bun in the oven" neither of which he understood.

In May 1926, the country entered a volatile period. A General Strike was called by the

General Council of the Trade Union Congress in an attempt to force the government to act to prevent wage cuts and worsening conditions for coal miners. The government refused and almost two million workers from many different industries went out on strike in sympathy with the miners. Transport ground to a halt, schools were closed, and food supplies started to run out. Harry and Sidney stood and watched as hundreds of people marched along Oxford Street en route to the Houses of Parliament to protest.

'If they can go on strike, why can't we?' Harry asked his pal.

'What d'ya mean?'

'Well at some stage, when it re-opens, we will have to go back to school. Why can't we refuse?'

'They'd realise we weren't there.'

'I don't mean every day; I mean just now and again.'

'Oh, bunk off, play truant.'

'Yes.'

'Why not?'

The General Strike ended in a defeat for the unions just a couple of weeks after it began. But it left a lasting impression on Harry. Although just seven years old, it was clear that Harry had a scheming brain incorporating leadership qualities that many older boys would have envied. This manifested itself in a series of entrepreneurial scams he embarked on ably assisted by Sidney.

The horse and cart was still the most favoured form of transport for delivering goods to shops in the 1920s. As a result, horses' natural by-product was very much in evidence on the streets of London. Harry stood and watched his mother hand over some large silver coins to the man who regularly came to the house with sack loads of steaming, smelly horse manure for use in the garden. Within seconds, a plan formed in the boy's head. Here lay an easy route to riches. By gathering up quantities of manure Harry could sell it off at cut price to customers for pennies rather than silver. The returns would enable him to buy supplies of his favourite sweets, sherbet and liquorice. But first he needed to acquire the hardware. The large pram and some of the empty manure sacks in the shed could be used. An implement to pick up the muck presented more of a problem though. Then he remembered seeing a large shovel in the fireplace at Sidney's house. Harry persuaded Sidney to "borrow" the shovel and they set off on their new enterprise.

There was an abundance of raw material for

their new business. However, a row broke out between the boys after the first sack had been filled and placed in the pram. The outcome was that the business ended before it really got off the ground, literally.

'Why do I have to do all the shovelling?' Sidney asked. 'You've got the easy job pushing the pram. Surely, it would be fairer to take turns in shovelling?'

Quick as a flash, Harry responded: 'Well, the thing is that's it's your shovel, and my pram so it's only right that you should shovel, and I should push.'

Sidney was not convinced: 'No, I'm not having that Harry.'

The argument continued back and forth until Sidney became exasperated and swung the shovel at Harry. It just missed Harry who scooped out a hand full of manure from the sack and threw it at Sidney hitting him in the face. He followed up with a second salvo that landed on his body. Sidney screamed, started to cry, and ran off chased by Harry pushing the pram throwing more muck at his friend as he did so.

The next project proved slightly more successful and certainly less smelly. With a great deal of help from the gardener, Harry removed the wheels from the pram. They then took a plank of wood and affixed a wooden box to one end. Smaller pieces of wood were used to create axles to which the wheels were attached at the front and rear of the plank. The front axle had a large screw pin passed through the plank with a length of rope tied to it thus providing a means of steering the cart. The rear axle was static. Harry then proudly announced to his class that "the adventure of a lifetime" in his chariot would be available after school with departures outside Sidney's shop for just one penny a trip. About ten punters followed Harry and Sidney across Oxford Street eager to experience the ride. Things started a bit slowly with some reluctance by the assembled kids to be the first to get aboard. But once it got going, there was no shortage of school mates willing to part with their pennies. Naturally, it was Sidney who pushed the cart and Harry who collected the fares.

The venture went from strength to strength with a steady stream of customers each day after school. Sadly though, an unexpected hitch occurred that led to the cessation of the "Soho Chariot Rides" a name thought up by Harry. Herbie Steiner had initially been unwilling to join the throng of classmates round to Sidney's after school to take a chariot ride. He preferred to head straight for his house to do his homework. Eventually, curiosity got the better of him and off he went to experience "the adventure of a lifetime." Having handed over his one penny fare to Harry, Herbie climbed onto the cart. In an attempt to scare Herbie, Sidney gave it an almighty shove and pushed it at a much faster rate than usual along Dean Street. Herbie screamed for him to slow down but to no avail. The ride had only lasted some 20 yards when disaster struck. As the cart reached the corner of Bateman Street, a car was about to turn into Dean Street. Herbie panicked and yanked at the rope used to steer the cart causing the pin to which it was attached to fly out. Sidney lost his grip on the cart and fell flat on his face grazing his chin in the process. Herbie fared worse. The cart veered sharply to the left straight down the six basement steps of the Soho Working Men's Club. The impact threw Its passenger headlong onto the floor at the bottom of the stairs and landed with the one remaining wheel intact spinning on top of his prostrate body.

Harry and the other kids ran to the scene of the disaster jumping over a dazed Sidney as they did so. Hearing the commotion, the secretary of the Club rushed out of the building's basement door and went over to examine Herbie. Above, at pavement level, Harry and his mates looked anxiously on through the railings. Herbie was conscious and miraculously, apart from some minor abrasions, seemed to be alright. The problem arose when, with the help of the adult, he went to stand up. Herbie let out a blood curdling scream and collapsed back onto the floor. His left leg was broken just above the ankle. The man told Herbie not to attempt moving and went off to phone for an ambulance. The vehicle arrived shortly afterwards and took a sobbing Herbie to the Middlesex Hospital a few minutes away in Mortimer Street.

When Herbie Steiner reappeared at school a week later in a wheelchair, to his astonishment, he was more popular than he had ever been previously. The reason being that all his classmates were keen to write their names on the plaster cast on his leg.

It was not long after this accident that another occurred that ended badly for poor Sidney. However, this time it did not involve a money-making scheme. On a rare visit by Sidney to Harry's house, the latter showed his friend his father's photographic studio. Harry impressed Sidney with the knowledge he had gleaned from his Uncle Lenny about photography. He took one of the cameras and suggested they should go outside in the garden and play at being photographers. Bossy as always, Harry commanded that he would have the first go at being the photographer and Sidney should be his model. After a short time, it became apparent that this was a boring game.

'I know, I will pretend that this is a cine camera like they use to make films and I will be the cameraman directing you, the actor, what to do,' Harry instructed. 'But we need to create a scene that's exciting. Climb up on the greenhouse and slowly walk down the roof as if you are creeping away from doing a burglary.'

Sidney did as he was told and started to walk down the greenhouse with trepidation. Suddenly, there was a cracking noise and Sidney fell through landing on the rows of plant pots below.

Harry shouted: 'Cut!' which on seeing Sidney's arm, aptly summed up the situation. And, for the second time in a matter of weeks, the Middlesex Hospital's casualty department was called into play because of Harry's activities.

Instead of punishing Harry for his misdemeanours, as they had done in the past, Sara and Lenny decided to adopt a different psychology. They hoped that by focusing on his favoured past times he would become more amenable to knuckling down to the school subjects that he hated. Consequently, they took him to the cinema and music hall performances regularly. In addition, Lenny allocated more of his time to giving Harry guidance about photography and introduced him to a long-term friend, the artist, William Sickert.

The venue for cinema visits was predominantly the Tolmer Cinema, opposite Warren Street Station off Euston Road. Just a few years previously in 1924, it was converted from a Congregational Church. Harry loved all the films he saw in 1928, which included "Circus" starring Charlie Chaplin and "The Mysterious Lady" featuring Greta Garbo. But his out and out favourite was "The Cameraman" a comedy starring Buster Keaton, which told the story of a man in Hollywood who was so in love with a girl working at MGM Studios that he attempts to become a movie cameraman to be close to her.

Although Sara had effectively ended her business connections with the music halls following Davide's death, she still received complimentary tickets to shows at The Palladium, Holborn Empire, The Coliseum, and the Hackney Empire. Harry looked forward to accompanying his mother to performances as the seats allocated were always the best, nearest the stage where he could get a great view of his idols. These included some of the biggest stars of the day such as George Robey, Max Wall, Gracie Fields, Will Hay and the man who inspired Harry's "Chocolate Coloured Coon" act, G.H.Elliott.

Lenny endeavoured not to make his talks to Harry regarding photographic techniques sound like lessons. He went to great lengths to ensure these sessions incorporated as much fun as possible by taking his nephew to sites around London to capture images of famous landmarks and local people.

Since the late 1800s, Lenny had enjoyed a close friendship with William Sickert. The artist, whose studio in Camden Town was near Harry's home, had gained fame from his paintings of urban culture in London, especially music hall scenes. Wandering around Sickert's studio while his uncle chatted to the artist, Harry was fascinated by the paintings on the walls. Some of them depicted girls in the nude which reminded him of his secret encounters with Elsie the maid. During one of their visits, Sickert explained that it was his intention to change his style and subject matter after he had completed a portrait of Winston Churchill, the Chancellor of the Exchequer, who had become a friend. Instead, he would take black and white photographs, enlarge and transfer them to canvas, then paint onto the image. Harry liked Mr Sickert a lot but sometimes became a little scared of him when he spoke about his interest in the notorious murderer, Jack the Ripper.

For a short period, it appeared that Sara and Lenny's strategy was beginning to work as Harry's reading, writing and arithmetic improved. Sadly though, this renaissance lasted just a few months before Harry reverted to his old ways. His previously discussed plan with Sidney to play truant from school was resurrected. On these forays, the boys would spend a good deal of their time chatting to the prostitutes who operated around Frith and Manette Streets close to Sidney's parent's shop. The women were very friendly towards the boys and got them to run errands for them. In return, they would give the lads sixpence or sweets. It had been explained to Harry and Sidney what the ladies did for a living. Indeed, sometimes when they were talking to them, the girls would give them a pat on the head and say they would be back in a few minutes as they went off with a client. The only time things became a bit feisty was when arguments broke out between the prostitutes and their pimps. On these occasions the boys learnt a few choice words, but they knew never to repeat them in front of their parents or at school.

Lenny was beginning to lose count of the number of times that he was asked by Sara, following a phone call from the school, to retrieve Harry and Sidney. After he had found them, he marched them back to school for the inevitable appointment with the headmaster's cane.

CHAPTER 12 – HARD TIMES

Apart from some outstanding performances in the school plays and his work in art classes, Harry's reports from The Jews Free School did not improve between 1928 and 1932. Teachers' comments such as, "could try harder," "has the ability but does not use it," and "lacks concentration" appeared frequently on the annual appraisals.

On the home front, things took an unexpected turn for the worse which proved unsettling for Harry. Following her husband's death, Sara had placed her legal and investment matters in the hands of Davide's solicitors' firm, Abraham, Fischer & Partners. At yearly meetings at the company's office in the City of London, Sara was provided with an update of the various dealings that had been undertaken on her behalf. Each time it was pointed out to her that her financial position was rock solid, and she had nothing to worry about. All that was required of her was to sign a few lengthy documents that she did not really understand. As she trusted the company, she did so without question. It therefore came as a shock when at the 1932 update meeting Mr Abraham advised in a solemn tone that her wealth had been reduced to virtually zero because of the

Great Depression in America. Sara sat in total disbelief as the solicitor explained that for the years after her husband's passing, the USA economy boomed and therefore, increasingly bigger tranches of her money had been invested in that country's stocks and shares. The returns from these investments were considerable and the profits were reinvested in more American ventures. The Wall Street Crash in 1929 brought an abrupt end to the bull market but the stockbrokers handling Sara's finances had been confident that this scenario was a blip, and the market would bounce back rapidly. It did not. Consequently, Sara's fortune had been lost.

Mr Abraham apologised profusely but Sara was momentarily too stunned to react. When she did regain her composure, she asked for the documents detailing the transactions that had led to this situation. The solicitor had anticipated this request and handed over two large files. Sara opened the first and stared at the rows of figures. As far as she was concerned, they were incomprehensible. Mr Abraham detected this by the expression on Sara's face, so he proceeded to explain what the various columns of entries represented.

'Can you tell me why my total assets were invested in the American stock market? Surely it would have been more sensible to spread the investments across other countries, not just having all my eggs in one basket as it were.' Sara demanded.

'As I outlined, the brokers believed that the greatest profits were to be gained from US based companies. And indeed, they were proved correct for several years.' Mr Abraham replied.

'But why on earth did they continue to invest in America even when the market there collapsed? At that point it was clearly madness to back more projects in that country.'

In a somewhat condescending manner, the solicitor responded: 'Hindsight is a wonderful thing Mrs Levi, but sadly in stock market dealings, it is of no value.'

By now, Sara's initial shock had turned to anger.

'So that's it is it? I come here and you calmly advise me that I'm penniless, then I'm dismissed, and you move on to your next appointment. You seem to forget that when my husband was alive, he was your biggest client, and in no little way responsible for the growth of your business to where it is now.'

'Mrs Levi, I fully understand that you are upset but you are not the only client who finds themselves in this predicament.'

'Well, frankly, that's of no real comfort to me Mr Abraham. I don't suppose for one minute that you are in this position and must go home tonight to tell your family and friends that you are financially ruined?'

The solicitor went red in the face and tried to stutter an answer, but Sara picked up the files and stormed out of his office. As she did so, Abraham shouted.

'Mrs Levi, please wait, those files are our company property.'

Too late, Sara had left the premises and was driven off in the Lancia that was waiting for her outside.

'Are these *meshuggenehs* for real?' Lenny enquired as he went through the files with Sara that evening at Regent's Park. 'I'm no expert but I'm certain that some of the American companies listed here that your money was invested in over the past couple of years went bankrupt in the original crash in 1929. That was three years ago. How could investments be made in companies that no longer existed? Also, most worryingly, it appears from the files that you authorised the re-mortgaging of your Regent's Park house to create more monies for investments to be made.'

'I've no idea about any of this Lenny but will

you accompany me to Mr Abraham's office first thing tomorrow to ask these questions?'

'No problem, it will be interesting to see what that weasel has to say for himself.'

Sara and Lenny arrived at the offices of Abraham, Fischer & Partners the following morning and were surprised to find a small crowd of well-dressed people outside the door. Lenny made his way through the gathering to read a notice pinned on the large oak panelled door.

"The solicitors' company, Abraham, Fischer & Partners, has ceased trading with immediate effect from today's date, 28th July 1932. Enquiries pertaining to this company's business activities should be directed to the Law Society, Chancery Lane."

Lenny was about to address a gentleman standing by the door when the man said: 'You'll be wasting your time going round to the Law Society. Some people have already been there. Apparently, the directors of this firm have done a midnight flit. No trace of them at their homes or anywhere else. Bastards. I've lost every penny I had.'

Lenny made his way back to Sara, imparted the devasting news and they left.

Sara was a proud woman and was reluctant to

accept Lenny's offer to help her with money and find accommodation for her and Harry. However, she had no alternative until she could establish categorically whether she had any monies left. She felt responsible for being duped by the crooked solicitors. Somehow, she would need to find a new form of income to sustain her and Harry. The first step on that path would have been to sell the Regent's Park house but it appeared that she was no longer the owner. After sitting Harry down and explaining the situation to him, that evening, Sara turned her attention to the staff. With tears in her eyes, she advised Mary, the housemaid and gardener/driver what had occurred. Naturally, they too were extremely upset. Sara had been a good employer and if the new owners of the house did not require their services, finding another job would be difficult. Sara confirmed that she would be able to pay them their wages at the end of August but beyond that, she could not make any guarantees.

Neither Sara nor her employees had to wait long for their questions to be answered. The following morning, two representatives of Coutts & Co Bank presented their calling cards and requested a meeting with Mrs Sara Levi. They were shown into the drawing room by Sara and offered tea or coffee which they declined. In a polite but business-like manner, they explained to Sara that in return for substantial amounts of money paid to Abraham, Fischer & Partners, their bank held the deeds to her house. As proof, they produced documents bearing Sara's signature authorising the transaction. Sara pleaded that she had been tricked into signing the papers and in no circumstances would have done so if she had been aware what they meant. Whilst sympathetic to her accusations, the men could only suggest that she should take the matter up with the Law Society but advised that they needed the property to be vacated four weeks hence. In response to Sara's question as to whether they would require the services of her excellent staff they replied that this was unlikely as the house was to be occupied by an overseas embassy. They were not at liberty to disclose the identity of the country concerned. The men also stipulated that all furnishings should be removed from the property as these would not be needed by the acquiring party.

The same day, the 29th of July, was Harry's thirteenth birthday. As Harry's bar mitzvah party was scheduled to take place at Aunt Zelda's the following week, Sara had secured tickets for the pair of them to attend the opening of the Regent's Park Open Air Theatre for its inaugural performance, Shakespeare's

"Twelfth Night." Thankfully, some earlier rain had blown over and alongside his mother, Harry sat on a grassy knoll enthralled watching the actors play their parts. He particularly loved the way in which Viola disguised herself as a man to achieve her objective in the plot. Although the performance was very different from the music hall shows he had been to in the past, it merely served to confirm to Harry that his destiny lay as an actor treading the boards. And, as far as he was concerned, this could not come fast enough. Harry was aware that the school leaving age was 14 and he began counting the days for his next birthday to come round.

On hearing her son's aspirations, Sara was understandably unenthused. In her mind, she had conceived a plan for Harry to gain a scholarship to a grammar school and ultimately, progress to a place at a university. The reality was that this scenario was never going to happen. Harry's school reports continued to show no improvement and his "away days" with Sidney increased. It appeared that his only real talent was his ability to give the slip to the truant officers who patrolled the streets of central London.

As the remainder of 1932 unfolded, Sara and Harry moved into a terraced three-bedroom house in Whitfield Street, a few doors along from Lenny's fish & chip shop. Lenny had secured it on a rental basis from the man he had bought his shop from who owned several houses in the street. The house was generally in good repair. In addition to the bedrooms and bathroom on the first floor, it had small separate reception and dining rooms, and a kitchen on the ground floor. There was a small yard at the rear with an outside toilet located in the corner. Sara had transferred as much of the furniture from Regent's Park as possible and sold the considerable residue providing some welcome funds. She was extremely grateful to Lenny for his support through an exceedingly difficult period for her and Harry. To show her gratitude she suggested to Lenny that she would take on the onerous task of running his business accounts. Unusually for a girl from her background, she had taken a course in accountancy in her late teens before her marriage to her first husband. Therefore, with a small amount of brushing up, Sara was confident that she could handle the work without any problems. Lenny readily agreed but insisted that he would pay her a wage for her time.

Harry adjusted to his new surroundings well. He was delighted that his father's photographic equipment had been retained as well as his photographs and gramophone records. His attendance at school remained erratic but, on the days he did deign to show up, it was now just a fifteen minutes' walk from his new home.

With July of 1933 fast approaching and consequently, Harry's last days at school, Sara and Lenny spent hours discussing potential employment opportunities for the boy. Sara had given up on trying to convince Harry that he should continue his education albeit at a different place to the Jews Free School. He flatly refused to hear of this notion and stated that he would simply not attend any such venue if this decision was made. In the circumstances, Sara had no option than to fall into line with Lenny's proposal that Harry should start as a teaboy come messenger come stagehand at the Hackney Empire. Lenny knew the theatre manager who was prepared to give Harry a trial. The wages would be minimal, but it would at least provide Harry with an entry point to the profession to which he aspired, acting.

CHAPTER 13 – HI HO, IT'S OFF TO WORK

'Today is a reason for a double celebration Levi,' the headmaster, Mr Silver, said to Harry. 'I am retiring, and you are leaving the school. You have been a constant source of annoyance during your time here, but I wish you well for the future. Although, I would add that I do not believe that you will make anything of yourself.'

Harry shook the headmaster's hand and left his office without replying. A sense of joy was running through him. At last, he was free of the place that had been the bane of his life for so many years.

'Won't make anything of myself, eh? I'll bloody well show him. I'll make him eat his words, soppy old sod,' he said to himself as he went in search of Sidney.

The commute to the Hackney Empire was fairly straightforward. A short stroll from his home to Great Portland Street Underground Station, the Metropolitan Line to Liverpool Street, then a 20 minutes' walk to the Hackney Empire. The Manager of the theatre, John Harris, had been forewarned by Lenny that he would need to keep a close eye on Harry. He should be given a set of tasks each day and a check made to ensure he completed them. For his part, Harry was ecstatic to be working in a place that his music hall heroes had, and continued to, perform in. In his mind, it would not be too long before he would be joining them on the stage.

Initially, things went exceptionally well. Although menial, Harry carried out his duties with vigour. Making tea for the performers during rehearsals, running errands for Mr Harris, and learning the ropes, literally, as a stagehand, raising and lowering the curtains and sets. Harry was cock-a-hoop to receive his wage packet each week containing two pounds and 10 shillings in return for working nine hours a day, Monday to Saturday. After paying for his train fares and Sara taking 10 shillings for his savings box, Harry spent what was left on films for his camera and records. He generally met up with Sidney on Sundays. His friend had also left school but despite wanting to pursue a career like Harry, had been cajoled into working in his parent's shop. Sidney was not in the least happy with this development and relished his get-togethers with Harry to hear about the world of theatre. These chats usually took place while the boys were fishing in the Regent's Canal at Camden Town or en route to the Tolmer Cinema. At both locations they were often approached by men who wanted to get to know them in an intimate way by offering all sorts of inducements. However, the lads, fully aware of what these men were, ignored them, having been briefed on the subject by the prostitutes they talked to in Soho.

Soon after the trial period for Harry's job ended and his full-time employment at the Hackney Empire was confirmed, two momentous events occurred. The first was extremely pleasurable, the second, decidedly less so.

Shelly, an attractive eighteen-year-old brunette, was in the chorus line appearing in a revue at the theatre. She had winked at Harry several times as they passed over a number of days. A couple of Harry's co-workers had noticed this and ribbed him saying: 'You're well in there boy, she's a bit of a goer.' Harry now looked much older than his fourteen years. He was a handsome lad, almost six feet tall with jet-black hair, blue eyes, and the beginnings of a wispy moustache. His mother ensured that he left for work each day with good personal hygiene and was suitably dressed in clean clothes.

One afternoon, during a matinee, Harry was sitting on some sacks in a musty smelling area under the stage. He was listening to the actor

Stanley Holloway performing a monologue above. Like Harry, the audience was loving it and virtually every line was being greeted with thunderous applause.

A voice from behind said: 'Hiya, it's Harry, isn't it? Thought I might find you down here. I'm Shelly.'

Harry turned to see the shapely dancer. She was wearing a gun-metal grey sequined leotard, black fish-net stockings and was holding a pair of black patent tap shoes in her hand.

Giving a ballet-like twirl, Shelly announced: 'I'm on for the finale in 20 minutes, what do you think?'

Harry's face turned bright red, and his mouth gaped wide open as he attempted to reply. But before he could, Shelly sat next to him and started to slowly roll down her stockings. She removed them and then slipped the leotard off, placing the items in a neat pile on the floor next to her shoes. Now completely naked, Shelly placed her finger on Harry's lips as if exhorting him to keep quiet. A somewhat pointless exercise as the din from the auditorium was deafening and Harry was totally lost for words. Clearly expert in the art of seduction, Shelly swiftly removed Harry's trousers and underpants and began to caress his penis. It sprang to attention immediately and Shelly straddled Harry guiding his now fully hardened tool into her vagina.

Harry's eyes bulged as Shelly placed his hands on her ample breasts and moved up and down rhythmically on him to the sound of Stanley Holloway reciting: 'But brahn boots! I ask yer, brahn boots!' All Harry could think about in that moment was his childhood bedtime encounters with Elsie. Suddenly he experienced a feeling like nothing else he had experienced before. Simultaneously, Shelly climbed off and wiped the inside of her thighs with Harry's pants.

'It's better out than in when that moment arrives,' Shelly laughed as she began to put her costume back on. 'Your first time wasn't it, I could tell,' she giggled. 'Well, you can tell your mates that you are no longer a virgin. Got to fly, time for my daily high kicks!' She kissed Harry on the lips and whispered: 'See you around,' before she flounced back towards the dressing rooms. Overwhelmed by what had just taken place, Harry lay back on the sacks and heard tumultuous applause above denoting the end of Stanley Holloway's act. In a strange way he imagined the clapping could have also applied to his performance with Shelly.

The perfume that Shelly wore was very strong

and had permeated Harry's clothes. He became conscious of it on the tube journey home that evening and was concerned that the commuters would smell the scent and think he was a poofter. On arrival at the house in Whitfield Street, he rushed straight upstairs to get changed in case his mother smelt the perfume and started asking questions. He hung his clothes by an open window and shouted down to Sara that he was going to have a bath. Harry then had a good soak and scrubbed himself with Lifebuoy soap to ensure that no traces of Shelly presence remained on him.

In bed that night, Harry's thoughts centred on his romp with Shelly. What ecstasy. He couldn't wait to tell Sidney when they next met.

With a spring in his step on his way to work the following morning, Harry remained on cloud nine thinking only of Shelly. Surely, more sessions like yesterday's were on the cards. But while waiting for the train on the platform, he came down to earth with a bump. He saw a poster warning of the dangers of VD. He had seen these posters before and, at the time, looked up in the dictionary what VD meant. It was at that moment, the penny dropped. His engagement with Shelly could mean that he had contracted venereal disease. Shelly was obviously an experienced girl who had been with other men and could have transmitted VD to Harry.

This was a dilemma. Harry could not ask Shelly whether she had VD. Even worse, he could not broach the subject with his mother or Uncle Lenny. Going to see the doctor would be too embarrassing. And, certainly, Sidney would not be able to offer any advice. An added problem would be if Shelly approached him for another bout of sex on the sacks.

On arrival at The Empire, Harry learnt that the last issue he had worried about was already solved. Apparently, the revue featuring Shelly's chorus line was closing that day before moving on to a tour of provincial theatres. Therefore, all he had to do was to avoid Shelly for one day. However, that did not solve the bigger problem as to whether he had the dreaded VD. Reluctantly, he concluded there was only one option open to him. He would have to counsel his boss, the stage manager. To date, their relationship had not been very warm. The manager, a tall blond effeminate man named Hans Goeber, or "Hans by name, Hans by nature", as he was called behind his back. He was the fussiest character Harry had ever met. Every task that Harry was set by him was criticised. The man revelled in belittling Harry in front of other members of the backstage team and loved to play practical jokes on him. The most recent was when, having alerted his team in advance, he sent Harry to paint the last post. Not wishing to appear ignorant, Harry did not question his instructions and obtained a pot of red paint and a brush from the stores. He proceeded to go round his fellow stagehands to enquire where he might find the last post. Trying desperately to keep a straight face, each one directed Harry to a different part of the huge theatre. It was not long before Harry realised that he was the butt of his manager's tomfoolery and at the tea break, grudgingly laughed along with colleagues as to how he had been led a merry dance.

'Excuse me Mr Goeber, can you spare a few minutes for a word in private?' Harry asked his boss.

'Sure, step in here,' Goeber replied pointing to a small room.

Once inside with the door firmly closed, Harry said: 'I need some advice please, highly confidential, you understand.'

'That's fine by me, strictly entre nous,' Goeber assured his young subordinate.

'You know that chorus girl you all said was a bit of a goer, well, she was.'

'So, you got your leg over, eh? Nice one son.'

'I did Mr Goeber, I did. But that's where the problem lies.'

'How come?'

'I'm worried that I might have caught VD as a result of what happened.'

'Oh, I see. But you must have worn a condom?'

'What's that?'

'You mean you don't know what a rubber is? Like an ONA or a Durex?'

Harry's vacant expression revealed to Hans Goeber that another opportunity had presented itself to have some fun at the lad's expense.

With a look of deep concern on his face, the manager scratched his head and said: 'Blimey, no condom, eh? Oh dear.'

Fearing the worst, Harry's heart began to beat faster.

After further thought, Goeber earnestly said: 'I've heard from reliable sources that have experienced the same problem, that you have to get up at 5.30 every morning and run for a minimum of four miles. Then when you return home, get straight in a freezing cold bath and scrub your privates with carbolic soap for ten minutes. You must repeat the same exercise in the evening when you get in from work. Do this for two weeks and if you did have VD, it will be gone.'

'Thank you so much Mr Goeber, I will do exactly as you suggest. But please, please, do not tell anybody else about our conversation.'

'Of course not. Now get back to work Harry, there's plenty to be done.'

Feeling considerably reassured, Harry returned to his duties.

Goeber immediately left to tell his team about the discussion with Harry. But he warned them that if they let on to Harry they knew before the two weeks were up, they would be sacked.

Harry explained to Sara that he was taking up a fitness regime that included long runs and cold baths. For obvious reasons, he did not mention the carbolic element though.

Exhausted after his two weeks stint, Harry returned to work much fitter but with a red raw undercarriage. However, he was perplexed when his colleagues kept asking him the same question: 'Where's Arizona?' He always answered America, but they then responded: 'No - still in the barber's shop.' It was not until the joke had started to wear thin that one of his workmates spelt out the reason for their question.

'You're Harry and an ONA is a condom, right? So that's the joke, where's Harry's ONA? Still in the barber's shop because you didn't wear a condom. Get it? Your tackle must be highly polished after all that scrubbing. Hans Knees & Bumsy really got you there, didn't he?'

It took a while to sink in but suddenly it became clear to Harry. When he was in the barber's he had seen small packets on the shelf with ONA on them. Pointing to the shelf, with a smile, the barber would often say to the adult customers: 'Something for the weekend, sir?'

Harry knew immediately that bastard Goeber had told everyone about his problem. He vowed to himself that Goeber would get his comeuppance. Revenge would be sweet. As was usual, it did not take long for Harry to hatch a plan. Sidney's parent's shop primarily sold groceries, but certain other products were available such as medicines that did not require a doctor's prescription. Harry recalled that he had once asked Sidney's father what magnesium citrate was, having spotted a large brown bottle high up on one of the shelves. Apparently, many of the Solomon's customers were old and suffered from constipation. Sidney's father explained that the tablets in the bottle were a sure-fire way of opening their bowels very rapidly after taking a dose.

On Harry's next visit to Sidney, he revealed his plan and asked his friend to steal a quantity of the magnesium citrate tablets. Sidney duly obliged and handed a bag-full of the tablets to Harry when they met the following Sunday. After Sara had gone to bed that evening, Harry crept out into the kitchen and poured the tablets into a pestle and mortar. He then ground them into a fine powder which he tipped back into the bag, and thoroughly washed the pestle and mortar to remove any traces of the stuff. The following day at work Harry sprinkled the powder into the tea urn and gave the contents a good stir. He made sure that his first round of the theatre's staff with the tea trolley was restricted to Hans Goeber and his team of stagehands. As Harry filled the mugs with tea Goeber and his colleagues rubbed their privates in unison making mocking pain-like noises and laughing heartily. Harry just smiled benignly and moved off.

Harry returned to the kitchen and rinsed the tea urn with boiling water until it was completely cleansed before refilling it and proceeding on his rounds. As predicted by Mr Solomon, it took just fifteen minutes for the tablets to have the desired effect. Screams of pain and the sound of crashing boots emitted from the stagehands' lair in a frenzied stampede to the toilets. As there were only three cubicles, scuffles broke out between the eight men in the rush for the loos. Those who had lost the race to secure one were now defecating in their trousers. Despite his managerial status, Goeber was one of the losers and grimaced as he clutched his stomach in an unsuccessful attempt to stop the inevitable.

'Who's laughing now?' Harry screamed at Goeber. Unfortunately, his glee was short-lived. With all the commotion, he had not heard Mr Harris arrive behind him.

'That little bastard has poisoned us,' Goeber shouted at Mr Harris.

Turning to Harry, Mr Harris enquired: 'Is this true Harry?'

'I was merely getting my own back on him and the other morons who've been making my life a misery over the past few weeks. It wasn't poison, just some tablets that will keep them extra regular for a couple of days,' Harry replied.

'My office now Levi!' Mr Harris commanded in a tone that reminded Harry of his old headmaster.

'Do you appreciate the seriousness of your actions?' Mr Harris began.

Harry shrugged.

'I'll tell you then. You have effectively prevented the entire stage management team from working at tonight's and tomorrow night's performances. This means that the shows will have to be cancelled and refunds made to every customer who has booked a ticket. In addition, all the performers and other members of theatre staff will have to be paid even though they will not be at work. In other words, the company will lose a huge amount of money because of your stupidity.'

Harry attempted to justify his case and apologise for the consequences. But he was cut off before he could utter a word.

'Now get out and don't show your face around this theatre ever again. You're fired. Get out of my sight!' Mr Harris screeched pointing towards the office door.

CHAPTER 14 – REEL TIME

The journey home that evening was torturous for Harry. In his mind, he thought the other commuters on the tube were looking at him with disgust. Of course, they were not, but this thought was just one of several that were vexing him as the train made slow progress to Great Portland Street Station. How was he going to explain his sacking to his mother and Uncle Lenny? Especially as the latter had been so kind in finding him the job in the first place. Would Mr Harris reveal all the details of his actions to Lenny, including the encounter with Shelly which doubtless, Goeber would have now recounted to The Empire's overall boss? Mr Harris was obviously not going to provide Harry with a reference so how would he be able to get another job? The fact that Goeber had tricked him regarding the supposed cure for VD, was it possible that he may actually have the disease? So many questions with no answers.

As he made his way towards home in the drizzle that had dampened the pavements, Harry turned up the collar of his jacket and dug his hands deeper into his pockets. It was then that he remembered this was the evening each week when Uncle Lenny visited his fish

& chip shop a few doors away from Harry's house. There was nothing else for it, he would have to come clean, and tell his uncle about his misdemeanours at The Empire.

Harry stepped into the shop with his head bowed looking glum. Lenny was in his favourite place, behind the counter chatting to a couple of regulars. Spotting his nephew, he called over to him: 'Hello Harry boy, why the long face? Fancy a bag of chips?

'No thanks Uncle Lenny, can I have a word with you out the back when you are ready?

'Sure, go on through. I'll be with you in a sec.'

Lenny followed Harry in a couple of minutes later and said: 'Ok, spill the beans. Who's died?'

Harry then explained to his uncle in detail the events that had taken place at work over the past few weeks. He apologised profusely for his actions and the embarrassment he had caused. Lenny remained silent throughout until Harry had finished. Instead, as he had expected, of being shouted at, Harry was surprised to hear his uncle's response delivered in a calm manner.

'Sounds as though that bender Goeber had it in for you from the start. Give people like him a bit of power and they think they're God Almighty. That said, your revenge was somewhat extreme, especially as it has resulted in the theatre losing a pot load of money. Although I shouldn't laugh, the sight you have described of them all shitting themselves is pure gold. What occurred with the floozy, well, that's just part of life's rich tapestry. It's happened to you earlier than it usually does with young men but don't worry. I'll arrange an appointment with my doctor to check you over downstairs but I'm sure it will be alright. The main thing is, you should leave that part of the story out when you tell your mum the reason you are no longer at The Empire. In the meantime, I will put out some feelers about other jobs for you.'

'Thank you for being so understanding Uncle Lenny. I know I've let you down, but I will do everything possible to make it up to you.'

'Don't be daft. It's a lesson learnt for you. Just remember, if you are facing those sorts of problems again, speak to me before you do anything. Now get off home and see your mother. She'll be wondering where you've got to.'

Harry did as his uncle instructed. Sara was not quite so understanding as her brother-in-law though. And she was certainly not amused about the outcome of Harry administering the magnesium citrate into his colleagues' tea. 'You could have put them in hospital,' she said scornfully.

Having been given the all clear by Lenny's doctor, Harry was in a much better frame of mind. Sitting in Benny's, the barbers in nearby Gower Street, Harry was looking at the packs of condoms remembering the doctor's words about the necessity of wearing one on future sexual encounters. He had kindly given Harry a couple of packs for such an eventuality. It was then he overheard a conversation that Benny was having with the customer currently in the chair having his hair cut.

'Yeah, little wotsit nicked the cans of films and nobody's seen or heard of him since,' the man informed Benny.

'How long had he been in the job?' the barber asked.

'Only a few months. The thing is, he was a bright kid and I felt that he was beginning to get a good knowledge of becoming a projectionist. Let's face it, I'm up for retirement in a couple of years and he could have slipped into the role nicely.'

Listening to the two men talk, it quickly became apparent to Harry that the man worked in the Tolmer Cinema, just around the corner. He cleared his throat and said: 'Excuse me, I couldn't help but hear your conversation.

I live close by in Whitfield Street and I'm looking for a job.'

The man looked at Harry in the mirror facing him. He was in his early sixties with an abundance of grey hair that Benny was systematically applying his clippers to. He had a weather-beaten face with a flat nose at its centre. Like most men of his age, his teeth were deeply stained with nicotine. Addressing Harry, he asked: 'How old are you lad?'

'Sixteen,' Harry lied.

'Don't suppose you have any experience of working in a cinema, do you?'

'No, but I'm a regular customer at the Tolmer,' Harry replied.

Before any further exchanges could be made, Benny butted in. 'Young Harry's been coming here since he was a small boy. I know his Uncle Lenny and mother, Sara Levi well. He's also a bright kid. If you need help, it wouldn't do any harm giving him a trial.'

'Righty-ho, when you've had your locks chopped, pop round and see me. Just ask for Mr Purvis at the kiosk. Someone will direct you to the projection room.'

During the interview that followed in the afternoon, an instant bond was formed between Purvis and Harry who, had been careful not to mention his short tenure at The Hackney Empire. He simply intimated that this would be his first proper job since leaving the Jews Free School, but he never actually said as much. The job was essentially assisting Mr Purvis with his duties as the cinema's projectionist. A major part of the role entailed humping heavy cans of film up and down the fire escape at the rear of the building to and from the distributors' delivery vans. Additionally, Mr Purvis outlined there would be dirty tasks such as operating the projectors, oiling and greasing machinery, changing spools, rewinding film and splicing and cementing celluloid. But he would be taught these tasks as time went on. Inevitably, tea making and cleaning "the box" as Purvis referred to the projection room, were also involved. The wage was slightly less than what Harry was getting at The Empire but as it was a ten-minute walk from his home, there were no travel expenses to be paid. Harry was thrilled to accept the appointment and was told to report for duty the following Monday.

Sara and Lenny were delighted to hear that Harry had seized the initiative and with a little help from Benny the barber, had secured the job himself.

Harry settled in well with the Tolmer's

workforce which in addition to Purvis the projectionist, comprised a manager, Mr Higginbottom, a cashier, June, and two usherettes, Glynis and Cheryl. Unlike his last job, the group worked as a unified team and respected one another's roles. Harry was a quick learner and Mr Purvis was pleased with his ability to absorb information about the techniques required to operate the projection equipment. 1934 saw the release of some classic films including "Catherine the Great" starring Flora Robson and Douglas Fairbanks Jr; and "The Scarlett Pimpernel" featuring Merle Oberon and Leslie Howard who Sara had told Harry was a friend of his father's. Harry never tired of watching these films from "the box" albeit repeatedly during their run at the cinema. Indeed, he memorised scenes within the films and the way the actors performed them. He firmly believed this would be useful to him when he too became a star of stage and screen.

The usherettes, Glynis and Cheryl were sisters who lived further down Euston Road from the Tolmer in Kings Cross. The older, Glynis was eighteen and shortly after Harry's arrival at the cinema, she took a shine to him. They started to go out together and Harry introduced her sixteen-year-old sister, Cheryl to Sidney. As a foursome, the couples would spend Sunday walking on Hampstead Heath and Primrose Hill. The girls came from a C of E background so neither Sara nor Mr & Mrs Solomon, although they thought the sisters were nice enough, were particularly happy. They worried that if the relationships became more serious, it would mean having a *shiksa*, a non-Jewish girl, in the family. Their fears were unwarranted. Lust rather than marriage was the primary reason the couples enjoyed each other's company. Harry's stock of condoms was soon exhausted, so Sidney had resorted to raiding his parent's shop to maintain a steady supply. During the remainder of 1934 and into 1935, the four had some memorable encounters that when talked about over shandies in the Royal George pub near the cinema, always brought out howls of laughter. One that cropped up frequently they called "The Prick with the Stick" or "The Arse in the Grass." On this occasion they were engaged in a game of "Ladies & Gentlemen" as they referred to it, on Hampstead Heath. It was a dark October evening when having heard heavy breathing and groans coming from the bushes, a park keeper shone his torch and simultaneously, thrust his walking stick into the area. Direct hit. The stick rammed into Harry's bare bottom, he yelled and leapt to his feet leaving a bemused Glynis flat on her back, naked from the waist down.

'Dirty little buggers, worse than rabbits,' the park keeper exclaimed. 'What with your sort and the queers behind the Spaniards Inn. Get off with you now before I whistle for the police.'

Sidney and Cheryl who were just yards away in a separate wooded area, heard the shouting, quickly dressed, and beat a hasty retreat down the hill towards the bus terminus. Harry and Glynis were not so fortunate. Attempting to pull his pants back on, they caught round his ankles, and he fell forward into a clump of nettles. The stinging sensation around his private parts started instantly, and a string of expletives erupted from his mouth. In an almost identical manoeuvre, Glynis stooped to retrieve her panties but in doing so, tripped over Harry, falling headlong into the arms of the park keeper who immediately dropped her like a piece of filthy rag. Harry pulled Glynis to her feet and, hand-in-hand, the two of them staggered away from their nemesis, pulling on items of clothing as they went.

Harry's yearning to become a performer was still strong. But for the moment, in mid-1936, he was content with his lot at The Tolmer and his romance with Glynis. Photography remained an important pastime and he had become increasingly accomplished in the art. This was demonstrated at Mr Higginbottom's retirement party at the cinema. The softly spoken, kindly Yorkshireman, who had served his country in the trenches of the First World War, had worked at The Tolmer as manager since being demobbed from the army in 1918. A well-earned retirement now beckoned, and he could not wait to return to a small cottage in his beloved Harrogate with his wife, Gladys. The owner of the cinema, together with the Mayor of St Pancras, presented Higginbottom with a carriage clock as a leaving present and he struggled to hold back the tears as he made his farewell speech. As he finished and the sound of clapping died down, the Wurlitzer organ, installed as part of the cinema's refurbishment in 1929, slowly rose from the pit with the renowned artist, Arthur Jenkins, playing "For He's a Jolly Good Fellow." Throughout the proceedings, Harry took photographs of the gathering.

When the final bars of the song faded, the cinema's owner introduced the new manager. James Walker was in his forties. He was tall and muscular with dark slicked back hair, aquiline features, and well-manicured nails. He dressed sharply with a wide-lapelled double breasted grey pinstripe suit. This was a man who took care about his appearance. Walker had no previous experience in the entertainment business but had been the manager of a fruit and vegetable wholesaler based in

Covent Garden. Unlike his predecessor, he had not fought in the Great War, as he had been working in a reserved occupation, food provision. The fact that he had not been enlisted suited him fine as his political views were, particularly since the end of the conflict, pro German. An admirer of the German Chancellor, Herr Hitler, he was a member of the British Union of Fascists, and vehemently antisemitic. As such, Harry's cosy existence at The Tolmer was about to take a turn for the worse.

After the First World War, the countries of Europe declined economically leading to a depression creating widespread poverty. As a result, political unrest emerged and scapegoats, usually ethnic minorities, were sought on whom to place the blame. Fascism as an ideology grew rapidly, especially in Germany, Italy and Spain. And, in the latter, civil war had broken out on the day of Mr Higginbottom's party, 17 July 1936, with the better armed fascists predicted to be the ultimate victors. Up until this point in his life, Harry had not been either politically or religiously motivated. Under duress, he had accompanied his mother and uncle to the schul in Great Portland Street for the main Jewish celebrations. Sara had been a leading light in the women's suffrage movement but since her financial crisis, had virtually been dropped by her former friends in society circles. This situation also prevailed in respect of her late husband's show business clients and associates. Coming from a self-inflicted working-class background, Lenny's political sympathies had always leaned towards the Labour Party. However, with a business to run, he had little time for talking politics except the occasional banter with his customers.

The start of the James Walker era of management at The Tolmer did not bode well for any of the staff. Gone was Mr Higginbottom's laissez faire approach to staff relations. The new broom meant to sweep clean, even if it meant replacing the entire workforce with his cronies. As expected, Harry was the first to experience the new man's ire.

'Bloody lazy yid, those cans of film have been round the back for the past hour. They could have been knocked off. Where have you been?' Walker asked Harry.

'Sorry Mr Walker. I was on my lunch break getting my hair cut. The films are not usually delivered until much later in the afternoon.'

'Hair cut? You don't get your hair cut in the company's time.'

'Well, it grows in the company time,' Harry

quipped.

'Listen four-by-two, don't come the old acid with me or you'll be out of here before your feet can touch the ground.'

Following the ticking off Harry was determined not to go down the route of revenge as he did at The Empire. He decided it would be better to talk the matter over with Mr Purvis first and then counsel Lenny.

'I'm afraid we are all in the same boat Harry. He's a nasty piece of work and hell-bent on getting rid of us,' was the projectionist's response. 'Away from the cinema he's one of Mosley's Black Shirts and hates Jews so it's going to be even worse for you. It's a shame because you were shaping up well to take over from me when I go. But if I were you, I'd start looking for a new job.'

'But why does he hate Jews so much? I'm not very religious and it's not as if I'm going to take his job.'

'Those madmen Hitler and Mussolini have whipped up hatred against Jews in their countries, and that idiot Mosley is trying to do the same thing here.'

Despite Mr Purvis's explanation, Harry was still confused. Perhaps his uncle could throw more light on the matter.

Sitting in the back room at the Whitfield Street chippie, Lenny espoused his view. 'Sadly, the storm clouds are gathering all over Europe again, Harry. That *meshuggah* Adolf Hitler in Germany has got it in for the Jews. He's brought in legislation that boycotts the use of Jewish shops, organised the mass burning of books written by Jews, and banned German Jews from joining the country's armed forces. With all this going on, you can understand why Jewish people who can, are fleeing from Germany as quickly as possible.'

Harry considered his uncle's words for a moment before replying: 'I get that but why does Mr Walker hate me so much?'

'Because he's been brainwashed like most of the Germans that the world's economic problems are caused by the Jews. Hitler's doctrine of fascism has now reared its head in Britain with the MP, Sir Oswald Mosley, advocating that this country should follow Germany's lead and supress Jews living here. I know it may sound cowardly, but from what you've told me about your boss, it's just a matter of time before he finds a way to sack you. So, I think you should get out now.'

'That's all very well uncle, but where will I find another job? Things are not exactly rosy on the employment front now, are they?'

Lenny got up and walked through to the shop. He flicked through some sheets of newspaper on the counter used to wrap the take-away fish & chip orders and returned to the back room holding a selection. Putting them down on the table, he passed some to Harry and said: ‘Here you go, take a look at the situation’s vacant pages. I’ll do the same.’

A few minutes elapsed before Lenny piped up: ‘Here’s one in last week’s Jewish Chronicle. “Assistant Photographer required. Reporting to the paper’s in-house photographer, the successful candidate will carry out assignments throughout London’s Jewish communities covering topical events. Some experience of photographic processes including developing film, preferred. Apply to: The Editor, Jewish Chronicle, 20 Eastcheap, London, EC.” Sounds right up your street Harry boy.’

Harry was hesitant and said: ‘I’ll give it some thought.’

‘No, you won’t. That ad was in last week’s JC which means there will already have been a lot of applications. I’ll help you draft a letter now, then we will show it to your mother for her comments. You will need to pull a portfolio together too.’

'A what?'

'A portfolio. A selection of your photographs to show them if you get an interview. The ones you took at Mr Higginbottom's retirement party will be ideal as they are saying you would be attending bar mitzvahs and weddings to take shots for the paper. I would leave out some of those pictures of Glynis you've taken though. I don't think they're looking for glamour girl pictures,' Lenny added laughing.

Sara concurred with Lenny's suggestion and after making a couple of minor amendments to the text, ensured Harry finished the letter and posted it off enclosing the best photograph from the party at The Tolmer.

Following a week of having to bite his lip to stop him reacting to James Walker's constant jibes, Harry was delighted to receive a letter from the Jewish Chronicle inviting him to an interview with the editor.

Ivan Greenberg had held the post of editor at the Jewish Chronicle since the death of his father, one of the owners, a year earlier. He looked older than his forty years with a receding hairline and tightly fitting wire rimmed glasses that caused indentations on either side of his nose. His three-piece dark green and brown tweed suit was a little crumpled and his shirt collar and tie slightly askew. Judging by the heaped cigarette butts in the ashtray on his desk, he was a heavy smoker. He welcomed Harry warmly and, like any good journalist, had obviously carried out some research on the lad now sitting opposite him.

He opened the discussion by pointing out: 'My father Leopold often spoke about your father Davide. He met him on several occasions at the first nights of shows your father put on. You will be pleased to hear that my father generally wrote good reviews of the productions for the newspaper,' Greenberg smilingly advised Harry. 'Your father, rest his soul, was a generous supporter of many Jewish charities. I was sorry to hear that your mother fell victim to those shysters at Abraham Fischer.'

Harry was encouraged by the way the interview had started. Prior to the meeting, he had decided to come clean if questioned about references. He would truthfully explain what happened at The Empire, leaving out the tea urn incident, and at The Tolmer, stating antisemitism as the problem in both instances. However, he would add that Mr Purvis would be prepared to put in a good word for him. As it transpired the subject of references was not raised.

Indeed, Harry became more optimistic when Mr Greenberg praised the photographs that Harry had brought along. At this juncture, the editor called Harry Kessler, the JC's long serving photographer into his office.

'Harry One meet Harry Two,' Greenberg joked. 'I was impressed with these, what do you think?' he said to his photographer showing him the pictures of the retirement party.

Kessler was a short man, almost bald save a few strands of hair spanning from the left to right side of his large head. His waistcoat and trousers needed a good press, his shirt was open at the neck with sleeves that were too long but held back from slipping onto his hands by gold-coloured elasticated armbands. Brown scuffed shoes completed his attire. In a competition for best dressed man, James Walker would win outright. With a cigarette dangling precariously from his lower lip, Kessler examined the photographs.

'I agree Ivan, they're exceptional, the lad certainly has talent. But tell me son, do you have any experience of developing film?'

Harry spoke with a hint of emotion about recollections of his father's photographic studio and how his uncle had demonstrated the process of developing film. He went on to explain how he now carried out this work in his dark room at home in Whitfield Street.

The two older men exchanged glances of approval and after a short while, asked Harry to wait in the office reception on the floor below. Harry hardly had time to have a sip of the Russian tea the nice receptionist had made for him when he was summoned back to Mr Greenberg's office.

'Well Harry, we both have some reservations about your age, but we've decided to give you a trial.'

That word "trial" again, Harry thought to himself, remembering how things had backfired at his previous places of employment. Nevertheless, he was cock-a-hoop to receive the news that his application had been successful, especially as the wages would be more than he was currently earning. He shook hands with Messrs Greenberg and Kessler and agreed a start date in two weeks' time.

After telling his mother and uncle the good news, Harry went to work.

'No need to give me notice kike, you can piss off now. I'll pay you up to the end of the week. Money well spent to be rid of your sort,' was Mr Walker's response to Harry giving notice. 'Good news all round, I've also told the Kings Cross slags they can go, as well as that dopey tart of a cashier. The only one I'm stuck with is the old fart of a projectionist, but people with his experience are not two a penny,' Walker added.

Harry was concerned to hear Walker's comments about Glynis, Cheryl and June but was relieved to learn from his girlfriend that all three had secured jobs at the Regent Cinema further down Euston Road, opposite St Pancras Station. A distinctly more prestigious venue than The Tolmer. He was also greatly relieved to be away from his manager's stream of vitriol. Little did he know that their paths would cross again in the not-too-distant future.

CHAPTER 15 – BATTLE LOSS

Harry and Sidney were down in the dumps. They were sitting in silence at their usual spot on the bank of the Regent's Canal by Camden Lock, throwing the odd stone into the water. The loves of their lives, Glynis and Cheryl, had dispensed with them in favour of two firemen based at Euston Fire Station. Clearly, the girls had wasted no time in finding alternative sources of fun whilst working at the Regent.

Romance aside, Harry was happy with his new role at the Jewish Chronicle, or the JC as it seemed to be referred to by everyone. Harry Kessler, although outwardly personifying a gruff East End Cockney, was in fact a genuinely nice character with a heart of gold. He had spent the first couple of weeks following Harry's arrival mentoring him in the various etiquettes involved with taking photographs at Jewish weddings, bar mitzvahs and anniversary celebrations. As he had demonstrated in his past jobs, Harry was quick to absorb instructions, so Kessler was pleased with the mature manner in which he interacted with people at the various events. The older man was equally impressed with the quality of the work Harry produced and his willingness to stay on after hours to develop his rolls of film. Kessler reported this to his editor, and they agreed that Harry should be allocated assignments on his own moving forward.

It was 1936 and a steady stream of photoshoots ensued over the next two months with Harry enjoying the hospitality afforded to him at these social events. However, the hard news photo stories remained the sole province of Kessler. Therefore, Harry was surprised when, at the beginning of October, he was called in to Mr Greenberg's office and briefed on an assignment that was likely to be a major news story. He was informed that Mr Kessler was suffering from chronic bronchitis, probably from the twenty or so cigarettes he smoked each day Harry surmised. Anyhow, his doctor had signed him off from work for at least two weeks until his chest infection cleared. Meantime Mr Greenberg explained that Harry would have to hold the fort by working on news stories and a freelancer would be brought in to handle the social events programme. The editor then proceeded to give Harry the background on a march that was scheduled to take place in the East End at the weekend on Sunday 4th October.

It transpired that the British Union of Fascists, an overtly antisemitic organisation, led by Sir Oswald Mosley, was planning a march of 3,000 of his Black Shirts followers through the East End, an area of London with a predominantly Jewish population. Over 100,000 people had signed a petition to stop the march but the Home Secretary, John Simon, had decided that despite warnings that violence would erupt, it should be allowed to go ahead. To prevent any disorder, Simon had ordered 6,000 policemen to accompany the march. Mr Greenberg outlined to Harry that his sources had informed him that almost 100,000 anti-fascists, mainly Jews but also trade unionists, communists and the Irish community living in the vicinity intended to stop the march from proceeding along the planned route. He emphasised to Harry that under no circumstances should he put himself in danger. Although somewhat daunted by the prospect of being in the middle of a potential riot taking photos, Harry assured his boss that he would exercise care and get some good pictures for the JC.

It came as no surprise to Harry that Sara was not happy about her son being put in such a situation when he related his conversation with Mr Greenberg to her. 'Do you know what those Black Shirt thugs are like? They are animals. They have beaten up Jewish people, smashed their shop windows and set fire to their houses. How do you think they will react when they see you taking their picture doing these awful things?'

'Mother, be reasonable. Don't you see this is my big chance? If I say no, I will be condemned to taking photos of nice Jewish celebrations with the guests getting *shicker* for the rest of my life!'

Up until this point, Lenny had sat in silence at the table at Sara's listening to the argument swing back and forth. 'Just hold off for a second the pair of you,' he implored. 'I think I have a solution that will satisfy you both. As I understand it, the route of the march will pass directly outside my shop in Cable Street. Harry can take the pictures he wants from the doorway of the shop. Apparently, there's going to be hundreds of coppers on duty so they will stop any trouble the Black Shirts start. Besides, me and my staff will be on hand to protect Harry if anything untoward happens. My manager at that shop, Solly, is six feet five of solid muscle and the ex-heavyweight boxing champion of Essex. Even Mosley's hardest supporters would do a runner at the sight of him!'

Once again, Sara had been put in a difficult position by Lenny and was not best pleased about it. However, whilst reiterating her concerns, reluctantly acquiesced to her brother-in-law's proposal.

The following Sunday morning Harry set out at 7am from home. He had packed his Leica II camera he had bought second-hand the year before, and several rolls of film in his small shoulder bag. The Leica with its built-in rangefinder and lens focusing mechanism would be ideal for the task at hand. Alighting at Aldgate Station, a ten-minute walk from Lenny's shop, Harry was surprised to encounter huge crowds of local people and mounted police. The crowd was chanting: "They shall not pass," over and over again. The noise was deafening, and the police horses were becoming erratic in their behaviour. Indeed, the police's job to control the mob was being made more difficult because trams had been abandoned by their drivers, probably sympathetic to the anti-fascist cause, in the narrow streets around the station. Avoiding the piles of manure strewn across the street, Harry squeezed through the hordes of shouting people and took up a position in a tailor's shop doorway. The sign that swung in the slight breeze above the shop read "S.Gronofsky – Suits Made To Measure." He knelt, removed the camera from his bag and started to take photographs of the melee. Satisfied that he had enough shots, Harry moved on along Cable Street and came upon a barricade across the entire width of the road and adjacent pavements. The barricade stood about seven feet high and comprised items of broken furniture stacked in an interlocked fashion creating a sturdy structure. It was manned by dozens of anti-fascists in what incongruously appeared to be their Sunday best suits complete with collar and tie. They too were screaming: "They shall not pass," repeatedly. The expression on the men's faces was grim and determined. They obviously intended to adhere steadfastly to their mantra. Harry captured the scene on film and was sure that this would depict the drama of the occasion. There was a small gap at one side of the barricade that Harry attempted to pass through but was stopped by two hefty men who stood guard, surrounded by more bits of furniture to plug the hole when required. Only after Harry explained that he was going to his uncle's shop would they let him enter.

Before reaching Lenny's shop a little further along Cable Street, Harry took more shots of the reverse side of the barricade including the piles of cobblestones that had been uplifted from nearby streets. As he did so, he heard the clatter of boots and police whistles. All at once, he was shoved over by a phalanx of police officers as they rushed past with truncheons drawn. Their aim was to remove the barricade. The protectors of the edifice turned, picked up the stones and pelted the blue line that was rapidly approaching. Screams rang out as policemen hit by the barrage fell bleeding to the ground. Scuffles between the two groups broke out everywhere. More anti-fascists including women and children joined their comrades from the adjoining streets and shops. They were wielding an assortment of weapons including frying pans, chairs legs and brooms. By now, the police were severely outnumbered and began to retreat dragging injured colleagues with them as they went. The local people cheered and defiantly continued to chant: "They shall not pass."

Harry used two further rolls of film covering the entire fracas on camera. He was sure Mr Greenberg would be impressed with the results. Breathless with excitement, he finally arrived at his uncle's shop and banged on the door. Lenny unbolted it and yanked his nephew in before quickly re-locking it. 'Thank goodness. I've been worried sick. I had no idea it was going to be like this. I think your mother was right when she said you would be safer staying at home. No sign of Mosley and his nutters yet but things have already kicked-off.'

'I've got some great shots for the JC,' Harry said. Then sniffing the air asked: 'Why are you cooking fish and chips at this time of the morning uncle?'

‘All this fighting will give the locals an appetite and I’m going to feed them for free. ‘Power to the people,’ he shouted, and was echoed by Solly and the rest of the staff. ‘Now listen carefully Harry. You can take all the pictures you want from the upstairs window, but under no circumstances are you going out on the street again until this rumpus is over. Understand?’

‘Understood,’ Harry begrudgingly replied and trudged up to the first floor to inspect the room he was to use. In fairness, he thought, the view from the window provided a panoramic landscape encapsulating the barricade as well as the east and west sides of Cable Street on either side of the structure. He set-up his camera in readiness and returned downstairs to chat to Lenny.

‘According to my contacts, the BUF members will assemble at Tower Hill this afternoon and the march will split into four groups bound for separate public meetings across the East End. The main group, led by Mosley, will come past here,’ Lenny informed Harry over cups of tea. ‘You should be able to get some good shots of the posh ponce as he goes by.’

During the hours that followed until lunchtime, Harry stationed himself at the upstairs window. Glancing up, he saw a low-flying police spotter plane circling that was presumably sending messages to the senior police officers below regarding the locations and numbers of anti-fascists in the area. Using the rangefinder and focusing tools on his camera, enabled him to secure some excellent photos of the aircraft. Periodically, the police attempted two further sorties on the barricade. They were unsuccessful with injuries sustained by both sets of combatants.

Unbeknown to Harry and Lenny, Sir Oswald Mosley had arrived a short distance away at Tower Hill in an open-top black sports car surrounded by Black Shirt motorcyclists. His force had formed a column a half mile long in preparation for the march. It was here that Mosley was met by the Metropolitan Police Commissioner, Sir Phillip Game, who informed him that owing to the levels of violence already unleashed on his men, it was too dangerous for the march to proceed through the East End. He had made the decision to cancel it. However, if the BUF so wished, they could parade through the West End and hold their meeting in Hyde Park. Mosley was furious and threatened Game that he would make sure the Commissioner's position would be untenable after he had spoken to his Parliamentary cohorts. But Game stood firm and ordered Mosley to withdraw his supporters immediately.

The leader of the BUF sent messengers to the amassed Black Shirts to communicate the Police Commissioner's decision. However, large factions within the column chose to ignore the order to turn around and march towards the West End. Instead, these hot heads broke away and charged through the police lines without being challenged in the direction of Cable Street. Some were waving BUF flags, all carried weapons including knives, baseball bats and knuckle-dusters. Within minutes, they reached the barricade and serious violence erupted. The main protagonists were the Black Shirts and the anti-fascists with the police fighting both groups. Women in windows overlooking the street were emptying their chamber pots over the BUF members below who were hurling missiles up at them in response. A small group of Black Shirts managed to clamber over the barricade and fought with its defenders on the other side. It was during this engagement that one of the Black Shirts, James Walker, manager of The Tolmer Cinema, looked up and saw Harry at a window above Levi's Fish & Chip shop, taking pictures. He instantly made the connection between the name on the shop's window and his former employee, Harry Levi.

Walker called to a couple of his BUF mates, pointed up at the window and exclaimed: 'It's that dirty little Yid I told you about who I got rid of at work.' All three men scooped up bricks that were laying in the road and in unison, threw them at the shop window. Shards of glass flew into the shop. One hit Lenny in the neck and he fell down behind the counter. Brushing splinters out of his hair and off his shoulders, Solly grabbed a trough of boiling hot fat and jettisoned it at the three imbeciles gesticulating on the pavement outside. The three of them screamed in agony as the oil burned its way into their faces. Solly leaped through the gap in what had previously been the window and punched Walker and his colleagues relentlessly leaving them writhing on the ground from their injuries. He then climbed back into the shop to find Harry kneeling next to his uncle who was gasping for breath as blood gushed from his wound.

'We need to get him to a hospital fast,' Solly said. 'The nearest is The Royal London.' After jamming a clean white cloth into the gash on his neck, the two of them lifted Lenny up, carried him out the back door and headed via the narrow streets towards Whitechapel Road. By the time they reached their destination ten minutes later, Lenny was unconscious. The hospital's reception area and corridors were already full of people injured in the riot that was still raging in the nearby streets. Despite their injuries some people were continuing to fight inside the hospital with a few policemen trying to keep them apart. Chaos reigned. Solly tugged at the arm of a doctor who was rushing past and asked him to examine Lenny's wound. The medic pulled a grim face.

'His carotid artery has been severed. I'm afraid he is dead.' The doctor moved on leaving Harry and Solly in devastated shock. The tears rolled down Harry's cheeks. He had lost his father-figure, his confidante, his uncle, his friend. And it was all his fault. Lenny was buried shortly afterwards in a grave alongside his brother Davide's at the Hoop Lane Jewish Cemetery, Golders Green.

Harry's photographs for the Jewish Chronicle of the Battle of Cable Street as it had become known, received wide acclaim. Several national and regional newspapers had used the syndicated pictures and Harry was duly credited with his name appearing alongside them on the front pages. Ivan Greenberg entered the shots for the 1936 National Press Club Awards Photo Category, and they won the top prize. Sara sat next to the JC's editor and other journalists in the audience at the awards ceremony taking place within the striking black glass art deco façade Daily Express building in Fleet Street. She was so proud to see her son take the stage to receive the award presented by Lord Beaverbrook, owner of The

Express, amidst rapturous applause.

Harry Kessler did not return to the JC. Dogged by ill health, he took early retirement. Harry Levi was duly promoted to become the youngest photographic editor of a newspaper in Britain.

Harry's political naivety had been exposed by the Cable Street debacle. The true meaning of antisemitism had finally registered, and he had matured as a result. His work producing photos for the JC covering mainline topical stories considerably aided this development. One such example was when, in 1937, Harry was sent to Southampton Docks to take pictures of 4,000 Spanish children refugees' arrival on the liner Habana. Referred to as the "Basque Children," they were fleeing the Spanish Civil War that had started the year before. Although only a small percentage of the children originated from Jewish families, Harry was interested to learn that propaganda by the Nationalist side in the conflict, led by General Franco, cited the growing number of Jews and Freemasons in the Spanish population as a root cause for the country's problems. Franco's attempt to overthrow the Republican government was being supported by the German Chancellor, Herr Hitler, with the provision of armaments. Talking to the children through an adult interpreter who had accompanied them on the voyage, Harry heard about the International Brigades, set up by Communist International. These units comprised people from various countries, including Britain, who had gone to fight on the side of the Republican government. This information, combined with stories he had covered regarding Jewish German and Austrian refugees leaving their countries owing to increasing levels of persecution by Nationalists, moved Harry's political leaning further to the left.

This position was strengthened in 1938 when Harry was sent to interview the famous Austrian psychoanalyst, Sigmund Freud. Now over two years into his tenure at the JC, Harry had convinced Ivan Greenberg that he was more than capable of conducting interviews as well as taking the pictures required for an article. Like so many others that Harry had encountered, Freud had reluctantly fled his home in Vienna before being arrested by the Nazis who had recently annexed Austria. As Harry rang the doorbell of 20 Maresfield Gardens in Hampstead, where Freud now resided, he wondered how the great man had adapted to life in a Queen Anne style house in a suburban London street. The door was answered by a slim lady in her early forties. She wore her dark brown hair with a central parting in a bun and introduced herself as Anna Freud, daughter of Sigmund Freud. Harry advised her that he was from the JC for an appointment with her father and she guided him through a door to a small room on their right. Speaking with a strong German accent, she explained that her father had been suffering from cancer of the jaw for several years and therefore, found talking at length arduous. Although he was keen to give the interview to the Jewish Chronicle, Ms Freud suggested that Harry should steer clear of the subject of religion as her father was a confirmed atheist. She went on to say that she would be sitting in on the meeting and warned Harry that Freud would smoke his cigar throughout the interview.

'No problem. I have prepared some questions for the session. Apart from religion, are there any other no-go areas?' Harry asked.

'Not really but I think he will be keen to talk about the new book he has written that will be published here in Britain next year,' Ms Freud replied.

Harry was then shown into a much larger room further along the ground floor of the house that enjoyed views of the well-maintained garden, visible through long portrait shaped windows. Sigmund Freud rose from behind his large antique oak desk, placed his cigar in an ashtray and gave Harry a frail handshake. He looked older than his 83 years with slightly tanned skin, a small amount of neatly cut greyish hair, watery brown eyes and a closely trimmed grey moustache and beard. The renowned psychoanalyst greeted Harry warmly speaking like his daughter with a strong German accent. He then surprised Harry by immediately launching into a description of his Ashkenazi Jewish upbringing in Freiberg, a town in Galicia, part of the Austrian Empire. This was just the type of copy Harry wanted for JC readers and furiously took notes as Freud spoke. Harry looked at Anna Freud as much as to say, I thought he didn't want to talk about religion. But she simply smiled, shrugged, and raised her eyebrows.

Tea was brought in by a maid. Harry thanked her as he took a cup and was about to ask a question from his list when the old man embarked on a lengthy lecture-like ramble concerning the important part that sex played in his research of the human brain. In parts this became extremely detailed especially elements relating to libido and seduction. Whilst not embarrassed himself with such talk, Harry felt a little uncomfortable that there was a lady present. However, Ms Freud showed no reaction, as though she was used to hearing her father's pronouncements on this subject.

Eventually, Harry managed to get a word in edgeways by asking Freud a question that he had read recently in an article about the man. 'Is it true that you draw some of the inspiration for your work by reading Shakespeare?'

'Yes, that is true, I started reading the plays of Shakespeare when I was eight years old. As you can see behind me, they have pride of place on my bookshelf. The plots contained in them provided the raw material for my formative theories on psychoanalysis.'

Harry had a good idea of the answer he would get to his next question, Nevertheless, he felt it was worth a punt: 'It has been written that Princess Marie Bonaparte is one of your patients and that she was instrumental in securing safe passage from the Nazis for you from Vienna. Can you tell our readers who some of your other famous patients are?'

'My dear young man, the whole essence of the relationship between an analyst and his patient is confidentiality. You are correct that I have many well-known patients, but I cannot disclose their identities. The great granddaughter of Napoleon Bonaparte is an exception because she has told the press, not me, that she is a patient of mine. She is a good friend and indeed, helped with the arrangements for my departure from Vienna. Part of that arrangement was that I had to sign a document stating that the Nazis had treated me well. I must tell you that I signed the document but added a postscript that read, "I can most highly recommend the Gestapo to everyone." Freud gave a wry smile as he said these words.

Sensing Freud was tiring, Harry pressed on as he was certain that Anna Freud would intervene at any minute to terminate the interview. 'Can you tell me about your new book, due for publication here soon?'

'The book is entitled "Moses and Monotheism." It consists of three essays which are really an extension of my work on psychoanalysis theory as a means of generating hypotheses about historical events. I am fascinated by Egyptology, and everything related to it. The book hypothesises that Moses was not Hebrew, but actually born into Ancient Egyptian nobility and was probably a follower of Akhenaten, the world's earliest recorded monotheist.'

Harry nodded sagely but frankly didn't understand what Freud was talking about. However, he had taken down his comments word for word and would get his editor to explain them back at the JC office.

As Harry had anticipated, at this point Ms Freud interrupted and indicated that time was up. He was pleased that his request to take photographs of the eminent psychoanalyst on the couch adjacent to his desk that had been shipped over from his house in Vienna were met with enthusiasm. Likewise, other shots of Freud and Anna examining some of the antiquities that were dotted around the office that had also been transported from Austria. The final pictures taken were of the Freuds in the garden with the house as the backdrop.

Walking back down the hill to Finchley Road station, Harry's thoughts turned to Freud's comments on sex. His present location in Hampstead was not far away from the place where he had experienced coitus interruptus with Glynis on the Heath. He had been celibate for the past year since then apart from the occasional hand job. Time to get himself some female company again.

However, the more serious subject that dominated his thoughts was Sigmund Freud's warning about the spread of Nazism and the potential consequences for Jews if it took hold in Britain. He had seen the highly praised photographs of the Spanish Civil War taken by Robert Capa and David Seymour. Perhaps he could become a photographer for the British armed forces, if, as was likely, war was declared.

CHAPTER 16 – HIGH FLYER

"I have to tell you now that no such undertaking has been received, and that consequently this country is at war with Germany." Britain's Prime Minister Neville Chamberlain's words struck terror into Sara Levi's heart as she sat listening to the radio broadcast on 3rd September 1939 with Harry in the kitchen at their Whitfield Street home.

Harry looked dapper in his RAF uniform. Much against his mother's will, he had joined the service earlier in the year and had been trained as a reconnaissance photographer. He had left the Jewish Chronicle on good terms. Ivan Greenberg fully understood Harry's eagerness to serve his country against the Nazis and assured him that his job would remain open for him when he returned from the war, that even then, back in January, looked to be inevitable.

Since enlisting, Harry was based at Heston Aerodrome to the west of London. The RAF had recruited Sidney Cotton, an Australian inventor and aviation photography pioneer to head its No 1 Photographic Development Unit located at the Aerodrome. He was largely responsible for the development of early colour film and numbered amongst his close friends,

Winston Churchill. Cotton was regarded as something of a maverick by the RAF hierarchy and was often brought to book for flouting regulations. The men at Heston including Harry, loved him for this.

When questioned by his mother about his duties at Heston, Harry was economical with the truth, ever mindful of his pledge to secrecy in respect of military matters. Sara was therefore under the impression that her son was still undergoing training. The reality was that he had already flown on numerous missions as the photographer onboard a Blenheim Bristol aeroplane to film German military installations. In fact, just the day before their discussion, he had flown over and filmed the German naval fleet anchored at Wilhelmshaven. The film had already been delivered to British Naval Intelligence's office.

During his relatively short time in the RAF, Harry had become an expert in the operation of the small F24 (5x5 image) and the derivative but much larger F52 (8.5x7) aerial cameras. The former was used mostly for night photography with the aid of flash bombs. In planes like the Blenheim flying at high altitudes, up to 40-inch lenses were fitted to the cameras. Exposures typically required the use of a mounted intervalometer, set by reference to speed, altitude, and interval so that the photographer, or observer as they were referred to, could obtain the correct exposures by keying a switch. Great flight precision was needed especially for exposures for stereography and cartography, so Harry had to work closely with the pilot and navigator onboard.

Hearing the Prime Minister's radio broadcast, Harry decided that despite having been given three days leave, he should return to Heston immediately. He kissed his mother goodbye and she waved to him from the doorway as he disappeared round the corner from Whitfield Street into Warren Street. Sara stood on the step and started to cry wondering whether she would see her son again. Literally within minutes of Harry's departure, Sara was still standing at the front door wiping her tears when the air raid siren sounded. Visibly shocked, neighbours came out of their houses and made their way in an orderly fashion to the nearest shelter in Warren Street underground station. Sara followed them in a daze still thinking about Harry.

As it turned out, Sara did see Harry several times, albeit briefly on each occasion, in the ensuing months. Keen to "do her bit" for the war effort, Sara took a bookkeeping job for a firm in nearby Mortimer Street. The company, Morrisons, was a *schmuter* dress manufacturer whose office was located in what was called the rag trade area between Great Portland Street and Oxford Street because of the number of tailors shops. Morrison's office though was purely administrative. The factory was based in the East End and had switched its production line from making evening gowns to military uniforms. Sara enjoyed the camaraderie in the office and the work took her mind off Harry's wellbeing.

The war had begun disastrously for the British armed forces. Germany's well-oiled military machine with superior armaments rapidly pushed the British forces back to the beaches of Dunkirk in France just six months since its arrival. Over 300,000 men were stranded on the French town's sandy stretches of coastline awaiting evacuation back to England. Winston Churchill had taken over as Prime Minister after Neville Chamberlain stepped down through ill health. Churchill was desperate for more intelligence about the location of the German army divisions in relation to the trapped British troops. This information would enable him and the War Committee to ascertain whether the capture of the British forces could be prevented. He therefore instructed the Committee's most senior RAF member, Air Chief Marshall Lord Dowding, to issue orders to his reconnaissance units to fly sorties over the areas in France to obtain photographs of the German advance. Dowding duly telephoned Wing Commander Sidney Cotton at Heston Aerodrome and gave the order emphasising the urgency of the matter.

Closely examining his poker hand, Harry said: 'I'll raise you two bob.'

Addressing his comment to the third player in the game, Flight Sergeant Steve Nicholls; Pilot Officer Charles Morgan stated: 'He's bluffing.'

It was May 1940, the three men, all in their flying gear, were sitting in the wooden slatted mess hut at Heston around a small table with a pile of coins in the middle and half-drunk, blue-rimmed white enamel mugs of tea. Suddenly the door of the hut burst open, and Sidney Cotton strode in. The three men jumped to their feet and saluted their commanding officer.

'At ease men. Just had Dowders on the blower. Winnie needs pix of the Krauts' positions around Dunkirk PDQ. Get your arses in gear and get over there at the double. I've already briefed two other crews. They will be covering the land areas to the east and west of Dunkirk. You will need to take the central area. Here are your flight details. It's a night operation but it's not going to be a joyride. Jerry has got squadrons of Stukas and Messerschmitts strafing our boys on the beaches so as soon as they see you, they'll be on your tail. Good luck!'

As the door slammed behind Cotton, the three crew members looked at one another but said nothing. However, they were all thinking the same thing. This was a suicide mission. The German fighters were much faster and manoeuvrable than the Blenheim. Several of the RAF stalwart fighter/bombers had already been shot down in missions over France and Belgium. No bombs would be loaded for this flight, purely rolls of film and belts of ammunition for the Browning guns mounted in the wings and turret halfway along the fuselage. Both Harry and Steve Nicholls had been trained in the use of this latter gun whilst Morgan controlled the other guns.

The three Blenheims took off from Heston at 22.00 hours. They flew at low level 5,000 feet across the English Channel, then climbed sharply to an altitude of 25,000 feet on reaching the French coast. At this point the planes broke away from their formation and continued on individual flight paths. Harry took up his position on the cameras and started to take pictures as they flew over the German army units below. Inevitably, the flash bulbs used by the cameras attracted the attention of the anti-aircraft guns below and flak began to explode around the Blenheim. Mercifully, no German fighters appeared on the scene as

Harry raised his thumb to indicate to the pilot, Charles Morgan, that he had taken sufficient shots. As the aircraft turned to head for home, it was hit by flak. Shrapnel flew through the fuselage and the plane jolted ferociously. Steve Nicholls was killed instantly as pieces of shell fragments ripped into his head. Harry was hit by chunks of the molten metal in both legs and passed out. Fortunately, his oxygen mask stayed in place as the plane was still flying at a high altitude. Shrapnel had gone through Charles Morgan's thick sheepskin leather flying jacket and embedded itself in his chest. But he was still conscious struggling with the controls as the port-side engine was on fire causing the Blenheim to descend rapidly. Assessing the situation Morgan knew there was no chance of reaching England. If he did attempt this, it would almost certainly result in crashing into the Channel and probably dying. At this stage, he had no idea as to whether his crew members were alive. They were not responding to his calls, but he could not leave the controls for fear of the aircraft nose-diving earthwards. Bailing out without knowing whether Harry and Steve were alive was unthinkable. He decided that the only option was to attempt a landing.

Spotting the sandy beaches below, Morgan banked the plane towards them and throttled back the only working engine.

Initially, the Allied soldiers on the beaches awaiting evacuation boats thought the aircraft approaching through the gloom was German and prepared to open fire. It was only when their officer screamed: 'Hold your fire, it's one of ours,' that they lowered their weapons. Applying all his remaining strength, Charles Morgan steadied the plane and somehow managed to land it using the just visible line of the sea's incoming tide edge as his reference marker. The aircraft skidded along the wet sand at great speed, finally coming to a halt. The front wheel buckled, and the plane's nose tipped slowly towards the shallow seawater.

The British soldiers raced from their dug-outs and levered open the fuselage door. They released the crew from their seat belts and carried them along the beach to a medical tent. Steve Nicholls was pronounced dead on arrival. As well as the large wound in his chest, Charles Morgan had sustained a serious blow on the head from an altimeter gauge that had become dislodged on the impact of landing. Blood was pouring from the gash. Despite the intense pain he was feeling, the pilot managed to tell the army officer at his side the importance of the films still onboard. The officer gave orders for a party of his men to retrieve the cameras and they hurried back to the plane. Harry's legs were peppered with pieces of shrapnel. He remained unconscious. Both survivors were injected with morphine and transferred to a medical operating unit that had been set-up in a large house further along the beach. Sadly, Charles Morgan died on the operating table. The loss of blood from his wounds proved too severe. The operation to remove the shrapnel from Harry's legs was successful and when he awoke, he could hear the gentle lapping of waves on the side of the hospital ship Isle of Guernsey which was taking him and hundreds of other wounded soldiers back to Britain.

During Harry's two-week stay in the Naval Hospital in Portsmouth, Sara Levi visited her son several times. In true Jewish mother fashion, on each occasion, she came loaded down with bags of food. Far too much for Harry to eat, so the patients in the surrounding beds were always delighted to see her. Once the doctors were happy that Harry's wounds were healing, and his rehabilitation walking exercises were complete, he was discharged. However, he would have to use walking sticks and was told that he would not be able to resume active service in the foreseeable future. There was still a danger that the wounds could become infected. Rest was essential if a full recovery was to be achieved. Obviously, Harry was not best pleased to hear this news and was itching to get back in the air again. The thought of having to sit at home with his mother continuously fussing and making him endless cups of tea was driving him mad. Nevertheless, he knew he would have to comply if he wanted to return to Heston. The single upside of this enforced home stay was that Harry would be able to catch up with his pal Sidney Solomon, who, owing to poor eyesight, had not been called up. Much to his frustration, he had been enlisted to serve with The Entertainments National Service Association. ENSA was created to provide entertainment for the troops and factory workers. Sidney's role was to act as the stooge for Leslie Henson, a well-known comedian. Many of the acts included in these shows were substandard, hence ENSA obtained the nickname, "Every Night Something Awful."

Harry was only back in Whitfield Street a matter of days before an official looking envelope addressed to him, marked confidential, fell on the doormat. The letter was from the War Office and stated that his Commanding Officer, Sidney Cotton, had recommended that his expert knowledge of photography and filming should be utilised to assist the war effort. Therefore, as soon as he had recovered from his injuries, he should make an appointment to attend a meeting at the Ministry of Information in Malet Street, London, a fifteen-minute walk from his home. Harry was intrigued.

CHAPTER 17 – MARIE

Sara was pleased to hear the sound of laughter coming from the kitchen. Sidney was rattling off some of the jokes to Harry used in his act with Leslie Henson.

'Hitler and Goring are standing atop the Berlin radio tower. Hitler says he wants to do something to put a smile on Berliners' faces. So, Goring says: Why don't you jump?'

'General to Private: Have you come here to die? Private to General: No sir, I came here yester-die!'

'Knock, knock. Who's there? (Henson pretends to slap me in the face). Vie Ask Zie Questions!'

'Hitler visits the front and talks to a soldier. Hitler asks: Friend, when you are in the front line under artillery fire, what do you wish for? The soldier replies: That you, my Fuhrer, stand next to me!'

Smiling, Harry said: 'They're crap Sidney. Do the audience actually laugh at these jokes?'

'Depends. The factory bods usually sit stony faced as they've already heard the quips on the radio. The troops tend to be a bit more forthright shouting get off and rubbish.'

'Not terribly rewarding then?'

'Suppose not but at least I'm still in one piece

which is more than can be said for you.'

'You're not wrong there, but I'm hoping to be back properly on my feet soon.'

'What then? More sky's the limit stuff?

'Well, that's what I'm hoping but I have to wait for further orders. I'll keep you posted.'

Promising to keep Harry updated on his next ENSA show around different parts of Britain, Sidney bade his friend and Sara farewell, then headed for his parent's shop in Soho.

After just a couple of weeks at home reading magazines about the latest developments in photography and filming techniques, Harry felt much better. He had stuck rigidly to the exercise regime he was given before leaving hospital and had his wounds re-dressed at the nearby University College Hospital but was still walking with the aid of a stick. He told himself that now was the time to make that appointment to find out exactly what his Commanding Officer had suggested for him.

Harry stood in awe staring up outside Senate House, the imposing 19-storey Art Deco white Portland Stone-clad building in Malet Street that housed the Ministry of Information. Crikey, he thought, it stood out like a sore thumb compared with the surrounding low-rise buildings. Surely, a prime target for the Luftwaffe. Entering the bustling reception area, Harry was stopped by an armed soldier, one of several strategically positioned around the marble pillars and floor of the impressive hallway. Having presented the letter, he had been sent confirming the appointment to the soldier, Harry was directed to a uniformed female assistant who led him up four flights of stairs and pointed him to a door marked "Head of Films Division."

Kenneth Clark was a well-spoken man in his forties. He came from a wealthy Scottish family and had graduated from Oxford where he had studied history. Prior to the war he was the Director of The National Gallery in London. As the outbreak of war approached, Clark proposed to Winston Churchill that the contents of the National Gallery should be shipped to America for safekeeping. Churchill refused and ordered that the artworks would be hidden in a cave in Wales. A decision with which Clark vehemently disagreed. Following the closure of the National Gallery, Clark was appointed Head of Films at the Ministry of Information, or MOI as it was generally called.

Between draws on his pipe, Clark emphasised the important part propaganda would play in the war and how film could be used to influence opinions. Harry listened wondering where Clark's explanation was leading to. Finally, Clark stated that the Films Division was urgently in need of an assistant camera operator and that Harry had been highly recommended for the post. Before Harry could ask whether he would ultimately be able to return to active service in the RAF, Clark rose, shook his hand, and told him to report for duty the following day. As he ushered Harry out of the door, he said that the pay was good and that he should not tell anyone what his role at the MOI involved. He would be given a letter and had to sign to that effect. Outside Clark's office, Harry stood momentarily replaying in his mind what had just occurred. It appeared that his future had been pre-ordained by the powers that be. No point in arguing, just adhere to the words on the poster produced by the MOI he had seen on Clark's wall: "Keep Calm and Carry on."

Harry's first day working at the MOI was like a dream come true. He had read about Cecil Hepworth being one of the founders of the British film industry. Now, he was rubbing shoulders with him having been introduced to the great man by his new line manager, Peter Monckton. Apparently, the two men had worked together on several of Hepworth's films, the most recent being "Mist in the Valley," in 1923. This had been the last of Hepworth's films as a producer and director because his company had gone into receivership shortly after. He was now acting as a consultant to the MOI on the production of wartime newsreels.

Similar to most of the previous jobs he had held, Harry had a knack of being liked and taken under the wing of his boss. This certainly proved to be the case with Peter Monckton. From the outset, the older man, in his late fifties, began to teach Harry the tricks of a cameraman's trade. And once again, Harry's innate ability to pick up things quickly, came to the fore. Within no time at all, the pair of them were referred to as "The Master and his Apprentice," by colleagues working at Senate House. Every day, Monckton would reveal to Harry more secrets about studio lighting, sound levels, camera operating techniques, and the technical mysteries of film making. As a result, Harry found himself doing lots of tasks that somebody much more senior should have been handling. When he questioned his manager as to why he was imparting all this in-depth information, Monckton simply replied that he should keep quiet about it. Harry was quite happy to remain *schtum* but continued to wonder what the reason for this crash course in film production was for.

It was shortly after that Harry discovered the reason by accident. He was setting up the focussing on cameras for a filming session when he pointed something out in the lens viewfinder. Monckton couldn't see what Harry was referring to. Harry immediately thought, he is going blind. He's losing the most important asset for his job. He is training me to be his eyes.

Meeting Cecil Hepworth had proved to be a magic moment for Harry, but it was surpassed a few days later. Harry was in the reception area of Senate House chatting up Marie Jacks, one of the female uniformed attendants when to his astonishment, the Prime Minister, Winston Churchill, bounded through the doors clutching a bottle of Pol Roger Champagne and puffing vigorously at his cigar. He was preceded by his bodyguard, Walter Thompson, and followed by an entourage of secretaries and assistants. The purpose of his visit was a meeting with Kenneth Clark to discuss the filming of a speech that the PM had made in The Houses of Commons the day before. Apparently, extracts of the stirring speech, that had instantly become known as, "We will fight on the beaches," had been widely reported in the press and on BBC radio but the full contents, with Churchill delivering it, had not been seen or heard by the British public. The idea was to film the PM on the roof of Senate House, looking out across the London skyline as he made the speech. Stock footage scenes depicting words from the text such as seas, beaches and landing grounds, would be intercut. According to Peter Monckton, who attended the meeting and told Harry later, the bottle of champagne was a gift for Kenneth Clark as a peace offering in respect of the two men's falling out regarding the storage of the National Gallery's valuable artworks.

As it transpired, the film was never made. Churchill could not spare the time because the prospect of a German invasion of Britain had become imminent. However, one filming session that did take place occurred soon after the Prime Minister's visit, albeit that only the audio element was subsequently broadcast. General De Gaulle, the self-appointed leader of the Free French Forces, had fled to England following the German forces overrunning France. Churchill had authorised the filming despite the War Committee being unhappy about De Gaulle's status and credentials. The British Government was technically still communicating with the Vichy Government in France, established following the German occupation. The script for the General's speech denounced the members of the Vichy administration as traitors and called upon French soldiers to continue their fight against the Nazis.

On the appointed day for the recording, De Gaulle arrived at Senate House and was extremely aloof and rude to the staff. This behaviour from someone who was now dependent on the support of Britain was not well received. Word had reached Monckton and Harry before the "Surly Frog," as he had been nicknamed, arrived in the film studio. Without acknowledging the two-man film crew, De Gaulle marched over to the desk that had been placed in the centre of the studio and plonked his bulky frame into the chair behind it. He grabbed the large microphone on the desk and shouted "dépêchez-vous," at Monckton and Harry. Neither spoke French so did not understand the General's command to hurry up and get on with things. Harry was not too pleased with the Frenchman's action as he was wearing headphones to adjust the sound levels and was temporarily deafened by De Gaulle's bellowing. As Peter Monckton tried to explain by using hand gestures that they were almost ready to begin recording, the General sat back and referred to his notes. Meanwhile, Harry had slipped behind De Gaulle without him noticing. Monckton then nodded to Harry who banged the clapper board together as hard as he could next to the General's ear. Taken entirely by surprise, De Gaulle leapt up from the chair clutching his chest screaming: *"Putain de merde!"* Monckton and Harry exchanged conspiratorial smirks as the Frenchman demanded water to wash down some pills, he had pulled from his tunic pocket. With the help of Marie Jacks, now Harry's girlfriend, who spoke a little French and was called in to act as a translator, the filming was eventually completed. The pompous General then left the studio in the way he had entered it, head held high with his long nose in the air, without saying a word of thanks to the crew.

In the weeks that followed, Harry and Marie made several visits to the roof of Senate House for canoodling sessions. But try as he might, unlike some of his previous female acquaintances, Marie was determined to stay a virgin until wedding bells had chimed. She came from a Jewish family in nearby Goodge Street. Her father, a gentle Austrian who had lived in Britain since the turn of the century, had a tailor's shop in Hanway Street, round the corner from Harry's Alma Mata. And her mother was a fearsome character who hailed from Russian stock. Marie was a petite girl seven years older than Harry but looked much younger than her age. In addition to her looks, the things that appealed to Harry most was her sense of humour, kindness, and her ability to talk about virtually any subject in an authoritative manner. Although frustrated, deep-down, Harry respected her continual refusal of his attempts to get into her *hoyzn*.

At his 21st birthday celebration in July, Harry introduced Marie to his mother and to the friends and family members shoe-horned into the Levi house in Whitfield Street. Sara was delighted that Marie was a bright attractive Jewish lady but if marriage proved to be on the cards, felt that her son should be aiming higher up the social scale. Marie's parents were distinctly working class and local gossip she had gleaned without Harry's knowledge indicated that her older brothers were always in trouble before being called up into the army. Sara kept reminding herself that she was in no position to be snobbish. The circumstances she had endured since her husband's death were not exactly anything to be hoity toity about. Despite her doubts, Sara did not express her worries to Harry. Neither, for fear of worrying him, did she tell him that to do more for the war effort, she had taken on an additional role. Whilst still working at Morrison's during the day, three nights a week she had volunteered to become a fire watcher. This entailed standing on the roof of her firm's building and looking out for incendiaries dropped by German bombers during air raids. If she spotted these containers on the roofs of surrounding buildings, she would shout down to firemen in the street below to alert them to their existence. Whilst this was obviously a dangerous task, Sara was more than happy to carry it out in preference to taking shelter in the crammed conditions of Warren Street underground station.

A few months later, in September, the German Luftwaffe began what became entitled The Blitz on London. Thousands of bombs were dropped on England's capital daily causing widespread deaths and injuries. One night the bombing was particularly intense. Harry and Marie were standing on the roof of Senate House when a string of bombs landed to the west of their location. The impact shook the building and fires immediately sprang up where the bombs had landed. The sound of fire engine bells rang out as the machines from Euston Fire Station sped towards the blaze.

Staring at the fires lighting up the night sky, Harry said: 'I pity the poor buggers who copped that lot. Don't think there will be much left of anything round there.'

Little did he know that the building on the roof of which his mother had been standing had taken a direct hit.

CHAPTER 18 – SNAP!

Later that night, on his way home from work, as he turned the corner into Whitfield Street, Harry was concerned to see a policeman standing outside the front door of his house. He quickened his pace and addressed the officer as he approached: 'Can I help you?'

The policeman replied with a serious look on his face: 'Do you live here sir?'

'Yes, I do.'

'Are you related to a Mrs Sara Levi?'

'Yes, she's, my mother.'

'Can we please step inside sir?'

Harry unlocked the door and showed the officer into the front room parlour. He did not switch on the light as the black-out curtains were not drawn. Harry directed his guest to take a seat as he drew the blinds and lit a candle which created an eerie silhouette on the wall of the policeman who had not removed his helmet.

'Please sit-down sir. I'm afraid I have some very sad news. Your mother was carrying out her fire watching duties on the roof of a building in Mortimer Street earlier this evening when it was hit by a German bomb. The firemen found your mum's identity card in the rubble I am sorry to tell you that she was killed in the explosion.'

Harry turned white. 'It can't be her. My mother was not a firewatcher.'

'I'm sorry to contradict you sir but the firemen who work in that area have informed us that she was. And a very brave one at that.'

Trembling, Harry blurted out: 'But she never told me.'

'Perhaps she didn't want to worry you sir. You know what mothers are like.'

Harry put his head in his hands and started to sob.

The policeman rose and enquired 'Is the kitchen through the back? I'll go and make you a cup of tea.'

Harry nodded and the officer took his helmet off, disappeared, returning a few minutes later with two mugs of piping hot tea.

Having recovered some composure, Harry asked: 'Where have they taken her body.'

The policeman paused before replying. He knew he would have to choose his words carefully as he had done when imparting this type of information to people in previous weeks. 'The thing is sir, is that the building took a direct hit and was reduced to ashes. As a result, the identity card and we assume this necklace is all that remains of your dear mother.' He handed Harry the card and the necklace with the Star of David pendant. 'Although it's of no consolation, she would not have known anything about what happened. She died instantly.'

Both men sat in silence sipping their tea in the flickering candlelight. Finally, the officer stood up and patted Harry on the shoulder. 'Is there anyone you can call to be with?' Harry shook his head. 'Sorry sir, my condolences. But I must move on. I have the unenviable task of relating this kind of news to other families in the area.'

Harry heard the street door close as the policeman left. He began to cry uncontrollably clutching a photo frame containing a picture of his mother he recently took to his heart. He sat in the same position until dawn broke.

It was Saturday morning, mercifully, not a workday. Harry telephoned Marie but could hardly speak. Realising there was a serious problem, Marie went straight round to Harry's. She was devastated to hear of Sara's death but being a practical soul, persuaded Harry that he needed to inform his relatives and then speak to a rabbi to arrange a funeral. In something of a daze, Harry dutifully carried out Marie's suggestions. Rabbi Moyer from the Great Portland Street schul arrived in the afternoon and explained to Harry that a memorial service for Sara could be held at the synagogue but in the absence of a body, no burial could take place. However, it would be permissible for a headstone to be erected in his mother's name next to his father's grave at the Jewish Cemetery in Golders Green. When the stone was completed, a short service could be undertaken at the cemetery. In the immediate term, sitting Shiva could take place after the service but that it might be difficult for friends and family to attend during the prevailing Blitz conditions. Harry agreed and said he would like a memorial service to be arranged but not put relatives and friends through more risk by inviting them to sit Shiva at Whitfield Street. He would provide the rabbi with notes about his mother and photographs to be displayed around the room at the service.

Marie insisted that Harry stay with her at her parent's home in Goodge Street on Saturday night and Sunday. Her mother made a great deal of fuss of Harry and tried to tempt him with various dishes including his favourite lokshen soup, but to no avail, he had no appetite. Early on Monday morning, Marie accompanied Harry back to his house where he changed and then they walked to work. Peter Monckton was shocked to hear Harry's news and insisted that he should take compassionate leave. Harry thanked his boss but refused his offer saying he would prefer to remain at work as it would help to take his mind off things. Monckton had intended to impart some work-related news to Harry that he had just received from Kenneth Clark. But in the circumstances, he refrained.

Harry was pleased that many of his friends and relatives attended the service including Sidney and his parents, Peter Monckton, Ivan Greenberg and Sara's workmates from Morrisons. However, he was disappointed that despite advising them, none of his mother's so-called friends from her time when his father was alive had managed to come. Harry had invited attendees to come back to Whitfield Street for refreshments but very few took up the offer for fear of another air raid.

A week later, deciding that he could no longer delay talking to Harry about the changes that were planned at Senate House, Peter Monckton suggested that they go out for a drink and a chat.

Supping half pints of bitter in the Plough Tavern, a Victorian style pub with taped up windows opposite the British Museum, Monckton opened the conversation. 'I'm sorry to spring this on you so soon after your mum's passing but I had no choice. Remember at the beginning of this month when the Blitz started and we were trying to film an interview with the Secretary of State for War, Anthony Eden?'

'Only too well,' Harry replied. 'Some Jerry

bombs landed close by, the building shook furiously, and the cameras and equipment slid around the studio. We had to abandon the filming and get Eden down to the basement shelter pronto.'

'Exactly. It was because of that incident Eden spoke to Kenneth Clark and told him that the work we do was far too important to be ended by a bomb. He ordered that our unit should be moved out of London as soon possible to a suitable location. Me, you, and the team would all be expected to relocate.'

Swigging a mouthful of beer that left a thin white line on his upper lip, Harry enquired: 'Where would the new location be and when will the move be?'

'It's not been finalised yet, but the probability is in the countryside near Oxford early next month. It goes without saying that we are sworn to secrecy on the subject.'

Harry chewed this over in his mind for what seemed like an age before responding: 'I am not sure I can relocate boss.'

'Why not, you're a single talented lad and we need your skills?'

Harry gave a rueful smile: 'Last night I proposed to Marie, and she accepted.'

'That's brilliant news. Congratulations. I'll get another round in to celebrate.'

As Monckton made his way to the bar to order drinks, Harry sat thinking about the future. He urgently required money to pay for the rent as his wages would not stretch to cover that and other living expenses, including an imminent wedding.

Harry took the beer handed to him by Monckton: 'Cheers boss. I need to discuss what you've told me with Marie. I haven't even spoken to her parents about getting married. Everything seems to be going so fast.'

Holding hands, Marie and Harry sat on the sofa at her parent's place in Goodge Street and announced their intended marriage. In time honoured tradition, Harry had earlier taken Marie's father Samuel to one side and asked his permission. The answer was an immediate yes with a hint of relief. No questions as to how Harry was going to support his daughter were asked. Marie's mother, Esther, was less enthusiastic but did not show it. She was the business brains of the family and unlike her husband, her first thought was how the couple would exist on the meagre wages they were earning at the Ministry of Information. In her mind, Harry was a nice enough lad who had had a rough time with the loss of both his mother and father, but she was concerned about his stability in the longer term. And if they thought she and Samuel were going to splash out on a lavish wedding, they would need to think again.

In fact, the couple did not want a big wedding. Quite the opposite. Harry was not religious, and Marie was happy to forgo a ceremony at the synagogue followed by an expensive reception. It was agreed that they would marry at Marylebone Registry Office and invite close friends and relatives for drinks and cake upstairs in the Fitzroy Tavern in Charlotte Street. The pub, round the corner from the Jack's house in Goodge Street, was run by a friend of theirs, Judah Morris Kleinfeld.

Harry and Marie discussed moving to Oxford with the film unit but decided on just Harry's income, this would not be practical. It was decided with the agreement of Marie's parents that she would continue working at the MOI while Harry would seek employment in London. The couple would stay at the Jack's house until they were earning enough to rent their own place. Reluctantly, Harry gave his notice in to Peter Monckton who was sad to see him go but wished him and Marie all the best for the future. With Harry's departure, keeping his eyesight problem under wraps had suddenly become more acute.

Without telling anyone, Harry attempted to regain entry to the RAF but was rejected on medical grounds. Esther Jacks made it clear from the outset that Harry was not going to be allowed to sit around at home all day while her daughter went out to work. Consequently, Harry made himself scarce during the day on the pretext he was out looking for a job. The reality was that most days he was sitting in a pub far enough away from Goodge Street to make sure he was not spotted. On one such occasion, he was in the Lamb & Flag pub at the western end of Oxford Street making a half pint of beer last a long time when he met an old school pal of his and Sidney's. Danny Shelby had avoided call-up for military service as he had a club foot. He now spent his time as a snapper on Oxford Street taking pictures of couples as they walked along and then selling them the photo.

Smothered in an over-sized old fashioned double-breasted black Crombie overcoat that had seen better days, Danny took off his tweed peaked cap and woolly scarf, revealing his blonde hair, thin pale face, and bulging eyes. He sat down opposite Harry and shook his hand: 'Long time, no see *Mosher*,' were his first words. 'What have you been up to? It's been ages. I heard on the grapevine that you married the Jacks girl. Shrewd move. Nice bit of crackling, her old man's got the tailor's shop and all. Watch out for her brothers though, Rudi and Izzy, right pair they are. Hard nuts.'

Harry updated Danny on his RAF exploits and bearing in mind Peter Monckton's cautionary words, a limited amount of detail about his time at the MOI. He emphasised how he now needed to find a job and fast to avoid the lash of his mother-in-law's tongue.

'You used to be well into photography as I remember, worked for the JC didn't you? Still got your camera gear?' Danny asked.

'Matter of fact, I have.'

'Look, there's plenty of punters out there for both of us. You could take one side of the street and I'll take the other. Nobody knows if they are going to live until tomorrow with this war going on so these young lovers that wander up and down are mad keen to have their photo taken. Five bob for two photos and their address. I develop the pictures every night and pop them in the post the following day. You get the occasional *mamzer* who says you won't send the photos on but that's usually because they are with somebody else's missus. Cruise and schmooze. You were a dab hand with the spiel at that back at the Jews Free School,' Shelby laughed.

Harry thought the prospect of earning some money would certainly placate Marie and her mother. Without hesitation he said: 'You're on.'

At first things went well and Harry was raking the money in. However, ever since he was a child, he had suffered terribly from the cold. December 1940 saw freezing fog descend on London, followed by snow and ice. Harry noticed that these adverse weather conditions brought out a meanness in people and a reluctance to have their photo taken. Quite different from their attitude when it was warmer. The light faded early in the afternoons making the quality of the photos poorer. Therefore, Harry had taken to packing in work at lunchtime and retiring to the Lamb for some whiskies to warm up.

Marie, Harry, and Sidney were at a friend's pre-Christmas party in D'Arblay Street, Soho. Sidney had taken some leave time off from his ENSA tour and was not scheduled to rejoin it until after the festive break. To the delight of the other partygoers, Harry and Sidney performed an impromptu double-act comprising comedy sketches that they revived from years ago. Probably fuelled by copious amounts of alcohol everybody was in fits of laughter. Reliving his childhood performer days, Harry hammed it up by singing to the accompaniment of his purposely awful banjo playing. Sidney acted as his straight man, a role he was well-acquainted with working for Leslie Henson. When they finished to thunderous applause and calls for an encore, they were approached by a tubby man in a smart suit and a floral bow tie.

'In the business, are you, looking for work?'

Harry replied: 'No, just a bit of fun.'

'Your act certainly seemed to go down well. If you ever think of taking it up professionally, I can help,' the man said as he gave Harry a card, turned and left the party.

Harry and Sidney looked at the theatrical agent's card, giggled and carried on chatting with Marie and their friends.

A few days later, with an icy wind blowing down Oxford Street, having been told to piss off by virtually every couple he had tried his *spiel* on, Harry was freezing. Disgruntled, he loped into the Lamb & Flag where he had arranged to meet Sidney for a drink. Cupping his hands round a glass of whisky, he took a swig and pulled out the theatrical agent's card from his pocket. He tossed it down on the table and said to Sidney: 'What do you think? Just for a laugh, let's pop round to his office and see what he says.'

'Don't be daft, he was probably winding us up at the party. We haven't even got an act,' Sidney replied somewhat apprehensively knowing his mate's track record for landing them in trouble.

'You're probably right Sidney but we might be able to get a drink out of him for nix, and it will keep us out of the cold for half an hour.'

'You sound like a right *schnorrer* Harry. Okay,

let's give it a go. His office is only at the bottom end of Denman Street. Nothing lost, nothing gained.'

Climbing the rickety rackety wooden stairs with peeling theatres posters on the walls, hyped up by drinks from the pub, Harry and Sidney were in the mood for fun. They burst through the door at the top of the stairs which had "Jonny Preston Theatrical Agency" engraved on the glass panel in large black lettering. The woman sitting at the desk in front of them was in her sixties but trying to look thirty judging by her dress and heavy make-up. If there was ever an example of mutton dressed up as lamb, this was it. She didn't bother to look at them. She just continued to examine the paper in her aged typewriter and drag on her cigarette, the smoke from which was contributing to making the ceiling of the office an even deeper shade of dirty brown. Realising they had failed to make an impression, Harry and Sidney broke into one of their skits with the former plucking on an imaginary banjo. Finally, the receptionist begrudgingly glared at them and enquired: 'Have you got an appointment?'

'Actually, no, but if Mr Preston is available, we would like a quick word as he suggested we should pop in,' Harry piped up.

Sidney quipped: 'Is that the typewriter used by

Dickens?'

They both laughed. The receptionist didn't.

In the adjacent office they heard a phone crash down onto its receiver followed by a shout of "*farshtunkener chazer*!"

A silhouette appeared through the windowpane of the office where the outburst came from and its door opened. Jonny Preston recognised Harry and Sidney immediately.

'Ah, the *mushuganahs* at the party. Come on through.'

The receptionist gave an exasperated sigh as they went past her.

'Your lucky day,' Preston advised. 'I've just had a call from the Theatre Royal Brighton, they urgently require a comedy act for a run that starts next month.' He pulled out a standard contract from his desk drawer and placed it in front of the lads. 'They will arrange digs near the theatre.'

Harry and Sidney carefully read the contract. It seemed straightforward and they noted that Preston's agency would receive ten percent of their earnings. On enquiring how much they would be paid, Preston said it would be a minimum of £8 per week each but they would need to agree the final amount with the theatre manager on arrival in Brighton.

'Just sign at the bottom and I will fill in the rest

of the details when you phone me with them,' the agent said handing them a pen.

With a mixture of excitement and naivety, they winked at each other, signed, and shook Preston's hand. He poured them a double scotch from a bottle and three glasses he had taken out of a dusty filing cabinet.

In unison, the three of them exclaimed: '*Mazeltov*!

CHAPTER 19 – BARE ESSENTIALS

'But Brighton,' Marie shouted. 'It's not exactly round the corner, is it? You could have talked it through with me first.'

'I know, I'm sorry, but it will save me getting my goolies frozen off every day in Oxford Street,' Harry responded. 'Besides, it will give us more income, and you will be able to come down at weekends. Come on, it's something I've always wanted to do.'

'Me, me, me, that's what it's always about with you isn't it? Mr Selfish.' 'Call that a proper job? Hamming it up like a couple of *schiemiels*. You and that putz Sidney don't even have an act!'

'Look, you and your mother have constantly been on at me to get a proper job so we can get our own place. Now I'm trying to do that, suddenly, I'm Mr Shyster.'

Marie stormed out of their tiny bedroom on the top floor of her parents' house, slamming the door loudly as she went. Harry sat on the bed wondering what he needed to do to bring Marie round. Meanwhile, Mr and Mrs Jacks had been sitting in the living room below listening to the raised voices coming from above. Neither exchanged a word as the front door banged denoting Marie's departure from the house. Esther Jacks concealed a smile behind the magazine she was reading. Moving to Brighton would get that shyster out from under her feet she thought. However, she was concerned about how this would affect his relationship with her daughter. Samuel Jacks continued to read his newspaper.

Harry and Sidney hurriedly set about putting together an act. Like most performers of the time, they stole material from other artists' repertoire but changed it slightly to avoid accusations that their act was totally cribbed. They rehearsed continuously for days before taking the train to Brighton to meet Albert Rose, the manager of the Royal. Rose was a legend in show business. He was a patient kindly man who had helped many novice performers become more professional, and in some cases, famous. It was mid-January 1941 and the theatre's pantomime run was coming to an end. The Royal had a great reputation for its pantos and this season had been no exception. Despite the threat of air raids, the 1000 seat theatre was virtually full for every performance including matinées.

Having sat in the front row of the stalls watching them rehearse, Albert Rose beckoned Harry and Sidney down from the stage to join him.

'I like the act but a few tips. You're rushing your lines. I realise that you're a bit nervous, but you need to pause every now and then to give the audience time to laugh. After all, you are a comedy act. I appreciate that you are the straight man Sidney, but you must speak up and look at the audience as though you are confused after some of Harry's quips. It will add to the humour you are trying to convey. I've got a couple of tickets for you to see Max Miller round at the Hippodrome. The "Cheeky Chappie" lives in Brighton and is the best in the business with his timing. Just sit back and learn. Lastly, I am due to finalise the posters today on which you will feature for the show. The name of your act, "Levi & Solomon," sounds like a firm of Jewish solicitors. What about, "Wally & Solly?" that's going to be much more memorable.'

Harry and Sidney agreed and headed off to the digs that the theatre had arranged. Albert Rose had told them that the theatre would cover the cost of their rent at Mrs Simkins guest house in Preston Street but the wages of £8 per week each was non-negotiable. He didn't mention that "Wally & Solly" would appear at the bottom of the show poster in barely readable sized text.

The lads were only too pleased to take up Albert Rose's offer to see Max Miller perform. They loved every minute of the show. Dressed in his customary stage outfit of white trilby hat and multi-coloured suit, Miller was a tour de force. Part of the comedian's act was to start by asking the audience which one of his two joke books he should use for the performance. The white one or the blue one. As usual, the crowd opted for the blue book containing the naughty jokes. Miller's material was cleverly constructed. By using innuendo or leaving out the last words of a joke, he could get away with risqué stuff. He never swore outright during his act, but the audience knew the meaning, and laughed uncontrollably. One of the jokes Harry and Sidney particularly liked was:

Adam and Eve in the Garden dwelt,
They were so happy and jolly.
I wonder how they would have felt,
If all the leaves had been holly!

Miller's style of delivery was regarded as perfection amongst his fellow comedians, and he would often follow up a saucy joke with the line:

"Ere, it's people like you that give me a bad name!"

Invigorated by Max Miller's sublime performance, Harry and Sidney continued to refine their act. When the big night arrived for their debut, they were confident until standing in the wings of the stage waiting for their cue to come on. Both were nervous wrecks. Worryingly, neither could utter a word. Overcome by nerves, they had temporarily dried up. The compere introduced them as “Wally & Solly,” a zany new comedy duo from London who were destined to take show business by storm. Bottom of the bill, they were scheduled as the first act on stage. Topping the bill that night was the singing and comedy act, Flanagan and Allen, who had achieved great success with their much-loved theme tune, “Underneath the Arches.’ Bud Flanagan had been one of the coffin bearers at Harry’s father’s funeral and having made the connection to the aspiring comedian, had been giving Harry tips and encouragement during rehearsals.

Harry and Sidney bounced onto the stage and were greeted by a mild ripple of applause from the audience. That was except for one lady sitting in the front row of the stalls who stood clapping and whistling loudly. Marie Levi was making her presence felt.

All things considered; their nine-minutes performance went well. The duo had heeded the advice from Albert Rose and Bud Flanagan by slowing their delivery and seeking audition approbation as they went through their routine.

After watching Flanagan and Allen’s barnstorming finale performance that included not only “Underneath the Arches,” but other hits of theirs such as “Run Rabbit,

Run," and "We're Going to Hang out the Washing on the Siegfried Line," Marie, Harry and Sidney raced out to the Colonnade Bar next door to the theatre and ordered drinks to celebrate the arrival of "Wally & Solly." Harry had dismissed the idea of sneaking Marie into his and Sidney's room at the guest house. Although they were married, it would have proved a tad awkward with Sidney sleeping there and Mrs Simkins was something of a prude. Instead, Harry had booked them into a B&B off Regency Square. When they got back there, the adrenalin rush from his stage debut considerably aided Harry's between the sheets performance. An encore took place a few hours later prior to a much-needed hearty breakfast to restore the couple's energy levels.

The run at the Royal went smoothly and although Harry and Sidney were strapped for cash most of the time, they were having fun. Marie came down to Brighton every weekend and Harry always welcomed her warmly, especially at the B&B. Not wishing to become a piggy in the middle, at the weekends, Sidney found himself at a loose end during the day on Saturdays and Sundays. Unlike Harry, Sidney had never been very good at chatting up girls. Despite numerous efforts to become better acquainted with some of the showgirls in the cast at the theatre, these encounters generally ended after the first date. He was also facing increasing pressure from home to give up his show business aspirations and return to Soho to manage the family business as his father was now suffering from a debilitating illness. Things came to a head when the show was approaching the last days of its run. Harry had continuously badgered Jonny Preston to see if he had secured Wally & Solly another engagement but to date, there had been no joy. Therefore, Harry was surprised to receive a call from their agent to advise that he could get them a booking at the Glasgow Empire in mid-March for three-weeks. Harry told Preston that it was almost certainly a yes, but he would have to discuss it with Sidney.

Sitting in the Colonnade Bar, Harry was about to tell Sidney when Bud Flanagan walked in with Max Miller. Having prized themselves away from back-slapping well-wishers at the bar, carefully holding their drinks to avoid spillage, Flanagan guided his companion to Harry and Sidney's table, and they sat down. Flanagan introduced Max who was now resting before starting his next tour around London and the south of England. When Harry had finally got over the shock of sitting next to the "Cheeky Chappie," he asked him for his opinion of taking up the booking in Scotland. His response was less than enthusiastic.

'Your agent's taking the piss isn't he? The

audiences in Glasgow are notorious for not taking prisoners, particularly English ones. I can name you a hundred acts who have died a death up there. Some have been reduced to tears after being booed off and having had rotten fruit thrown at them. Trust me boys, stay well away. My agent once offered me a stint at the Empire, but I told him I wasn't interested in missionary work!'

All four of them laughed at this comment but Harry could see that Sidney was not going to agree to a move north. After another couple of rounds of drinks, and the exchange of lots of one-liner jokes Flanagan and Miller departed.

'I'm sorry to let you down Harry but I cannot come to Scotland with you. Dad's taken a turn for the worse and Mum can't cope with the shop. I've got to call it a day on our Wally & Solly act. I hope you understand,' Sidney said almost in tears.

The bond of friendship was strong between the two of them and Harry replied: 'There's nothing to be sorry about mate, let's be honest, we were never going to top the bill at the Palladium, were we? Family always comes first. You must return home as soon as our run finishes in Brighton in a few days' time.'

'But what are you going to do Harry.'

'I don't know. Obviously, I need to talk to Marie before making any moves. Don't want to get my head bitten off like last time. One thing I cannot be doing though is going back to live at the Jacks in Goodge Street. No way, it'll drive me *meshuga*.'

Albert Rose was sympathetic when Harry related this news. He said it would not be advisable to rush into going solo. The double act had worked well, and he would scout around to see if he could find a suitable replacement for Sidney. Rose concurred with Max Miller that Harry should give Glasgow a wide berth: 'Stick to the south, it will be much safer, believe me,' he added. He went on to say that when the current run at the Royal ended, obviously, the theatre could not continue to pay Harry's rent at Mrs Simkins guest house. However, he had a proposition that might tide Harry over until he could re-establish his act. He was aware of Harry's first-class credentials as a photographer and earlier that day, he had come from a meeting with the managers of Brighton's other theatres. They had decided to sack the theatrical photographer they jointly used as he had become unreliable owing to a serious drink problem. Rose would suggest that Harry take up the role. In return, Harry would receive expenses to cover the cost of developing the film and have the rent paid at a basement flat that Rose knew was about to be vacated in Brunswick Square, Hove. As the photography work would mainly take place in the evenings, Harry would be free to do other jobs during the day.

Harry was extremely receptive to Albert Rose's proposal. Although it was a temporary blip on his path to stardom, it meant he didn't have to go back to living in Goodge Street. He phoned Marie immediately to tell her that they would finally have a place of their own in the posh end of Brighton. Always the sensible one, Marie was cautious. She said it sounded great, but she would need to see the flat and then set about finding a job in Brighton to supplement their income. As usual, Harry ignored Marie's comments and confirmed to Rose that he was keen to take up his offer.

Thankfully, everything turned out for the best. Marie fell in love with the little unfurnished flat. After descending the stairs from the pavement, on entering, it had a combined sitting and kitchen area, a bedroom and bathroom. The small garden at the rear was shared with the flats above. Despite the fact it only had an eye level view of Brunswick Square from its window, and even that was sometimes obscured by people's legs as they walked past, the couple settled in quickly. Marie's parents helped by buying some second-hand furniture for the flat. Harry had always been a dog lover and by way of celebrating the move, bought a beautiful Alsatian puppy which he named

Goldie.

Harry was delighted to be able to remain in his beloved show business circle taking photographs of the leading stars of the day. Albert Rose came to the rescue again when Marie had difficulty in finding work locally. Through a contact, he got her the job as assistant box office manager at the Hippodrome Theatre. Whilst the wages from this were a help, they did not compare with what she had been receiving at the Ministry of Information. After a few weeks, Marie stressed to Harry that he would need to find work during the day to make sure that they stayed solvent. Harry seemed happy enough to play with Goldie during the day giving him regular walks to the nearby pubs. But eventually, he agreed that he would have to meet Marie's wishes. It therefore came as something of a relief when he received a call from his old school chum and Oxford Street snapper. Danny Shelby had moved down to Worthing not far along the coast from Brighton. He found the sea air, and the punters, much more agreeable than London's West End. Danny had landed himself a nice little earner by taking photos of people posing next to somebody dressed up as Rupert Bear, the Daily Express's mascot.

Rupert Bear had become a national icon since his introduction in a comic strip in the newspaper. In the face of fierce competition from its rival, the Daily Mail, the Express was using Rupert as a promotional vehicle at seaside resorts around the country. The idea was that on seeing the bear, children would rush over and want their picture taken with him. A photographer would be on hand to take the photo that would appear to parents or the hosts of evacuees to be free until the snapper, after taking down the subject's name and address would advise there was a charge. Naturally, at this point with their kids pleading, the unfortunate adults would have no option but to pay up. The plan was that the photographer kept half of the payments for his services but as all the transactions were in cash, so not audited, there was considerable room for manoeuvre on the amount returned to the Daily Express.

Danny had heard that the Express had found this promotion to be highly successful in boosting readership and therefore, was expanding its operation to more resorts. Rupert would soon appear on the promenade at Brighton and the Express was seeking a reputable photographer to assist. Harry thanked his pal and quickly contacted the Express securing the role as the official Rupert Bear photographer in the Brighton area. By a remarkable coincidence, the man recruited by the Daily Express to dress up as Rupert was the photographer who had been dismissed by the Brighton theatres. For some reason, the newspaper's local agent had failed to take up references and had appointed Allan Fox following an early morning interview at which the applicant had disguised the smell of alcohol on his breath with copious amounts of mouthwash and told a pack of lies regarding his employment history.

Fox was a short rotund character with a shock of unruly grey hair, a bulbous red veined nose, and puffy cheeks. His limited capability with a wet razor was clearly visible resulting in semi-healed nicks arounds his face. Frankly, with the addition of a beard, his appearance would have been more suited to Father Christmas than Rupert Bear.

Their first meeting occurred on an unusually hot day outside the entrance to the West Pier. Harry instantly recognised Fox and vice a versa as they had seen one another occasionally in the Colonnade Bar but never formally met.

'Was it you who got me the tin tack as the theatres' photographer?' Allan Fox slurred.

'No, I think you managed that all on your Tod Sloan,' Harry replied sharply.

'Any ideas where I can change into this stupid costume?' Fox said waving a tatty suitcase under Harry's nose.

'Your best bet is probably the Gents on the pier.'

Fox trundled off and after what seemed like ages to Harry, returned in the costume walking in a distinctly bow-legged fashion. The fluffy white head, thick red sweater, woolly yellow checked trousers, and white boots were already attracting grinning glances from people on the pier.

'These fucking trousers are two sizes too small, their killing me under the crutch,' Fox moaned.

Harry stifled a laugh as he knew if he started, he would find it difficult to stop.

'Look, you better cut out the swearing, we're going to be encountering loads of kids. Their parents are not going to be too pleased hearing a bear with a sore head,' Harry joked.

'Very funny,' Fox remarked through the mouthpiece in the bear's head that was already beginning to make the incumbent sweat profusely.

Within seconds of emerging onto the promenade, Harry and Fox were encircled by a group of children chanting: 'Rupert, Rupert, Rupert!'

They were quickly followed by parents who together with the children all carried their gas mask packs. Harry swung into action with his camera and some slick sales patter. The demand to have photos taken with Rupert was non-stop and Harry was just about coping with doing the shots, then obtaining names and addresses plus payments. After almost two hours, Harry and Fox had hardly moved from the spot where they started. The latter was becoming increasingly agitated as some of the kiddies were finding it funny to give Rupert a kick in the shins. This combined with the release of last night's drinking binge through his pores was causing perspiration to run down his legs.

'I urgently need to have a break,' Fox mumbled to Harry.

'Ok, but don't be too long, we've got a queue of punters eager to give me their cash.'

What Fox did not tell Harry was that the break was just not to towel himself down, it was to top-up his alcohol levels from a whisky bottle he had in his suitcase.

After twenty minutes, much to the annoyance of the ever-growing assembly of children and adults, Rupert had not reappeared. To placate them, Harry said he would go in search of the errant bear. With his camera swinging from side to side on the lanyard around his neck, Harry ran along the pier towards the Gents toilet. Like the Palace Pier at the other end of the promenade, the West Pier was only accessible to half its length. The wooden slats beyond that point had been removed to prevent the Germans using it as a landing stage in the event of an invasion. He was halfway there when he saw Fox in full costume standing on one of the long benches that were built into the seaward sides of the pier. Fox was singing "The Teddy Bears' Picnic" at the top of his voice and clutching an empty bottle of whisky in his white paw style glove. A small crowd had gathered and were loving the impromptu performance.

Harry shouted: 'Fox, get down and come back with me now!'

Everybody laughed as a man in the crowd piped up: 'Blimey mate, a fox, a bear, are you starting a zoo on here?'

But the hilarity instantly turned to screams as Rupert toppled backwards and fell over the side. Luckily, the tide was in, and the sea was becalmed. The drop between the pier and sea was about twelve feet. Fox hit the water creating a huge splash and rose to the surface, face up, still singing and clutching the bottle. Two Home Guard soldiers who were erecting barbed wire defences on the beach below the pier saw the incident, dived into the sea, and swam out the short distance to where Fox was located. He was still singing when they dragged him onto the stony beach seemingly oblivious to what had happened. Several onlookers took photographs. One of them, an enterprising would-be journalist, rapidly made her way up to the promenade and hailed a taxi.

The editor of Brighton's Evening Argus was delighted to pay the young woman £10 for the story and her roll of film. This was a godsent opportunity to make fun of the Daily Express which was encroaching on the Argus's patch. The later edition of the newspaper's front-page headline read: "Rupert Bear Washed Up on Beach." The tongue-in-cheek article that accompanied the picture of Fox being escorted by two policemen went on to state that Rupert had been arrested for being drunk and disorderly whilst disguised as a bear.

The Express's hierarchy in London was not amused to read the story. Their local agent was fired for hiring Fox, but Harry was retained. A replacement Rupert was recruited, and a new costume provided. This one fitted perfectly and Harry and his new, much better-behaved sidekick, resumed working the seafront. The cash began to roll in again just like the adjacent waves.

CHAPTER 20 – MIDNIGHT FLIT

The extra income derived from Harry's Rupert Bear exploits was keeping Marie happy. Little did she know that not all the money her husband earnt was reaching the household budget. Harry had always been a light smoker. Woodbines was his brand of choice. However, his habit increased, and he switched brands to the dearer Park Drive as he considered the name to give him an upmarket profile. Like his father-in-law, he was also now partial to a cigar. Spending on these items combined with more visits to the pub and Brighton Races meant that much of the additional money coming in was going straight out. Two other factors then occurred simultaneously that resulted in fewer people visiting the seafront. The summer season was coming to an end and the Daily Express had advised Harry that they were winding up the Rupert promotion until next year. Apart from an air raid that had killed over 50 people the year before, Brighton, as a small town, had been spared the Luftwaffe's bombs. This situation now changed and just the week before bombs had fallen in Park Crescent not far from the Palace Pier, destroying a newsagent's shop and a row of houses.

Eventually, Harry had to tell Marie that his work for the Express had ended. Her reaction was that he would have to tighten his belt and cut back on some of his "luxuries." Harry was surprised that Marie was aware of these indiscretions, but she always seemed to know what he was up to. Of course, he reassured her that he would limit his spending in future whilst at the same time having no intention of doing so. Before long Harry's financial situation worsened. Gambling debts had accrued with one of the gangs at Brighton Racecourse who were notorious for seeking retribution from debtors via a razor. Every time there was a knock on the flat door, Harry became nervous and asked Marie to answer it. He would add: 'If it's anybody for me, tell them I've gone back to London and won't be back for a while.' Naturally, Marie was not happy about this development and rows became a regular part of their daily life. To escape this domestic turmoil, Harry went out for walks but was constantly looking over his shoulder to see if he was being followed. He started to use different pubs and always took Goldie with him in case he was confronted by a gangland thug.

It was on one of these walks that he bumped into Max Miller who lived nearby in a large Georgian villa at the northern end of Brunswick Square. Harry knew where Miller lived but never mentioned it when they met at The Colonnade Bar as he didn't wish to appear as if he was after an invite to the comedian's home. But Miller was aware that they were neighbours because Albert Rose had told him he had found Harry and Marie a place in the Square.

'Hello neighbour, just the man I wanted to see,' Miller said bending down and giving Goldie a stroke. 'Those photos you took of me in my dressing room at The Hippodrome in my stage outfit, loved 'em.'

'Thanks Max, good of you to say,' Harry replied, somewhat taken aback.

'Thing is, I get hundreds of requests a week from fans asking for a signed photograph of the Cheeky Chappie. Can you give me a good price for a thousand of the one of me playing the guitar and a thousand of the head and shoulders version?'

'Sure, no problem. I'll do my sums at work in the morning and give you a ring. Can I have your number?'

Miller gave Harry his card and scribbled his home telephone number on the back. 'Don't phone before 10 though, I'll be under the covers with the missus!' The comedian laughed and waved Harry goodbye as he made his way towards the seafront.

Harry couldn't believe his luck, turned on his

heels and returned to the flat to tell Marie the good news. They had not parted on the best of terms earlier, but she had calmed down and was delighted to hear that some extra cash would be coming in.

‘Two things Harry. Firstly, you are not going to fritter this money away on the horses and the pub. Secondly, just think about what’s happened for a minute.’

Harry gave Marie a vacant expression and shrugged his shoulders.

‘If a star like Max Miller wants a couple of thousand photos, what about all the other stars out there? Surely, they must want photos as well?’

The penny having dropped, Harry said: ‘You’re right. I hadn’t thought about it like that.’

‘The problem is that there’s only three theatres in Brighton, so our scope is limited,’ Marie added. ‘But if we move back to London, with all the theatres there, we could be coining it every day. I could do the knocking on dressing room doors with the sales pitch, and you could take the pictures and develop them. We’d have a thriving business on our hands.’

Harry’s reaction was instantaneous: ‘You’re a bloody genius Marie Levi.’ He swept her up and kissed her on the lips as he carried her into the bedroom.

They had only been at it for a matter of minutes when there was a loud thumping at the front door. Fortunately, they had turned out the lights so the flat was in darkness. Harry put his finger to his lips and signalled to Marie not to move. Goldie was barking furiously. A gruff voice from outside shouted: 'Mr Levi, I am here on behalf of my boss. You have not paid him the £50 debt you owe from the race meeting last month. Full payment must be made by the end of this week otherwise I will be round with some associates to see you on Saturday. You have been warned. Pay up or else.'

Harry and Marie remained motionless in bed as they heard heavy footsteps on the stairs going up to the pavement. Goldie continued to bark. After ten minutes Marie exploded with a stream of obscenities directed at Harry. The peace between the couple had been short-lived. She instructed Harry to tell Albert Rose what had happened the following morning. She would telephone her parents and inform them that they would be returning to Goodge Street imminently. Harry's worse nightmare had come to fruition.

The first thing he did the next day was to phone Max Miller after 10 with a price for the photos. The comedian agreed without haggling which made Harry think he had not charged enough.

Anyway, he said he would run the pictures off and pop them in at Miller's house the following day. He explained that he would need cash on delivery.

Albert Rose let Harry explain about the visit he had received the night before and how it had come about. He remained silent until Harry had finished although he already knew the situation having been told by a bookie friend of his.

'The trouble with you Harry is that you are your own worst enemy. I got you a job here and you began to earn some decent money on the side. Great, but you pissed it up against the wall. I helped you out by finding Marie work, and the pair of you a place to live. I even got Max Miller to order some photos from you. I did all of these things because your father, God rest his soul, helped me out a great deal years ago, and I feel that by helping you, I am repaying that debt in a small way.'

Harry had never felt so ashamed. He sat; head bowed without saying a word.

Rose continued: 'You are a talented boy Harry with real potential on both the entertaining and photography fronts. But you need to grow up and fast. Get into the real world. I will pay your gambling debt. You will print the photos for Max using the equipment and paper we have here. I will take the money from Max as a down payment on what you owe me for getting the mob off your back. You will then pay me the remainder of the £50 in monthly instalments. Do a midnight flit from the flat and move back to your in-law's place. There's a lot more work to be had in London. Like Max, I'm sure the stars of the West End shows need a constant supply of photos for their fans. I will put out a few feelers for you with my contacts.'

Harry was overcome with emotion. He hugged Rose and thanked him saying he would repay him. Albert Rose simply smiled, and they shook hands before Harry went off to start printing the photographs of Max Miller.

On their return to London, Marie was greeted with open arms by her parents. The reception for Harry was decidedly frostier as Marie had told her folks the reason for their hurried move back to Goodge Street.

Once again, Albert Rose came up trumps for Harry. He contacted his longstanding friend Frank Littler who ran the Society of West End Theatre Managers. Rose asked him if he would get his Society colleagues to provide Harry and Marie with access passes so they could go backstage at shows to ascertain if the stars appearing required bulk quantities of photographs for them to autograph and send to their fans. Littler was only too pleased to help and replied that he would raise the matter at the Society's board meeting that week. However, he told Rose to bear in mind that some of the theatres had been bombed and not reopened so the opportunities for Harry and Marie would be somewhat limited. Following the meeting, he phoned Albert Rose to confirm that his request had been granted and that Harry should pick the passes up from his secretary at his office at the Drury Lane Theatre.

Harry and Marie were cock-a-hoop on receiving this news from their guardian angel and collected the passes immediately. Typical of his impulsive nature, Harry suggested they get to work that evening.

'Hold your horses,' Marie said. 'For once, just think it through before rushing into things. Let's say we obtain an order for a few thousand pictures on our first outing. How are we going to get them printed with a quick turn-around? We don't have the equipment or materials to handle such a sizeable order. The last thing we want to do is mess up our very first assignment. Don't forget, showbusiness is based on gossip. If word got around that we can't deliver, we'll be finished before we've started.'

'As per usual, you're right but how are we going to crack the problem? To give the impression that we are a legit set-up, we need a West End studio base with all the necessary equipment, business cards, phone line, the works. I didn't see a tree with money growing on it in Goodge Street and something tells me your parents are not going to stump up the cash.'

'Ha ha, very funny. But I might have a solution. Mum's sister, my Aunty Bunny, is married to Stanley Lee. He owns the posh butchers on the corner of Romilly Street in Soho.'

'Is that where the meat is on the ceiling? The steaks are too high!' Harry joked.

'You've been watching Max Miller too much. No, Uncle Stan owns the whole building. I've heard mum say that apart from the shop on the ground floor, all the floors above are empty. With the bombing going on, businesses are moving out of London in their droves. The place would make an ideal studio. It's massive.'

Marie made arrangements to meet Uncle Stan and together with Harry, they went round to see him the following day. Stanley Lee was an old-fashioned entrepreneur who had made good by building a business that delivered high quality meat to discerning customers, both individuals and restaurateurs. He also had a soft spot for his niece who he regarded as the brightest spark in the Jacks family. Indeed, on several occasions, he had tried to coax her into joining him in his enterprise as he and Bunny were childless. After listening to the youthful enthusiasm Marie and Harry put forward about their plans, he made them a proposal. They could use the first floor of his building rent free, and he would loan them the money required to purchase the equipment and materials for their new venture. He would require repayment of the debt in monthly instalments beginning three months after the business had launched. The amount of the monthly payment would be agreed after the equipment had been bought. As it was "family," Stanley would not charge any interest on the loan. He would even recommend Harry and Marie's photographic services to his customers, many of whom were vain and wealthy, so he felt would be keen to be captured on film.

Straight from the meeting after a thorough recce of the first-floor space, Marie and Harry decamped over to the French House pub in Dean Street and sat down with two half pints of shandy. Business-like as always, Marie pulled a notepad and pen out of her handbag and said to Harry: 'Right, let's start by making a list of the stuff we are going to need for the studio.'

Harry considered her comments, then responded: 'On the plus side, those huge windows will provide tons of natural light during the day for studio-based work such as portraits. Thankfully, the windows all have black-out blinds so I will be able to do commissions on the evenings when we are not trawling theatres for work. I've got the cameras but for the studio area we will need special lights on stands, umbrella reflectors, a range of pull-down backdrops and a selection of props such as pot plants, and toys if I am doing shots of kids. Sourcing the equipment for the dark room is going to prove trickier though. Manufacturers have, at the government's behest, switched production to war related items. Therefore, getting enlargers, printers, development tanks, a dry-mounting press, electric print dryers, lenses etc will be a real headache. And the chemicals we require will be equally difficult to get our hands on.'

'Why don't you speak to Peter Monkton? You left the MOI on good terms with him. He might be able to give you a steer,' Marie suggested,

Monkton was pleased to hear Harry's voice when he called and initially hoped that he might have reconsidered the possibility of him and Marie moving to Oxford. However, once he had resigned himself that such a move was not on the cards, he gave Harry some useful information. Just prior to Harry's return to London, a large film production firm in Wardour Street in Soho that carried out some work for the government had sustained considerable damage in the Blitz. Consequently, the company could not carry on its operation from that location and was seeking to dispose of the equipment that was still intact. Harry was also interested to hear that to boost morale amongst the armed forces, the government was sanctioning certain photographers to be permitted to have access to supplies of chemicals used in the film development process. The reason for this was that soldiers' wives and girlfriends were keen to have photographs taken of themselves to send to their loved ones who were away fighting. Monkton said he would speak to the powers that be and get Harry added onto the list of approved photographers so he could obtain the necessary chemicals. He ended their conversation by saying that Harry owed him a drink next time he was in London.

Once Harry had found out the contact at the Wardour Street film company, he fixed an appointment for him and Marie to meet with him on site. Mainly through Marie's charm offensive and the fact she was wearing a tight jumper, a cheap price was negotiated for the equipment required for their new studio. Helped by Sidney and a couple of other friends, it was then transported the few streets away to the studio in Romilly Street. Levi Photography was open for business.

CHAPTER 21 – SAILING INTO THE WINDMILL

The fledgling business started well with Harry and Marie quickly becoming an integral part of London's theatreland. They made friends by supplying half bottles of whisky to the all-important stage door keepers who tipped them the wink about which stars were in an approachable mood and those who were not. The tactics adopted by Harry and Marie proved successful. Having boned up on the production, the newspaper reviews and the stars' background, Marie would introduce herself to the principal players in their dressing rooms. She would then talk effusively about the show and how much the stars' fans were enjoying it. Continuing with this line of ego massaging patter, she would name-drop shamelessly, mentioning the quantities of photographs other celebrities had ordered. Wherever possible, Marie would include the names of rivals of the star she was pitching to. Inevitably, on hearing that so-and-so had placed substantial orders, they would follow suit. Marie would then summon Harry into the dressing room who would set-up a series of shots. If time permitted, sometimes, he would take pictures of the person in costume on stage.

The war was taking its toll on the London theatre scene. Some theatres had closed because of bombing, others were still undergoing repairs from bomb damage. Most young actors, directors and stagehands had been called-up for military service. Audiences were severely depleted for the same reason. Although the Blitz had effectively ended in 1941, people were worried about going out to the theatre in case bombing suddenly recommenced, and cost was also a factor in these difficult economic times. Many of the productions, whilst starring well-known actors such as John Gielgud and Alec Guinness, were serious Shakespeare plays with more limited public appeal. But some populist shows did emerge. For example, "Blithe Spirit" written by Noel Coward made its debut in the West End at the Piccadilly Theatre. Margaret Rutherford played the role of the clairvoyant Madame Arcati. Another production, "Brighton Rock" starring Richard Attenborough and Dulcie Gray at the Garrick Theatre also proved a hit with the public. Both shows proved highly profitable for Levi Photography, but the latter made Harry shudder when he saw it as it depicted gang warfare in Brighton. A subject he knew only too well about.

The theatre work represented the main source of income but demand for personal portraits was steady and contributed worthwhile sums. Harry and Marie were pleased with the fruits of their labours and began to make monthly repayments to Stanley Lee. Marie also insisted that Albert Rose's outstanding debt should be settled, and a cheque was duly despatched. The business continued to thrive into 1943.

One evening Harry was about to lock up the studio and head for home when he received a telephone call that would prove a turning point in his life. The voice at the other end of the phone announced himself as Vivian Van Damm. Of course, Harry was aware of the famous impresario who ran the Windmill Theatre in Soho. But he thought it was Sidney playing a silly prank and went along with it dramatising his responses for effect between drags on his ciggie. It was only when the caller referred to Harry being recommended by his friend, Albert Rose, that he realised that the call might be genuine. Harry immediately switched tact and became extremely business-like. Van Damm asked Harry if he could pop round to see him as he had a proposal. Harry arrived at the Windmill ten minutes after replacing the telephone receiver.

The Windmill Theatre in Great Windmill Street was originally a cinema. It was purchased in 1930 by Mrs Laura Henderson, an eccentric wealthy widow. A programme of plays and films did not resonate with audiences and losses were incurred. Mrs Henderson then hired Vivian Van Damm as manager. He introduced Revudeville, a combination of revues and vaudeville in shows that ran daily from 2.30pm to 11pm. The acts included singers, dancers and showgirls performing popular numbers. Although a slight improvement in finances was achieved, losses continued. It was not until Van Damm introduced glamorous nude females on stage during the acts that things started to take off. His idea was inspired by the Folles Bergère and Moulin Rouge in Paris. Van Damm skilfully navigated round the British censorship laws by pointing out that as nude statues were not considered obscene, providing his showgirls remained in motionless poses on stage, no objections could be made. As a result, the Windmill Girls became a huge commercial success for the theatre. Performances carried on throughout the Blitz and the theatre adopted the motto: "We never close," which was often humorously changed to: "We never clothe." All 320 seats were regularly fully booked for every performance with audiences comprising mainly young soldiers on leave and "interested" adult men.

The Windmill was one of the few theatres that Harry and Marie had not included on their forays for business as the shows did not feature famous stars. Standing outside the front door, Harry could not believe the length of the queue waiting for the next show. It meandered down to the bottom of Great Windmill Street round into Shaftesbury Avenue. An excited air of anticipation rose from the crowd of men. As Harry approached the front door, he was met by cries of: "Can't you see there's a queue mate?" A burly doorman then re-directed Harry to the stage door. After gaining entry, his eyes came out on stalks as he stood back to allow a string of scantily clad girls trot past on their way to the dressing rooms. The stage door keeper's voice from behind quipped: 'Don't worry pal, you get used to it after a while!'

Vivian Van Damm spotted Harry in the narrow corridor motionless like one of his girls. He was smartly dressed, of medium height and build, tanned with short neat, slicked back hair, bushy eyebrows, and thick black rimmed glasses, similar to Harry's but more rounded.

'Harry Levi, I presume? Come into my office.' Putting his arm around Harry's shoulder, he led him towards a large red painted door. 'I've heard great things about you from Albie down in Brighton. I gather you've done your bit for the war effort and have the scars to prove it. I remember your father, a legend in the business. The governor here, Mrs Henderson, knew him and your mother.'

'Thank you, Mr Van Damm, very kind.'

'Please, please, VD, it's what everyone calls me. I know what you're thinking but it's ok, I don't mind being referred to as the abbreviation for a sexual disease,' he guffawed. 'Well, look at us, a couple of Yiddisher boys trying to make a living. I come from a Dutch Jewish family, and I gather yours originated in Italy.'

'You are well informed Mr, sorry, I mean, VD.'

'I make it my business to find out about the people I deal with,' the impresario advised. 'I need someone to become our official photographer. To start with, I want some tasty topical publicity photos of our girls. Bookings have been booming but the competition has finally cottoned on to the fact that you can get round the Lord Chamberlain's censorship laws. Both the Piccadilly and Pavilion are planning to copy our format by using nude tableaux vivants which could dilute our traffic. Thereafter, I want to have a local photographer that I can call on at a minute's notice to get shots that we can use for publicity in the papers. As I say, we have to up our game to ensure the money keeps coming in.'

'Not a problem VD, but surely you could run into problems by putting the pictures in advertisements and on posters?' Harry asked.

'You're right. They can't be totally naked, but I want to be as near to that as you can possibly get.'

'Ok, I'll pull together some ideas for different poses and run them past you together with my charges. Is it alright if I have a look inside the theatre as I need to check whether the lighting is good enough. Otherwise, I will have to do the shoot at my studio.'

Van Damm chuckled and checked his watch: 'It's almost change over time between shows. Follow me and you will witness the famous Windmill Steeplechase.'

Harry looked bemused but did as he was instructed. Both men stood in the wings of the stage as the band played its last song. The curtain dropped and the naked girls trooped off. In front of the thick dark red velvet curtains, the compere announced that the performance had ended. Van Damm told Harry to peek out into the auditorium. He was astonished at the sight of men scrambling over the seats from the back to the front of theatre. Their objective, to claim a better seat nearer the stage for the next show.

Harry was now faced with a predicament. He knew Marie would not be happy to hear he was going to be taking photos of nearly naked girls, even if it meant good money. His in-laws would be even less enthused, despite the fact it might hasten Harry and Marie being able to raise enough cash to find a home of their own.

He was still pondering his dilemma when the solution presented itself on his arrival back at Goodge Street. A tearful Marie greeted him at the front door and ushered him into their room at the top of the stairs.

Sounding choked, Marie said: 'Pop collapsed at work and was taken by ambulance to the Middlesex. The doctor thinks he has had a stroke. They are doing tests and we will know more tomorrow. Mum is at the hospital at his bedside.'

Hugging Marie, Harry replied: 'Oh darling, I'm so sorry to hear that.' He decided that if he was going to discuss the Windmill project, now was not a good time. The last thing he wanted was to ignite an argument at such a delicate moment. The following day, Marie's mother was advised that her husband would be kept in hospital for a few days for observation and if everything was in order, he would be discharged. Then it was essential that he convalesced, preferably away from London. This news presented a problem for the Jacks. Whilst not poor, the family did require the income from the tailor's business they owned. Esther Jacks was an accomplished seamstress and more than capable of managing the shop on a day-to-day basis. But she would not be in a position to do this if she was caring for Samuel at a location outside London. Esther contacted a cousin who had a nice house near the coast in North Devon and it was agreed that Samuel could stay there until fully recovered. She then discussed the matter with Marie, and it was decided that her daughter would look after her father in the West Country, while Esther ran the shop. A doctor friend of the Jacks with a large comfortable car agreed to transport Samuel and Marie to the Devon countryside. Although petrol was rationed, it could still be obtained by certain people such as doctors.

Marie told Harry about the plans saying it would only be for a few weeks, and then she would be back. Harry outwardly expressed his concern but said he understood. Inwardly, he breathed a huge sigh of relief. He would not now have the difficult task of explaining to his wife why he was getting young women in a state of undress to pose for pictures. Harry immediately set about preparing ideas for the photo shoots at the Windmill. When Harry presented them, Van Damm was impressed. The first featured a chorus line of four attractive Windmill Girls in skimpy satin lace trimmed basques sporting army tin helmets and gas masks, doing a high kick. Another pose included members of the troupe in low-cut blouses and short pleated skirts waving small union jack flags. Each girl wore a uniform hat of the armed services. A third set-up was a variation on the last by inserting a uniformed soldier, sailor and airman into the shot. The final concept was a further variation with the girls kneeling behind stacked sandbags outside the doors of the theatre, all pointing rifles. Large Union Jacks were draped on the doors.

'These will certainly send out the message that the Windmill is patriotic and doing its bit to boost morale for our boys,' Van Damm said to Harry. 'It will also give our competitors something to think about. You better get cracking as soon as you can because I want to use the photographs for posters and advertisements. Come round on Saturday morning at 9, that will give me a few days to select the models and get the props you need. Just one more thing. To keep the boss on side, make sure you do a couple of set-ups with Mrs Henderson surrounded by some of the girls but in more conservative costumes.'

Harry was delighted with VD's enthusiastic response to his proposals. He had inflated his quote for the work knowing that the impresario would haggle. Indeed, this proved to be the case, so Harry ended up getting the price he wanted.

Samuel Jacks was discharged from hospital with strict orders to rest. Marie pushed him in a wheelchair and helped him into the back seat of the doctor friend's car that was waiting outside. Harry and Esther Jacks waved them goodbye as the car headed off to Devon.

Harry arrived fifteen minutes before 9am at the Windmill on Saturday. Having gained access via the stage door he was surprised to find nobody around. He knocked at VD's office but there was no reply. He did the same thing on the dressing room door but although receiving no response, he heard voices from within. Harry opened the door and froze on the spot at the sight of several girls in various stages of undress. The girls didn't bat an eyelid at Harry's presence. They merely smiled at him and carried on chatting amongst themselves. From the centre of the group the voice of an older lady sitting at one of the dressing tables dabbing a powder puff on her cheek boomed out: 'Good morning, Mr Levi. I am Mrs Laura Henderson, the owner of The Windmill.' The woman said holding out her hand in a queen-like fashion as if wishing it to be kissed. Harry shook her fragile hand and estimated her age as late seventies. She had grey hair, in a bobbed style, parted in the middle. Her pudgy face was thick with make-up which although intended to disguise the large bags under her eyes, failed.

A little flustered, Harry eventually replied: 'Err, I'm sorry to burst in, I couldn't find anybody but heard voices from in here.'

'Don't worry, the girls are used to men invading their territory, in more ways than one,' Mrs

Henderson quipped. The girls giggled at this comment. 'Big mouth VD probably told you that I knew your mother and father, they attended many of my soirees. I was sorry to hear of their passing. My condolences.'

Harry thanked Mrs Henderson but thought it was a pity that the woman had not enquired after his mother when she was experiencing difficult times following his father's death. However, with the prospect of ongoing business from the theatre, he did not mention this.

Vivian Van Damm then poked his head round the dressing room door: 'Morning Mrs H, Harry. Come on girls, get a move on. We haven't got all day. We need to get these photos done before the first show at 11 o' clock.' As the girls bent over and pulled their costumes and stockings on, Harry was finding it difficult to control the swelling in his trousers.

'Morning VD. Can you show me where you're thinking of me doing the first shoot so I can assess the light levels etc?'

'Sure, follow me.'

Harry was relieved to escape from the gaggle of giggling girls and the domineering Laura Henderson. The two men meandered round the dusty breeze block corridors and came to the stage, in the centre stood an ornate throne with a faux ermine cape, sceptre and crown placed on it.

Van Damm pointed at it: 'What I was thinking was the old bag sitting there in her robes, surrounded by the girls. For this one I've told the lasses to wear their silky long evening dresses with a split up the side so they can show a bit of leg. Once we've got that one out of the way, we can give the Queen Bee her marching orders and move on to the sexy shots.'

By the tone used by both VD and Mrs H when referring to each other, Harry quickly established that there was no love lost between them.

'I'll require more light around the throne,' Harry advised VD.

The impresario walked over to the wings and flicked some switches: 'How's that?'

'Perfect,' Harry shouted as his voice echoed around the empty theatre.

The first shot went smoothly, and Laura Henderson disappeared on the pretext of having to do some accounts work. VD gave Harry a thumbs up sign behind her back.

The set-up involving the inclusion of some of the girls' boyfriends in their uniforms proved trickier. Naturally, the girls were used to having their photos taken but the men were cumbersome and were a bit tetchy about taking instructions from Harry regarding how to pose. As predicted by VD, the shot of the chorus line of girls wearing tin helmets and gas masks doing a high kick was the most impressive. Harry realised that leaving the outside photo until last was a mistake. A queue for the 11 o'clock show had already gathered and as the girls in their revealing outfits knelt behind the sandbags, holding replica rifles, a group of lads at the front of the queue, obviously the worse for drink, started to shout lewd comments about the girls. Harry managed to secure a few shots before VD summoned his burly security men and an altercation broke out with fists flying. The girls screamed and ran inside the theatre. Harry was knocked to the ground but managed to cushion his fall in a way that protected the camera from smashing on the pavement. He scrambled to his feet and swiftly followed the girls into the safety of the foyer. He had barely set foot inside when one of the girls, pretending to be shaking with fear, threw her arms round him.

'Ooh, that was all a bit scary,' she whispered in Harry's ear, placing her tongue in it as she spoke. 'Any chance you can take some photos of me on my own at your studio? You see, my boyfriend is in the army and he's away somewhere in Europe. He has asked me to send him some saucy pictures of me to show to his mates. Of course, I'll pay the going rate for the photos.'

At first, Harry was somewhat taken aback by the request. But as he had been told by Peter Monkton, women wanting photos to send to their men in the armed forces was now commonplace. The fact that Marie was in Devon and therefore would not be popping into the studio, made it easy for Harry to agree. Also, the butcher's shop below the studio closed at 5.30pm every day so the staff would not see any comings and goings after that. Working in the evenings would provide another benefit. Harry would not have to endure more bowls of lokshen soup cooked by his ever-critical mother-in-law. Instead, he could avail himself of egg, bacon, and chips at the café he frequented along with the market traders in Berwick Street.

'My name's Sherry, Sherry Brown. My boyfriend jokes that his schooner's always full up when he sees me,' she squealed cheekily. 'What's the address of your studio?'

Harry gave Sherry one of his cards and said she should pop round that evening at 7.30. She smiled and wiggled off towards the dressing rooms. Harry admired her pert bottom as she did so.

CHAPTER 22 – IN VOGUE

'Bit chilly in 'ere, innit,' Sherry observed on arrival at the studio. She draped her raincoat on a chaise longue that Harry had positioned in front of a drop-down screen depicting a countryside scene with trees and fields.

Harry smiled and said: "Can I offer you a drink to warm you up before we start? Maybe a whisky?'

'That would be lovely,' Sherry replied.

Harry poured scotch into a couple of tumblers, and they clinked glasses. 'Cheers,' they said in unison and sat down on the chaise.

'Have you modelled for a photographer before?' Harry enquired.

'Not professionally, just the usual stuff at the seaside and family gatherings. But, of course, I pose at every show at the Windmill for all the pervs in the audience playing with themselves under their coats!'

Harry laughed. 'You must get lots of offers from those blokes desperate to take you out?'

'Yep, but after a while, you become oblivious to it. Christ, if I agreed, I'd spend more time on my back than standing up,' Sherry yelped, simultaneously gulping down her drink in one.

Pouring her another, Harry outlined what he

had in mind for the shoot. 'I was thinking about shots of you in various positions on the chaise with the screen behind. You know, sort of Clara Bow style.'

Sherry gave Harry a quizzical look: 'Clara who?'

'You must have heard of "The It Girl" the famous American actress in silent movies? Those black stockings and high heel shoes you are wearing will work nicely. I've got a short sparkly flapper dress in the props room that should fit you. Topped off with a bandana with a feather protruding, a long string of pearls, and you waving a long cigarette holder. Perfect. But mind out for that big machine in there, it's my old enlarger.'

Sherry laughed at the word enlarger: 'Sounds alright. Thing is, it's not exactly sexy, is it? I want the pictures to get my boyfriend excited, not to send him to sleep. Like me, odds on, bet he's never heard of your Clara what's her name?'

Harry was stunned by Sherry's directness. However, on reflection, he thought that she would only have been a baby in Clara Bow's heyday. 'Well, I'm sure that we can come up with a compromise. Nip into that room over there and slip into the dress. It's on the rail. You'll find the other props I mentioned on one of the shelves.'

A few minutes later, Sherry reappeared looking

quite the vamp.

Striking a statuesque pose with the long cigarette holder at arm's length, in a deep voice, she purred: 'How's that?'

'Wow, if that doesn't get your man going, I don't know what will,' Harry gasped.

Sherry had a beautiful figure, and the short dress accentuated her long legs. It fitted snugly around her peach shaped bottom that Harry had admired earlier in the day. She had removed her bra. Her ample breasts were straining below the shoulder straps revealing small areas of the sides of her chest. Sherry had applied too much bright red lipstick and in doing so, had left some on her pearly white front teeth. Her blonde curly hair cascaded down just below her ears. She had a silky complexion with a button nose and steely blue eyes.

Recovering his composure, Harry said: 'Let's get started then.'

'You're being a bit forward, aren't you?' Sherry giggled.

Harry ignored the comment. He directed Sherry to lie on her stomach on the chaise propping her head on one elbow, sticking a leg up in the air.

'Put the cigarette holder close to your lips as though you are smoking. Look at the camera and smile.'

At this point, Harry noticed the lipstick smudge on Sherry's teeth. He pulled out a handkerchief and went over and gently removed the smear. He was checking the light levels before shooting when he heard boisterous laughter and bottles chinking outside the studio in the stairwell. He motioned to Sherry to keep quiet and tiptoed over to the door. He opened it abruptly and was astonished to see Stanley Lee with his arm around a young woman. He was holding a carrier bag containing a couple of bottles. Clearly, the couple had both been imbibing.

Equally stunned as Harry, Stanley instantly withdrew his arm from his companion. Somewhat hesitantly, he said: 'Hello Harry, didn't realise you were working here in the evenings. I am showing this lady the flat upstairs. She's interested in renting it. Bunny doesn't know so please don't mention it to Marie or Esther.'

Harry winked at Stanley: 'Don't worry, I won't. Just take care on those stairs. The cleaner was in earlier, they're a bit slippery.'

Not half as slippery as me Harry thought to himself as he closed the door. That encounter could definitely be used in future negotiations with his landlord.

Sherry had retained her pose and looked at

Harry: 'What was all that about?'

'Oh, just the people upstairs, a little the worse for wear. Right, smile at the camera please.' Harry peered at Sherry through the viewfinder and took several shots. 'Ok, you wanted something sexier. Sit up. Cross your legs. Slip the left shoulder strap down.'

'Oops,' Sherry exclaimed as her left breast escaped the confinement of the dress.

'Not exactly what I was thinking, but if you are alright with that, I will take the pictures.'

'Go for it,' Sherry answered. 'But as you've seen one, I might as well display them both. Half of the male population of London has at The Windmill.' She removed the other strap and the dress crumpled to her waist. Harry stood momentarily fixated on the size of Sherry's nipples. They were huge and erect.

Desperately trying to stay cool, Harry instructed Sherry to dispense with the cigarette holder. 'Now, cross your legs and put your hands on your hips. Bring your head forward slightly and pout. I want a real come and get me expression.'

Sherry obliged and wiping beads of perspiration from his forehead, Harry fired off a further series of shots.

'Without wishing to sound crude, my boyfriend likes a bit of rear-guard action, if you get my drift,' Sherry explained. 'How about one of me bending over the chaise with my bottom in the air and head turned back towards the camera?'

Harry considered the suggestion at the same time thinking this assignment had already gone way beyond his usual jobs. 'We can certainly give that a go. But it would work better without your dress on.'

Stepping out of the dress and hanging it on a tripod, she said: 'You're a very naughty boy Harry.' Sherry then adopted the pose. Her bright pink knickers provided a contrast to the black stockings and suspender belt she was wearing. Looking at the camera she cooed: 'Ready and waiting.'

With trembling hands, Harry gripped the camera and pressed the shutter a few times. 'Can you part your legs a bit wider? It will work better that way.'

'Open Sesame!' Sherry cried out.

'Not quite right,' Harry murmured. He walked gingerly towards the bent over figure doing his best to conceal his erection. As he gently patted Sherry's inner thighs to extend the gap, she turned suddenly and kissed him on the lips.

'A girl has needs too,' she whispered, pulling him down on top of her onto the chaise longue.

As Harry indulged himself on her

mountainous breasts, Sherry fumbled with his button flies until his fully stiffened cock emerged. Cupping it in her hands she commented: 'Now that's what I call an enlarger.' Sherry had obviously come to the studio with the intention of having sex because she took a condom out of the top of her stockings, tore off the wrapper, and slipped it onto Harry's penis.

Harry reciprocated by removing Sherry's pants and for fun, pulled them onto his head. At the sight of this, she laughed out loud as he got down to work. After a vigorous fifteen minutes, with both parties satisfied, Harry withdrew. He went over to the table, lit two cigarettes, and gave one to Sherry. He then replenished their glasses with whisky. Sitting side-by-side, Harry enquired: 'What if your boyfriend asks who the photographer was that took the pictures? If he's the jealous type, I don't want him to come round here when he's on leave and punch my lights out.'

'Don't bother yourself with that my lovely,' Sherry advised. 'I'll tell him it was some old codger photographer who took them in the dressing room after one of the shows. And after I got the prints, he went back to his home base up north.' Pausing for a puff on her ciggie and a pull of her drink, she continued: 'I know I said I would pay the going rate for the prints of the photos you've taken, and I will. But it occurs to me that if I can coax some of the other girls to come and get shots done for their lovers, you could be making a pretty penny out of it. How about you refunding me my payment if I persuade at least four of my fellow performers? I can add that you may be prepared to show them your enlarger during the visit. I would of course say, I highly recommend it!'

'It's a deal,' Harry responded, and by way of cementing the agreement, they put down their drinks, extinguished their cigarettes and embarked on a second round of sex.

'This time, you'll need to do rhythm,' Sherry instructed. 'I don't have any more Johnnies.'

Sherry kept her side of the bargain, and in no time at all, was refunded the payment for her photos. A steady stream of Windmill girls made evening visits to the studio. Almost all of them requested the additional service that Harry provided as part of the session. Everything was going swimmingly from Harry's point of view until he received a phone call from Marie saying her father was feeling much better and subject to an examination by a local doctor, she would be bringing Samuel home the following week. Harry feigned delight at this news but realised he would have to curtail his extracurricular evening jobs immediately. It had certainly proved lucrative, albeit that the daily dose of sex with nubile beauties was exhausting him.

The Windmill's dressing room gossip about Harry Levi's sexual prowess inevitably reached the ears of Vivian Van Damm. He called Harry in for a meeting.

'I'm the last person to be a prude but shagging the merchandise is a non-starter Harry my boy,' VD told Harry in a schoolmasterly tone. 'I don't need problems from these tarts' boyfriends coming round to complain that their little darlings have been subjected to total exposure and worse by you. I've got enough on my plate as it is. It's 1944, the old biddy Henderson is on the verge of croaking it and the fucking Nazis are raining Doodlebugs on London. I'm sorry mate, but you're fired. Good luck with your business. If I can put anything outside of Windmill stuff your way, I will.'

The phone rang, VD picked it up and indicated to Harry the meeting was over by waving and pointing towards the office door. Well, that's sorted that problem out Harry thought to himself as he trudged back in the rain to the studio. He picked up a salt beef bagel from his favourite café en route. Marie arrived back from Devon with her father a few days later.

'Mum says you've been getting home late while I was away,' Marie observed over dinner on her first night back. 'Theatre work?'

On hearing this Harry almost choked on a spoon of sauerkraut he had just swallowed: 'No, just some orders for reprints,' he lied. 'I've also been out touting for business but Hitler's V1 rockets are playing havoc with people's lives. They are frightened to venture out for family photos or to go to the theatre. They're spending most of their time in basements or air raid shelters.'

'In other words, the French House and Fitzroy Tavern's tills have been benefitting from Levi Photography,' Marie retorted sarcastically.

'Don't be like that. It's been hard without you. I've missed you. I'm pleased you are back and that your Pop's on the mend.'

Fully aware of Harry's voracious sexual appetite, Marie was expecting a rousing welcome home in bed that night. She was wrong. By the time she had cleaned her teeth, changed into her nightie and slipped under the covers, he was fast asleep snoring.

The next morning Harry awoke to find Marie was gone. Scratching his head then his bottom, still half asleep, Harry went downstairs and found Samuel Jacks sitting in an armchair.

'Morning Pop, where's Marie?'

'She's gone to the shop with Esther to do some accounts work. It got behind in her absence. She said she would see you at the studio this afternoon and not to forget to take Goldie with you, he needs some exercise.'

'Thanks, I'll see her there then.'

When he arrived at the studio, the phone was ringing. He rushed over to it but by the time he lifted the receiver, the caller had rung off. Shit, he said to himself as he went to make some tea. Almost immediately, the phone rang again, and he picked it up.

A female voice enquired: 'Good morning, is that Mr Harry Levi?'

'Speaking.'

'My name is Audrey Winter. I am the Editor of British Vogue. I understand that you are the photographer who took the pictures on the Windmill Theatre's advertisements and posters.'

'Yes, that's correct,' Harry replied.

'They are just the sort of thing I need for a project I have in mind for the magazine. However, the models will have more clothes on.' Audrey Winter laughed as she said this. 'Would you be interested?'

'Most definitely,' was Harry's enthusiastic response.

'Can you come round to my office in Bond Street tomorrow morning at 11?'

Without hesitating Harry said: 'That time is good for me. I look forward to seeing you then.'

Not for the first time, Lady Luck was smiling on Harry Levi.

When Marie called in at the studio that afternoon, Harry couldn't wait to tell her the exciting news about the potential business opportunity with Vogue. Naturally, she was delighted to hear this and at Harry's request, gave him as much information as she knew about the magazine. The sterling job that Audrey Winter had been doing since she took over as editor in 1940, had been widely publicised. She was a formidable woman who, at the outset of the war, petitioned the government to allow the publication to continue distribution despite the rationing of paper. The politicians agreed as they were anxious to keep the fairer sex onside in the knowledge that they would be needed to become an important part of the war effort. In addition to serving in the armed forces, women would replace men, who were away fighting, in many other roles such as working in munitions factories, driving public service vehicles, and farming to produce food for the nation. Whilst the magazine continued to cover women's fashion trends, as clothing was rationed, the articles tended to concentrate on how existing clothes could be adapted to create new looks. Vogue's monthly editions also included developments in the war, approaching the subject from a woman's perspective. It was this aspect that Audrey Winter wanted to discuss with Harry.

At the Vogue office the following day, the editor greeted Harry effusively. They sat down in armchairs next to a round table adjacent to her desk. A secretary brought in a tray of tea and biscuits, placed it on the table and retired.

Audrey Winter was in her late thirties. As you would expect for a woman in such a position, she was immaculately attired and well spoken. She wore a dark green velvet dress adorned with a large star-shaped diamond brooch. A double strand choker pearl necklace graced her long, elegant neck. She had a fresh complexion with an enchanting smile which extenuated her slightly protruding teeth. Her deep brown eyes were a stark contrast to her short blonde curly hair.

'I was pleased that you were able to come in to see me so promptly,' Ms Winter began. 'To be candid, we have something of a dilemma on our hands. Shortly before the war began, we had to sack our house photographer, Cecil Beaton, for some inappropriate antisemitic references he made in the copy accompanying his photos in one of our US editions of the magazine. A huge row blew up, and as a result, the board had no option but to let him go. We have used several other photographers since then. Most recently, I took on an accomplished American photojournalist, Lee Child. You may have heard of her. Anyway, she pleaded with me to send her to Europe to cover the war for us. She has been doing a splendid job, but this has left us without anyone here at home to carry out UK based assignments. That's where you come in. What I have in mind is a series of articles in the remainder of the 1944 issues spotlighting women in different roles who are making a significant contribution to the war effort. I want to cover a wide spectrum of occupations ranging from politics to nursing. We will provide you with the women contacts and it will be up to you to capture them in photographs that positively depict their role. You will need to submit outline copy to support the pictures which we will knock into shape before it goes in the magazine. What do you think?'

Harry took a sip of tea before answering. 'I am confident I can deliver exactly what you require. I carried out similar work for the Jewish Chronicle before the war and received an award from the owner of the Daily Express for one of my pieces. But you mentioned on the phone that you wanted specific types of shots.'

'Yes, that's right. I want images that encompass the war. For example, a female politician standing next to a bomb site or a woman volunteer ambulance driver tending to casualties. But I still want to retain a fashion element in some of the articles. I envisage these would include women working in tailors' shops changing garments to give them a new styling. It was your shot of the Windmill Girls in the gas masks that gave me the idea for this in the first place.'

After more discussion between the pair, and Harry dispensing a great deal of schmooze, it was decided that he would be retained on a trial basis for the first two articles. A decision would then be made if he would be required to continue. A sizeable fee was agreed for the work and Harry left the Vogue office with a spring in his step as he set out for the studio.

CHAPTER 23 – A STICKY END

Harry's first Vogue assignment was at a munitions factory in Wootton Bassett near Swindon. He travelled there by train from Paddington Station in London. On arrival at Filling Station no.12, the factory's official title, he was met by the manager, Mr Sallis, a tall thin balding man with a weak handshake and bad breath. Sallis explained that he had selected one of his more attractive female workers or "munitionettes" as they were referred to for the shoot. He then led Harry to the location he had allocated for the photos to be taken outside the entrance to the factory.

Stroking his chin, Harry politely explained that this was not what he had in mind: 'I am sorry Mr Sallis, but this is not suitable. My brief is to capture women in their work environment. I need to photograph the lady at her workplace carrying out her duties.'

'With respect Mr Levi, you do realise what this place is, don't you? We must operate with maximum security and safety regulations. One small error inside the factory and we could all be blown to kingdom come. Besides, I would have to shut down the entire production line while you take your shots.'

'I fully appreciate your concerns but an image

of a woman standing outside a factory will simply not be acceptable to my editor. She has gone to great lengths to get clearance from the Ministry of Defence for this job. And they, incidentally, are keen to have these articles run in Vogue to boost morale. I don't think their hierarchy will be too happy if I return without the photos required.'

Sallis thought about this for a moment and clearly did not want repercussions from his bosses. He reluctantly agreed to permit Harry entry inside but on the strict understanding that he would be closely supervised at all times. 'Ok, you'll have to give me a few minutes to sort things out in there. Wait here and I will come back for you when it's ready. But please work as quickly as you can. I cannot afford a long hold up of the production line,' the manager said testily.

To placate Sallis and speed up the proceedings, Harry prepared his equipment for the shoot outside in readiness for when he was summoned. Fifteen minutes elapsed before Harry received the signal from Mr Sallis that it was in order to enter the factory. The first thing to hit Harry was the overpowering smell of chemicals. The second was pure astonishment at the sight of the female workers. If only he had colour film which was in short supply during the war. The areas of the girls' faces, and hair not covered by masks and berets, was yellow.

Seeing Harry's expression, Sallis said: 'That's why they are called "Canary Girls." It's the sulphur they're handling that turns the skin yellow.'

On being introduced, Harry could see why the worker, Lily Winslow, had been chosen by the manager. Despite the manly overalls, she had an amazing figure and a pretty face which like all the other girls, had a jaundiced complexion. Her workstation could not have been in a better position if Harry had selected it himself. There was an abundant level of light and on the wall behind her was a large war poster proclaiming, "Mightier Yet! Back Up The Fighting Forces." With the impatient Sallis hovering close by, Harry lost no time in getting Lily to pose in different positions. He grinned as he instructed Ms Winslow to place both her thick rubber gloved hands around a large shell casing and smile suggestively at the camera. It would probably not be used by Vogue, but he imagined if he was shooting it in his studio with Lily in her underwear, it would be stunning.

Having finished the shoot, Harry thanked Lily and in answer to her question, advised that hopefully, the article would appear in the month after next issue of Vogue. He then followed Sallis back to the manager's office.

'Thank you so much for your co-operation, Mr Sallis, I will be sure to tell my editor,' Harry remarked without any intention of doing so. 'Before I go, I just need some information from you about Lily and the girls' jobs. You see, I have to send some copy with the photographs back to the magazine.'

Looking concerned, the manager replied: 'Well I cannot go into too much detail, Official Secrets Act etc.'

'I appreciate that but just some outline information will suffice. Of course, I will mention you in my submission,' Harry lied.

On hearing this Sallis perked up. 'As you have seen, the ladies are fiercely patriotic. They put in long hours, eight in the morning until eight at night, seven days a week. The work is extremely dangerous. They are handling explosive materials all day. You probably read about that dreadful accident at the Royal Ordinance factory in Kirby, Lancashire where two women workers were blown apart and several others badly injured.'

Harry nodded and said: 'No doubt about it, these ladies are very brave. But surely it must be difficult for them working in such conditions to retain some degree of femininity? The reason I ask is that this is the sort of thing that Vogue would be interested in including in the article.'

'Hmm, that's obviously difficult for a man to answer. I'll get Lily to come in and see what she has to say on the subject.'

Mr Sallis stuck his head out of the office door and instructed his secretary to get the foreman to bring Ms Winslow up.'

Lily Winslow did not disappoint. She provided Harry with just the kind of material that Audrey Winter required. She talked about how at the end of the day, covered in grime, on returning home she would bathe and then coat her nails with iodine to harden them. Lily spoke passionately about the shortage of cosmetics but was not too concerned as the yellowing of her skin was a small price to pay when men were being killed daily in the quest for victory over the Nazis.

Harry left the factory with some first-class images and pages of notes giving a woman's perspective of the war. Just what the doctor, or more accurately, the editor, ordered he thought on his journey back to London. His predictions proved to be accurate. Audrey Winter was impressed with Harry's submission and advised him that his copy only required minor amendments. She then proceeded to brief him on his second assignment.

'You are going to have to watch your Ps and Qs with this one Harry. Elizabeth Conroy is one of our top models. She is thirty-five, the oldest daughter of the Duke of Kendal and something of a socialite with a reputation for fast living. Her husband, Peregrine Conroy is the MP for Chester. He is well regarded in government circles and during the war, has been regularly posted overseas to represent Britain. They have a small estate near Chichester in Sussex. Elizabeth is a volunteer pilot delivering new and repaired planes to airfields around the country. She also manages the production of camouflage netting for gunnery units at an outhouse on the estate. A third string to her bow is beekeeping. There are over 100 hives in the fields producing vast quantities of honey. I think you will agree, quite a character with all the makings for a great photo story. The main shots should be of her in her flying gear in and next to planes. Apparently, she has already arranged the necessary pass for you to gain entry with her to RAF Westhampnett near Goodwood. Other shots should include the camouflage and bees. Over to you.'

The packed train taking Harry to Chichester stopped at every station en route. As one group of passengers disembarked, they were immediately replaced by the same number boarding. Emerging at Chichester Station Harry heard the honking of a car horn and turned to see an attractive woman wearing a silk patterned headscarf, large sunglasses, and an RAF flying suit standing up in an open top British Racing Green MG sports car. She was waving frantically at him shouting: 'Mr Harry Levi, over here.' Harry picked up his equipment and walked over to the car.

'Mrs Conroy?' he enquired.

'At your service, and please, Elizabeth,' she replied in a distinctly posh voice.

Harry lifted his gear into the space behind the seats and climbed in.

'Pleased to meet you,' he said.

His bottom had barely touched the beige leather seat when he was jolted back, and the car roared out of the car park. With a broad grin on her high-cheeked boned face, Elizabeth Conroy swerved around the closing level crossing gates just before they slammed closed. Harry was already getting the impression that the drive to Mrs Conroy's home was going to be undertaken at break-neck speed. Hopefully, it would not be too far away he thought. His wish was answered when the driver, yelling to be heard against the noise of the wind, said: 'First stop RAF Westhampnett. It's only a 10-minute drive. I've obtained permission from the Wing Commander of the base to have access to a couple of the planes so you can get the photos you require. Then we can head over to my place to take the other shots Audrey wants.' She leaned across Harry and ran her left hand along his thigh before opening the glove compartment and pulling out a pass which she pushed firmly into his lap brushing her hand across his crutch as she did so.

Harry's immediate thought was that this was not an accident, but he said nothing as the car continued to hurtle along at high speed.

'Audrey told me you are ex RAF,' Elizabeth Conroy bellowed. 'Invalided out I understand. Bad luck, eh?'

Before Harry could reply, the MG skidded to a halt at the gates of the RAF base where they were confronted by an armed guard.

'Hello Mrs Conroy, passes please.'

The pair of them showed their passes and the guard signalled to two other guards to open the gates.

Elizabeth drove past a row of heavily camouflaged hangars and pulled up alongside a Supermarine Spitfire. Grabbing a flying helmet from under the driving seat, she took off her sunglasses and scarf, and placed them on the dashboard and made her way over to the plane. 'These beauties are the reason we won the Battle of Britain,' she exclaimed patting the fuselage before clambering up on to its wing. 'How do you want me? And be careful how you answer that!'

Harry rapidly pulled out his camera from the

car and began focussing it. 'Left hand on hip and the right holding the helmet down by your side, please.'

'How's that? I'm good at holding helmets you know,' she giggled.

Harry ignored the overt sexual innuendo and asked her to unzip her flying suit a little. Elizabeth purposely lowered the zip to her waist partially revealing her bra-less breasts.

'Very nice, but not really suitable for Vogue,' Harry quipped.

Elizabeth laughed and raised the zip higher.

Harry took some different poses then requested Elizabeth to get into the cockpit and to put on her helmet. He climbed onto the wing and shot a series of close-ups of Elizabeth with and without flying goggles in place. As he helped her out of the cockpit, she hugged him tightly pretending that she needed to steady herself. Without consulting Harry, Elizabeth summoned a couple of mechanics who were working in an adjacent hangar and asked them to stand on either side of her holding large spanners. Begrudgingly, Harry had to agree it made for a good picture. Clearly, this was a woman who liked to be in charge of things.

'One down, one to go,' she said as they went back to the car and travelled a short distance to a new location.

Harry had never seen a P-51 Mustang fighter close-up previously. The plane was a joint American/British design made in California. The RAF had been using the planes extensively since 1940 at its bases.

'I thought it would be a good idea to give the Yanks a bit of kudos in the article,' Elizabeth explained. 'After all, they are an integral part of the war effort and will ultimately help us to eliminate the Hun.' She whipped out an American flag from the boot of the car and posed in various positions around the plane draping the Stars and Stripes across her body.

On the way to Elizabeth Conroy's house, she talked non-stop about her exploits delivering aircraft to bases around Britain. She had learnt to fly on her father's estate as a teenager and loved the adrenaline generated by piloting aircraft of all shapes and sizes. She joined the Women's Auxiliary Air Force when war broke out and despite having received very little training, had flown over fifty different types of aircraft. One of the funniest experiences she recounted was when coming into land at a base, she spotted lots of men running for cover. Naturally, she assumed that the airfield was about to be attacked by the Germans. But it transpired that the male pilots had all been sunbathing in their underwear and had just been told that a woman ferry pilot was about to land.

As the car approached the house from a long straight drive, Harry gawped at the sheer size of the property. In sprawling mock Tudor style, complete with chimneys modelled on that period, according to Elizabeth, it was built in the early 1900s. How the other half live Harry thought to himself.

'We've got the place to ourselves,' Elizabeth advised. 'I've given the staff the weekend off. As it's such a brilliant day weather-wise, I thought we'd start over at the hives. We will need to get kitted out first though. There are some suits in a shed over in the field by the hives. Not afraid of bees, are you?'

'Not something I've encountered in large numbers,' Harry responded. 'You don't tend to get swarms of them in Soho,' he joked.

Elizabeth ushered Harry into the shed and pointed to some bee suits hanging on hooks. 'You should find one to fit you.' She turned and was making for the door when Harry enquired.

'What about you?'

'Oh, I won't bother, I will keep this flying gear on. I just need a hooded veil and a pair of thick gloves,' she said about to leave the shed.

'Frankly, it would be better if you were wearing a suit for the photos. We already have a selection of shots with you in that outfit.'

'I had not thought of that. Of course, you are right. I'll be back in a minute and change.'

Harry had just stripped down to his underpants and was considering which of the suits was likely to fit him best when Elizabeth came back in. 'Nice legs,' she remarked eyeing him up and down. Totally unselfconsciously, she kicked off her flying boots, unzipped the flying suit and stepped out of it. She took the leather helmet from of one of the pockets and put it on. Her dark brown eyes narrowed in on Harry's pants which now contained a large bulge. 'Come fly with me,' she whispered. Harry wasted no time in taking up the invitation and boarded after minimal foreplay. As they were writhing on some coconut matting on the floor Harry let out a yelp.

'You haven't come, have you?'

'No, I've been stung on the bum,' Harry complained.

'Just one of the hazards of beekeeping,' Elizabeth laughingly blurted out. 'Don't fret, I'll rub it better later.'

Already hot from his exertions, Harry donned the bee suit and lumbered uncertainly into the field. The heat hit him immediately and he decided he needed to complete this part of the shoot as quickly as possible. Also in her bee suit, Elizabeth had removed the outer casing of a hive and was examining a frame covered in honeycomb. Harry was finding it difficult to operate the camera with the heavy gloves on, so he removed one to enable him to press the shutter button. He had just completed a nice sequence of shots when he was stung on the hand.

'Bugger, you should get danger money for this,' he screamed.

Elizabeth replied: 'I agree but someone has to do it. Since sugar rationing began, the demand for honey has shot up. It is not just used as a substitute for sugar. Honey has other properties that are useful as an antiseptic and help to reduce scarring. The Ministry of Food is keen for beekeepers to extend their colonies to attract more bees that will in turn pollinate the crops. All part of the drive towards Britain being self-sufficient in food production. I receive about two shillings and sixpence for every jar I make, and that helps towards the running of the estate.'

'Thanks for the lecture but I'd like to get out of this clobber as soon as possible. I'm melting in here.'

'Typical man, always complaining. In the shed there is a cold-water tap and a towel. Douse yourself down and change back into your civvies. I'll finish off here and join you shortly. We can have some tea and cake over in the house before doing the netting pictures.'

Harry was happy to agree with this suggestion as he was famished.

Seated in the drawing room while Elizabeth prepared the refreshments, Harry viewed the surroundings and was impressed. Fine paintings adorned the wood panelled walls, the grand piano displayed several rows of framed photographs on it, and the furnishings were of high quality. The entire place screamed under stated elegance.

Elizabeth returned carrying a tray bearing an exquisite bone China tea service and a fruit cake. Since meeting her, this was the first opportunity that Harry had had to see Elizabeth wearing something other than a flying suit or a beekeeping tunic. He certainly liked what he saw. She was wearing a plain white silk blouse, tight black slacks, and ballet pump style flat, burgundy-coloured slip-ons. Her long auburn hair was topped with a pale blue grosgrain head band.

Gesturing towards the piano, Harry said: 'Nice photographs. Is that your husband in some of them?

'Yes, that's Perry. Lovely chap but he bats for both sides. Mainly, the other side. He's in his element at the moment.'

'Why's that?'

'He is on a government posting working at our

embassy in Tunisia. Lots of young local bum boys to occupy his spare time.'

That explains Elizabeth's sexual appetite Harry thought.

Having finished the tea and cake, Elizabeth asked: 'Do you want me to change into something different for the netting shots?'

'No, what you've got on will be fine,' he replied. 'We already have ones of you in working outfits, I want to capture the feeling of the lady of the manor doing her bit for the war.'

Carrying his equipment, Harry walked down a semi made-up road alongside Elizabeth. As they rounded a bend in the road, a large brick outhouse appeared. Elizabeth pulled open a small door which was part of a much bigger wooden double door that was used to allow lorries in to enable the camouflage netting to be loaded. Rays of sunlight were shining through a few tiny windows located high on the walls. This gave the interior a hazy appearance. Rows of netting hung from beams that crossed the barn-like structure just below the pitched roof. The wall at the far end was lined with shelves where jars of honey were neatly stacked. The scene was ideal for the set-up Harry had in mind.

'Stand behind the netting and hold onto it with your arms apart and press your face into one of the gaps,' Harry instructed Elizabeth.

She did as she was asked and poked her tongue out looking at the camera.

'No tongue thank you,' Harry said.

Complying, Elizabeth replied: 'We will see about that in a minute.'

Harry took some further shots of Elizabeth in different poses around the netting and the machines used to produce it. He was about to pack away his camera when Elizabeth piped up: 'Harry, I have a favour to ask. I would like you to take some pictures of me naked with the netting wrapped around me.'

'Something tells me Audrey Winter will not be interested in those,' Harry joked.

'Don't be silly. They are strictly for me. I have my reasons. Please be a good boy and do as I ask. I will pay you for the film.' She did not wait for a response and removed her blouse and slacks. She was not wearing any underwear. 'You will need to help me position the netting.'

Trembling with excitement, Harry did as he was instructed and fumbled a new roll of film into his camera. He shot his subject from various angles with her standing and lying down. For the final sequence he stood over Elizabeth with his legs apart and took close up photos of her from the chest up. Cheekily, she extended her tongue in some of them. It was at this point that she reached up and unbuttoned

Harry's trousers. Pulling his hard cock through the gap and addressing it, she said: 'I have plans for you.' Then looking up at Harry, she purred: 'Be a poppet, strip off and put your camera on the tripod. Position it so it can take a timed exposure with both of us in the frame.'

'Hang on a minute, if those pictures were circulated it could spell the end of my career, as well as divorce proceedings,' Harry remonstrated.

'Don't be ridiculous. I want you to position it in such a way that your head is not shown, just mine with your impressive enlargement.'

After several attempts, moving back and forth from where he and Elizabeth would be located to check the position through the lens, Harry was about to press the timer when Elizabeth stopped him and said: 'Wait a second, I need to get a prop.' She walked over to the shelves and picked up a jar of honey. Removing the lid, she dipped her fingers in and began smearing Harry's erect penis with the sticky contents. 'Now go and set the timer for ten seconds.'

Harry carried out the instruction and returned to Elizabeth who was kneeling on the piles of netting. With Harry standing, she started to lick the honey from his knob whilst counting to herself. Smiling, on reaching eight, she opened her mouth wide and sucked his cock. The camera shutter clicked but Elizabeth held the position slowly moving her lips up and down Harry's extension until he could hold back no longer, clasping her shoulders, he came.

Spitting out the contents in her mouth Elizabeth enquired: 'How was that big boy?'

Harry had never experienced fellatio before. Still in a state of ecstasy, he was unable to utter a word.

Examining Harry's penis, Elizabeth giggled: 'Apologies, but I must have gone a tad heavy on the lipstick. I'll need to get a scrubbing brush on that!'

Harry looked alarmed until Elizabeth reassured him, she was kidding and that she would only use soap.

It was getting late by the time they arrived back at the house and Elizabeth advised that Harry had missed the last London train. He did not object to her suggestion that he would have to spend the night with her until he could catch a train tomorrow morning. He telephoned the Jacks house. Mercifully, Marie was out so he was not questioned closely by Pop as to his whereabouts. Harry just said he had been delayed on the job and would be back tomorrow. As he replaced the receiver, he thought to himself that on the job was a good description of what he would be doing overnight. His assumption proved to be accurate. Elizabeth's demands were intense. Intercourse took place when they went to bed, again in the middle of the night, and once more when they woke. As a result, Harry caught up on some much needed sleep on the train journey back to London.

CHAPTER 24 – GLAMOUR

Audrey Winter was extremely pleased with Harry's work on the Elizabeth Conroy article. Whilst suspecting that Harry had provided more than just photographic services, for Vogue's best-loved model, she continued to award Harry regular assignments around the UK. The income from these projects supplemented by family portraits, theatre shoots and the occasional clandestine glamour session, meant that Levi Photography's bank balance was in the black for once. Unwittingly, Marie and her parents were delighted that Harry seemed to have knuckled down to become a model husband. Indeed, everything was looking rosy for Harry until the end of the war. On 7 May 1945, Germany surrendered. The Prime Minister, Winston Churchill, declared a national holiday for the following day. Celebrations took place throughout Britain on what was designated Victory in Europe or VE Day. Huge crowds gathered outside Buckingham Palace to see King George VI and the Royal Family wave from the balcony.

Like many other London based businesses, Audrey Winter organised a party at Vogue's office to which Harry, and the great and the good of society, was invited. He was in awe when introduced to the famous American novelist, Ernest Hemingway, whose wife, the journalist, Martha Gellhorn, had been covering the war as a correspondent for Vogue. Hemingway, a bear of a man, was already intoxicated and was loudly regaling Harry with his escapades in the Spanish Civil War and, more recently, the Second World War, which he had covered as a correspondent for various publications. Their conversation was interrupted by Gellhorn who pushed past Harry and slapped Hemingway on the face. She followed this with a string of expletives accusing her husband of adultery with the Time Magazine journalist, Mary Welsh, before storming off. Hemingway did not react but merely winked at Harry and slurred that it was all true.

Stunned by the incident, Harry was about to offer solace to the great man when he felt his arm grabbed and was pulled away. Turning, he was surprised to see Elizabeth Conroy holding an open bottle of Pol Roger champagne. She led him through several doors to a staircase which they ascended to the floor above and went into an office marked "Editor." Elizabeth took a long swig from the bottle and passed it to Harry who did likewise. 'This is Winnie's favourite tipple, so if it's good enough for him, it's good enough for us,' she exclaimed.

'Long time, no see, big boy,' Elizabeth said as she undid Harry's trousers and pulled down his pants. She then swept the top of a desk clear of papers and laid back on it with her legs apart. Harry climbed on her and pushed his member in causing Elizabeth to let out a scream of delight. They had only been in action for a matter of minutes when the office door opened and Audrey Winter, accompanied by a weeping Martha Gellhorn entered. The two women stood opened mouthed at the scene in front of them. Harry rapidly withdrew and slid off the desk but as he stood, his foot caught in the trousers round his ankles, and he fell backwards with his tackle waving wildly as he did so. Seeing this slapstick performance by Harry, Elizabeth burst into uncontrollable laughter. She swung her legs off the desk, straightened her pretty dress and said:

'Apologies Audrey but our celebrations got a little out of hand. Too much bubbly!'

Still in a state of shock, the editor failed to respond as Harry pulled his trousers up and Elizabeth took his hand and led him out of the office.

Harry did not remember much about the rest of the evening. He accompanied Elizabeth to the Café Royal in Regent Street where they consumed more champagne before staggering out the back door into the Regent Palace

Hotel across the street where Mrs Conroy was staying. In the early hours of the following morning, Harry quietly dressed and left the room leaving Elizabeth fast asleep. With a thumping headache, Harry needed to concoct a plausible excuse for Marie. Instead of heading back to the house in Goodge Street, he decided to go to the studio. After making himself a couple of cups of black coffee, he set about developing some films he had taken the previous day prior to attending the Vogue party. The film included shots of people celebrating in The Mall with Buckingham Palace in the background as well as others depicting revellers dancing outside the Houses of Parliament. He would show them to Marie and explain that he had been commissioned by the Daily Mirror who wanted photos for their late morning edition. Hence, unable to get a cab, he had to walk to the newspaper's office in the City and wait until they were processed. It was then so late, he decided to sleep at the studio rather than disturbing her and her parents in the early hours.

Harry was sleeping on the studio sofa when Marie came in and shouted: 'What happened to you last night?'

With his best exhausted hang-dog expression, Harry related the story he had pre planned. Initially, Marie did not believe a word of it but on seeing the prints on the worktop, she changed her mind. She made some coffee, and they chatted about the positive upturn in the company's finances. After half an hour Marie explained that she was needed at the Jacks' shop for a while but would see Harry for dinner later. She had only been gone a matter of minutes when the phone rang. Harry had a shrewd idea who was calling. He was not wrong when he heard Audrey Winter's voice at the other end.

'Good morning Harry. You've doubtless guessed the reason for my call? By now, Martha Gellhorn will have told half of London about her experience in my office yesterday. Unfortunately, you have put me in an impossible position. As much as I would like to, I cannot afford to dispense with Elizabeth Conroy's services. I have been very happy with the work you have carried out for the magazine. In fact, if it was not for your part in the carnal coupling on my desk, I would probably have found the occasional project for you in the coming months. But as Lee Child has now returned from covering the war in Europe, she will resume her role as Vogue's main photojournalist.'

Despite his hangover, Harry pleaded his case eloquently. He explained that the combination of VE Day euphoria, copious amounts of alcohol and Mrs Conroy's demanding nature, had caused his fall from grace. He tried to reassure the editor that such a situation would never occur again. But for once, his charm offensive was to no avail.

'I'm sorry Harry but my decision is final. I have instructed our accounts department to settle any of your outstanding invoices with immediate effect. Goodbye.'

As 1945 rolled into 1946, things became increasingly tougher for Levi Photography. Harry tried desperately to replace the lucrative Vogue business but without success. Although West End theatres were slowly getting back to normal after the war, austerity was biting hard, and the public were slow to react. Broadway musicals such as "Gentlemen Prefer Blondes," "Carousel," and "Call Me Madam," were imported from the States but the lead roles were filled by British actors which proved less appealing to theatregoers. Even the arrival of the American smash hit, "Annie Get Your Gun," failed to stimulate mass interest. This situation had a knock-on effect for Harry. Whilst he was still obtaining work from some of the stars of these shows, it was not in the volumes that he required to maintain a steady cash flow for the business. This, coupled with the fact that since the war unemployment was high, it meant that many would-be photographers decided to take up the job. Hence the competition for Levi Photography intensified considerably.

Things were no better on the home front. Rows with Marie and her mother about the lack of money became a regular occurrence which led to Harry sleeping at the studio more often. It was on one such occasion that Harry was awakened around midnight by a gentle tapping on the studio door. Thinking it was Marie who had had second thoughts about the verbal roasting she had unleashed on him, Harry padded over and partially opened the door. He was flabbergasted to see Sherry standing there.

'Good to see you again. It must be two years since we last met,' Harry said ushering her in. 'How are things with you?'

Sherry forced a smile and replied: 'To tell the truth, a bit shit. I'm sorry to get you up at this time. But I was walking by after my last show, saw the light on and thought you might be able to help.'

Harry signalled for her to sit down. 'Fancy a drink? I haven't got any scotch so it will have to be beer or a cup of tea.'

'Tea will be fine.'

Harry made two cups and sat down next to Sherry. 'Now, tell me all.'

In between sips of tea, Sherry related her story.

Her boyfriend did not return from the war. She heard via a friend of his that he had shacked up with a French girl and he was living with her in some unpronounceable named village in the Dordogne. He didn't even have the decency to write to her and advise he would not be returning. Far from being heartbroken, Sherry explained that she was well-shot of the bloke. Harry was surprised to learn that although distinctly working class, her parents, Mr and Mrs Brown, who lived in Essex, were reasonably well off. Indeed, her father's scrap metal business had profited from the war. Sherry was still performing at The Windmill. But ever since her brief encounter with Harry, she had felt that there must be a way to make more than the meagre wages she received. It was this subject that had dominated her thoughts over the past two years. Sherry believed that the saucy pictures scheme she came up with involving her Windmill colleagues and Harry could be a profitable business if adapted differently. She based her thinking on the fact that The Windmill continued to be packed for every performance with men desperate to see naked girls. It therefore followed that around Britain there must be hundreds of thousands of such men who could not visit The Windmill. If Harry and Sherry could produce a magazine featuring pictures of girls in various stages of undress, and sell it, in her opinion, there was money to be made.

Harry listened patiently to Sherry's idea without commenting. He was somewhat relieved that it had not turned out to be what he expected, a request for a loan of money.

'Lovely idea Sherry but I have a few questions. Firstly, how would we get the models? Surely, they would have to be paid. Then how would we print the magazine? We would have to pay a printer and one that would be willing to work on such a risky project. Finally, there's the issue of selling copies. Newsagents would not be prepared to display the magazine on their shelves.'

Sherry had clearly thought through such objections prior to calling in to see Harry.

'To start things off, I'd get my mates at The Windmill to model. They would do it based on being paid a fee once we had sold a certain number of copies. There's a dodgy printer I know near home that owes my dad a big favour. We could do a deal with him on a profit share from which he could recoup his costs. I appreciate that we could not expect to sell the magazine over the counter in shops. It would have to be done through mail order by placing advertisements in certain newspapers. The printer's place would be the address to which punters would send their cheques to receive a copy in a brown envelope marked confidential.'

'Bloody hell, I'm impressed, you've certainly thought this through in detail,' Harry replied. 'But how are your mum and dad going to feel about their darling daughter running a dirty magazine business in the pages of which she will feature?'

'My folks are very liberally minded. They know I display my threepenny bits at The Windmill every day but have never said I shouldn't. And another thing. We must not use the word dirty in the context of the magazine. From the outset, it's important that when challenged we always refer to it as art. That's how Mr Van Damm got round the rules and look how much money he has made out of it.'

Harry smiled at this last point but chose not to contradict Sherry because in essence, she was right. It seemed to him her proposed business opportunity was worth a punt. Of course, details of the profit splits would need to be agreed but other than his time and the cost of film, he would not have to put any money into the venture. His only concern was keeping the details of the associated activities away from the prying eyes of his wife and mother-in-law.

Finally, Harry said: 'I like it a lot.'

'Are we talking my idea or something else?' Sherry asked cheekily.

'Both actually,' Harry replied laughing.

As per her previous visit to the studio, Sherry had come prepared for sex. The pair of them wasted no time in cementing the deal on the chaise longue.

A few days later, a meeting with the printer at his works in a seedy back street of Romford, took place. Nick Howard was a short man with a huge beer belly. His brown work coat was spattered with ink and judging by the odour he emitted, he had not seen a bathtub for several days. Clearly the favour he owed to Sherry's father was substantial as he had no problem with agreeing to fund the costs of the paper, ink, and printing 20,000 copies of a 24-page magazine. He would also provide the money for the advertisements, postage, and envelopes to fulfil orders. In return, he wanted all the income from the first issue which, at two shillings and sixpence a copy, would hopefully yield £2500. For reprints and subsequent editions, he proposed that Harry and Sherry would receive one shilling per copy sold. Harry thought this was a fair deal as essentially, the printer was taking all the financial risk. He was about to shake hands with the printer when Sherry stopped him. She argued that Harry would have to buy the film and pay the models so the split of profits should be 50/50 for any reprints of issue one and future editions. Following a certain amount of moaning by

Howard, the deal was agreed, and he shook hands with Harry.

Harry was stunned with the way Sherry had handled the meeting. As the weeks past and they saw more and more of each other, Harry realised that he was falling in love with the business-like beauty from Essex. And Sherry had the same feelings for Harry. She knew full well that Harry was married but that did not deter her.

True to her word, Sherry arranged for her pals from The Windmill to model for the photos required for the magazine. Harry could not carry out many of the shoots at his studio for fear of being interrupted by a visit from Marie. Instead, Sherry arranged for most of the pictures to be taken at the theatre when Vivian Van Damm was not around. Having selected the photos to be used, Sherry and Harry met with Nick Howard to discuss the layout and captions for the images. Thankfully, the printer had washed on this occasion, so Harry and Sherry were not at pains to keep their distance from him. Sherry suggested that the magazine should be entitled "Glamour." Harry had done a good job in creating different set-ups which ensured there was a wide variety of shots. Howard was impressed with the quality of the photos, so much so that Harry and Sherry had difficulty in deflecting his attention from them. He said he would get to work on the layout and deliver the proofs to Harry's studio within the next week. Unlike printers Harry had had dealings with in the past, Howard personally brought the proofs to the studio on schedule. Bar a few minor amendments to some of the captions, Harry and Sherry gave their approval. They were particularly taken with the font the printer had used for the title "Glamour" that incorporated a graphic of a camera next to it.

Just three days later, a box containing two dozen copies of the magazine were delivered to the studio with a letter from Nick Howard stating that a steady stream of cheques was being received at his office in response to the classified advertisements he had placed in a range of newspapers. Despite the fact that they were not going to receive any payments from the first print run, Sherry and Harry were pleased that sales of the magazine had taken off. The week after they were even more ecstatic. Harry received a call from Nick Howard advising that supplies of the magazine were exhausted, and he was reprinting a further 20,000 copies as cheques were still pouring in. Another week passed and the printer called again in a state of high excitement. Apparently, cheques were arriving by the sack load every day and he had taken on a couple of part timers to handle the mail outs. He confirmed that he was printing 50,000 more copies and told Harry he should be planning the next issue. Before ringing off Howard said he was putting a cheque for £4375 in respect of Harry's share of the reprints made out to Levi Photography in the post. Harry thanked him but stated that the cheque should be made out to Sherry. The last thing he wanted was Marie questioning him about what such a large payment was for.

Overjoyed with what he had just learnt, Harry could not wait to tell Sherry the good news. She was due to call in at the studio within the hour. Shortly afterwards there was a knock at the door, and he rushed over to open it shouting Sherry's name as he did so. He was met by a large fist that hit him in the face sending him sprawling backwards with blood pouring from his nose. Looking up he saw Marie's brothers Rudi and Izzy standing over him.

'No, it's not your slapper. We're here to give you a slapping and some news,' Rudi said.

'Izzy added: 'Thing is, Soho's such a small community, there's always gossip. You simply can't get away with shagging somebody without your missus eventually finding out.' He then stamped on Harry's balls causing him to scream out in agony.

As Harry writhed around clutching his scrotum, Rudi laughed: 'Well they won't be of much use to you and your whore for a while.' He then pulled Harry up, head butted him and dropped him back on the floor. Blood started to run from the gash on his forehead caused by Rudi's action.

'Marie's filing for a divorce. She never wants to see you again,' Izzy shouted, at the same time kicking Harry in the chest.

As Harry curled up into a ball expecting further blows, he heard the brothers smashing up the studio before the door slammed and they left.

CHAPTER 25 – A ROYAL FLASH

'Christ Almighty, what's happened?' was Sherry's first words after Harry had managed to drag himself over to open the door.

'Marie's brothers,' Harry said, barely able to reply through his puffed facial features.

'Bastards. I assume the reason was me?'

'Yeah.'

Sherry righted an upturned chair and directed Harry to sit. She then set about cleaning up the wounds on his face.

'It's not just my mush,' Harry slurred as he dropped his trousers to display his testicles that were already starting to swell.

'Blimey, they look painful,' Sherry observed.

'Hurry, get me a bowl.'

Sherry returned just in time as Harry threw up into the receptacle.

'I don't think you need stiches in the cut on your forehead, but we better get it checked at the Middlesex. We'll also get them to look at your balls and make sure they've not broken any of your ribs.'

'I hope the nurse is pretty,' Harry spluttered.

In the taxi to the hospital, Harry told Sherry about the good news regarding "Glamour."

Although she was delighted to hear this, she was more concerned about Harry's condition.

It was not a nurse that examined Harry's undercarriage in the accident department but a male doctor. He advised that the swelling would remain for a couple of weeks before going down. The same applied to Harry's nose which the doctor confirmed was not broken. The medic stated that Harry did not require stitches in the cut to his head but would arrange for a nurse to bandage it. His ribs were badly bruised but not damaged. Knowing the injuries were the result of an assault, the doctor urged Harry to report the matter to the police. Harry said he would think about it.

Back at the studio, Sherry phoned Sidney Solomon who popped round to help her clear up while Harry slept after taking some pain killers prescribed by the doctor. Later, she called The Windmill to say she was sick and could not make the evening performances. After Sidney left, Harry awoke, and he was chatting to Sherry when there was a knock on the door. Harry instructed Sherry not to open it but ask who it was. The reply came back that it was the landlord, Stan. Harry nodded to Sherry to let him in. Sherry then went into the other room to make some tea.

'I'm sorry to hear what happened Harry. The staff in the shop downstairs heard the commotion and saw Rudi and Izzy leaving. 'That's not all. Esther has told Bunny that I must evict you.' Stan said nervously, knowing that Harry might remind him of his escapades in the flat above. He was therefore relieved when Harry replied:

'Sure Stan, I understand. No problem. But do you know anybody who has some accommodation suitable for a studio.?'

'I'll have a word around. I have a couple of people in mind. I'm sure somebody will have rooms they are keen to rent. And don't worry about the outstanding rent you owe, we'll call it quits,' he said winking.

Less than twenty-four hours later, Harry received a call from a contact of Stan's. He had a suite of unfurnished rooms to let on the first floor of a property he owned in Tisbury Court, off Wardour Street. It was located a few streets away from the current studio. Harry arranged to view the place the following day. Standing outside looking up at the red brick building, Sherry and Harry were intrigued to see a huge hand painted sign on the façade that had become coated with grime. It depicted a smart waiter with text beneath in English and French advertising clothing for catering staff. Above the sign in bold lettering were the words "2 Little Crown Court." Talking to the landlord inside, they ascertained that the sign had been there since the late 1800s and the name of the street had been changed to Tisbury Court just before the war. The apartment was twice the size of the premises in Romilly Street. It comprised a spacious well-lit living area with two large bedrooms, a kitchenette, and a bathroom. The rooms had been recently decorated and a slight smell of paint still lingered. Overall, perfect for photographic work, Harry thought to himself. Flushed with the knowledge of the cheque received for the reprint of Glamour, acting on impulse, Harry was about to agree the rent of £6 per month. But not for the first time, Sherry took control and negotiated the landlord down to £5 per month.

Helped by Sidney and some other friends, Levi Photography was on the move once again. Over a weekend the contents of the old studio were transferred to the new. Certain items that had been smashed beyond repair by the Jacks brothers were replaced following a swift shopping spree by Sherry and Harry. This sortie included the purchase of some new clothes for Harry as he had no intention of trying to retrieve the ones in the wardrobe at Goodge Street. The couple then treated their friends to drinks and a fish and chips supper as a thank you. Everything seemed to be falling into place nicely but there was one thing that was troubling Harry. He had always been an animal lover and he was saddened by the fact that he was not going to see his beloved dog Goldie again. During the beating, the Jacks brothers had made it clear that the dog would be staying with Marie. Sensing the dilemma, Sherry brought her cat, Tiddles, from her parent's home to live at the new studio with her and Harry. Tiddles was a sleek tabby cat and rapidly adapted to life in Soho. Prostitutes operating out of rooms in the surrounding streets adored him spoiling him with titbits such as chicken livers, rabbit, kidneys, and even steak. Conversely, the local restaurateurs were not so enamoured, as they often had to chase the cat out of their kitchens after he had sneaked in to scavenge food left on the worktops.

In a peculiar way, Tiddles helped Harry and Sherry to integrate into the local community. Whenever they ventured out, people would stop them to talk about Tiddles and his exploits. Almost all the comments were complimentary, except for the occasional restaurant owner threatening to cut the cat's balls off it kept stealing food from them. Unsurprisingly, in a short space of time, Tiddles svelte-like appearance turned into that of a lumbering fat cat. Nevertheless, Harry loved him wholeheartedly and took some superb photos of his pet. But Tiddles was not the only reason for Harry's emergence as a "face" in Soho. He had always been a magnet for quirky characters and there was no shortage of them within the Soho village. The local "brasses" were very fond of Harry. Whenever they saw him in the street they would stop and chat about their business activities as though it was an everyday office job. Comments such as, "bumper day, have done 20 tricks but feeling a bit tired now, going for a lie down, alone," were commonplace. Not all the street walkers came from a working-class background. One was a well-spoken lady in her mid-thirties who was always turned out immaculately. She only worked her patch Monday to Friday. The reason Harry ascertained was that she went home to a large mansion in the country she had inherited, at weekends. If her staff at the mansion received telephone calls for her on weekdays, they would inform people that madam runs a company in London during the week. They had no idea what that business was.

Prostitution in the area was not restricted to females. Homosexuals cruised the streets dressed in what was a type of uniform. It comprised a large, brimmed fedora hat, a velvet cape, silk shirt corduroy trousers and brown boots with Cuban heels. Like the ladies of the night, they too showed great affection towards Harry, but not in an overtly sexual way. They loved to banter with him and Sherry in the pub regaling them with camp jokes whilst sipping a port and lemon. Inevitably, Harry would get the occasional request for photographs to be taken of them in full drag in the studio. This he did without question providing they paid. However, he drew the line when the costume, or lack of it, was too extreme. He also dismissed any suggestions from these "queens" for twosome "action" shots. Harry knew that if the photographs ended up in the hands of the police and were traced back to him, he could be sent to prison as homosexuality was illegal.

It was not just sex workers who crossed paths with Harry. There was the bizarre case of the Canadian millionaire who aspired to be a renowned thespian, starring on the London stage. This chap arrived at the studio with suitcases full of costumes and on the production of a wad of five-pound notes, asked Harry to photograph him in different poses. At the end of the day-long shoot, the Canadian instructed Harry to bring the proofs to his suite at The Savoy, and he would select which ones he wanted. This Harry did a couple of days later, and to his astonishment, the millionaire ordered several prints of virtually every set-up. Calculating the cost of the materials in his head, despite the luxurious surroundings in which the meeting was taking place, and the champagne and canapes he had been plied with, Harry was concerned about final payment. Airing his worry in a polite manner, the Canadian pulled out a large wad of notes and handed them to Harry without even counting them. Harry subsequently delivered the prints. The man advised him that he was liaising with a leading theatrical director who was arranging for him to take the lead role in a production that would initially run at a small theatre in East Anglia before moving to the West End. Naturally, on hearing this, Harry was sceptical, as he had found out that the millionaire had no previous acting experience. He then asked Harry to take pictures of the dress rehearsal and the first night. Harry was about to decline when the man offered a staggering amount of money for his services. Never one to look a gift horse in the mouth, Harry accepted the assignment.

Taking shots around the Theatre Royal in Norwich at the dress rehearsal, Harry's suspicions regarding his paymaster's acting credentials were well-founded. It was apparent throughout the performance that the male lead had no aptitude for learning lines. The director and cast members made no comment about the man's total lack of ability because like Harry, they were being paid handsomely. The first night was a disaster. Hilariously, the review in the Norwich Evening News stated that the best performance of the night was that of the prompter who spoke more lines than the leading man. The production closed after just two further performances.

On his return to London Harry was pleased to learn from Sherry that the printer, Nick Howard, had been in touch and was anxious to receive a set of photos and captions for the next issue of Glamour. Not wishing to use the models from the first edition of the magazine, Harry and Sherry thought they would struggle to find new girls willing to pose. They were proved wrong. Letters enclosing a photograph from ladies around the UK were being received at the printers requesting an audition. The majority added that they did not require payment. Sherry diligently replied to them all stating Levi Photography would hold their details on file and be in contact if appropriate. She then selected the best submissions, discussed them with Harry and arranged for the girls to come to the studio for a session. This system gained momentum and the material for the next issue was delivered to the printers on schedule. The print run of 100,000 copies sold out in just over a week so Nick Howard reprinted another 25,000. But the printer pointed out that he was finding it increasingly difficult to cope with handling individual requests and payments for copies of the magazine. In response, Sherry proposed that Glamour should offer readers the opportunity to buy a subscription to the magazine. By making one payment for twelve monthly issues, it would boost cash flow, create reader loyalty, and importantly, reduce administrative costs. It was therefore agreed that the next issue would include a subscription form.

As income from sales of Glamour grew, Harry and Sherry rightly concentrated on this aspect of their business. This meant that their work on family portraits and at theatres reduced. However, when Harry received a telephone call from the famous impresario, Val Parnell, he simply could not resist accepting the project. Topping the bill at the 1947 Royal Variety Show were Harry's comedy idols, Laurel and Hardy. Parnell wanted Harry to be the official photographer for the event being staged at the London Palladium on 7th November. The show would take place in the presence of His Majesty King George VI, Her Majesty Queen Elizabeth and their daughters, the Royal Princesses, Elizabeth and Margaret. The brief for the photographic requirements fell into three parts. The first was for shots of the performers during rehearsals so that photos could be issued to the press for pre-event promotion. The second was for images of the acts on stage on the night. And the final sequence was for the stars in the line-up after the show being presented to the Royal Family by Val Parnell. It was agreed that Sherry would assist Harry during the shoots. Her role would be to take the rolls of film to the stage door and hand them to a runner. He would deliver them to the Levi studio nearby where an assistant would develop them in readiness for Harry to decide which ones should be sent by a motorcyclist to the various newspapers.

The first phase of the plan went relatively smoothly except for an issue with Tommy Trinder, the much-loved comedian, who was compering the show. The incident demonstrated that performers can be extremely superstitious. Trinder refused to let Harry take his photo stating that every year, the hit of the Royal Variety Show was a comedian who had not had his picture taken at the dress rehearsal. Thankfully for Harry, other performers on the bill such as The Crazy Gang, Wilson Keppel & Betty, The Dagenham Girl Pipers, Gracie Fields, and Laurel and Hardy, did not object. Without doubt, the highlight of the session for Harry was getting to chat to Laurel and Hardy. They were a delight and explained that Stan Laurel had written a special piece for the night. Laurel of course was no stranger to the boards having left Britain with Charlie Chaplin years ago to perform with Fred Karno's Army at theatres around America. Oliver Hardy had played villains in films before teaming up with Stan Laurel to form the most famous comedian duo in the world. After 40 years in show business, they were touring the UK and had been warmly received by audiences.

The big night finally arrived. Sherry and Harry looked fabulous in their evening dress wear, in Harry's case, hired for the event from Moss brothers in Covent Garden. Harry was given a special position away from other photographers outside the Palladium to ensure that he secured shots of the Royal Party arriving in their limousine being greeted by Val Parnell. Inside, in the foyer, Harry took more photos of the Royals being introduced to the theatre staff. Once the Party had taken their seats in the Royal Box, Harry obtained some good pictures of them with a long-range lens camera he had set up earlier on a tripod in the wings of the stage. As he finished a roll of film, he passed it to Sherry who whisked it out to the stage door. This procedure followed intermittently through the various performances. At the end of the show, Harry obtained some great shots of the King and Queen smiling as they shook the hands of the stars in the line-up. The main part of their work for the evening completed, Harry and Sherry hurried back to the studio to begin sifting through the prints that had been developed so far. As they burst through the door laughing, the pair were alarmed to see the look of dismay on the studio assistant's face.

'Sorry boss but all the photos you took of the performers in action on stage tonight have not come out bar a couple of Tommy Trinder.'

'Shit,' Harry shouted. 'What about the ones of the Royal Family before and after the show.'

'All ok,' the assistant replied.

'Thank God for small mercies,' Harry murmured. 'But what am I going to do? The papers are going to want some shots of the acts.'

Harry knew instantly what he had done. He had taken the shots of Tommy Trinder from the orchestra pit. But In his rush to take the other artists from different angles around the auditorium, he had re-set the camera on the wrong synchronisation which led to the flash operating before the lens shutter opened.

Nobody said anything until Sherry piped up: 'Calm down love. Let's think about it for a moment. You took lots of pictures of the stars performing at the dress rehearsals, didn't you?'

'Yes, I did but how does that help? Harry snapped.

'The main photos the press want are the Royals and you've got plenty of those. I know they also like to run a selection of the acts too, but they tend to crop them. On that basis, how would they know whether they were taken on the night or at the rehearsals?'

'You're right but they also like a couple of photos of the audience. Obviously, I took a few but I did that while I was doing the acts. So, they have not come out either.'

'Surely, you have sections of the audience on the film from the camera you set up in the wings to get the shots of the Royal Box?'

At this point, the assistant chimed in: 'Those ones were not spoilt and are useable. We could mark them up, so the photo editors just use the audience areas if they want to.'

Breathing a sigh of relief, Harry said: 'Seems like I've been dealt my "Get Out of Jail" card. Maybe there was something in that superstitious stuff Tommy Trinder was on about!'

Sherry and Harry then packed up the prints together with the applicable captions, inserted them in separate envelopes and sent the motorcycle despatch rider who had been waiting outside to the newspaper offices in and around Fleet Street.

CHAPTER 26 – FILM FESTIVAL

As sales of Glamour went from strength to strength, Sherry's father, a seasoned East End businessman, urged his daughter to formalise the deal between Harry and Nick Howard. The reason for his prompting was that he did not trust the printer. He felt that unless there was a legally binding contract in place, ultimately, Nick Howard might renege on the existing, somewhat loose agreement. Predictably, the printer was standoffish when the subject was broached by Harry. However, Harry persevered, and Howard reluctantly agreed to a meeting to discuss the matter. In doing so, the printer planned to adopt delaying tactics as he had his own agenda to maximise his share of what had become a highly profitable enterprise. But Sherry anticipated the "iffy inker," as her father called Howard, would try to manoeuvre things to his advantage. She therefore suggested to Harry that they should get an old Jewish friend of his, Michael Mankowitz, who had become a successful solicitor, to draw up a contract and accompany them at the meeting. As expected, the printer rejected the terms of the new agreement that was rightly weighted financially in favour of Levi Photography. But when the solicitor forcefully pointed out that whilst printers were two-a-penny, without the photographs of the models, there was no magazine, Howard relented. The contract was duly signed, and Levi Photography was registered at Companies House with Sherry and Harry listed as directors and shareholders.

Harry had never been good with managing money. As fast as the profits rolled in from Glamour, he spent it. Pricey presents for Sherry included jewellery, designer clothes and a fur coat. The latest equipment for the studio was purchased as well as some smart new suits for himself. Perhaps the most sensible element of this spending spree was renting a luxurious flat on East Heath Road in Hampstead. The property, on the top floor of a three-storey block, had commanding views across Hampstead Heath and the surrounding area. It was located a ten-minute walk from Hampstead underground station. This enabled Harry and Sherry to travel to Leicester Square every day and walk the short distance to the studio. The total journey time was half an hour. However, his newfound wealth had given Harry ideas above his station. The experience of commuting on busy trains in the morning did not appeal to him. He had never learnt to drive but an opportunity for him to be chauffeured around London arose soon after the move to Hampstead.

During daylight hours, Soho remained a relatively safe area. Its streets were thronged with locals living their Bohemian lifestyle, market traders, office workers, shop assistants, and waiters from the numerous restaurants. Added to this mix was the daily influx of visitors from other parts of Britain and overseas, all keen to experience the atmosphere they had read about. This included characters such as Prince Monolulu and The Happy Wanderers. The Prince, a self-styled horse racing tipster, was instantly recognisable by his brightly coloured clothes and his cry of:" I gotta horse." By handing over half a crown to him, he would whisper to the donor the name of a horse that was running at a race meeting on that day. Monolulu was not really a Prince. His real name was Peter McKay and he came from the West Indies. Conversely, The Happy Wanderers were genuine musicians. Mostly retired, they formed a band and travelled into London each day from the suburbs. Playing traditional jazz tunes such as Basin Street Blues and Honeysuckle Rose, they marched around the West End collecting tips from passers-by. To avoid being arrested as vagrants, they had to keep moving, hence their name.

But Soho at night took on a more sinister complexion as the crime capital of London. Prostitutes and their pimps loitered on street corners. Rival gangs regularly clashed and open warfare had intensified between them as the new decade arrived in 1950. Throughout the 1940s, these gangs battled it out to become the underworld's top dog. The contenders included Jack Spot, Billy Hill, the Elephant Gang, and the Whites. Following a series of bloody engagements between the protagonists, it was Billy Hill and his mob who emerged victorious. This led to a string of daring robberies of jewellery shops in Bond Street and Regent Street. The police knew that Hill was responsible but unsurprisingly, witnesses at the subsequent identification parades "failed" to pick out the gangster.

Harry had always been at pains to avoid any contact with these villains although both parties would acknowledge the presence of each other with a nod whilst drinking in the local pubs. It was on one such occasion when a former member of Hill's gang pulled up a chair at the table where Harry and Sherry were sitting enjoying a drink in the French House. Introducing himself as Big Jock, the man was in his late thirties, heavily built, at least six foot-four with a rotund pock-marked face which had a deep scar down the right cheek. He had unkempt ginger curly hair and greenish eyes. He sported a smart suit, shirt and tie, and well-polished shoes.

His heavy Scottish accent pronounced: 'Mr Harry, isn't it?'

Sheepishly, Harry nodded.

'Word's out your magazine is doing well. So much so that there's a few faces who are anxious to get involved. Now I take it that you and your good lady here wouldn't welcome such interference?'

Again, Harry nodded his agreement.

'Well, I have a proposition for you. Having left Billy Hill's entourage, on good terms I'd hasten to add, I am looking for a job. I don't want big wages, just enough to tide me over for a while. I would act as a deterrent to anybody who was thinking of muscling in on your business. I could also act as your chauffeur. I have honed my driving skills on jobs undertaken for Billy that required a speedy service, if you get my drift?'

'I don't need an immediate answer, tomorrow will be fine. See you then.'

The man mountain slipped away from the table and left the pub.

Sherry was the first to speak. 'Well, he certainly put the wind up me. Scary bloke.'

Not usually lost for words, Harry hesitated for a minute before replying: 'I'll check him out but it's worth considering. I don't want to be walking around Soho looking over my shoulder all the time. With him by our side, I don't think anyone is going to trouble us.'

That evening, Harry made some discreet enquiries regarding Big Jock. The man had a quite a reputation. Indeed, he was no longer a member of Billy Hill's notorious mob. The reason being he had taken the rap for a heist by Hill which exonerated his boss who the police were desperate to charge. As a result, Jock MacGregor had served a two-year jail sentence and had just been released. Billy Hill was indebted to MacGregor for not grassing on him and had offered to take him back into the gang, but the Scot had declined. Frankly though, this incident was the most innocuous on his criminal record. The others included charges of GBH, all involving the use of razors. It appeared that his speciality was using these weapons to carve the victims' initials on their face. Harry concluded that if you needed a bodyguard, Big Jock fitted the bill to a tee.

Early the following morning, Harry answered a knock on the studio door.

'Morning Mr Harry. I hear you've been checking up on me. All satisfactory I hope?' Macgregor walked in handing Harry a bacon sandwich and a cup of espresso coffee as he did so. 'I brought you breakfast.' Surveying his surroundings, he commented: 'Nice place you've got here. Security needs to be tightened up though. Better locks on the door and windows. That old safe should be replaced with a new one. At the moment, it would be too easy for someone to gain entry and help themselves to your expensive equipment. I'll have a look at your Hampstead pad later to see what's required there. I've got a mate who can do the work for you on the cheap. I understand you don't have a car so we will have to sort that as soon as possible. I can then start to drive you and Miss S around town whenever you want.'

Harry was impressed by the burly Scotsman's forthright assessment of the situation and the fact that he knew about the Hampstead flat. After a brief discussion about hours and payment, Harry was pleased that he had secured the services of a man who could provide protection for himself and Sherry, should the need arise. He did not have to wait too long before his new employee's usefulness was called into play. Two men, who in appearance, could have doubled for Laurel and Hardy, turned up at the studio one morning and asked for a few minutes of Harry's time. Citing the success of Glamour, they put the case that the studio set-up would provide the ideal location for their pornographic photographs business. All Harry had to do was take the pictures of the models that the two gents would arrange. A payment of £600 per week in cash would be paid for three months guaranteed work. As with previous approaches of this type, Harry refused outright. He had heard about similar cons where the first month's payments are made but then blackmail was used to keep the photographer in tow on a minimal payment. The men pleaded for Harry to reconsider his decision and although the conversation was still amicable, it looked as though it was about to turn threatening. At this junction, Big Jock, who had been listening in the adjoining room burst in and hauled the men off their chairs and dragged them over to the door.

As he threw them down the stairs, the Scot shouted at the cowering duo: 'Yer hearing's nay sa good, is it? The man said no! Now piss off and don't come back.'

Having organised the implementation of the security measures he recommended for the flat and the studio, MacGregor arranged a meeting at a car dealership in Berkeley Square. He escorted Sherry and Harry to the showroom and suggested that they should have a test drive in a new dark green Rover 75. Petrol rationing had just been lifted for the first time since the war and was sold at three shillings per gallon. As a result, car sales were beginning to increase. Sitting in the sumptuous leather seats in the back of the car, listening to the radio, Harry and Sherry were bowled over by the smooth ride the car provided. With Big Jock at the wheel, the salesman who was sitting next to him in the front was giving the prospective purchasers all the patter. This included a list of film stars such as Grace Kelly, who had recently bought the luxury cars. He didn't need to bother. Harry and Sherry were sold. On arrival back at the showroom, Harry wrote a cheque for £950 on the understanding that MacGregor could pick up the car the following day. Thereafter, commuting to work on the tube ceased. Harry and Sherry were chauffeured into the West End everyday like royalty.

The new car and the other displays of wealth indicated that Harry's fortunes had seen a meteoric rise. This had not gone unnoticed. Once more, the Soho gossip mill was at full tilt. Word reached Marie regarding these developments for whom life had not been so kind. Her father had died, and her mother had become stricken with diabetes which prevented her from working. Hence, Marie had been forced into taking over the running of the Jacks shop full-time. Her brothers had married and moved out of London so could not provide her with support. She still had feelings for Harry but was aggrieved that she was struggling financially. Marie was sure that Harry was aware of her circumstances but had never been in contact to see if he could help.

It grated that she had played such an integral part in achieving the success, the fruits of which, Harry was now reaping. She therefore decided to consult a solicitor about divorce proceedings and maintenance payments. A search by the lawyer Marie retained of Levi Photography's accounts recorded at Companies House showed that the directors, Harry Levi and Sherry Brown, were receiving substantial amounts from dividends. Clearly, the business was doing extremely well. This information, coupled with the evidence that Marie provided regarding Harry's adultery and the precarious state of her finances, prompted the solicitor to advise Marie that there were sound grounds for divorce and maintenance payments.

'Bloody bitch,' Sherry exclaimed having read the letter from Marie's legal adviser that Harry had passed to her.

'We made a fatal error formalising the registration of the company. It meant that people have access to the accounts.' Harry replied. 'But in fairness, she has a point. She did help me through some difficult times, and I was a complete bastard by screwing around.'

'That's all very well but the success of Glamour magazine was down to our hard work. It was nothing to do with her. Why don't you get Jock to pay her and her brothers a visit?'

'Don't be ridiculous. If I did instruct the big

man to do that, it would be traced back to me immediately. Besides, I don't hold any grudges towards her or even, Rudi and Izzy. She's a decent sort and has obviously hit on difficult times. I am sorry for that.'

'Trouble with you is you're too soft.' Sherry insisted.

'Calm down. I want a divorce. It will make things easier between you and me. Both personally and business-wise. What she is asking for in terms of maintenance is no great shakes. I can afford it. What's the point in contesting it and attracting negative publicity for Levi Photography? I'll get on to Michael Mankowitz and tell him to settle.'

The remainder of 1950 ran reasonably smoothly for Harry and Sherry. Glamour's circulation continued to grow and the number of pages in each issue was increased from 24 to 36. There was no shortage of models wanting to feature in the publication, so Harry was kept busy. Britain was still in the grip of post war austerity. The General Election saw the Labour Party returned for a second term but only just. The Prime Minister, Clement Atlee's, previous huge majority was reduced to a mere five seats. The Government's plans for the Festival of Britain, scheduled to take place over five months in the summer of 1951, were well advanced. Essentially the Festival would operate in various locations around the country. But its cultural hub would be on London's South Bank between Waterloo and Hungerford Bridges. Here, a spectacular series of pavilions were being built to promote British science, technology, architecture, industrial design, and the arts. The aim was to give the public a feeling of a successful recovery from the war. An additional objective was to boost the Labour Party's dwindling popularity. The directors of Levi Photography were also considering ways their company could derive benefits from the Festival at which large numbers of businessmen would be visiting London.

Conversations about the Festival of Britain with some of his business contacts proved thought provoking for Harry. The consensus was that there would be companies who had exhibits on show at the Festival who would be sending their executives to London to represent them on their stands. There would also be firms arranging for their senior employees to visit the Festival to seek out ideas to develop for their organisation. Both sets of businessmen, staying in London's big hotels during the event, would be at a loose end in the evenings. They would be on expense accounts from their companies so would have money to play with. And Soho would be an obvious attraction to many of these executives.

Harry recounted the visit of the "Laurel and Hardy" characters that he had sent packing. If he could produce his own short films featuring models he was using for Glamour, and hire a venue to show the movies, it could be a money spinner. The knowledge Harry had gleaned from producing propaganda films during the war meant that he could do most of the work involved himself, thereby keeping costs to a minimum. When he talked the idea through with Sherry, she was enthusiastic. She had no reservations that Harry could make the films, but astute as ever, questioned how the businessmen would be made aware that they could attend showings. Newspaper advertising would prove too costly. Besides, some of the publications would be reluctant to carry such an advertisement for fear of criticism of being party to denigrating London and the Festival. Following further consideration of the conundrum, resourceful as ever, Sherry came up with a suggestion.

'Have you heard of, Les Clefs D'Or?' she asked Harry.

'Is that French? I was only in the country a short time after being shot down, so I didn't pick up any of the lingo,' he responded laughingly.

In an exasperated tone, Sherry said: 'Of course it's French. It's a membership organisation comprising concierges of all the big hotels over there. Anyway, they've just formed a branch in London and called it the Society of Golden Keys. The members are all hall porters who help guests at their hotel with tickets for shows, trips to tourist spots and other extras for gentlemen staying such as female company etc.'

'Very nice but how does that fit in with our scheme?' Harry enquired.

'Simple. We get the iffy inker to print off a smaller size cover of the current issue of Glamour that's out at the time the Festival is running. We then have details of the film show dates, timings, and venue on the other side of the leaflet and deliver them to the Golden Keys bods.'

'Got it. But one thing. I assume these porters are wheeler dealers, aren't they? What's in it for them to hand the leaflets to male guests?'

'First, we'd get to the bloke who calls the shots for the Golden Keys in London and offer him a sweetener to make sure he endorses our venture to his members. We'd get the porters to put their hotel stamp on the leaflets and tell their punters to present it at the door of the venue. At the end of each show, we would tot up the numbers of leaflets and which hotel they came from. We would pay ten per cent commission on every booking received to the porter. They'd want cash so Jock could run me round the hotels, and I'd drop the money off.'

Harry kissed Sherry on the forehead and said: 'Sounds like a goer. I'd better get cracking on the plans for the films.'

'While you are getting things going on that front, I will start scouting around to find a suitable venue where we can show the films. It will have to be big enough to seat about a hundred punters. I don't think we need to complicate matters by having a bar because that will mean applying for a liquor license. Let's face it, there's plenty of boozers and clubs round here where they can get a drink before and after the shows. I'll have to factor in the cost of renting the venue, printing the leaflets, a couple more heavies to work with Jock in case of trouble, and what you will be spending to produce the films. I can then calculate the charge for the tickets.'

Harry duly set about writing scripts for the films. For this task, he enlisted the help of his old friend Sidney Solomon as he wanted to incorporate an element of slapstick into the productions along the lines of their stage act. Whilst the main part of the films would feature attractive models undressing, providing titillation for audiences, Harry felt that it was necessary to inject a bit of humour around the central premise. He therefore wrote in cameo appearances for himself and Sidney. The two friends subsequently spent many hours giggling in Soho pubs developing the scripts. The result was four half hour films. Harry decided that he would require the most up to date 8mm film equipment before shooting could begin. There was also the question of locations for the shoots to be addressed as they could not all take place in the Levi Photography studio. The titles of the four productions dictated the type of backdrop that would be needed. They were, "Shop Around" with scenes in a London store; "All Change" on a train; "A Midsummer Night's Scream" romps in a forest, and "Doll Flanders" set in a 17th century British colony in Virginia.

Meantime, Sherry had secured a venue for showing the films in the basement of a building in Walker's Court, a narrow passage just a stone's throw away from the studio. With the knowledge of the rental costs of the property and the budgets she had obtained for the various parts of Harry's work, she was then able to set a price for the entry tickets. This she based on achieving an average of seventy per cent occupancy at each of the two performances that would feature two films per evening, six nights a week for the five months duration of the Festival of Britain. Bearing in mind that the price of a ticket for a London cinema was around two shillings, Sherry's charge of one pound appeared high. However, she was convinced men would be prepared to pay the inflated price as they would much rather be watching a saucy picture rather than the typical romantic slush showing in West End cinemas. After deducting costs including printing leaflets and the commission paid to hotel hall porters, Sherry estimated a £10,000 net profit for Levi Photography. Not bad she thought for less than half a year's work.

In fact, Sherry's projections were surpassed. It transpired that occupancy at the performances averaged almost eighty per cent as audiences were boosted by non-Festival related attendees who had seen advertisements for the film shows in early 1951 issues of Glamour magazine. Further income was derived from sales of the films at £5 per copy to subscribers of Glamour after the Festival. When all of these components were taken into consideration, the final amount of profit was slightly over £15,000. In true hedonistic fashion, to celebrate, Harry and Sherry threw a party in Walker's Court basement before they vacated the premises, for everyone who had been involved in the project including friends, the models and the hotel concierges. The event became a part of Soho legend with Humphrey Lyttleton's jazz band blaring out, gallons of alcohol consumed, frenzied dancing and debauchery in the darker alcoves.

CHAPTER 27 – THE CONSORTIUM

'You see Mr Harry, the FST, are trying to fit me up as one of Billy Hill's gang that did the Eastcastle Street job a few days ago,' Big Jock explained.

Harry looked at him non-plussed: 'FST?'

'The Fucking Sweeney Todd, the Flying Squad rozzers,' MacGregor replied.

The Eastcastle Street robbery had created a major sensation in government circles and amongst the public. It had taken place at four o' clock in the morning on 21st May 1952 in a quiet road that ran parallel to Oxford Street on its north side. The heist had been carried out with military precision by Hill's mob who were dressed as masked gangsters on the pretence of making a film. Over £280,000 was stolen from a Post Office mail van. Winston Churchill, who had recently become Prime Minister as leader of the Conservative Party, was enraged by the audacity of the raid and ordered hundreds of police officers to solve the crime. The police were fully aware that the robbery was masterminded and executed by Billy Hill but had struggled to come up with any convincing evidence. This, even though Hill was flaunting his bravado by inviting members of the underworld to his suite at The Dorchester

Hotel to quaff champagne under washing lines pegged with five-pound notes strung from the ceiling.

'As sure as eggs is eggs, the bastards are gonna come for me and I have no intention of spending another few years of my life banged up in prison for something I didn't do. When they arrive, tell 'em as far as you know, I've gone back to Scotland to visit a sick relative who's at death's door. Of course, Mr H, that's not where I'll be,' Jock said with a grin on his face and was about to say where he was heading to when Harry stopped him.

'Best I don't know where you are going to lie low. That way nobody can squeeze the information out of me if you get my drift,' Harry advised. He then went over to the safe and took out a wad of notes and pressed them in the big man's hand. 'I'm really sorry we have to part like this. You've done a great job for us Jock. Good luck mate.'

Literally within two hours after MacGregor's departure the door of the studio was battered down and a group of uniformed policemen rushed in led by a man in a smart trench coat and dark green trilby hat. Two of the police officers grabbed Harry's arms as if he was about to escape, which was impossible even if he had wanted to.

'Good afternoon Mr Levi. My name is Detective

Inspector Hancock of the Metropolitan Police's Flying Squad,' the trench coat man stated, showing Harry an identification card encased in a black leather wallet. 'We are given to understand that you employ a man name of Jock MacGregor who we wish to interview in connection with an investigation we are undertaking.'

Unflustered, Harry answered: 'Was it necessary to break down my office door to ask that question? It's going to cost a fortune to have it repaired.'

'Never mind your woodwork problems Mr Levi, just answer my question. Does MacGregor work for you?'

'Well, if your goons can release their grip and my blood can circulate again, I might be able to reply.'

The detective nodded at the officers who were restraining Harry and they let go of his arms.

'Yes, Mr MacGregor has worked for me for the past couple of years.'

'In what capacity may I ask?'

'He carries out several duties. Chauffeur, banking, security guard, courier, administration.'

'You knew he had a criminal record longer than your painful arms when you took him on Mr Levi?'

'Indeed, I did. But he assured me that he had turned over a new leaf and wanted to make a fresh start in life. On that basis, I decided to give him a second chance. Certainly, his work has been exemplary and as far as I'm concerned, has been squeaky clean since he joined us.'

DI Hancock laughed out loud. 'You've heard the expression about leopards not changing their spots? Well, serial criminals like MacGregor are no different. So, let's stop pissing around, my time is precious. Where is the big Scottish git now?'

'He's on compassionate leave.'

On hearing this, the detective and his entourage laughed even louder. 'He's what? That Sweaty Sock doesn't have an ounce of compassion in him.'

Sounding affronted, Harry replied: 'It's true. He went back up to Scotland a couple of days ago. Apparently, one of his relatives is at death's door and he wanted to say his goodbye to them.'

'Hmm, that's jolly convenient, isn't it? Just at the time a major robbery happens up the road, MacGregor scarpers to Jock Land. Don't tell me, he didn't give you details of this relative of his, or where they live?'

'That's very perceptive of you detective, he did

not.'

'Don't come the old acid with me sunshine otherwise I might tell my associates here to leave you with something to think about in your hospital bed.'

'It's true though DI Hancock,' Harry remonstrated. 'In the past he has mentioned about having friends in the Glasgow area but I'm not sure whether that was his destination. He simply didn't disclose any further information.'

'Ok lads, we're obviously wasting our time here. Let's go.'

As they trooped out, Hancock was the last to leave. He tossed a card at Harry: 'If he does contact you Mr Levi, phone me on the number on that card immediately. If you don't, and I find out, you could end up sharing a cell with the Scottish prick once we've caught him.' The DI then trampled over the remains of the smashed door purposely stamping on parts of it to cause further splintering.

From that day on, Harry never heard from Big Jock again. The police did not apprehend him, nor did they manage to prosecute Billy Hill who retired to a life of luxury in South Africa on the proceeds of the Eastcastle job none of which were recovered.

On analysing the commercial success of the Festival of Britain from Levi Photography's perspective, the films Harry had made offered considerable potential for development. He had certainly enjoyed producing them with Sidney and following discussions with Sherry, it was decided that another four shorties, as Harry liked to refer to them, should be made. However, Sherry suggested that the sales of these films should be kept separate from the magazine business. Naturally, the shorties would continue to be advertised in Glamour. But the administration and payments would be handled at the studio, rather than by the printer, Nick Howard, who was overcharging for the work involved with fulfilling orders for the films. Sherry had been on about employing a secretary to carry out clerical work at the studio and this could be part of her duties. Similarly, the replacement for Big Jock could assist with the admin, but Sherry thought this appointment could wait. She and Harry would have to revert to commuting to and from work by the tube for the time being.

Trisha Sutton was the perfect fit for the job as secretary. She was a very attractive recently divorced thirty-year-old. Mrs Sutton lived not far from the studio in Holborn. Although facially her looks were like the film star, Ava Gardner, she was a little fuller in the figure than the Hollywood siren. Her interview with Sherry had gone well. Thankfully, Trisha was not prudish about the business conducted by her new employer. She came with first class references which Sherry had checked with the companies who had provided them.

Whilst contributing greatly to the bar takings of the French House pub, Harry and Sidney wrote scripts for the four short films. Shooting commenced and as previously, walk-on parts were created for the two friends in each of the films. Unlike their earlier counterparts, which were, in the main, sex romps, these films incorporated more sinister themes. The horror movie genre had become popular, and the scripts reflected this. The titles were purposely a double entendre to raise the curiosity of the target audience. "The Grim Peeper," "Esmerelda Gets a Hump," "The Phantom of The Rude Morgue," and "Fangs For The Memory." The setting for all the films was Hever Castle in Kent. Built in 1270, the Castle was the home of Anne Boleyn, wife of King Henry VIII and mother of Queen Elizabeth I. Surrounded by a moat and over 100 acres of land, it was the ideal backdrop for the eerie atmosphere that Harry wanted to create. Through a friend of a friend who worked for the owners of the castle, the wealthy Astor family, Harry negotiated a deal that would make the castle available for the filming. This would take place when the Astors, and most of their staff, were away in Italy for their annual break abroad.

A convoy of two cars and a van made its way to Hever. The cars carried four female models and two male actors who were lookalikes of the famous horror film stars, Bela Lugosi and Lon Chaney Jr. The van driven by Sidney, had Harry, the filming equipment, and costumes onboard. The filming was completed on schedule in eight days. Much fun was had by everyone present in the evenings when some heavy drinking took place and rampant sex between the models and the actors that would definitely not have been suitable for inclusion in the shorties' footage. Whilst willing participants in the drinking sessions, Harry and Sidney stayed well clear of the intimate interludes.

With the editing of the films complete, as planned, advertisements were placed in Glamour to announce their availability. The response was unbelievable. Stocks were exhausted rapidly, and more copies were hastily produced. Some Glamour subscribers were so desperate to buy the films that they started turning up at the studio ready to hand over their cash. Sherry was happy to facilitate this demand. For security reasons, she arranged for a hatch to be built adjacent to the new studio door with a buzzer installed. That way, enquirers could be dealt with without having to allow them into the studio. A wise decision judging by the state of the unsavoury characters that called.

The phenomenal profits from sales of the shorties continued to accumulate throughout the remainder of 1952 and into the following year. This led Harry and Sherry to believe there was potentially even larger sums to be made from the production of longer, feature length films. As part of this move, they would rent or buy a Soho property, like the Walker's Court premises, to show the films. The venue could also act as a club for live strip shows and a shop to sell films, magazines, photos, and other products. However, such a strategy would require substantial financing. Far more than was in the Levi Photography coffers, albeit they were distinctly healthy. The company had long since abandoned its theatre and family portraits business to concentrate on the magazine and films. Whilst the time was right to further expand their sex industry operations, finding the money to make this happen was another question.

The answer manifested itself in somewhat peculiar circumstances on 2 June 1953. Three million spectators were lining the streets of London, most waving small Union Jack flags, and a further 27 million people around Britain were watching the Coronation of Queen Elizabeth II on television. Although the procession was passing within a quarter of a mile from where they were sitting, Harry and Sherry were happy viewing the event in front of their TV in the studio, sipping champagne. With the windows open, the couple could hear the cheers of the nearby crowds standing in the drizzling rain. The BBC commentator, Richard Dimbleby, was describing the scenes to viewers when there was a knock on the studio door. Sherry and Harry exchanged glances as they were not expecting any visitors.

Sherry quietly stepped over to the wall hatch and opened it slightly to see who was at the door. Standing outside were two extremely well-dressed young men, carrying briefcases. They were quite different in appearance from the usual callers wanting to purchase a film.

'Can I help you?' Sherry enquired.

'Sorry to bother you on this auspicious day,' one of the men replied in a well-spoken voice. 'But we were hoping to speak to Harry Levi. We have a proposition that we think he will be interested to hear. It involves the production of feature films with a substantial budget. His friend, Vivian Van Damm, suggested we should get in touch. Is he around?'

Taking two business cards from one of the men, Sherry slid the hatch closed and passed the cards to Harry who had heard the conversation. He nodded his approval to Sherry who went over to the door and showed the men in.

'Good afternoon Mr Levi. Thank you for seeing us. Once again, apologies for interrupting your viewing. My name is Jonathan Styler and this is my colleague Clive Diamond. As you will see from our cards, we are solicitors working for the firm Goldmann & Co. We represent a consortium of businessmen who are keen to open a specialist cinema in Soho. And they would very much like you to make the films that would be screened at their new venue.'

Harry turned down the sound on the television, invited them to take a seat and offered them a drink. They sat but declined the drink.

Gesturing towards Sherry who was standing by the window smoking, Harry said: 'You are aware that we did something similar last year?'

'Yes, indeed we are, and from what we have gleaned, it proved successful,' Styler responded. 'To be candid, that's what gave our clients the idea. But with the greatest amount of respect, our scheme would be on a much grander scale. For example, our cinema would be more of a club. Entry would be by membership only. In addition to films, both feature length and short, there would be live striptease shows, a restaurant, bar, and shop.'

Harry smiled at Sherry then looked at the solicitors: 'We have been considering such a project ourselves. The main constraint though has been financing.'

'Well, the brief from our clients was solely to talk to you today about the making of the films. But, if you wish, we can certainly discuss the possibility of you joining their consortium.'

Before Harry could answer, Sherry jumped in: 'That would depend on the terms. But before we get to that, we'd like to hear more about these substantial budgets for the films. And who exactly the people in the consortium are."

Unfazed, Styler replied: 'Of course. We fully understand. There would need to be much more detailed meetings on that subject. Meantime, reverting to your question about the financing of the films. We are authorised to disclose to you that the consortium has earmarked an initial budget of £350,000 for the first three productions.'

On hearing the figure, Harry just managed to supress a whistle: 'Gentlemen, I'm naturally flattered that your consortium has chosen to approach me. However, I have received such proposals in the past and declined. The reason for this was that the content of the films would have landed me in an institution at His Majesty's Pleasure. Although as of today, I suppose that would be at Her Majesty's Pleasure.'

'Mr Levi, let me assure you that the productions

the consortium have in mind are purely of the "naturist" documentary type and therefore, within the law.'

'What about scripts, casting, make-up artists, location and travel costs, camera equipment etc? If you are talking feature films, I'll need 35mm cameras and film. All my stuff previously has been shot on 8mm.'

'All items for further discussion Mr Levi but I would suggest with the budget allocated, this would not prove problematic.'

'My partner and I would have to discuss the matter. Then, if we decide to go to the next stage, we will need to meet your consortium members before making a final decision.'

'We will relay your response Mr Levi and will be in touch. Thank you for your time.'

The two solicitors rose in unison, shook hands with Sherry and Harry and left.

Harry's euphoria was quickly tempered by Sherry: 'Don't let's get too carried away. It sounds too good to be true. I know I'm naturally suspicious but why were they reluctant to tell us the names of the businessmen? Also, how come their plan was identical to ours? Has somebody been rabbiting about our intentions? Did you let the information slip during the filming of the shorties last year? You know what Sidney's like after he's had a few.'

'Look, get serious, think what we could do with that budget. After costs, we'd be making an absolute packet. Rolls Royce and holiday in the South of France, here we come! What harm is there in at least having a meeting with these bods? Let's face it, if we smell a rat, it's kiss my *tokhes* and we walk away.'

Sherry remained sceptical. Deep down she had a nasty feeling that not replacing Big Jock with someone similar was a mistake. Somebody with the inside track of the movers and shakers on the Soho scene, would be invaluable at this moment.

The subsequent meeting with the consortium members and the two solicitors took place in a private conference room at the Cumberland Hotel, Marble Arch. The four businessmen investing in the cinema project introduced themselves individually and gave Harry and Sherry an overview of their other business interests. Judging by the extent of their empires and the contributions they were making to charities; they were all extremely wealthy. None of the companies they owned were in any way related to the leisure industry. The firms covered all sorts of sectors such as food imports, furniture manufacturing, property development, and ship building. Whilst they agreed that Levi Photography's experience in the glamour market would assist greatly with their plans, initially, their wish was for the contract to be restricted to the making of the films. If this proved to their satisfaction, consideration would be given to Harry and Sherry's company becoming a member of the consortium, if they so desired. Discussion then turned to the type of films the executives had in mind. It was clear that they had done their homework on the subject. The central theme of the productions should be the promotion of the benefits of naturism in a documentary format. By adopting this stance, nakedness of the actors would be acceptable to the censors. Showing the films at a private members' club venue would obviate the necessity of the productions having to carry a British Board of Films Censors certificate. It was envisaged that the first two productions would be shot in Britain. The third would possibly be filmed overseas to add an exotic dimension to the storyline. Levi Photography would have overall responsibility for the making of the films, but the consortium would have final sign-off on scripts and budgets. A draft contract containing these points was handed to Harry and Sherry who said they would talk it through with their solicitor and revert to Goldmann & Co as soon as possible.

At Harry's behest, Michael Mankowitz carried out extensive research into the consortium members and their companies. He couldn't find anything untoward and confirmed that they were Kosher. Coincidentally, they were all in fact Jewish. Likewise, the contract seemed in order although he did suggest a couple of amendments. Firstly, to clarify that if any losses were incurred in the production of the films, they would be the sole responsibility of the consortium. Levi Photography would still receive its fees for the work carried out. Also, to insert a clause stating that on satisfactory completion of the films, Levi Photography would be considered to become a partner in the core business, not just the film making element.

Despite their solicitor's comments, Sherry still had a niggling doubt that there was something not quite right about the set-up. Predictably, Harry was gung-ho to sign the contract. As things turned out, Sherry was to be proved right.

CHAPTER 28 – PORN AGAIN

Once these amendments to the contract were agreed by both parties, a drinks reception to celebrate the signing was held at the Cumberland Hotel. It was here that Harry and Sherry were advised that plans for the cinema club were well advanced, and they would be kept up to date with developments. Meantime, they were urged to get on with the script and casting for the first film. The pair wasted no time in roping Sidney Solomon in for ideas sessions at the French House pub. However, this time, Sherry was involved in the process, so the bar bills were decidedly lower than on previous occasions. As the duration of the film would be one hour long, the script needed to be much more detailed than those produced for the shorties. Most of the content for these had been made up as the shooting took place. Following a good deal of discussion over several days, an outline script was produced. The concept for the new film would centre around two friends, attractive female models, who worked as civil servants in an office in Whitehall, London. The girls lead a somewhat hum drum 9-5 existence handling boring shipping orders. Their lives were devoid of fun, and they yearned to break free and experience the great outdoors. They quit their routine jobs and embarked on a journey that took them to East Anglia where they encountered various characters at locations of historic interest. These included a tour guide in the Roman town of Colchester Essex, an artist highlighting the Constable connection at Flatford Mill and an archaeologist at Sutton Hoo, both in Suffolk, and an actor performing on Cromer Pier, Norfolk. Inevitably, all of these meetings included scenes of nudity which leads the two friends to join a naturist colony adjacent to a sandy beach near Great Yarmouth in Norfolk. The thinking behind this approach by the scriptwriters was that by including locations with a cultural background, a documentary style format could be achieved, thereby keeping the censors onside.

The consortium approved the script and much to Harry and Sherry's surprise, the budget submitted. To keep as much money as possible for themselves, Harry and Sherry had already agreed that she would play the part of one of the two friends in the film. That way her fees could be charged to the budget. Obviously, Sidney would have to receive a fee for the roles Harry had in mind as he would need to pay somebody to run his shop when he was away filming. However, there were other opportunities to generate more income for the Levi Photography pot from the budget. For example, a contact of Harry's ran a nudist camp in Norfolk. This was the reason he had written such a location into the script. This contact had said that his place could be used for the filming for a minimal sum as long it was paid in cash. Other costs such as hotel bills, travel, and backhanders to custodians at the filming sites could be "adjusted" to ensure the Levi share was maximised. The only thing that Harry and Sherry were not able to legislate for was the British weather. The spring of 1954 produced some of the wettest, drabbest conditions on record. As a result, the shooting schedules became protracted. Farcical scenes occurred as the actors and crew literally tried to film in between cloud breaks. Tempers became frayed as Harry screamed instructions through his loud hailer whilst fiddling with his light meter. The actors, particularly Sherry and Jackie Pike, the model hired as Sherry's "friend," complained that their boobs were turning blue from the cold in the nude scenes. The upshot of these delays was escalating costs. After the first location shoot in Colchester, Harry thought he would need to hire some muscle as part of the team. Although the filming was at night with the Roman ruins lit by arc lights, word soon circulated around the local pubs that a film was being made featuring shapely girls. This prompted groups, mainly men, to gather to ogle. Occasionally, things turned nasty with lewd comments and whistles shouted from the onlookers, meaning filming had to be halted. Thankfully, there was no repeat of this behaviour at the other locations as they were more rural and sparsely populated.

Despite these challenges, the filming was finally completed and following some lengthy editing sessions, was ready to be shown to members of the consortium. The screening took place at the soon to be opened premises purchased by the businessmen to house the club. Entering the building, on Dean Street, Harry and Sherry were amazed. From the moment they stepped off the pavement under the portico supported by two cream coloured Ionic style pillars and went through the heavy oak double doors with brass fittings, the impression given was pure class. The extensive reception area continued to reflect this aura. A marble floor of alternating black and white squares was surrounded by oak panelled walls which were adorned with gold framed oil paintings of naked women. The front of the large solid counter to one side was covered with bespoke wine-red chesterfield padded leather. It was big enough to accommodate four receptionists behind it. The overall effect was that of a St James's gentleman's club. Without doubt, this was a cut above other clubs in Soho which tended to be cramped, sleazy dives with poor sanitary arrangements and nicotine encrusted ceilings.

Harry and Sherry were greeted by two attractive female receptionists who guided the couple into the main cinema area, accessed by a door in the same style as the reception counter. Here, at the front of the rows of 250 banked plush red seats, the members of the consortium and the Goldmann solicitors rose from where they were sitting to welcome them. They then invited Harry and Sherry to sit with them and a signal was made to start the film. Two other men in the back row below the projection room remained seated and were not introduced to the couple.

A round of applause broke out from the businessmen when the film ended, and Harry was congratulated with handshakes and pats on the back. As this was happening, Harry glanced up to the back of the cinema and noticed that the two men seated there earlier, had gone. In the discussion that followed, it was explained to Harry and Sherry that the position regarding the film had changed slightly. There was now an aspiration to make the production more widely available at cinemas around Britain. To achieve this objective, certain parts of the film would require further editing to meet the British Board of Film Censors approval. Sequences that included glimpses of Sherry and Jackie's pubic hair would have to be masked out.

Likewise, flashes showing Sidney and the other actors' genitalia would have to be obscured. Harry was quick to point out that this would entail reshooting sections of the film which, together with the hire of an editing suite, would mean additional costs. Responding on behalf of the consortium, the solicitor, Styler, stated that this was understood. And the extra costs would be more than compensated by the greatly increased revenues received from the film's wider distribution. He also stressed that work should commence on the other two films contracted as soon as possible. The only subject left for debate was the title that Harry had given to the film. It was generally felt by the consortium members that "Naturally Bare," would not get passed by the censors. Several alternatives were put forward, but Sherry politely suggested that such an important decision should not be decided by committee. She proposed that more research was required with input from some of Levi Photography's trusted contacts who were the target audience. This was agreed and the meeting was about to end when Harry asked what the club was going to be named. Styler replied that it was to be called "The Cineworld Club." Harry and Sherry were underwhelmed by this news but did not express their opinion as the solicitor took them on a tour of the premises which included the restaurant, bar, and private rooms on the upper floors. All of which were as equally luxurious as the other areas of the building.

Harry and Sherry had concerns that even after the edits were carried out, the film would not be acceptable to the censors. Nevertheless, spurred on by the receipt of a cheque for £29,750 in full payment for the film and the thought of more money coming their way from the changes, they proceeded with the work. Harry had a friend in Wardour Street who owned a Steenbeck editing machine, a massive piece of equipment. It had four spools that enabled the user to load the reel of film and the reel of sound simultaneously to carry out the edits on a frame-by-frame basis. This was a time-consuming exercise as it required marking up the film in the appropriate places, cutting, then inserting the new segments and splicing the ends together with tape. To avoid travelling to all the locations again, Harry shot the revised scenes with close-ups in the studio and undertook the editing. The amended film was then submitted to the consortium who were delighted with the outcome. They also accepted the new title, "Back to Nature Girls," that resulted from Sherry's research. A fortnight later, Harry received a call from Jonathan Styler advising that following a series of meetings with Arthur Wilkins, Head of the British Board of Film Censors, "Back to Nature Girls" had received a certificate of classification for distribution under the documentary category. Harry and Sherry were dumbfounded. Clearly, the consortium had friends in high places. This notion was confirmed at the grand opening of the Cineworld Club which included the premiere of "Back to Nature Girls."

On arrival at the event in September, Harry, Sherry and Sidney, in their best evening dress finery, mixed with the great and the good of British society, as well as show business celebrities and the press. Post war rationing had ended two months earlier but judging by the amounts of champagne and caviar being consumed, this would not have previously affected any of the guests present. It was noticeable that although the members of the consortium and the Goldmann solicitors were attending either with their wives or mistresses, they maintained a low profile. The comedian, Tommy Trinder, who Harry had met previously at the Royal Variety Show, had been contracted to perform a short act before introducing "Back to Nature Girls." The end of the film was greeted by hearty applause and Trinder invited the guests to return to the reception area for more food and drinks. Here, Sherry was immediately surrounded by male admirers who were obviously keen to speak to the woman who had bared her all in the film they had just watched. Elsewhere, Sidney was pinned in a corner by a few ladies who were making comments about his nice bottom that had appeared prominently in parts of the film. The press photographers then got Harry, Sherry, and Sidney to pose together. It was something of a new experience for Harry to be on the other side of the camera during this session. But it did not take the snappers long to break the threesome up and focus their lenses on Sherry separately for most of their shots.

Shortly after the flash bulbs had stopped popping and the photographers were hurrying back to their publications, Harry was approached by two men who introduced themselves as Frank Leach and Harry Fink. They had emigrated from Vienna before the war and after serving in the British army, opened an art gallery in Bond Street. The pair enquired if Harry would be interested in having his photographic work displayed in an exhibition at their gallery. Previous exhibitions they had organised included paintings by Monet, Renoir, Sisley, Degas, and Van Gogh. The current one they were running featured pottery by the artist Picasso. Harry expressed his surprise that they would consider exhibiting his photography but agreed to arrange a meeting to discuss the possibility at their gallery.

Reading the newspaper reviews of the film

over breakfast with Sherry the following morning at the flat in Hampstead, Harry was disappointed. The arts critics who had attended the premiere took a puritanical stance, condemning it as smut. The only one that had any praise was the Jewish Chronicle that hailed the production as a breakthrough in cultural cinema and referred to the fact that the director, Harry Levi, was a former employee of the publication. The article referred to Harry as the "King of the Camera," a moniker that would stick in the future.

The year that followed, 1955, proved even more profitable for Levi Photography. Sell-out performances daily of "Back to Nature Girls," at the Cineworld Club and other cinemas around the UK, brought pressure from the consortium to produce the next two films. Safe in the knowledge that the format of their first production had been passed by the censors, Harry, Sherry, and Sidney adopted a similar approach for scripting the new films.

The first involved a romp around Scottish historic locations combining serious and humorous elements. These included the "stealing" of the Stone of Scone, an oblong block used in the coronation of Scottish monarchs from Westminster Abbey and returning it to Scotland. This real-life incident had occurred a few years earlier. Mayhem was unleashed in the filming with "Nessie" the Loch Ness Monster, a specially constructed huge rubber replica, chasing female naturists swimming in the Loch. Cawdor Castle provided the location for a re-enactment of sequences from Shakespeare's play Macbeth. Scenes depicted the witches, played by semi clad females and Sidney as Banquo's Ghost. Other places featured in the schedule included connections to the poet Robbie Burns, the warrior William Wallace, and the fictional village of Brigadoon, the centrepiece of Lerner and Lowe's hit musical. Unlike the previous year's summer, the weather was sweltering. However, this brought with it clouds of midges that played havoc with the shooting as the actors and crew tried to avoid being bitten by the insects.

The second production in Paris, demanded considerably more logistical planning and the need to obtain permissions to film at certain locations. It proved to be much more of a challenge than the two previous films made. To start with, the French people encountered, such as the police and staff at the locations were generally surly and refused outright to converse with Harry and the crew in English, albeit that many of them could speak it. Fortunately, Harry had anticipated this problem and engaged the services of a good-looking young Parisian girl, Monique, as an interpreter. She was extremely shapely and dressed in the latest chic fashions. These attributes combined with her persuasive charm assisted the film crew's cause considerably when dealing with the authorities. Naturally, the Eiffel Tower featured prominently in the early scenes but most of the shooting had to be done at night under powerful lights to keep the number of onlookers to a minimum. Sequences on a tourist bateaux-mouche boat on the river Seine were much easier to arrange as the vessel could be hired for the sole use of the cast and crew. Likewise, the contracting of a river-side traditional open-air dance hall without the public admitted, enabled the actors to appear in nothing but boaters as they waltzed to the music of an orchestra. Harry abandoned an attempt to resurrect the idea from one of his former shorties for a shoot at Notre-Dame Cathedral featuring actors as Quasimodo and Esmerelda. The officials at the French Ministry of Culture who were responsible for the running of the Cathedral, despite wads of French Francs being waved in front of them, responded with a firm, "Non." The working title given to the film by Harry was "Nature Girls: An Eiffel in Paris." He hoped that the censors would not pick up on the wordplay around "Eiffel" and "Eyeful."

Once again, Sherry and Sidney starred in the

films. However, more actors and models were drafted in this time as it was felt that audiences might become bored with seeing the same people playing different characters in all of the films. Both the new productions were finished on time, but the French one badly overshot the budget allocated. Despite this setback, the films were endorsed by the consortium and finally, after some edits, approved by the censor. Levi Photography netted £52,300 for its work making Sherry and Harry extremely happy, and the latter to embark on another spending spree.

The year ended on a high note with the launch of the Scottish based film entitled," Nature Girls: Windy Kilts." And the opening of Harry Levi's photographic exhibition at the Mount Gallery in Mayfair. Harry had produced a special series of photographs for the exhibition. They included shots of his leading models in poses completely different from the raunchy ones he submitted to Glamour. These images were more artistic and classical in style. The day after the exhibition launch party, attended by members of the aristocracy, politicians, and London's upper-classes, queues formed outside the gallery. However, the visitors eager to view the photographs were mainly from the other end of the capital's social spectrum. They were predominantly men whose knowledge of art was extremely limited. Indeed, most thought that the impressionists were comedians who mimicked famous people.

The success of the exhibition led to the publication of a glossy coffee table book of the photographs entitled "Naked" with an introduction by the Duke of Bannock, a co-owner of the gallery. Following its publication, Harry spent several days at the gallery signing copies of the book for visitors wishing to purchase a keepsake of their attendance. To each signature, Harry added a small drawing of a camera, like that on the front of Glamour magazine, which he had adopted as his personal trademark.

Harry's ever-growing reputation as Britain's leading photographer and film director had made him a celebrity. He regularly appeared in the newspaper gossip columns. The trouble with all this newfound fame was that it went to Harry's head. His personality changed. He became egotistical. Whilst out walking in the streets, he would deliberately seek to be noticed by members of the public. In fact, if he thought someone had recognised him, he created an imaginary camera with his hands in front of his face, said "smile," and made a click noise as though he was taking a photo. When Sherry was with him, she was embarrassed by Harry's behaviour and asked him to desist. But much to her annoyance, he continued.

Harry's status as a celebrity was further enhanced in 1957 when he received an approach from the Labour MP, Frank Longford. The pair had met briefly at the Mount Gallery launch. The politician subsequently invited Harry to a meeting over lunch at the Garrick Club. Thankfully, Harry had decided to put on suit for his visit to the club in Covent Garden. However, he was not wearing a tie. The hall porter advised that this was necessary to comply with the club's dress code and loaned one to Harry. He then led Longford's guest to the ornate dining room the red walls of which were covered in portraits of notable club members. Longford rose from the table and greeted Harry like a long-lost friend. The man was regarded as something of an eccentric. He was in his fifties, tall and thin, mainly bald with a few tufts of hair sticking up from the sides of his head. This, together with his large round steel-rimmed spectacles made him resemble a clown minus the red nose. Longford had held several government offices when Labour was in power and had gained notoriety as a campaigner for social reforms.

He opened the conversation: 'Thank you so much for sparing the time to meet me, Harry. I know you are a busy man. Please call me Frank.'

'To be candid, I was intrigued and honoured.

What a magnificent place this is. I've passed by the door many times but never been in.'

'Yes, isn't it. It was founded in 1831 and named after the famous 18th century actor, David Garrick. It was established for the patronage of actors, artists, authors, and musicians. As you can see on the walls, some of them are looking down on us.' Longford then pointed out paintings of Dickens, Rossetti, and Elgar.

The conversation was interrupted by the arrival of a waiter to take their lunch order.

Longford said: 'I can recommend the roast beef from the trolley. Alternatively, if you prefer fish, the Dover sole is usually excellent.'

Harry opted for the sole whilst the MP stated a preference for the beef. Longford ordered a half bottle of Chateau Neuf Du Pape for himself and a half bottle of Chablis for his guest.

As Harry continued to view the opulent surroundings, his host launched into the reason he had invited him.

'You may have heard that I have been asked by the government to head up a commission of inquiry into the possible relaxation of the laws relating to homosexuality and pornography. I'm putting together a powerful committee including Mary Whitehouse, a schoolteacher who has positioned herself in the press as the country's spokesperson on the decline in moral standards, the Bishop of London, Henry

Campbell, the journalist, Malcolm Muggeridge, and Dr Janice Smith, a Harley Street psychiatrist.'

Harry smiled and replied: 'With all due respect, I suggest they would all hold the same view as you, good Christians who want to retain the status quo, totally opposed to reforming laws around these subjects.'

'Almost spot on my boy. That's precisely the point. They are all a bit like me, old farts. Although I do feel that some reforms are necessary. What we need is to get some younger people on the committee to provide an alternative view. That way the final report can be more balanced and representative of the thinking of today's generation. I've already got the skiffle singer, Lonnie Donegan, to come onboard, and a bright young psychologist, Dr Anita Milner. I'm still waiting for a reply from the thespian and male model, Quentin Crisp. Although he's not young, he is, how can I put it, more inclined to the company of men than women. Hence, he would be able to express the opinions of that community.'

Holding back a chuckle on Longford's last comment, Harry said: 'I did a bit of research on you before coming today. You are a Labour MP, and we currently have a Conservative government. Would they be interested in taking your report seriously?'

'Absolutely. It is they who have requested that I instigate the commission.'

'You saw some of my work at the Mount Gallery exhibition, didn't you?'

Longford interjected: 'I certainly did, and for research purposes of course, I have since purchased a copy of the exhibition book. I've brought a copy along and would appreciate if you could sign it.'

Harry was surprised by this admission but was happy to sign the book. He then explained his concerns about joining the committee: 'The thing is that the exhibition portraits were shot specifically for that reason, to exhibit in a gallery. Most of my work for magazines and films is of a more explicit nature. It's produced for men seeking titillation.'

'I understand that a sort of sex substitute,' the MP responded loudly causing some diners at nearby tables to look across at him. 'Well, I don't have any issue with that. Sex is an integral part of life whether it's actual or simulated. Personally, I have a good sex life. And I've got eight children to prove it,' Frank Longford chortled, again prompting raised eyebrows from fellow diners. 'Providing nobody is harmed as a result, I don't see a problem.'

Harry could not believe how open his host was being on a subject that most people from the upper classes preferred to discuss in hushed terms. And then only with close members of their family. 'I'm still not sure I am the right man for you Frank. Essentially, my reputation has been built on selling this type of material to make a living. What I'm trying to say is that I'm from the other side of the tracks to you and most of the members of your committee.'

'I disagree. Society is changing rapidly. Things that were taboo to speak of in public pre-war are now becoming more commonplace. Just look at some of the articles in The News of the World. It's vital that the government recognises this and considers amendments to the laws pertaining to them.'

The exchanges continued throughout the rest of the lunch and after, in the lounge area where the two men drank coffee and brandy. Frank Longford cleverly incorporated comments in his pleas that stroked Harry's ego such as how sitting on the commission would enhance his reputation. Harry was finally convinced by the MP and agreed to participate.

Longford chaired the first meeting of the group and outlined the objectives of the inquiry and the research that was required to be undertaken. However, it almost ended in disarray as Mrs Whitehouse rounded on Harry accusing him of profiting from immoral earnings. Throughout her outburst Harry sat back in his chair and grinned, causing his antagonist to become even more incensed. The chairman managed to restore calm and reassured everyone that ultimately all their views would be debated before the final report was submitted. He then requested Harry and Dr Anita to do some fieldwork by visiting sex shops in Soho, or as he referred to it, "the square mile of depravity." The aim of the exercise was to purchase magazines that the panel could review at the next meeting.

The doctor and Harry hit it off from the outset. She was vivacious with long black hair, a pretty face that did not require any make-up and a perfectly proportioned figure. A good salary allowed her to dress in the most current fashions. The pair found it difficult to contain their laughter as they jostled amongst men in these establishments who tried to avoid eye contact with their hats pulled down onto their foreheads. At one shop, the proprietor asked the couple why they were buying so many magazines. Dr Anita replied that they were doing some important research, to which the man responded: 'That's what they all say!' As expected, at the next meeting called to look through the magazines bought comments such as "disgusting" and "an affront to common decency" from the more traditional panellists. Whilst the liberaltarians said "live and let live." The divided opinions did not alter following visits by the group to strip clubs around Soho. A few months later Frank Longford advised that he felt the panel had gathered enough information from its research in Britain. But to make the report more comprehensive he believed, how homosexuality and pornography were considered overseas should be examined. He therefore arranged a trip to the red-light district in Amsterdam. To his disappointment, only Harry and Dr Anita Milner volunteered to join him on the excursion. Their experience was a total contrast to the activities they had encountered at the clubs in London. Performances at the clubs in the Dutch "City of Sin," were much more explicit. Actual intercourse took place on stage, between heterosexual and homosexual partners. Sometimes these included members of the audience. Harry joked under his breath: 'Now that's what I call audience participation.' Whilst the doctor and Harry giggled during these shows, Longford was appalled, and on one occasion, returning to their hotel, he was physically sick in the street.

Back at the hotel, Frank Longford made his apologies and retired to his room, declining the offer of a nightcap from Harry and Dr Anita. The pair continued to chat and drink Scotch into the early hours. During their time together, despite the fact he was taking pictures and filming some of the most beautiful girls in Britain posing naked on virtually a daily basis, Harry had remained faithful to Sherry. It was therefore totally unexpected when he suddenly had the urge to make a pass at the shapely fun-loving doctor, who he had become attracted to. Perhaps it was the drink, viewing the shows, being away from home, or a combination of all three, that prompted Harry. As a heavy drinker, Harry was able to manage the alcohol consumed much better than Ms Milner. Seeing his companion was about to nod off, Harry suggested: 'Time for Bedfordshire, I think. We have an early start tomorrow.'

The doctor rose unsteadily to her feet and almost slumped back into her chair when Harry grabbed her arm and supported her over to the lift. Once inside, with no other occupants present, Harry planted a kiss on Anita's lips and was gratified to feel the warmth of her reciprocating rather than a rebuke. As Harry led the doctor along the corridor to her room, she swayed from side to side and between giggles, hummed the tune of Lonnie Donegan's "Puttin' on the Style.' Arriving at the door, she fumbled in her handbag for the key, but could not insert it into the lock. After several attempts, Harry took charge and opened the door but in doing so, released his grip on Anita who fell headlong into the room. Unhurt, she rolled over onto her back and burst out laughing. Kicking the door closed, Harry picked her up and placed her gently on the bed. He began kissing her on the lips and neck, fondled her breasts, and undressed her. Meanwhile, Anita slurred the words of "Puttin' on the Style," instead of humming them. Meeting no resistance to his actions, Harry assumed the doctor consented to what was about to follow. He pulled his clothes off and slipped on a condom. She seemed fully cognisant of what was occurring as he made love to her although her part in the sex was somewhat passive. But she did continue to sing and wave her legs around a bit during the ten minutes before Harry came. Both then fell asleep.

They awoke with a start at the knocking on the room door.

'Dr Milner, are you awake? It's Frank Longford. I've tried to rouse Harry but there's no response from his room. I guess he's gone down for breakfast.'

Staring at Harry in a bemused manner, Anita replied: 'Sorry, I've only just got up. I'll be down to join you shortly.'

She waited until she heard the footsteps padding away then spoke: 'What happened last night? Did we, you know?'

'I think we both overdid the Scotch,' Harry explained.

‘I realise that, but did we have sex? If we did, I hope you took precautions,’ Anita asked.

‘Yes, don’t worry, I did. The evidence is in the bathroom bin.’

‘I must have been really drunk. You have to believe me. It’s not the sort of thing I do usually.’

‘Me either. But the thing is, I think I’ve fallen for you.’ Harry said.

‘I like you a lot too, but you’re married.’

‘Well, in actual fact, I’m not.’

There were no further exchanges as they showered together. Harry then left and headed for his room for a change of clothes.

After three days of exhaustive research, the trio flew back to London with suitcases filled with the sexually explicit material collected. At their debriefing with the other members of the committee, once again, things turned acrimonious. Mary Whitehouse could not contain herself listening to Frank Longford’s detailed description of what the research team had experienced in the clubs they visited. She stormed out of the meeting declaring that she wanted no further part of the inquiry. It soon became apparent that consensus would not be reached amongst the committee about the recommendations that should be made in the final report. To try and placate everyone, without reference to Government officials, Longford extended the remit of the inquiry. However, the inclusion of issues that had no direct relevance to pornography or homosexuality such as sex education in schools made the 500-page report rambling and inconclusive. It was dismissed by Parliament and the press with one journalist describing it as, “a thousand parts chaff to one part wheat.”

Despite agreeing a cooling off period, Harry, and Anita Milner, embarked on an affair shortly after the report was published.

CHAPTER 29 – LOOK BEFORE YOU LEAP

Surprisingly, it was the consortium that started to press for negotiations to commence regarding Levi Photography joining its ranks as a partner. Their move came immediately following the premiere of "Nature Girls: An Eiffel in Paris." The film received marginally better reviews than its predecessors, but this had no effect on the phenomenal box office takings at cinemas around Britain. The Levi company had fulfilled its part of the contract by producing the three films. The consortium had checked Levi Photography's financial status and knew it would not be able to stump up the cash required for partnership. But they coveted the Glamour Magazine business. And with Harry now an established celebrity, the consortium saw an opportunity to utilise the positive publicity surrounding him to its own ends.

A meeting was convened between the consortium, its solicitors and Harry, Sherry and their legal advisor, Michael Mankowitz. The Cineworld Club concept had successfully been expanded to include venues in Birmingham, Manchester, Newcastle and Glasgow. To become a partner in their leisure industry business, the consortium outlined it was seeking an investment of £100,000 from Levi Photography. Harry, Sherry and Mankowitz adjourned to a separate room to discuss the proposal.

Sherry opened the conversation: 'That's us buggered. We don't have that sort of money, so let's come clean and tell them, thanks but no thanks.'

'Hold on a second. If we used the Glamour operation as our contribution, perhaps they would accept that?' Harry retorted.

'Wait a minute.' Mankowitz interjected. 'You are not the sole owners of the Glamour business. You seem to be forgetting about Nick Howard's stake.'

'We could buy his share out,' Harry said.

'With what Harry, peanuts? Your latest spending extravaganza has left the bank account low on funds,' Sherry advised.

'Okay, I know I've splashed the cash recently but one of my better decisions, that you agreed with, was to buy the Hampstead flat. I could use that as collateral to get a bank loan to raise the money to buy Howard out.'

'What if Nick Howard won't sell? Glamour has been a lifeline for him.' Mankowitz asked.

'Everyone has their price. We just need to convince him it makes sense,' Harry responded.

Becoming irritated by Harry's usual failure to think things through properly, Sherry sounded a note of caution: 'Look, we already have a decent business with Glamour and the prospect of making more films. We also have a nice property that we own. Why should we risk everything on this deal?'

'I've gone through the consortium's financial accounts and the projections it is making,' Mankowitz pointed out. 'There's no doubt that the profits to be had by Levi Photography, as a partner, would be many times greater than from your current operations. However, at the end of the day, it's a big decision. And it must be made by you.'

Seeing that the discussion had reached an impasse, Harry suggested: 'Let's go back in and sound them out regarding the Glamour idea. If they reject it, then that's it. We walk away, and I promise I will not mention the whole thing again.'

Looking somewhat relieved, Sherry agreed and the three of them re-joined the meeting with the members of the consortium. Although they were fully cognisant of the Glamour business financials, the consortium feigned ignorance, and advised they would need to get their accounts team and solicitors to consider the matter. They would then revert to Harry for further discussions regarding the proposal.

A week later, Harry received a telephone call from Jonathan Styler of Goldmann & Co. He said that the consortium was prepared to accept the proposal but there was a proviso. Its searches had uncovered that in addition to Sherry and Harry, there was another shareholder in the Glamour operation. The deal could only move forward if Glamour Magazine was totally owned by the consortium. In other words, it was not prepared to have Nick Howard involved. Harry replied that he understood the consortium's position and would get back to them with an answer as soon as possible.

Michael Mankowitz's warning regarding Nick Howard became evident at the subsequent meeting at the printer's factory. Despite Harry's offer, which increased several times during the conversation, to buy out his share of the business, Howard was intransigent. Resigning himself to the fact that the Levi Photography would, regrettably, not be becoming a partner in the consortium, Harry contacted Styler to advise him of Nick Howard's decision. He shared the news with Sherry and Mankowitz and assumed that was the end of the road for the deal. It therefore came as something of a surprise when, just a few days after, he was contacted by Styler who told Harry that Mr Howard had had a change of mind. Following a great amount of soul searching and consultations with his family, the printer had provided written confirmation to Goldmanns that he was relinquishing his involvement in Glamour with immediate effect. Harry asked the solicitor how much Levi Photography would have to pay for Nick Howard's shares, but Styler said that this had been taken care of. However, to cover the arrangement with the printer, the consortium wanted Harry to sign a lien on his Hampstead flat. They also required Harry to become the public face of the consortium. If he consented to both stipulations, a contract for partnership would be drawn up.

Excited by this news, Harry could not wait to tell Sherry and Michael Mankowitz. The latter stated that this sounded like an ideal solution, subject to contract of course, as Levi Photography would not have to pay interest on a bank loan. But Sherry still had reservations. She could not understand why Nick Howard had relented from his dogmatic position literally within hours of the meeting at his place. As always, anxious to progress things, Harry dismissed her point and requested Styler to send the contract to Mankowitz's office. On receipt, he and Sherry sat down with the solicitor and went through it. Everything appeared to be in order and Harry instructed

Mankowitz to proceed. The contract signing took place the following week in one of the Savoy Hotel's private rooms. Glasses of Laurent Perrier Rose Champagne were raised to celebrate Levi Photography formally becoming a partner in the consortium. On leaving, Harry picked up one of the unopened bottles of champagne and said he wanted to present it to somebody as a gift.

Outside, Harry asked the doorman to hail a taxi from the rank adjacent to the hotel. Once he and Sherry were inside, he gave the driver the address of Nick Howard's printing works.

'You fucking bastard. Come to gloat?' Howard screamed at Harry from a badly bruised and swollen face that had traces of dried blood from cuts on parts of it

Harry and Sherry were stunned by the printer's appearance.

'Nick, what the hell happened?' Harry asked.

'Don't come the innocent with me. You know exactly what happened, you sent them.'

'Nick, please believe me, I have no idea what you're talking about. Sent who? We have come here today to thank you for agreeing to sell your share in Glamour. I brought a bottle of bubbly so we could toast you.'

'You sent your Yid gangster mates Jack Spot and Moishe Blueball to "persuade" me to sell. I told them no and this was the result,' Howard said pointing to his face. 'They then got me to sign some documents, threw a big bag of tenners on the floor and warned me if I grassed on them, my missus and kids could disappear.'

Harry tore at his hair and almost tearfully exclaimed: 'I knew nothing of this Nick. I was assured by the solicitors representing the consortium who now own Glamour that they had come to an arrangement on a final settlement with you. I am not a violent person. There's no way I would have been a party to what has happened to you.'

'As far as I'm concerned, you and your tart are just a couple of two-faced liars Harry. But if there's any truth in what you've said, you've dropped yourself in deep shit. The people in your consortium are just a front. The whole thing is run by Jack Spot's criminal gang. Now get out of my sight. Get out!'

Harry and Sherry sheepishly left the champagne on a desk as they departed the factory and boarded the taxi they had told to wait for them. They were in a state of shock at what they had just learnt and said nothing on the journey back to Soho.

Staff had gone for the day by the time Sherry and Harry arrived at the studio. They sat down with a cup of tea to discuss what had occurred at the printing works.

‘What have I done?’ Harry whined. ‘You didn’t clock those two blokes in the back row of the first showing of “Back to Nature Girls,” did you?’

‘No, I didn’t,’ Sherry replied.

Harry paused before saying: ‘It was dark but I’m sure one of them was Jack Spot’

‘What, “the” Jack Spot?’ Sherry asked.

‘Yes, the Jewish East End gangster who’s head of London’s underworld. He runs gambling at the racecourses, drinking and gaming clubs, vice rings and protection rackets.

‘Bloody hell, you think he’s part of the consortium?’

‘Well, according to Nick Howard, yes. I can’t think why else he would be present at a private showing of the film. And clearly, he did not want to be introduced to us.’

‘So let me get this right Harry, you are saying that Levi Photography is now part of a crime syndicate. Correct?’

‘Honestly, at this moment I don’t know what to think. But on the evidence, it would appear that’s the case. I will go round and see Michael in the morning to get his opinion. He was the one who checked out the consortium and told us it was kosher.’

The following morning, Harry decided to walk to his solicitor’s office in Bedford Row,

Holborn. He had a hangover from the half bottle of Scotch he consumed the night before and wanted to clear his head. Shortly after leaving the studio, he went into a telephone box and called Anita Milner and arranged to meet her for lunch after he had seen Michael Mankowitz. The session with the solicitor proved inconclusive. Mankowitz insisted that he had carried out comprehensive searches on the consortium members' companies and there was no hint of impropriety. There were certainly no signs of a connection to the criminal underworld. He tried to placate Harry by stating that he would instigate further research. But this time, recruit the services of a private investigator who would speak to his streetwise contacts about Jack Spot's activities. Harry was not particularly reassured by the solicitor's comments. He had hoped to hear categorically that London's top gangster was not bankrolling the consortium his company had just joined.

Harry started to pour out his woes to Anita over lunch in a café in Theobald's Road round the corner from Mankowitz's office. Afterwards, he suggested that they go to her flat in nearby Gray's Inn Road, for coffee so that he could finish the story. As it turned out, he had an ulterior motive. He persuaded Anita that it would help to calm him down if they could discuss it in bed. Although at first reluctant, Anita finally succumbed to Harry's pleas and the couple spent the rest of the afternoon engaged in two lengthy periods of love making.

Quite unexpectantly, Harry and Sherry received an invitation from Sherry's parents to join them on a holiday. Concerned that their daughter had been working non-stop for the past two years without taking any time off away from the business, the Browns wanted the couple to have a fortnight break at a house they had rented on the coast at St Malo in France. With everything that was going on in respect of the consortium partnership neither Harry nor Sherry were keen to accept the invitation. However, after discussing the matter, it was agreed that Sherry would go. But as Harry was snowed under with photographing models for the upcoming editions of Glamour, he would have to decline. Obviously, this decision suited Harry fine as he would be able to spend more time with Anita during Sherry's absence.

Only a day after Sherry's departure, Harry received news he had been dreading. Sitting in Michael Mankowitz's office Harry looked at his solicitor's grim facial expression which gave an indication of what was to come.

'Our detective friend's digging has unearthed some worrying information. It would appear the consortium members' companies are money laundering outlets for Jack Spot's illegal gambling operations,' Mankowitz advised. 'The talk is that he wanted Glamour to augment his Cineworld Clubs and vice businesses.'

Harry put his head in his hands and said: 'I don't get it. Why didn't he just set-up a competitor magazine of his own?'

'That's not the whole story Harry. He wanted you, Mr Celebrity, as the front man for the consortium. As well as having you on call to produce more films for his cinema chain and supply photographs for the magazine he now owns.'

'This is a bloody nightmare, Michael. How do I get out of it?'

'That's not going to be an easy thing to achieve. People that have crossed Spot in the past are now residing in concrete pillars supporting bridges on the new motorway in Preston. He has eyes and ears everywhere, and lots of friends in top positions. They include MPs, senior police officers, judges, solicitors, entertainers; you name it, and he will likely have them in his back pocket. I think your best bet for the moment is not to do what you usually do.'

'What do you mean?'

'I mean don't act like a *mushuganah* and rush into doing something stupid. Bide your time and see what happens. An opportunity might arise for you to extricate yourself from this mess without ending up brown bread. Keep me posted on developments but always on a face-to-basis. Apparently, that bastard can have your phone tapped by his pals in the force. And for god's sake, keep *schtum* about your concerns. As I've said Spot has loads of informants on his payroll.'

'Message received loud and clear,' Harry said. He shook hands with Mankowitz's and left. Later, he met Anita for dinner and then took her to the theatre to see "My Fair Lady,' a musical starring Rex Harrison and Julie Andrews, that had recently opened in the West End. During the interval, Harry was approached by several people who had recognised him. He did his trademark camera simulation to all of them which made Anita cringe in the same way as Sherry. The pair then went back to Anita's place for the night.

The Soho Fair was scheduled to take place the following weekend and Harry had been serving on the organising committee in the preceding months. The Fair was a popular annual event organised by local businesses. It included an open-air art exhibition in Soho Square, dancing to jazz bands in Golden Square, food and drink served by restaurants from stalls outside their premises, and a parade with floats around the narrow streets. Levi Photography would have a float under the banner of "Soho Visual Arts Club," a thinly disguised name to promote photography as an art form. The flat back lorry would have props to depict a seaside scene. It would carry some of Harry's models in swimsuits throwing a beach ball to each other and handing out leaflets to the crowds. Harry would be onboard pretending to take pictures of the girls with a camera. Each year, the highlight of the Fair was the Waiters' Race. This event involved around seventy waiters from Soho restaurants in their uniforms carrying a half bottle of champagne and two glasses on a tray in a race starting in Greek Street and finishing at Soho Square.

The day before the Fair, Harry picked up the phone and was immediately nervous when he heard Jonathan Styler's voice.

'Hello Harry. Hope everything is good with you. The consortium understands you have a float in the Soho Fair. Is that right?'

'Yes indeed. It's something we do to keep onside with the local community,' Harry confirmed.

'Very laudable. The consortium thinks it would be an ideal opportunity to show your support for it by handing out leaflets to the crowds.'

'In fact, we are already intending to do that. It's just a bit of PR for photography as art really. One side of the leaflet talks about that and the other, a few points about how to take better photos.'

'Good stuff. But the consortium would like you to also distribute pamphlets promoting the Cineworld Club.'

Harry took a deep breath before answering: 'Well that could prove a bit tricky. You must realise that this is an event attended by thousands of people, some of whom are families with children. Leaflets with details of a gentleman's club being seen by kids might not go down too well with the police, or the organising committee.'

'I appreciate your concern Harry but there's no need to worry. The pamphlets don't have any pictures of naked girls on. They are very tasteful. Besides, you will brief the lasses on your float to only hand the leaflets to men along the parade route.'

Harry was about to counter but Styler continued in a tone that was more order than request: 'The thing is, a leading member of the consortium is planning to run the bookie's stand for the Waiters' Race. He and his associates want you to display a board on your float showing the odds for the contestants in the race.'

'As far as I'm aware, the local Italian bookmaker, Albert Dimes, operates the betting stand for the race,' Harry advised.

'That arrangement will change by tomorrow, Harry. It would be in everyone's interest, especially yours, that the consortium's wishes are complied with. The leaflets will be delivered to your studio this afternoon. The board with the odds chalked on will be placed on your float just before the parade sets off.'

Harry started to reply when the line went dead. He was shaking and poured himself a large scotch to steady his nerves. There was no doubt in his mind that the leading consortium member Styler was referring to was Jack Spot. Harry's first task as part of a criminal organisation had been allocated.

As per Styler's dictate, the leaflets were delivered. And in fairness, whilst not exactly tasteful, they were in no way offensive. Harry stayed at the studio overnight as he had to be up early the following morning. Sherry telephoned from France to wish him luck for the Fair. She asked why he had not answered when she called the flat on previous evenings, but Harry made excuses about working late and staying in town. The sun was shining brightly, and the weather forecast predicted a very hot August day. Perfect Harry thought, it would prevent any gripes about being cold from his models in the bikinis he had arranged for them to wear instead of the swimming costumes originally planned. Walking up

Greek Street towards Soho Square, he was surprised to see Albert Dimes setting up his bookies stand. Spotting Harry, he beckoned him over and in a thick Italian accent said:

'Hiya Harry. Good day for it eh?'

'I hear you have some lovelies lined up to be on your float.'

'That's right. It should raise the blokes' temperatures higher that the weather.'

The two men laughed.

'Harry, you know that bastard Spot tried to get me to handover my betting booth to him for the duration of the Fair. I told the guys he sent to tell me to fuck off. I've been doing my bookies thing for donkey's years at the event and I'm not relinquishing it to that Yiddish wanker. No offence meant Harry.'

'None taken, Albert. I see what you mean though. Let's hope an outsider wins the race and you have a profitable day. Must go and get my float ready now. See you later.'

Harry continued up Greek Street before turning right into Manette Street through to Charing Cross Road where the floats were parked in readiness for the parade. A couple of set designers that Harry had hired from the Prince's Theatre in Shaftesbury Avenue were already securing the props in place on the flat back lorry that would be the Visual Arts Club float. Harry greeted them and checked they had brought the boxes of Cineworld and Visual Arts leaflets he had asked them to pick up from the studio. The boxes were stacked neatly behind some large cardboard palm trees at the driver's cab end of the vehicle. The designers were putting the finishing touches to a wood log-look bar structure made of thick cardboard. Their next task was to spread sand on the floor of the truck to create a beach effect. The last things to be placed onboard were the sun loungers, cocktail glasses, and beach balls.

The six models Harry had contracted for the day arrived an hour later. They had changed into their bikinis at the studio under the supervision of Trisha Sutton and walked round to the float in t-shirts and shorts. As Harry briefed them on their duties, hundreds of people poured out of Tottenham Court Road tube station and from the buses, all heading to the Fair. Shortly after, the parade moved off slowly, north up Charing Cross Road, west along Oxford Street and then South into Soho Street and Soho Square. It comprised twenty floats, vintage cars, and a Messerschmitt bubble car. Music blared out from the skiffle group playing on the 2 i's Coffee Bar float and jazz from the band on the Marquee Club float. Others carried the Soho Fair Queen, a huge barrel organ, and staff from restaurants and bars handing out free samples to the crowds.

Volunteers rattling buckets walked alongside the floats collecting charity donations for the House of Barnabas Chapel in Soho Square. Contributions would be put towards stained glass windows in the side apses that needed replacing.

Amidst the cacophony of noise, a bulky figure was pushing his way through the crowds with one purpose in mind. Jack Spot was sweating profusely, his long strands of combed across hair were stuck to his head. Nobody but nobody ignores an order from the head of London's gangland. Failure to rectify this situation would show weakness on his part to his competitors. Albert Dimes was going to pay for his misdemeanour. Spot reached the bookies' stand but there was no sign of Dimes. Two of the Italian's men were taking bets from members of the public keen to have a flutter on the Waiters' Race.

Jack Spot had a good idea where his adversary would be hanging out. The Bar Italia in Frith Street was the epicentre of the Italian community in the area. Spot's assumption was correct, bursting through the café's door, he rushed over to Dimes who was sitting at a table in the corner drinking coffee, and started to punch him. Now Dimes, whose real name was Dimeo could handle himself. He was a small-time criminal who in addition to his bookmaker's business, organised illegal bare-knuckle fights where gambling took place. As the two men traded blows, tables and chairs were turned over, and other customers fled the café. With honours equal, both men pulled out knives and proceeded to slash at each other. The café owner, who had been cowering behind the counter, suddenly jumped up and smashed a bottle of Campari over Spot's head. As he did so, the gangster fell forward stabbing Dimes in the chest as he did so. The Italian stumbled and plunged his knife into Spot's back before hitting the floor.

News of the fracas travelled fast around the surrounding streets and police on duty to marshal crowds at the Fair were quickly on the scene. An ambulance was called, and the two men lying in pools of blood and Campari, were taken to hospital.

Harry heard about the fight when he returned to Soho Square after the parade had ended. He stood and wondered how this would affect him and the consortium. If Jack Spot was dead, it could provide an escape route for Levi Photography. Harry continued to ponder the possible outcome as the Waiters' Race reached a climax with screams of excitement from the spectators. He bought an ice cream and started walking to Anita's flat in the searing heat.

CHAPTER 30 – CARRY ON REGARDLESS

It transpired that Jack Spot and Albert Dimes recovered from their injuries. But as they were discharged from hospital, both men were arrested. At the trial, the vicar of St Barnabas, the Reverend Basil Andrews, testified that Dimes had started the fight. This development together with the appearance of Spot's stunning wife Rita, made a positive impression on the male judge and jury. And ultimately, Dimes and Spot were acquitted. The result was that it was not just the combatants who were in stiches, it was London's underworld as well. The Rev. Andrews was known to the criminal fraternity as "the knocking parson," who had a reputation for defaulting on his gambling debts. He had been paid to lie on behalf of Spot by Moishe Blueball.

This whole debacle had an adverse effect on Jack Spot's status as the self-appointed head of the underworld. He had become a laughing stock and could see that a challenge from gangs in the East End and South London was imminent. Literally overnight, he upped sticks and retired with his wife to the Costa del Sol in Spain. The empire he had built over several years, including the consortium, was sold off.

The relief was palpable for Harry. Levi Photography was no longer part of a criminal organisation. To counter this however, his sources of income, including film making for the consortium, Glamour Magazine and the Cineworld Clubs had all gone. In addition, his ownership of the Hampstead flat had disappeared in the fire sale of Jack Spot's assets. Harry would have to revert to paying a rent to the property company that had acquired it. To compound matters, Harry was also having problems with his relationships.

Sherry had returned from France looking suntanned and relaxed. But she quickly became suspicious of Harry's activities during her absence. She found out from chatting to Elsie, the cleaning lady who worked at the flat, that Harry had hardly been there while Sherry was away. Casually talking to Trisha Sutton, with whom Sherry had become friendly since employing her, she gleaned that Harry had not been staying overnight at the studio either. Obviously, this information was contrary to what her partner had told her. Things came to a head in a blazing row between the couple at the studio.

'What do you take me for Harry? I'm not an idiot. You told me you'd mainly been staying in town which I naturally assumed meant here at the studio.'

Becoming agitated, Harry shouted: 'That's right.'

'You're a liar. Trisha says you have not been bedding down in the studio.'

'Well, not every night. I did get back to the flat occasionally.'

'No, you didn't. Elsie said you haven't slept there at all. You just left your dirty washing there. And that was only once.'

'Sherry, please calm down. Don't you see I've been at my wits end worrying about this whole business with Jack Spot and the consortium.'

'Your big end is all you've been interested in. And the question is, who have you been putting it in? Who is she? Who have you been shagging while I was away?

'Don't be ridiculous, you know you're the only one for me. I love you.'

'I don't believe you. You might as well come clean. I'll find out her name eventually.'

'Trisha and Elsie must be mistaken; I have been sleeping at the studio.'

'I trust their word more than yours. Why would they lie to me? I pay their wages.'

'I don't know. Maybe they've got it in for me for some reason.'

'Now you're the one who's being ridiculous. Why on earth would they have a downer on you?'

Harry remained silent.

'What's up? Cat got your tongue?' Sherry screamed. 'I'm going home to Mum and Dad's. Don't contact me until you're prepared to tell me the truth.'

Harry pleaded: 'Sherry, please don't leave. I need to talk to you about the business.'

'What's there to talk about Harry? You fucked up big time. As usual, Mr Ego had to drop us in deep doo-doo by signing up for membership of London's most notorious criminal gang.'

Sherry stormed out in tears slamming the door behind her. Harry sat on the sofa for a few minutes before rising and pouring himself a large scotch. He drank several more then fell into a deep slumber. This time he really was sleeping at the studio. Waking three hours later feeling dreadful, he went into the bathroom and looked at himself in the full-length mirror. The stress of the consortium issue had taken its toll. His face was gaunt with dark lines around his eyes. Grey flecks had started to appear in his hair. It was apparent that he had also lost some weight as his ribs were more pronounced.

Still in a morose state of mind, Harry decided he would pop round to Anita's to unload his woes. He wouldn't bother to telephone but surprise her with a bunch of flowers he'd buy on his way there. He walked up to New Oxford Street and boarded a bus. It had only gone two stops when it slowed to walking pace behind a queue of traffic. Further ahead there was a band playing and singing. Passengers on the bus were craning their necks to see what was going on. Harry asked the conductress who replied:

'Another one of those bloody ban the bomb Campaign for Nuclear Disarmament marches. Plays havoc with the traffic. They're probably walking to St Paul's. Don't see the point personally. Can't see the Russians taking any notice of CND before dropping the bomb on us. All I know is that we'll be back late to the depot, so I'll miss me tea before having to turn around and go out again.'

Harry decided it would be quicker to walk and soon found himself alongside the marchers who were singing "Brother Won't You Join The Line?" At the front of the march, he spotted Canon John Collins of St Paul's and the philosopher, Bertrand Russell. Both had featured in newspaper articles recently

Round the corner from Anita's flat was a florist where Harry bought a bunch of mixed roses. He knocked on her door holding the bunch behind his back. There was no response and Harry was about to move off when the door opened ajar. Clearly surprised to see Harry, Anita was dressed only in a flimsy silk dressing gown.

Before she could speak, a male voice boomed out from inside the flat:

'Who is it? Come back to bed.'

Anita's face went bright red. 'Harry, I'm so sorry. I was not expecting you.'

'That's pretty obvious, isn't it?' Harry replied as he tossed the flowers on the step, turned, and walked off.

Harry waited while Sidney closed up his shop. He too had been jilted a few days previously by his girlfriend, so the pair of them went off to drown their sorrows. Harry had become a member of the Colony Room in Dean Street. It was one of a number of private drinking clubs that had sprung up around the area to get round the licensing laws that stated that pubs had to close at certain times. The Colony was run by Muriel Belcher, a foul-mouthed woman who had managed to attract well-known actors, artists, writers and creatives generally, as members. In fact, Belcher came from a wealthy Midlands family of Portuguese Jews. She was brought up as a lady. However, after she moved to London, all traces of her strict upbringing disappeared.

Having climbed the stairs that led to the club, Harry was signing Sidney in as a guest when the host's dulcet tones rang out from where she was seated on a stool at the bar sipping a gin and tonic. She was fifty but looked ten years older and had black hair tied back tightly in a bun. Her dark semi-circular eyebrows accentuated a furrowed forehead and long angular face. Her skin tone reflected her Iberian heritage.

'Look what the cat's dragged in. Hello, it's cunty Levi the porno snapper and her latest lover.'

Harry laughed and shouted back: 'Good to see you too Muriel.'

Belcher's rudeness was legendary in Soho. As a term of affection, she referred to all male members as "she." And the stronger the profanity used was an indication of how much she liked the person.

As he and Sidney made their way to a vacant table in the corner, Harry acknowledged some of the regulars drinking around the room including the painter, Francis Bacon. The Colony's décor was awful. The moss green carpet and originally white, but now cream walls and ceiling were badly stained. Spilt drinks and nicotine being the main culprits for this look. The front and backdrop of the bar were covered in bamboo with plastic palm trees positioned at each end. The ill-conceived idea was to give the place a Caribbean theme to make Belcher's Jamaican girlfriend, Carmel, feel at home. The place was notorious as a hot bed of gossip and having a terrific atmosphere.

Muriel Belcher slid off her mock leopard skin

topped bar stool and moved unsteadily over to the table where Harry and Sidney were seated. Between draws on her cigarette perched precariously in a holder, she slurred:

'This bloke was in asking for you earlier Harriet.' Belcher threw a business card down. 'Something about a new film he's making. Said can you give him a call.'

Harry picked up the card which stated Peter Rogers, Film Producer. The name rang a bell, but he could not think where he had heard it.

'Cheers Muriel.'

'Too fucking right cheers Harriet. That will be a large G&T for your host's personal delivery service. I'll put it on your tab which by the way, is looking a bit serious. Payment on your next visit, we're not the fucking Provident you know.'

Belcher then wobbled back to her place at the bar.

On the stroke of 11pm, Muriel Belcher screamed: 'Closing time. Drink up and fuck off back to the sewers where you live.'

The members duly negotiated the stairs down to Dean Street, some better than others. The effects of the scotch he had consumed in the afternoon, followed by the session with Sidney, had left Harry in a state where he could barely stand. His friend supported him as they walked back to the studio. There, he deposited Harry on the sofa and left.

"Good morning, Harry,'

Rubbing his eyes, Harry squinted up at Trisha Sutton.

'What are you doing here?'

'I work here. Remember? I run the place when you're indisposed. Which recently, seems to be most of the time.'

Harry pulled himself up into a sitting position, scratched his head, and asked: "What day is it?'

'Tuesday,' came the secretary's stern response. 'I'll go and make you a strong coffee.'

After drinking the beverage, Harry had finally gathered his thoughts.

'Thanks for dropping me in it with Sherry,' he said sarcastically. 'You're aware she's buggered off back to Essex I suppose?'

'Yes, she called me to advise what had happened between you. But let's get one thing straight. I did not tell tales about you. I was asked a question by Sherry as to whether you had spent nights staying here and I told her the truth.'

'Well, that's not quite correct, is it? I did stay here.'

'Yes, you did but that was just one time. The night before the Fair. And that's exactly what I told Sherry.'

More conciliatory Harry replied: 'Ok, ok. I messed up and now I regret it.'

'I know I shouldn't talk to my employer like this but here goes. The trouble with you Harry is that you can't keep it in your pocket, can you? Instead of appreciating what you've got, you always must go in search of another conquest. You're like an overgrown teenager on heat. You don't think about the consequences that your actions might have. Sherry was the best thing that has happened to you. Just grow up. That's my piece said. I'll get on with some work now. There's a stack of bills that you need to pay.'

Harry knew deep down that Trisha's Sutton's comments were accurate. He just couldn't bring himself to accept them. He shuffled into the bathroom for a triple "S," and a change of clothes. When he emerged, the phone was ringing. The noise was not helping his thumping headache. Trisha held her hand over the mouthpiece.

'It's a Peter Roger's secretary. Are you available for a lunch meeting with him today at Schmidt's at 1 'o clock?'

With a quizzical expression on his face, Harry was about to ask Trisha to find out more details when he remembered the card that was given to him at the Colony the night before. At the same moment, despite his hangover, he recalled where he had seen Peter Roger's name. He was the producer of the film "Carry On Sergeant" that he had taken Anita to see a couple of weeks ago.

'Fine, say I look forward to seeing him there.'

Walking through Soho towards Fitzrovia for the appointment Harry thought to himself that this Rogers must be a bit of a *schnorrer*. Surely, L'Étoile, the restaurant almost opposite Schmidt's in Charlotte Street would have been a more suitable venue for lunch. It was a favourite of the film producer Alfred Hitchcock and Hollywood stars such as Gregory Peck. Conversely, Schmidt's was known as a dining on a budget place. The restaurant was an institution in the area which historically had been the German quarter of London. And its location was often referred to as Charlottenstrasse.

The pungent smells of Schmidt's Delicatessen hit Harry's senses as he approached the establishment. The cause of this aroma was the array of continental sausages hanging above the counter laden with German bread, jars of pickled cucumber and tins of various European produce. The restaurant, on the first floor, had wooden floorboards on which surly waiters, reputed to be the rudest in London, wearing black waistcoats and long white aprons scurried between tables. In the centre of the room was a wood and glass booth where a female cashier sat. During the war, Schmidt's owners had put posters in the windows stating they were British, not German.

Looking around the restaurant Harry spotted a man waving a napkin and beckoning him over. Harry's eyes lit up when he saw that the man was accompanied by a gorgeous blonde who he immediately recognised as Leigh Madison, an actress who appeared in "Carry On Sergeant."

Peter Rogers cut a suave figure. Immaculately dressed in an expensive light grey suit. His well-groomed dark hair was tinged with grey, but his tan, tight facial features and white teeth gave him the appearance of someone younger than his forty-four years.

At just twenty-four, Leigh Madison was stunning, and Harry was having difficulty in not staring at her. Her blonde curly hair sat neatly on her shoulders and her pale complexion with a spattering of freckles was accentuated by her dark arched eyebrows. Sparkling blue eyes and a perfect small nose completed the picture.

'Thanks for coming at such short notice Harry if I may call you that. I'm Peter Rogers and this is my friend, the actress, Leigh Madison.'

'Pleased to meet you both,' Harry said shaking hands with Rogers and kissing Miss Madison's hand as he sat down.

Before anyone could utter a word, they were

pounced upon by a waiter who barked the specials of the day out and waited impatiently for their orders.

'Please give us a moment to look at the menu, my guest has only just arrived.'

The waiter walked away briskly muttering under his breath.

Rogers poured Harry a glass of Riesling and smiled: 'I love it here. The ambience is much better than Elena's Étoile or Bertorelli's. Damn sight more reasonable too.'

Harry agreed but knew his suspicions about the film producer being a tight wad had been confirmed. All three of them opted for the bratwurst and sauerkraut and as they ate, Peter Rogers explained the reason he had asked to meet Harry.

'Have you seen my latest film, "Carry On Sergeant?" It's only been on release a few weeks but the response to date from the critics and filmgoers has been extremely encouraging.'

'I have, and I thoroughly enjoyed it. I thought you were great Miss Madison. In many ways, it reminded me of my recent films but less risqué.'

'That's exactly why I wanted us to talk. I've seen your productions and I believe that you would be the ideal man to direct my next film. You have a flair for comedic situations. And you know how to capture the actresses at just the right angles if you get my gist. Leigh here is going to star in the next film together with most of the cast that were in Sergeant. It will also be a Carry On but set in a hospital. If it proves as popular as the current film appears to be so far, we could make lots more Carry On productions in the future based on different themes.'

'Sounds interesting but why aren't you using the director from Sergeant?' Harry enquired.

'Gerald's a nice guy but frankly, rather temperamental. The actors complained that he was too exacting and wouldn't give them any leeway to occasionally interpret the script a little off-piste. Kenny Williams was particularly critical of his behaviour in this respect. I'm keen to keep a steady ship with the actors and crew in harmony for the next film. Isn't that right Leigh?'

The actress was somewhat taken aback to be brought into the conversation as if she was merely present for decoration. But she wholeheartedly agreed with the producer's comments before resuming eating.

Harry finished his glass of wine which was quickly topped up by a waiter that was hovering close by.

'Well, of course, I'm flattered that you have thought of taking me on as the director. It would depend on several things though. I currently have a few offers I'm considering,' Harry bluffed. In reality, he desperately needed income.

'I understand. I was sorry to hear about the problems you had with that consortium you were involved with. However, I'm hopeful you will be able to look favourably on my proposal after thinking it through. Perhaps you would like to come out to Pinewood Studios to meet the cast. We are doing script read-throughs now. Afterwards, quite separately, we can talk about money and terms?'

Harry was miffed that Rogers had found out about his ill-fated venture with the criminal syndicate. But was not really that surprised as like most industries, gossip was rife within the film making sector. Following a bout of such gossiping over the dessert of apple strudel and coffee, Harry arranged to meet Peter Rogers at Pinewood and said farewell to the producer and the actress.

When he arrived back at the studio, his decision to attend a follow-up meeting proved to be timely as he thumbed through the pile of unpaid invoices on his desk. Amongst them was an official looking envelope marked strictly confidential/addressee only, with an Essex postmark. Trisha, who had left for the day, had not opened It. The letter was from Sherry's father's solicitors. The contents stated that Harry's business partner had resigned her directorship of Levi Photography and that Companies House had been notified accordingly.

Any thoughts that Harry might have had regarding a reconciliation with Sherry had gone.

CHAPTER 31 – LIFE BEGINS AT FORTY

My God, what an outfit, Harry thought to himself as he travelled back in a taxi to Slough Station from Pinewood Studios. He had received a warm reception from the cast and crew of Carry On Nurse. The read-throughs of the parts of the script he had sat and listened to alongside Peter Rogers, were entertaining and included a few double entendres. The best exponent of these was Kenneth Williams who had the part of Oliver Reckitt, a patient in the hospital. His gurning was extraordinary and had other cast members in fits of laughter. He had a large head with sharp features and a slim body which gave the overall impression of a reincarnated Dickens character.

Williams was a compulsive gossip and during a break, took Harry to one side and told him about the leading cast members. According to Williams, several members of the cast were at it like rabbits at every opportunity. Also, that Harry should beware of Charles Hawtrey who was a homosexual constantly chasing young men. And Sid James was so saddled with gambling debts he had to accept every work offer to pay them off. His final piece of advice was to be aware that the producer, Peter Rogers, was in Williams words, as tight as a water rat's arsehole. Apparently, the senior actors were on a standard contract for each film of just £5,000. Bearing in mind his lunch meeting, this information came as no surprise to Harry. Later in the day, Rogers had said when they met in his office that the maximum he could pay Harry to be the film's director was £10,000. Considerably lower than the industry norm for such a project.

Harry was in no position to refuse. He had accepted the offer subject to contract which Peter Rogers advised he would have drawn up and delivered to the Soho studio as he wanted Harry to start immediately. With his bills mounting daily, Harry had tried to negotiate an initial payment, then the remainder of his fee to be paid monthly. However, Rogers would not accede. He said he would need to see how Harry performed and the fee would be paid in equal monthly amounts retrospectively.

Since Sherry's departure, Trisha Sutton had added the role of bookkeeper to her office duties. The day after the Pinewood meeting, she sat down with Harry, and they went through the accounts. The picture was gloomy. She told Harry that the landlords of the Hampstead flat had been in contact and in a forceful manner pointed out that unless the outstanding rent was paid in full, they would have no option but to evict Harry. A similar call had been received from the owner of the garage in nearby Poland Street. Harry's car had been in storage there for months as Harry did not drive. The garage's unpaid invoices needed to be settled immediately otherwise the car would be seized in lieu of payment. These were the main debts that required action as well as arrears on the studio's rent. Other invoices pending ranged from camera equipment purchased to basic items such as the daily milk deliveries.

'How did you get on with the bank manager last week?' Trisha asked.

'Not well,' Harry replied. 'He was not prepared to provide a loan as I did not have any collateral. I mentioned the car, but he was not interested. The bastard also mentioned the fact that Sherry resigning as a director had not helped my cause. He'd obviously been making enquiries at Companies House. The meeting ended on a sour note. I lost it a bit by reminding him that he was only too happy when the cash was rolling in from the films we made. However, now things were stretched, he didn't want to know.'

'Hmm. Not sure that was the right thing to say. Something tells me he's not going to be sympathetic towards Levi Photography in the future. Clearly, you are going to have to make some unpalatable decisions.'

'Like what?'

'Firstly, you'll have to move out of the flat and sell some of the contents like those expensive paintings you bought. That will be one major expense saved. You can live here at the studio like you used to. Secondly, from your first month's fee from the Carry On film, you must pay the garage what they are owed and sell the car. The cash you receive should clear the flat and studio rents together with most of the incidental amounts such as the Colony Room bar bill. That ghastly Belcher woman keeps reminding me of it every time I bump into her in the street. After that, it's essential that you set aside what you require to cover the bills each month from your fee payments. From what you've told me, it sounds as if this Carry On contract could be a rolling thing with a new film produced every year. That will put you on a sound financial footing moving forward. In addition, I know you will baulk at this, but you will have to go back to doing some photographic assignments.'

'As always, good advice Trisha. Much appreciated. I'll get onto it tomorrow.' If he was considering putting any action off, the post the following morning made him think again. A letter from his ex-wife Marie's solicitor stated that if the outstanding maintenance payments were not addressed, court proceedings would be issued.

Over the subsequent months Harry adhered to Trisha Sutton's advice and the company's financial situation improved. However, it was still far from stable. On a positive note, the filming of Carry On Nurse went well. Shooting finished early in 1959 and plans were made for the premiere at the Carlton Cinema in London's West End in March. Applause rang out at the end of the film from the audience of celebrities and critics. The cast and crew of the film were in an exuberant mood when they decamped from the premiere to the nearby Café de Paris for the after-show party. Everyone had imbibed on champagne at the cinema and as more was drunk at the night club along with wine and spirits, the gathering became more raucous. Hardly anyone was sober.

During the filming at Pinewood Studios, Harry had struck up a friendship with a young camera assistant called Lola. It was an entirely platonic relationship that had not gone beyond chats over cups of coffee in breaks between filming. She was fascinated to hear about Harry's career in photography and films and aspired to follow a similar path. Lola was in her late twenties and dressed in a boyish style with caps, sweaters, and slacks. She was extremely attractive with shiny brown hair tied in a ponytail. Sitting together at the dinner table, Harry suggested that they get some air outside and have a cigarette. Both were intoxicated. As they rose from their seats, the partygoers started to hoot and whistle making lewd comments which the couple laughed at as they headed for the back door. However, one member of the ensemble, Charles Hawtrey, who was not drunk noted the departure of the pair and nodded at a man sitting at another table. The man, who was carrying a canvas bag, rose and followed Harry and Lola. Hawtrey was furious about Harry's constant rebuttals of his amorous advances during the filming and was intent on getting revenge.

Once outside in the deserted dark alley behind the venue, Harry started to kiss Lola who could barely stand. Meeting no resistance, he lifted her sweater, loosened her bra and proceeded to gently caress her breasts. For the first time in such a situation, his tool was failing to rise to the occasion. The amount of alcohol he had consumed had obviously taken its toll. He unzipped his flaccid penis and asked Lola to take him in hand. Giggling loudly, she complied and in a somewhat haphazard manner embarked on a series of jerky motions. Just as the desired result was beginning to occur, the couple were startled by a flash bulb which was swiftly followed by another.

'Oi, come back here,' Harry yelled as the

photographer ran off. Letting go of Lola he attempted to give chase but stumbled landing face down and gave out a scream as his penis connected with the paving stones. Harry picked himself up and went back to Lola who had slid down the wall and was singing "Rub-a-dub dub." With his ardour now gone, Harry helped Lola readjust her clothing and the pair staggered back to the party. They were greeted by another round of bawdy cheers and table thumping as they slumped back in their chairs. Charles Hawtrey merely smirked.

Harry had almost forgotten about the strange incident that had taken place behind the Café de Paris until he picked up the News of the World newspaper a few days later. The headline that bannered the top of page three read, "What a Carry On!" Underneath was a picture of a startled Harry and Lola with the area of his penis blanked out. However, the position of Lola's hand clearly showed what was happening. The caption stated: "Carry On Nurse film assistant gets to grips with director Harry Levi." The short article that was written below was filled with double entendres that had been cleverly cross-referenced to the film.

Harry was dumbfounded. Who would want to do this? He could have understood if there had been a blackmail attempt, but there had not. Lost in thought, the telephone rang.

Kenneth Williams whining voice screeched: 'I told you to beware of that poofter Hawtrey, didn't I?'

'Was it him then?' Harry replied.

'Course it was. Bloody little snake. He wanted to drop you in the S, H,1, T with Rogers because you wouldn't play ball. Or rather with his balls,' Williams opined.

'Can I prove it was him?' Harry asked.

'He's too clever for that. If you challenge him, he will deny it. He will probably say it was your own fault. That you should keep your cock under control.'

The day after, Trisha arrived at the studio and handed the daily newspapers to Harry that she had bought on the way in.

'You need to read through these. They've all got articles citing the incident shown in the Screws of the World yesterday. It was just the excuse they'd been waiting for to run these types of articles. Banging on about how films like the Carry Ons are lowering the country's moral standards and the behaviour of people like you are ruining young people's minds.'

Harry groaned at the verbal onslaught: 'It was just a bit of fun. We were both pissed. Nothing happened. Just a bit of slap and tickle.'

Trisha bristled: 'Bloody hell Harry. How many times do you have to be told? Just as you're getting back on the financial straight and narrow, you end up caught with your pants down. You realise this will not go down well with Peter Rogers, don't you?'

'You know the old saying. All publicity is good publicity. This will boost box office takings for Carry On Nurse, not harm them,' Harry chuckled.

'Let's hope you are right,' Trisha stated before starting her office duties.

Just before five o' clock, the phone rang. Trisha's raised eyebrows said, I told you so, as she advised Harry it was Peter Rogers for him.

Harry smiled feeling sure Rogers was about to congratulate him on achieving so much publicity for the new film. The reality was quite the opposite.

'I've been inundated with calls and letters from the media and protest groups. All were taking the tact that the film I produced is smutty and that was bound to happen if I employed a porno director.'

Harry was stung by this accusation and hit back: 'That's their opinion, the public love the film.'

'You may be right, but I must do something to get myself out of the mess you've created. I'm sorry Harry but Nurse will be your first and last Carry On film. I cannot risk another storm like this when the next film is released.

Harry was stunned by the producer's comments: 'This is all a storm in a teacup Peter. It will blow over in a few days. You know the old saying, today's news, tomorrow's chip paper, and all that. Rest assured; box office revenues will not be hit.'

'I have consulted our publicity company and they have told me that the only way out of this predicament is to let you go.'

Harry was about to remonstrate when the line went dead. He looked at Trisha with a hangdog expression. She simply shrugged and carried on typing.

As Harry had predicted, the furore regarding his antics and the aligned debate on Britain's moral standards evaporated after a few weeks. He had received a call from Kenny Williams revealing that Peter Rogers had reinstated the director of Carry On Sergeant to undertake the work on the new production, Carry On Teacher. Williams was not best pleased as he intensely disliked the man and would have much preferred Harry to continue in the role. He went on to say that he would speak to his colleagues in the business and recommend Harry for film and photography work.

Despite these kind words, Harry had to face up to the fact that he was unemployed and had no option but to act on Trisha's words of wisdom.

Therefore, he put out feelers to his contacts on the picture desks of newspapers and magazines and a steady stream of assignments came in. The income would at least enable him to keep the wolf away from the door and pay essential bills. Most important of these was Trisha's salary as he had come to rely on her more and more in recent times. Indeed, he had become very fond of her.

Throughout the following months of 1959, Harry covered a wide range of projects as a photojournalist, very much in the vein of his time at Vogue. These included the opening of the Mermaid Theatre in the City of London, the first crossing of a new invention, the hovercraft, between Dover and Calais, and the launch of the British Motor Company's new concept car, the Mini. There were also two local Soho music themed stories: The release of pop star Cliff Richard and The Drifters record, "Living Doll," the group had risen to fame performing at the 2 i's Coffee Bar in Soho, and the opening of Ronnie Scott's Jazz Club in a basement in nearby Gerrard Street. But perhaps the most ironical job of all was on Harry's 40th birthday the 29th of July. He was sent to photograph the MP Roy Jenkins and Lord Justice Birkett outside the Houses of Parliament holding copies of the newly introduced Obscene Publications Act.

The year ended on a surprising note. After a whirlwind romance, Harry proposed to Trisha, and they were married at Caxton Hall Registry Office in Westminster. Sidney Solomon acted as best man. There was a generally good response to the invitations sent out but Harry was disappointed that many people did not reply. These tended to be acquaintances he had met during the period when he was a regarded as a celebrity by the press. Now things had changed, it seemed these contacts no longer wished to keep in touch. He likened the situation to what his mother experienced when his father died.

The wedding reception was held at The Goring Hotel a little way further down Victoria Street. In an amusing speech at the event, Trisha highlighted anecdotes explaining how she had tamed her man who was finally ready to settle down. Whilst outwardly endorsing the bride's words with applause, most of the guests present doubted that Harry would ever live up to Trisha's expectations.

1960 arrived and Kenneth Williams came up trumps by keeping to his word about introducing Harry to some of his showbiz and literary pals. Harry was commissioned to take the photographs for books beings produced by the BBC featuring two of their most popular radio programmes, "Hancock's Half Hour" and

"The Navy Lark." Williams starred in the former alongside Tony Hancock, Sid James, and Hattie Jacques. And of course, Harry knew James and Jacques from his ill-fated time filming "Carry On Nurse." Whilst the Nurse trio were great fun to work with, he found Hancock a morose and difficult character. This surprised Harry as the star of the show was a comedian by trade. It was as if he was acting the part he played in the programmes of a down-at-heel man living in a run-down house at 23 Railway Cuttings, East Cheam.

Conversely, "The Navy Lark," cast were a joy to work with. The main stars, Leslie Phillips, Jon Pertwee and Stephen Murray were a bundle of laughs. The sitcom depicted the life of the crew onboard a fictional Royal Navy frigate, HMS Troutbridge. Harry was able to get creative with shots including maritime related material obtained from the BBC props department.

Two more opportunities that emanated from Kenneth Williams followed shortly afterwards. The first involved a subject dear to Harry's heart. Battersea Dogs Home, the charity, wanted to produce a calendar to sell to raise money towards the running of the place. Harry had always had a soft spot for animals. His last cat, Tiddles, had finally died, probably of overeating. Before that, his dog Goldie had remained with his ex-wife, Marie, when they split up. Harry had an extensive portfolio of shots of both pets and took this along to his meeting in Battersea. The custodians of the home were impressed and briefed Harry on their requirements for the calendar. Although the establishment was called a dogs home, the charity wanted to communicate to potential donors that the place also cared for cats. Therefore, they emphasised the calendar should reflect this by featuring an equal number of each species. Apart from that stipulation, Harry was given carte blanche as to how the animals were depicted.

Whilst he appreciated it was not exactly a ground-breaking idea, Harry suggested that he should photograph the animals in scenes reflecting the seasons of the year. For example, a dog sitting in a deckchair on a beach wearing a straw hat for the month of August. To keep costs to a minimum, Harry advised that he could take most of the shots in his studio as he had background screens and props that could be utilised.

To his amazement, Harry thought the shoots went well. The animals were ferried across to the studio on different days escorted by a handler from the Battersea Dogs Home. In the main, they were well behaved and reacted well to Harry moving them into various positions to achieve the desired results. The only setback was on the occasions when the animals had a call of nature and Trisha was begrudgingly called upon to clear up their mess.

Kenny Williams second introduction was altogether a different proposition to that of the charity calendar. The comedian had had dealings with the founder of Penguin Books, Sir Allen Lane, when writing a book of amusing short stories published by the company. From their chatting while filming Carry On Nurse, Williams was aware of Harry's involvement a few years earlier with the MP Frank Longford's government commission on pornography and homosexuality. Penguin was facing prosecution for its planned publication of D H Lawrence's novel, *Lady Chatterley's Lover*, Williams thought Harry's knowledge gleaned working on the commission would be invaluable to the publishing company. He could have a dual role acting as a consultant but also taking photographs of the Penguin Books senior executives and their defence counsel for use by the press.

Whilst Lane was enthusiastic about Williams's suggestion, Penguin's defence barrister, Gerald Gardiner, was less so. He argued that involving Harry Levi, a man with a questionable history in the production of controversial films and magazines, might have a detrimental effect on the company's case. A compromise was reached in as much as Harry would be retained as a consultant but kept in the background. He would not be asked to carry out photoshoots, or to act as a witness for the defence during the trial. Penguin had already lined up some noted authors and dignitaries for that purpose.

The Director of Public Prosecutions brought the case against Penguin Books under the Obscene Publications Act which had come into force the previous year. The trial commenced at the Old Bailey in London in October. Despite the fact that the author of the book, D H Lawrence, had died thirty years earlier, the authorities had been looking for an opportunity to ban his works. Penguin's intention to publish *Lady Chatterley's Lover*, was the perfect conduit. Passages in the book covering sexual intercourse between Lady Chatterley and her gamekeeper, Mellors, when read out in court were described as obscene by the prosecutor, Mervyn-Griffiths QC. His words: "Is it a book you would even wish your wife or servants to read," brought laughter amongst the jury and reflected the out-of-touch views of the upper classes.

The prosecution fought on gamely to the end. Even the judge, Mr Justice Byrne, in his summing-up erred on the side of the prosecutor by saying the low price of the book would make it available to all and sundry. Thereby, in an aloof manner, inferring even the working class would be able to buy a copy. It took the jury just three hours to unanimously determine that Penguin was not guilty of producing an obscene publication. Contrary to legal tradition, the judge did not thank the jury for their verdict.

The outcome of the case was widely reported by the media as the advent of an era of sexual freedom. The book sold over two million copies within the weeks following the trial.

Harry was paid handsomely for his contribution in helping Penguin Books to win its legal battle. However, the whole exercise had reignited his desire to get back to producing films and magazines with sexual themes. He was in no doubt that there was a public appetite for this sort of material. And the Lady Chatterley trial had proved there was now less likelihood of falling foul of the Obscene Publications Act.

CHAPTER 32 – THE ESTABLISHMENT

As to be expected, having helped to get Levi Photography back on a sound financial footing, Trisha was not enthused about her husband's entrepreneurial aspirations.

'Get real darling, we do not have the money needed to re-enter the film or magazine business. You're talking big bucks,' she pointed out.

'I realise that but I'm sure that if we dig around, we can find backers,' Harry said.

'What? With our track record. It's not exactly glowing, is it?'

'That's history. People would have forgotten about that by now.'

'Something tells me not. You seem to be forgetting the bank manager's comments when you last touched him for a loan.'

'Well, he's just a silly old fart. A dying breed. No different from that snooty lot who prosecuted Penguin. They won't accept things have changed. They no longer rule the roost. It's the public, the working class, who set the agenda now.'

'Yes, but that snooty lot you refer to are the ones with the money. Either them or the gangsters like those you came a cropper with as part of the consortium.'

'Ok, ok, no need to rub it in. I screwed up. But I won't get caught like that again. Once bitten and all that.'

'We're doing ok. You did some profitable jobs last year. Let's build on that and not take unnecessary risks.'

'I'm sure Kenny Williams might know some potential backers he could put us in contact with.'

'He's already done so much for us. Don't push it. Be content with what we've got.'

This was the first major disagreement the couple had had since they were married so Harry was anxious not to take it to another level. He bit his lip and acquiesced. However, he firmly believed they were missing out on the new wave of public liberalisation towards sex. He was determined to develop his dream despite his wife's pessimism.

Kenneth Williams still lived with his parents in Marchmont Street, Bloomsbury. Harry arranged to meet him nearby his home in the bar at the Tavistock Hotel in Tavistock Square. It was built ten years before and was the first hotel to be constructed in London after the Second World War.

Harry was the first to arrive for the meeting. He sat in the lobby and admired the fusion of greens and pink colours that had been used to decorate the place. Williams made a grand high camp entrance soon after. He played up to the hotel staff who knew him well with his trademark catchphrase, "Oh, stop messing about," in his whiny nasal voice. The two men shook hands and embraced.

'Thanks for coming Kenny, what will you have?'

'Just a cuppa for me please luv. I've got to be at Pinewood later for rehearsals on the new Carry On. It's called "Carry On Cruising." Bloody stupid plot as usual and same crap wages but I have to keep a straight head.'

Harry ordered a scotch for himself and tea for Williams.

'Thanks again for those introductions last year, they worked out really well.'

'My pleasure dear boy. Least I could do after the way you were stitched up by that little creep Hawtrey.'

'You followed the Lady Chatterley trial I guess?'

'Me and the rest of the British public. A triumph for common sense. Finally put all those old fogeys in their place,' Williams cackled loudly.

'The thing is, I think there's still much mileage to be had out of it,' Harry half whispered.

'Ooh, tell me more.'

'You know I had film and magazine businesses.

They were very lucrative. Trouble was, I got duped by some nasty shysters.'

'Yes, I do recall reading about it. You're well out of that,' Williams exhaled.

'Now the law has been relaxed regarding the contents of films and publications, I believe there's big money to be made from projects that will titillate the public's appetite.'

''ere. I hope you're not tapping me up for some dosh. I haven't got a pot to piss in. Still living with mum and dad round the corner. The miserable amount I get paid for my film work by that tight arse Peter Rogers would not buy a roll of film, never known make one.'

'No, of course not. I'm not angling for that. I just thought you might know some legit and I emphasise, legit, potential backers for such a project?'

'Off the top of my head Harry, not really. The only people who might be worth a try are the ones investing in The Establishment Club that's scheduled to open in Greek Street.'

'I heard something on the Soho grapevine about that."

'One of the bods behind it is Peter Cook. He used to write stuff for my act but has since climbed the greasy pole somewhat. Bit of a piss artist but a nice guy though, a very funny man. I'll let you have his number.'

On that note, Williams made his apologies and departed for Pinewood. Harry ordered another scotch, pulled out a cigarette and mulled over the interesting information that had been imparted.

'I thought we agreed that you were not going to contact Kenny,' Trisha asked.

Harry was immediately on his guard when hearing this assuming Williams had phoned while he was out with the telephone number he promised.

'Oh that, it was just a quick drink for an update. He wanted to tell me about the latest shenanigans on the set at Pinewood. You know what an inveterate gossip he is.'

"So, you didn't ask him for help sourcing backers then?'

'Not directly, but he did give me some interesting info that could lead to some photography work on our doorstep.'

'And what might that be?'

'You've heard of that bloke Peter Cook, the one who was in that satirical show "Beyond the Fringe" with his university mates?'

'What about him?'

'According to Kenny, he's opening a club called The Establishment, in Greek Street. They're bound to need pictures of the opening and the acts performing there so I thought it would be good to get in early to see if there's some work for us.'

'Sounds like it's worth following up. Cook's number is on the pad,' Trisha advised.

Harry breathed a sigh of relief: 'I'll call him later.' He waited until Trisha popped out to pick up some groceries and then made the call. Fortunately, Kenneth Williams had alerted Cook that Harry might be in touch, so the comedian was happy to fix an appointment to meet the next morning at 10. The location was the office of the new satirical magazine, "Private Eye," in Carlisle Street, Soho.

Puffing at a cigarette and holding a tumbler of vodka, Peter Cook was sitting in a tiny room with peeling wallpaper. His long legs were crossed, propped on the desk with his brown Chelsea boots displaying a hole in each of the soles. Dressed in a sandy coloured safari jacket and jeans, he greeted Harry as if they had been chums for years.

'Pull up a pew and park your bottom,' Cook said in a posh accent with a slightly nasal tone. 'Ken has filled me in on your background. I'd heard of you of course, mainly through the newspaper coverage on those nudie films you made. Also, your time on Longford's porno committee. Seems you are a bit like me, an antidisestablishmentarian,' he guffawed. 'Fancy a drink? What's your poison?'

Even for Harry, 10 o' clock was a bit early, so he declined but asked for a black coffee. Cook bawled his request out and a dowdy looking young man in T-shirt and jeans, appeared a few minutes later with the drink in a chipped mug.

Harry then outlined his vision for a combined film and magazine company and that he was seeking investment from suitable backers. He had come well prepared and pulled out papers with financial projections for the new company that he had put together in recent weeks. But before he could continue, Peter Cook stopped him.

'Look Harry, I'll be frank. I'm up to my eyeballs in projects at the moment. As Ken has told you, I'll shortly be opening a club in Greek Street. We've met a lot of problems with the council about planning etcetera. The establishment has got wind of the news that we are going to be taking the piss out of them, especially the politicians, so they are making life difficult. But we've got some great acts booked. Comedians and musicians, so we are confident the club will be a winner. Then, there's this place, the magazine. I'm going to be taking a controlling interest in it shortly. And on top of all that, I'm contracted to do some television work with my dwarf mate, Dudley Moore. I simply do not have any spare time or cash for anything else. Besides, nudie films and mags are not really my bag.'

Harry sighed and began to gather up the documents he had laid out on the desk when Peter Cook chimed in again.

'However, I have recently come across a couple of gentlemen who could be interested in your venture. They are going to provide a service at The Establishment Club when it opens. Would you like me to mention your scheme to them?'

'That's very kind of you Peter. What are their names?'

'They are twin brothers who have their fingers in many pies in the London area. Their names are Reginald and Ronald Kray.'

The surname rang a vague bell with Harry, and he handed his business card to Cook for him to pass on to the twins. Before he left, he managed to tie up a deal with the comedian that he would provide photographic work for the club's opening and circulate the prints to his newspaper picture desk contacts. In return, he would reduce his fee and he would be granted membership of The Establishment.

Feeling pleased with the outcome of the meeting, Harry decided to walk round to Sidney's shop and tell him the good news.

'The Krays Harry, have you taken leave of your senses?' Sidney exclaimed.

Harry looked bemused. 'Why?'

'I thought you of all people, who's supposed to know everything that goes on in Soho, would have heard of those pair of East End gangsters. They muscled in on this area after Jack Spot did a midnight flit.'

'Shit, I thought the name was familiar, but I was so desperate not to turn down Peter Cook's offer of an introduction, it didn't register with me.'

'It doesn't surprise me that they've got their hooks into Cook's new club. They are obviously going to be providing "protection" for the place. I think one of them is in prison currently serving a short sentence for GBH.'

'What shall I do Sidney? Trisha will go ballistic if she finds out.'

'If I was you, I would just keep *schtum* for the time being. If what you tell me about Cook being so snowed under with other things, he might forget to pass your details on. Let's pray that's the case.'

'I could call Peter back and ask him to forget it. I could say that I've dropped the idea as something else has come up.'

'Well, that's a bit sudden, isn't it? You only left him ten minutes ago. Whatever you think is best. It's up to you.'

In a state of extreme anxiety following Sidney's comments, acting on impulse, Harry telephoned the Private Eye office and asked for Cook. He was informed that he had just missed him, but they would ask him to call Harry back as soon as he returned.

'Damn,' Harry said. He left Sidney's and headed back to the studio hoping Cook would contact him sooner rather than later.

Harry told Trisha about the positive news of securing the photography work for the opening of the new club. Unsurprisingly, he did not recount details of the other part of his meeting. The rest of the day passed uneventfully, and Harry hoped that Sidney's words about Peter Cook's busy schedule might prove to be correct. His peace of mind was shattered the day after when Trisha passed him the phone with a quizzical look on her face saying it was a Mr Hart regarding Harry's meeting with Peter Cook.

Richard Hart stated he was speaking on behalf of his cousin, Reginald Kray. He advised that Mr Kray would like to meet with Harry. Trying desperately not to show his nervousness to Trisha, Harry could not start to make up a story why he no longer needed to meet. He therefore agreed to a meeting later in the week at the suggested venue, an East End pub, The Blind Beggar in Whitechapel.

In the days leading up to the trip to the East End, Harry made some discreet enquiries about the Krays. What he heard was far from comforting. Apparently, the twins were treated like royalty in the East London community. Anyone who had disrespected them or their family over the years were either no longer around or bore the scars of their encounter with the pair. Their criminal activities included murder, armed robbery, arson, protection rackets, assault, money laundering and gambling. It was muted that they were even connected to the US mafia. The only glimmer of hope for Harry that came out of his conversations was that the Krays were keen to improve their public image. They craved to be treated like celebrities, seen at high profile events with film stars and entertainers. It occurred to Harry that this latter wish could prove to be a possible escape clause for him.

The Blind Beggar was a spit and sawdust type London pub. It had a redbrick façade with a double arch entrance supported by three mock Grecian pillars. It had some history to it. An inn had been on the site since the 1600s and William Booth, the founder of the Salvation Army, had made his first sermon there in 1865. Looking around the place on entering, Harry did not think it was the sort of place Booth would frequent nowadays.

Richard Hart welcomed Harry and introduced him to Reginald Kray who was sitting at a table flanked by two burly cohorts. All three had a pint of beer in front of them. Kray insisted Harry should call him Reggie and ordered a large scotch for him. He was a pugnacious looking character with thick black hair greased back in a slightly flattened quiff. He wore a smart navy suit, white shirt and a narrow black tie.

'I've heard a lot about you Harry from some of my Soho people. All good I would hasten to add. That's how I know you're partial to a drop of the gold watch.'

Harry smiled and thanked Kray for the compliment as he was handed his drink by the barman who had brought it over.

'Peter Cook tells me you are wanting to get back into the dodgy film and magazine business. Is that right? I would have thought being turned over by that shitbag Spot would have put you off that idea.'

Harry took a deep breath and launched into his well-rehearsed fawning speech.

'Firstly Mr Kray, sorry, Reggie, I need to make an apology. I know how valuable your time is, so I do not want to waste any of it. I think Peter misinterpreted our conversation. I only said I was considering going down that route again. Since our meeting, I've had second thoughts and decided to give it a miss and concentrate on my main earner, photojournalism.'

Kray's expression changed from a smile to a grimace on hearing this. He gripped his beer glass more tightly and Harry feared it might be coming his way imminently. Swiftly picking up on this, Harry moved on to what he prayed would be his trump card.

'You see, in that capacity, I've met some of the world's best-known Hollywood and British film stars, as well as singers, comedians and the like. Not to mention topflight politicians and socialites. If you so desired, I would be happy to photograph you and your brother with these people at major events. Gratis of course.'

Reggie Kray's facial contours returned to their previous smiling mode.

'I'm sorry to learn you've ditched the filming idea because I think we could have been of some assistance with substantial wonga to get you up and running again. But I understand your reasoning. We'd be very happy to take you up on your offer of getting us in the press with different VIPs. That will certainly help us with our public relations.'

By this time Harry was sweating profusely and could feel his shirt sticking to him under his corduroy jacket. He gulped down his drink and politely parted from the table leaving one of his cards for Reggie Kray saying he would be in touch as soon as a suitable photo opportunity arose. Once outside the pub, he almost threw up and hastened towards the tube station.

The Establishment Club opened a couple of months later. Harry was the only photographer allowed entry to the party. He took a series of shots of the star guests attending and was careful to ensure that the Kray Twins, Ronnie had been released from prison a few days previously, featured in most of the pictures. All the major newspapers and magazines ran the photos. Peter Cook and the Krays were delighted with the results. Harry was relieved.

As the months of 1962 rolled by, Harry became more convinced that his film and magazine business should be resurrected. His reasoning for this was that there were definite signs that sexual permissiveness in Britain was increasing. The lyrics of pop music songs by groups such as the Beatles underscored his theory. In addition, a film, the James Bond secret agent thriller, "Dr No," and a novel featuring a more downbeat spy, Harry Palmer, in "The Ipcress File," both included sex scenes.

These thoughts arose again when he received a call from another contact of Kenneth Williams with a potential offer of work. The caller's name was Stephen Ward, an osteopath who lived in Wimpole Mews, Marylebone. On the phone, Ward's manner was furtive, as though he was afraid somebody might be listening in to the conversation. When Harry pressed for more details of what was required, Ward suggested that this would be better discussed in person at his flat.

Stephen Ward's flat was in a cobblestone mews, a short distance from the back entrance of D H Evans department store in Oxford Street. Inside, the place was spacious and tastefully furnished with thick carpets and drapes. The furniture was ultra-modern in light wood and on the walls, framed drawings signed by Ward were displayed. Obviously. He was an accomplished artist as well an osteopath.

Ward was 50 of slim build and around 5 feet 10 in height. He had black hair heavily oiled with no parting, receding back in two places, on a high forehead. His nose was slightly hooked and his face thin with a square jaw. Dressed casually, he was well spoken and wore sunglasses which was somewhat disconcerting as they were meeting indoors. Harry thought it impolite to ask why.

Ward poured Harry a scotch and a gin and tonic for himself. They sat opposite one another in two white egg chairs which Harry considered quirky as well as comfortable. Adopting the same furtive tone as he had used on the telephone, Ward lent forward and started by saying:

'Thank you for coming. I want to make it clear from the outset that everything we discuss today is strictly confidential between you and me. Whether you take the job or not, I want you to swear that you will not divulge details of our conversation to anyone in the future.'

'Fine by me. You have my assurance on that score,' Harry replied.

'Good. The thing is, I have unwittingly become embroiled in a situation that could prove embarrassing for many people. The government included.'

Intrigued to hear this, Harry also leaned forward, almost causing his chair to swivel on its base.

In a hushed tone, Ward began his story. He explained that after serving in the army during the war, he set up a business as an osteopath treating patients from the upper echelons of British society. This, together with sales of his art, had provided a decent living. It had also enabled him to become friends with many distinguished people. As a result, he was invited to attend and organise parties for the rich and famous. The problem he now faced stemmed from this background.

One of the close friends he had made was Lord Astor, the owner of Cliveden, a stately home in Berkshire. Two years earlier, at a party there, he introduced a young showgirl, Christine Keeler, who had been living at Ward's home, to John Profumo, the Secretary of State for War, in the Conservative government. A torrid affair between the pair started and was ongoing. Assignations took place at Ward's flat and a boat house on the Cliveden estate. However, complications arose when Keeler, at the same time she was seeing Profumo, began an affair with another friend of Ward, Yevgeny Ivanov, a Soviet military attaché. MI5 suspected Ivanov as being a spy and were concerned that official secrets might be communicated as part of the love triangle that had evolved. Ivanov and Keeler's trysts also took place at Ward's flat.

Stephen Ward feared that he could be used as a scapegoat if details of the affairs came into the public domain. Therefore, he was anxious to secure some form of bargaining chip to prevent this happening. He wanted Harry to set up a camera hidden in the loft of his flat above the bedroom where Keeler entertained her two lovers. In addition, he required Harry to lie in wait in the woods near the boat house at Cliveden, and take photos with a long-range lens, of Keeler and Profumo entering and leaving the house together. Harry would be required to keep the films in his safe as Ward did not want them in his possession in case his flat and security boxes were searched in a raid.

After digesting what he had heard Harry said: 'Christ, that's a very big ask. Your mention of MI5 started the alarm bells ringing to me. Do I really want to get myself involved in something that could backfire for me as well as you?'

'I will pay handsomely for your time and silence,' Ward quickly replied.

'But would you expect me to get up in the loft and wait for the action to begin? I could be up there for hours.'

'No, absolutely not. I am talking about a video camera that you would set up but that I could activate when, as you put it, the action is taking place.'

'I'd have to purchase the equipment and that sort of gear doesn't come cheap. Ikegami has only just brought out a new video model and it's expensive.'

'I appreciate that but as I say, money is no object. I'm desperate to get myself some security that could keep me out of prison.'

'How would I know when to be at Cliveden? I don't want to spend any more time than I need to be laying in wet grass with the possibility of a gamekeeper putting some buckshot in my arse.'

'Not a problem. I always know when the boat house is being used as I rent it from Lord Astor. I will alert you to give you time to get there and set up in readiness for their arrival.'

'But you realise that it will only be shots of the participants entering the house. There would not be any pictures of what's going on inside.'

'I have considered that, but the Cliveden photos combined with the Wimpole Mews videos will demonstrate that these activities were happening for a period of time at different locations.'

Harry was about to give his answer of thanks, but no thanks, when Ward, sensing this said:

'I would be prepared to pay you £5000 plus the cost of equipment and any expenses incurred such as transport to Cliveden, hotel accommodation if you need to stay in the area, and films.'

'When would I be paid?' Harry asked.

'All transactions must be in cash. No invoices or cheques that could be traced back to me,' Ward insisted. 'I would pay you fifty per cent up front to enable you to purchase the equipment and the remainder, plus expenses on completion of the job. But remember, this is on the condition that details of what we have agreed are restricted to just you and I.'

'You have a deal, Stephen.'

The two men shook hands and Ward went into another room. He returned a few minutes later and handed Harry an envelope.

"There's £2500 in this. I'll be in contact. I will use the name Wilkins when I call your office. I will merely give a time for us to meet here at the flat, and not mention any other details.'

As Harry opened the flat door on his way out, he bumped into a tall, auburn haired attractive girl about to enter. He immediately recognised her as the subject of a portrait in one of the framed drawings on the flat's walls.

'Hi I'm Christine,' she said.

Harry smiled and replied: "Harry Levi, pleased to meet you.' He let her pass and the door closed behind her.

Over the weeks that followed, Harry completed the assignment to his client's satisfaction. The films were locked in a security box that Harry had rented in the vault at Selfridges store together with the total proceeds of the job, £6000. He did not want to keep these materials in his studio safe as Trisha would have become inquisitive. Harry only hired the video camera but told Ward he had had to purchase it. Ward did not want it left on his premises, so Harry returned it to the hire company therefore making additional profit for himself.

CHAPTER 33 – FAMILY FORTUNES

Harry kept thinking about the money in the security box and how he could use it to start his new business. But he knew he would require more capital to achieve his aim. In the meantime, he would have to carry on working and not give Trisha any hint of the nest egg he had acquired.

Out of the blue, Harry was asked to meet with Barbara Hulanicki and her husband, Stephen Fitz-Simon. The couple had recently married and were living in a flat in Kensington Square where the meeting took place. The exterior of the building housing the flat looked very grand as Harry approached it. The interior of the flat was quite the opposite. It was untidy and smelt of burnt food.

Hulanicki was of Polish extract and had gained considerable experience as a freelance fashion illustrator for Tatler and Vogue magazines. Fitz-Simon was earning good money as an advertising agency executive. Despite the tatty surroundings, the pair were well dressed in the most modern clothing and sported trendy hairstyles. They were both in their mid-twenties and epitomised hip sixties style. Over coffee they explained to Harry that they were in the process of producing a catalogue that would revolutionise women's fashion in the UK.

'Our business will be different from anything currently operating in the British fashion market,' Barbara Hulanicki explained. 'But to make it a success, we will require the highest quality photographs of our models. That's where we hope you can help us.'

'So, effectively, you are talking about a mail order catalogue operation?' Harry asked. 'Not exactly ground-breaking, is it? Companies like Kays, Freemans, and Grattan, have been around for ages.'

Replying to Harry, Stephen Fitz-Simon said: 'You're right. Those outfits have been selling using mail order since the beginning of the century. But their ladies' merchandise is staid and frumpy. And it not just women's wear they are offering. They are flogging everything under the sun.'

Taking up the reins of the conversation, Hulanicki interrupted: 'What we deliver will be a million miles away from those companies' tired old concepts. We will be targeting a younger audience that are seeking clothes to reflect the exciting times we are living in. Our items will be brightly coloured, trendy, and most importantly, affordable. Not haute couture.'

Characteristically sensing an opportunity,

Harry switched his initial negative stance to one of positivity: 'Sounds exciting. I was commissioned to photograph a new group called the Rolling Stones, at the Marquee Club in Oxford Street, near my studio the other night. Rhythm & Blues is not really my thing, I'm more into jazz, but I liked them a lot. The youngsters dancing there were just the type of customers your goods will appeal to. But how will you get the catalogue to them?'

'Stephen has already got that worked out. Tell him Stephen,' Barbara instructed her hubby.

'The plan is to advertise the catalogue in newspapers such as the Daily Mirror, Daily Sketch, the Express and Evening Standard. We will concurrently run a publicity campaign in these publications. People will order a copy and we will mail the catalogue out. The beauty of it is it will fit in a standard house letter box, not like those hulking great things from the mail order companies. We've come up with a name for the company, "BIBA." What do you think?'

Harry considered the question, and replied: 'Well, it's certainly different. It should stand out and be memorable. Just right. Catchy. Where did you get it from?'

'It's my sister's name,' Hulanicki said. 'I'm glad you like it.'

Terms were agreed for the first round of photoshoots and Harry left feeling pleased with himself. He walked over to the other side of Kensington Square and went into the Greyhound pub. After ordering a large scotch, he lit up a Romeo y Julieta cigar, which had become his preferred choice of smoke. Trisha would be delighted to receive the news that he had secured a big legitimate piece of work. Personally, Harry was sceptical about whether "BIBA" would be a success, but providing he was paid, it didn't matter to him. However, he thought here was a young couple setting up a mail order business on a shoestring. And it was not so different, apart from the content, from his magazine operation. Surely, there was some way to restart this business again without the backing of the Krays or their like.

Harry had never been a great one for family ties. Over the years he had kept the slimmest of contact with relatives from both his mother and father's sides of his family. More out of a sense of duty to his parents than anything else, he had attended the occasional funeral when elder members of the tribes passed away. These events proved difficult for him. They ranged from the ultra-religious aspects of Judaism to the now more widely accepted liberal ceremonies. Harry was approached by people who knew him from the period of his celebrity status, but he had no idea who they were. Small talk was not one of his attributes so in most instances, he would get away from such gatherings as quickly as possible after the burial.

He was therefore surprised to receive a letter from a Manchester based solicitor advising that he had been named as the main beneficiary in the will of his great aunt Naomi. At the meeting with the solicitor, Harry learnt that she had lived to the age of 101. She was related by marriage to his mother's uncle, a successful businessman. Although Harry had had little contact with the lady since his mother died, apparently Naomi had followed Harry's career avidly. She loved the spirit he had shown through his various ups and downs. And as her direct descendants were all deceased, she had bequeathed her entire estate to her great nephew.

Harry had to contain himself when the solicitor read out the details of her estate. The house, set in five acres of parkland, its contents plus cash held in bank accounts and stocks and shares came to a total value of around £250,000. Seeing the shock on Harry's face, the solicitor poured Harry a glass of water. He accepted it graciously but would have preferred something stronger.

On the train up to Manchester, Harry had travelled second class, on the return to London, he booked first class. More befitting the status afforded him by his now beloved great aunt. During the journey he began planning his re-entry to the magazine and film business. His thoughts also drifted to other items he could spend his newly acquired money on. Priorities would include the latest photographic equipment and some new suits made to measure by an old friend at the tailors, Pennarts, in Old Compton Street.

When Harry burst through the door of the studio, it gave Trisha quite a start. He rushed over to her and hugged her tightly singing: 'We're in the money, we're in the money!'

'What on earth are you on about?' Trisha asked.

'My great aunt Naomi has left me a small fortune, bless her.'

'Sit down and I'll make us a cup of tea.'

'Bugger the tea, go out and get some champagne.'

'Just calm down and sit down. Please explain. Who is the great aunt? You've never mentioned her before,' Trisha commanded.

'Oh, she was on my mother's side of the family. Lived to over a hundred. Married to a wealthy businessman. Nobody to leave all her *gelt* to, only me.'

'What sort of money are we talking about?'

'After everything is tidied up, round about a quarter of a million. We're rich. Levi Photography will very soon be back in the film and mags biz. What's more I'm going to buy back my Hampstead flat from those bastards who took it away from me. '

In her customary level-headed manner, Trisha ignored Harry's second demand for champagne and made a pot of tea. Whilst overjoyed to hear his pronouncements, she feared that this newly found wealth would return him to the excesses of the past. She gave him a cup of tea and sat down beside him.

'Obviously, this is fantastic news darling but let's not rush into things. Firstly, I assume you will not be seeing any money for a while as probate will have to be gone through. Did she have a property. And if so, where?'

'Yes, a stonking big place in acres of grounds in Cheadle on the outskirts of Manchester.'

'Well, as I guess we will not be moving in there, it will take time to sell it and get the cash from the sale.'

'I realise that but that's no reason to put my plans on hold,' Harry remonstrated.

'Until we see sight of a large slug of the money, there's every reason to do just that. We don't want to start running up huge debts which we will unnecessarily have to pay interest on,' Trisha pointed out.

'Same old, same old. You're putting a dampener on things before I've even had any of the dosh.'

‘No, I’m not. I’m just being sensible. You’ve just agreed to that “BIBA” assignment. You don’t want to appear unprofessional and ditch it because you’ve come into money that may not be available for some considerable time. You must stick to your word.’

Without realising it, Trisha would rue the day that she uttered those last words.

Although not in agreement with his wife’s advice, Harry decided to adhere to her suggestion. For the time being anyway.

The first series of “BIBA” shoots took place in a beautiful house in Holland Park, London. It was owned by friends of Stephen Fitz-Simon and was ideal for Harry’s purposes as it had high ceilings, an abundance of light and plain walls. Barbara Hulanicki had selected the models. All young girls between 17 and 20 years old. She had brought racks of clothes made to her designs. They were a mix of dresses, trouser suits and accessories including bags and hats.

Harry was impressed with the range, but one outfit in particular caught his eye. And moreover, the model who was wearing it. Sarah Jane North had black shoulder length curly hair, brown eyes, high cheek bones a slim nose and dimpled chin. She was just 18 but had the poise of a much older woman. Her tanned skin was a perfect contrast to the small red and white polka dot bra and matching shorts she was wearing. Hulanicki had placed a long white Hawaiian style garland around her neck with a large matching floral piece behind each of her ears. Not for the first time, Harry was bitten by the love bug.

At the end of the shoot, Harry was packing away his equipment and asked Sarah Jane if she would like to join him for a drink. He left his gear in a corner in readiness for the next day's work and the pair walked down to The Mitre pub a short distance away. They opted for a table in the corner and Sarah Jane asked for a vodka and tonic. Harry had his usual, a large scotch. As they chatted Harry learnt that Sarah Jane was privately educated at Roedean School near Brighton. Against her parent's wishes, she had decided to go into modelling rather than attend university. Nevertheless, her parents were paying the rent on a mews flat in nearby Notting Hill that she shared with another model. She called Harry famous which bolstered his ego no end. He ascertained that she did not have a boyfriend currently. When she asked whether he was married, he lied saying he was but separated from his wife. After another round of drinks and more conversation, Sarah Jane left but agreed to meet Harry for dinner the following day. Clearly their age difference of twenty-two years did not present a problem for her.

During the weeks that followed, Harry took Sarah Jane out for dinners and visits to the cinema. He used the excuse to Trisha that the "BIBA" sessions were taking much longer than anticipated. Harry was smitten but despite his continuous attempts to get his young escort into bed, she resisted. One evening, after a dinner at which several cocktails and glasses of wine had been consumed by both, things changed. Expecting the usual peck on the cheek and a thank you at the entrance to the mews where Sarah Jane lived, Harry was about to head for the tube station.

'Fancy coming in for a coffee?'

'Lovely, thanks,' Harry instantly replied in case she changed her mind.

'My flat mate Margot is out tonight so we'll have the place to ourselves. Can't find my key. We will have to go in through the garage.'

Sarah Jane lifted the creaky up and over door and closed it behind them. She switched on a light that revealed the garage was being used as a storage facility rather than for a car. Cardboard boxes and tea chests were stacked everywhere. They then went through another door and up a narrow staircase. The walls on either side were covered with diagonal strips of wooden slats painted red, white, and blue.

'Come through into the living room and make yourself at home. I'll get some coffee. I could certainly do with some,' Sarah Jane said in a voice that had become a little slurred.

Harry looked around. The spacious room had a thick dark red carpet, matching curtains, and cream walls. The mahogany furniture was old fashioned but the pictures on the wall were modern. A chintzy two-seater sofa, an armchair, coffee table, television, record player and radio completed the ensemble. His eyes homed in on a drinks cabinet in which were a few bottles including one of scotch.

Sarah Jane returned with a tray bearing two cups of coffee, a small jug of milk and a bowl of sugar.

'Cheeky I know, but ok if I help myself to a scotch?' Harry asked.

'Sure, go ahead.'

Harry poured two glasses of scotch knowing full well that another drink would probably make Sarah Jane less defensive to his advances.

The couple sat on the sofa and sipped their coffee and drinks. Harry put his arm around Sarah Jane but as he did so, she got up and put a record on. 'It's the Stones new single, have you heard it?' she enquired.

'Funnily enough I have but not on a record. I heard them play it when I did some pictures of them at the Marquee Club recently.'

'Wow, what were they like? I think their singer,

Mick Jagger is dishy.'

'They were a nice bunch of lads. I thought the music was a bit on the loud side, but I did like it.'

Sarah Jane laughed.

'What's so funny?' Harry asked

'You, saying about the loud music. That's all the thing now. The bigger the amplifiers, the better.'

'That's all well and good but if things go on like that, the younger generation will be queuing up for hearing aids.'

'You sound just like my dad.'

Harry was taken aback by this comment but didn't show it. His thoughts were very much focused on one thing, and it was not pop music. As The Rolling Stones record blared out, he regarded its title, "Come On," as an invitation.

Having finished their drinks, Sarah Jane simultaneously became giggly and sleepy. Seeing this development, Harry proceeded with his well-honed seduction technique. He began by gently kissing Sarah Jane on the forehead, cheeks and pulling back her thick hair, behind the ears. Moving onto her mouth, he slowly manoeuvred his tongue around her lips before inserting it between them. From then on, it was all downhill, literally. Harry removed her blouse and bra continuing to kiss her neck and small, pert breasts. Sarah Jane was not wearing tights, so the only remaining item of clothing was her panties which were rapidly removed as Harry became more excited. There was no resistance from Sarah Jane to these actions, therefore, Harry decided to continue with his exploration. He began kissing her clitoris which made her giggle louder. Meantime, the record played repeatedly as the needle arm kept returning to the disc when it ended.

Owing to the size of his erection, Harry struggled out of his trousers and pants almost toppling onto Sarah Jane in the process. At this point, not suspecting that things would go in this direction, Harry realised he had not brought his condoms.

As Sarah Jane admiringly caressed his penis, Harry said: 'I haven't got any Johnnies.'

'Don't worry, I'm on the pill.'

'Bloody hell, I thought only married women could get them.'

'Ways and means darling, ways and means. Roedean girls are always prepared,' Sarah Jane whispered into Harry's ear.

Sarah Jane seemed keen to increase the pace of Harry's up and down rhythm in time with the beat of the song and cooed:

'Don't "Come On" too soon Harry.'

At this point their lovemaking came to an abrupt halt as a shrill scream rang out from the living room doorway. Harry whipped out his tool but could not stop himself coming, squirting semen all over Sarah Jane as he did so.

Wiping Harry's sperm from her face, Sarah Jane said without a hint of embarrassment:

'Margot. I didn't think you'd be back until much later.'

'I'm so sorry SJ, I didn't realise you had company. Aren't you going to introduce me to this upstanding member of the community?' she quipped.

Sarah Jane laughed as Harry simply stood with a gormless expression holding his erect sticky penis.

'Margot meet Harry. Harry meet Margot.'

'I'll leave you two to it. But next time, please keep your activities to your bedroom SJ. It's going to be the devil's own job getting those stains off the sofa,' Margot joked as she flounced away.

'What shall we do?' Harry enquired.

Looking at Harry's tool she replied:

'Well, I'm not letting that go to waste.'

She took Harry's hand and led him to her bedroom to continue where they had left off. As Harry achieved re-entry, he wondered how many others had been in his current position viewing the walls that were covered in posters and photoprints of pop stars.

Over the weeks that followed the intensity of the affair grew. Harry was finding it difficult to fob Trisha off about the time he was spending away from the studio. The "BIBA" photoshoots excuse was starting to wear thin with Trisha asking for more details.

Similarly, Sarah Jane was receiving questions from Margot and other friends about why she was so hung up on Harry.

'Let's face it SJ, he's no spring chicken. He's old enough to be your father,' Margot opined.

'Oh, leave it Margot. He's lovely and he treats me like a lady. Not like some of those other geeks I've been out with.'

'Yes, but they were not married, were they?'

'I've told you all that. He's separated from his wife.'

'Hmm, why does he never stay overnight with you then? He always has to scurry back to his studio on the pretext he has a backlog of work.'

'It's because he is a busy man. He's in demand. People like Barbara and Stephen want his services.'

'Seeing your face when you finish a session with him, they're not the only ones in need of his services,' Margot joshed.

'Ok, I admit it, he's a great lover. What's more, I

love him, and he loves me.'

'Well, I'd take it easy if I were you. The rate you're going at it, he might peg out bearing in mind his advanced years.'

'Ha, ha. Not much chance of that. He's like a rat up a drainpipe every time we're together.'

'Ok, but don't forget to keep taking the tablets though. You don't want to end up having to buy children's wear from "BIBA."'

Sarah Jane had grown used to Margot's lectures on men and generally dismissed them. However, on this occasion, some of the things she had said resonated. The next time she met Harry for dinner she probed more deeply than she had done previously.

'We never seem to go to places in the West End. It's always restaurants, shops, and cinemas around this area. Why is that?

Harry considered the question carefully delaying his answer by placing another piece of steak into his mouth.

'No particular reason. It's just that I think the places around Kensington and Notting Hill are better than up west. Besides, it's much nearer to your flat for our night cap,' he responded in a jovial tone winking.

'Yes, but I'd like to come to your studio occasionally for our night cap.'

'Forget that idea. For one thing, the place

is always in a mess. Coupled with the fact the neighbours on the other floors are nosey parkers. Some of them are good friends with my wife and I don't want her to know about us yet.'

'But why not?'

'It's complicated but I will try to explain. You see I was fortunate to be left some money by a great aunt recently. It has not come through yet. Likely to be another year. But I do not want my wife to get wind of it, otherwise the cost of the divorce will go up astronomically. She will want to squeeze every last penny she can out of me. My plan is to keep the details of the bequest secret, get the divorce through and then settle down with you. If you will have me of course.'

'Oh, I see. That certainly puts a different perspective on things. I fully understand your dilemma. And yes, of course I want you. I love you, Harry.'

"And I love you my sweet.'

CHAPTER 34 – BACK IN THE OLD ROUTINE

Harry had always had a belief that his mother somehow acted as a guardian angel to him from beyond the grave. Whatever the problem that arose in his life, a solution would emerge to solve it. He was hoping the current predicament he had landed himself in with two women, would prove no different. It was true that Trisha had helped him get the business back on track, but his lust for the nubile Sarah Jane was insatiable. The trouble was that he had lied to both and maintaining those falsehoods was becoming increasingly difficult.

Until this point in his life, Harry had been mentally strong. He had survived the highs and lows in his career as well as the injury he sustained during the war. Furthermore, the effect of his father dying when he was very young, and the fact that he had heard so many conflicting accounts about the man, had not helped matters. Certainly, he was adept at compartmentalising his emotions. But he was now unable to supress the feelings he was experiencing. At over forty years old, he felt he had reached a crossroads and he could not decide which route to take. All these things had conspired to make him unhappy. He needed to take action to rectify his disposition. But what?

As had happened in the past when faced with a dilemma, Harry decided to defer to his oldest friend, Sidney Solomon. Having gone through the various permutations with Sidney in the Coach and Horses pub in Greek Street, his friend wisely sat on the fence with his response. He feared that by recommending a specific solution, it might come back to haunt him if it turned out to be the wrong one.

During their conversation Harry had not mentioned the £6000 in the Selfridges deposit box or the circumstances that had resulted in it sitting there. Consequently, when he talked about restarting the film and magazine business, Sidney concurred with Trisha's view that to proceed with such a venture at this juncture, even considering the promised substantial inheritance from his great aunt, would be highly risky.

In the knowledge that he had the seed money available to create a new business, Harry made an appointment to see his bank manager. He took the business plan he had shown to Peter Cook and the correspondence from the Manchester solicitor regarding the fortune he was going to inherit. It was the latter that proved key in the discussion. Asked how long it would be before he received the proceeds of his great aunt's will, Harry obviously put an optimistic slant on his reply stating it would be in the next few months. The bank manager agreed to match Harry's £6000 with a £6000 loan that he felt would be more than adequate to produce the first issue of a magazine. As Harry had the mailing list from his previous operation, the banker was confident that the new venture would rapidly fill a void in the marketplace for such literature. Harry was amused that the man knew so much about the glamour magazines market but did not say anything.

Concerned that Trisha would see any letters from the bank regarding the new business, Harry asked the bank manager to create a separate account for it. He also advised him he was in the process of moving out of the studio. Until further notice, Harry stipulated that all correspondence should be sent to him c/o Sidney Solomon's shop.

The first thing he needed to do was to find a printer and designer. Bearing in mind what happened previously, approaching Nick Howard in Romford was not an option. Whilst working on the "BIBA" project, he had established a good rapport with Barbara Hulanicki's printer whose factory was in Park Royal, West London.

Brian Statham was the complete opposite to

Nick Howard in appearance. He was tall, thin and wore a shirt and tie under his brown work coat that did not show a trace of ink or dirt. The man was softly spoken, and Harry was having trouble hearing him above the noise of the printing presses that were running at full speed. Statham showed Harry into his office that was on a raised platform at the far end of the building up a flight of wooden stairs. The office was like the factory below, extremely tidy. Over mugs of tea, the two men started to discuss Harry's plan.

'I'm sure you are aware of this Harry, but things have moved on since you produced Glamour magazine. The relaxation of the law surrounding these types of publications a few years back has, how can I put this delicately, made the contents more explicit.'

'I realise that Brian. That's why I've come up with a concept that will satisfy customers beyond the titillation that Glamour provided. The research I have undertaken indicates that more deviant sexual activities are in vogue these days.'

Statham's pale cheeks reddened on hearing Harry's comments.

'Not my bag of course. I'm old school,' Harry hastened to add.

'Hang on a minute Harry. Before we go any further. I'm not about to start printing stuff that is totally obscene. I've got my reputation to think of. Fashion magazines like I do for Barbara and Stephen, fine, but hard-core pornography, no.'

'Trust me Brian. I'm talking art, not porn. It just going to be a bit different from tits and bums.'

'Ok, but I would need to see it first before pressing the buttons on my presses.'

'Naturally, that goes without saying. But I'll need someone to do the design. What about that guy who does the "BIBA" mag?'

'No problem. I will set up a meeting for you here.'

After agreeing the costs of producing an initial 10,000 print run of the first issue and establishing a mail order fulfilment operation, Harry walked back past the huge Guinness factory to Park Royal underground station.

Regarding the Trisha and Sarah Jane issue, he decided to maintain the status quo for the time being. He realised this was a high-risk strategy but was still at odds as to who he should jettison, and who he should stay with.

The remaining months of 1962 passed in a frenzy of activity for Harry. Preparations for the magazine had gone well. Harry had enlisted the help of Sarah Jane, Margot and some of their girlfriends to produce the photographs for use in the new publication. To avoid the work taking place at his studio under Trisha's scrutiny, Harry persuaded Sarah Jane to let him use her garage as the location for the shoots. He purchased a selection of leather, PVC, and rubber outfits for the girls to wear. In addition, he bought an assortment of whips, ropes, handcuffs, and canes for props. After lengthy discussions with the designer, Harry decreed that the title of the magazine would be "Spank." The masthead would be an image of a cane being bent by a pair of female hands as though ready to be used.

Brian Statham's initial anxiety on seeing the photos to be included in the publication were placated after he had shown them to his solicitor who confirmed that they did not contravene any laws.

Once in circulation, sales of the magazine soared with reprints required almost immediately. Based on this success, a subscription order system, managed by the printer was introduced, more streamlined than that created for Glamour. A celebratory party was organised by Sarah Jane for her friends with champagne paid for by Harry. However, at this juncture, a problem manifested itself. Harry had exhausted the entire £12,000 in the budget on getting things to this point. Despite his best efforts to convince Brian Statham to produce a second issue, he categorically refused without a bank guarantee of payment. Harry even offered a profit share from future editions, but the printer stood firm.

Harry's only option was to see his bank manager again. Examining the figures from the first issue of "Spank," and sales forecasts for the next editions coupled with details of the growing subscriptions income, the manager was impressed. Harry embellished his request for a further loan by stating that research amongst subscribers showed there would be definite demand for a series of short films based on the "Spank" format. On hearing this, Harry noted beads of perspiration on the banker's head. Obviously, the mention of such a project had excited him. When questioned about the date his inheritance would come through, Harry lied saying it was imminent. Safe in the knowledge of the substantial funds that would shortly hit Harry's account, the bank manager agreed a further loan of £12,000. He confirmed that he would write a letter to Brian Statham advising his decision.

Harry was elated and spent the evening in bed with Sarah Jane drinking champagne in between bouts of sex.

The following day, Harry was watching the television at home in the studio sipping a scotch. Trisha was in the kitchen preparing dinner when she shouted through to him:

'Have you seen the front page of the Sunday Mirror? It's on the table.'

'Not got round to it yet. I'm watching "The Avengers." Honor Blackman's got a great bum.'

'Those bloody politicians, always at it,' Trisha said.

"What do you mean?'

'That cabinet minister, Profumo, he's been shagging some 18-year-old tart. Dirty old bugger. Denying it of course. They're trying to put the blame on some poor sod. He's an osteopath. Stephen Ward, or something like that.'

On hearing this, Harry almost dropped his drink. He leaped up, picked up the newspaper and started to shake as he read.'

'Apparently, she was also having it off with some Russkie at the same time. MI5 are worried that defence secrets could have been leaked to him during pillow talk,' Trisha added.

As Harry read through the newspaper article, his nervousness intensified. It appeared that John Profumo had made a statement to the House of Commons that the allegations of an affair with Christine Keeler were baseless. Stephen Ward had also issued a statement collaborating Profumo's account of the matter. Both men acknowledged the fact they had met the Russian Yevgeny Ivanov but insisted that this was purely at social events. Harry knew these assertions to be false. The proof resided in his Selfridges security box.

'Sorry darling, I've just remembered, I've got a job round at The Establishment Club this evening,' Harry lied. 'I'll be back in an hour. Pop my dinner in the oven. I'll have it when I get back.'

He picked up his camera bag, pulled on a jacket and was out of the door before Trisha could answer. If anybody knew what exactly was going on with the Profumo affair, Peter Cook would.

Cook was in his usual position at the Club perked on a stool at the bar, legs crossed, smoking with a glass of vodka and tonic next to him. It was early and there were only a few members dotted around at tables. Dudley Moore was playing a solo piece on the piano with no sign of the bass player and drummer in his trio.

Peter Cook greeted Harry effusively waving him over to him and ordering a scotch for Harry from the barman.

'Haven't seen you recently,' was Cook's opening remark.

'Been tied up working on my new mag,' Harry replied.

‘Good for you. So, you didn’t need the help of my friends in the East.’

‘No, I didn’t, but thanks anyway for the introduction.’

‘The way things have turned out here, just as well. But I’ll elucidate on that topic another time.’

‘Knowing you are the font of all knowledge in terms of what’s going on in political circles Peter, I wanted to ask you about the balloon that’s gone up about the Secretary of State for War, John Profumo.’

‘What rock have you been hiding under Harry? Don’t you read the “Eye?” We’ve been covering it for ages. You obviously did not see our piece in the March issue including the thinly disguised characters, “Mr James Montesi,” “Miss Gaye Funloving,” “Dr Spook,” and “Vladimir Bolokov?” In other words, Profumo, Keeler, Ward, and Yevgeny.’

Harry did not want to admit that “Private Eye” was not essential reading for him, despite receiving a free copy as a member of The Establishment Club.’

‘I vaguely recollect seeing something but must confess, I didn’t make the connection.’

‘What’s your interest in it all Harry? Have you got any dirt we can use in the “Eye?” Strictly off the record of course. Or do you want to get the Wraysbury Slapper and Randy Basmati to model for your magazine, "Spank" isn't? With those two featured you could rename it "Spunk." They've seen plenty of it,' Cook joked.

Harry looked non-plussed, as well as being concerned that Cook had heard about his new venture.

'Do catch up Harry boy. Nicknames. Keeler hails from an outpost of civilisation, Wraysbury, a village near Heathrow. Mandy Rice Davies is her mate, a so-called "actress," best known for her horizontal roles. They're together in New York at present seeking work. What kind is debatable.'

'No, I was just intrigued about the whole thing. Also, about the osteopath. What's his name again?'

'You mean Stephen Ward. Manipulator to the rich and famous and shortly destined to become a patsy for Her Majesty's Government.'

'How so?'

'Well, rumour has it that Ward is going to be hung out to dry by Profumo, and Lord Snooty and His Pals.'

'Sorry Peter, I know I'm being a bit thick again, but Lord Snooty? I thought that was someone out of the "Beano"'

'Lord Astor, the owner of Cliveden where some of the shagging took place. There and at Ward's flat in Marylebone.'

'Ok, thanks for the update, Peter. At least I have some idea at what's going on now.'

'You need to keep in the loop Harry. Most of the British public are ahead of you on this one.'

Harry downed his scotch, thanked Cook again and headed back to the studio for his dinner. He was now in a heightened state of anxiety. What if Ward spilled the beans on the job Harry had carried out for him? Harry would be up to his neck in a scandal that was being investigated by MI5. Precisely what he had feared when considering whether he should accept Ward's assignment. Something told him this would not sit well with his bank manager.

Harry could not eradicate this thought from his mind during the weeks that followed. The press coverage of the scandal was incessant. The only consolation was that the second issue of "Spank" proved even more successful than its predecessor. However, the financial accounts showed that so far, the magazine had only reached break even after the set-up costs such as printing, mail order systems, props and naturally, wild parties with Sarah Jane and her friends. This meant that Harry was still indebted to the bank to the tune of £18,000. Not a problem as far as he was concerned because the inheritance money would more than cover the loan. His projections indicated a small profit from the third issue, but that would mean he would require another loan, albeit not as much, to produce the next edition. Fine if great aunt Naomi's windfall had arrived, but If it had not, the bank was unlikely to provide more support. In his opinion, the only way to resolve the situation would be to produce a short film. This could be sold to subscribers and bring in much higher levels of income, and therefore, profits. It had worked for Glamour, why not again? Annoyingly, the conundrum was funding.

A potential solution presented itself shortly afterwards. Harry was drinking in The Establishment Club when Peter Cook introduced him to the former boxer, Freddie Mills. He was five feet ten with thick black wavy hair and a flat nose. A legend amongst the public, Mills became the World Middleweight Champion in 1948 having beaten the American Gus Lesnevich in London. He only held the title for a year before retiring from the ring at the age of thirty having won 77 of his 101 bouts. Since then, he had done well for himself. Mills had invested in several properties and owned a Chinese restaurant in nearby Charing Cross Road which he was in the process of converting into a nightclub. The boxer had a penchant for appearing in radio and television programmes, as well as in variety theatre shows. His role was generally as that of a tough guy, but he also was a presenter on the BBC's pop music tv show, "Six-Five Special."

Harry and Mills rapidly became good friends and after explaining his film funding dilemma, the entrepreneur agreed to help with a loan. The interest rate was lower than the bank, so Harry was delighted. Although he was confident that such a well-loved character would not have any criminal associations, Harry decided to carry out some checks before accepting the offer. He was relieved to find that Freddie was squeaky clean in that respect.

Wasting no time after agreeing terms with Mills, Harry embarked on plans for the film. Sidney was drafted in to assist with the script and work commenced on dressing Sarah Jane's garage as a torture chamber. As much as Harry would have liked to hire somewhere similar to Hever Castle as he had done previously for filming, he knew he needed to keep costs to an absolute minimum. Props were acquired such as cobblestone effect wallpaper, a replica medieval wooden rack, chains, and metal rings for inserting into the walls. The lighting could be masked to give a dark and dank feel to the background. Much of the paraphernalia bought for the "Spank" photoshoots including costumes could be used for the new film. Ideally, Harry would have preferred to hire different people to feature in the production from those that had appeared in the magazine. Costs prohibited this too, so he had to settle for Sarah Jane and her friends plus Sidney. A couple of middle-aged male extras would be required to be on the receiving end of the punishments meted out by the girls.

The filming went without a hitch and was completed in just under a week. It was only 15 minutes in duration and was by far the most amateurish production that Harry had ever produced. Sidney took the part of a demented jailer ordering Sarah Jane and her cohorts to administer the whipping and spanking of the extras who were either tied to the rack or chained to the rings in the walls. The girls were scantily clad in leather and rubber outfits that were totally out of keeping with Sidney's medieval costume. From the first sequence, it was clear that the girls had no acting ability whatsoever. Despite these elements, Harry was sure that the film would appeal to "Spank's" subscribers. He was spot on. Within a few days of copies being advertised, the first batch produced sold out. Demand was outstripping supply.

As the money poured in, Harry was able to settle Brian Statham's invoices and make small repayments against his loans from the bank and Freddie Mills. However, he was still a long way short of paying back everything he owed. Still, he was not worried, certain that his inheritance could not be that far off from reaching him.

It was then that two events occurred starting a chain reaction that would change everything.

CHAPTER 35 - DOUBLE TROUBLE

On Tuesday 4th June 1963, John Profumo confessed he had lied to the House of Commons and resigned as Secretary of State for War and as an MP. He admitted that he had had an extra marital affair with Christine Keeler. Harold Macmillan's Conservative government was thrown into turmoil and the press were having a field day reporting on the lurid details of the scandal.

Naturally, Harry had concerns regarding this development but did not see how it would affect him. After all, only he and Stephen Ward knew about the films in Harry's possession. But his relaxed demeanour was short lived. A month later, Stephen Ward was arrested. It seemed that Peter Cook's prediction was about to come true. The politicians were determined to make somebody pay for the embarrassment the Profumo Affair had caused.

The charges against Ward were based on the fact that he had received monies from Christine Keeler and Mandy Rice Davies as contributions to household expenses for their stays at the Wimpole Street flat. The prosecution asserted that this was tantamount to living off immoral earnings. He was released on bail and the trial began on 22nd July. The case was weak but none of Ward's well-known society friends came forward to speak on his behalf. Other factors that would have helped the osteopath were not raised and the outcome looked damning when the jury adjourned on 30th July. That evening, Ward wrote letters to the authorities and the press. He then took an overdose of sleeping pills and was rushed to hospital. In his absence from court, he was found guilty of living off the earnings of prostitution, but several other charges were dismissed. Sentencing was delayed until he was fit to attend court. Stephen Ward died of barbiturate poisoning on 3rd August.

On reading the reports in the newspapers, Harry focused on the parts that referred to the letters Ward had written. He wondered whether he had mentioned the films Harry held in any of these missives. The answer came later that day.

Trisha opened the studio door after a series of loud knocks. A plain clothed policeman faced her displaying his identity card in one hand and an open document in the other. Two uniformed police officers stood behind him.

'Mr Harry Levi.'

Trisha called Harry to the door. As he arrived the policeman said:

'Mr Harry Levi. My name is Detective Inspector Craddock. We have a warrant to search your premises for materials belonging to Mr Stephen Ward, deceased.'

Before Harry could respond, the three policemen stepped into the studio.

'Now just hang on a minute,' Harry said as the policemen began opening draws and cupboards. 'What is it I'm supposed to have done?'

'I think you know full well what we are talking about, Mr Levi,' Craddock replied.

'But I don't,' Harry remonstrated.

'I should also tell you that simultaneously with this search, similar exercises are taking place at Mrs Levi's Holborn residence, and' the detective said in a purposely raised voice: 'Your mistress Miss Sarah Jane North's flat in Notting Hill.'

On hearing this. Trisha started to scream at Harry.

'You bastard. After everything I've done for you. Dragging me into your sordid escapades. I only kept my flat on so I could rent it to provide some more money for the business. Just as well I did. At least I've got somewhere to live because I'm not spending another minute here with you.'

Trisha picked up her coat and handbag and stormed out of the studio.

'That didn't go too well, did it?' DI Craddock quipped. 'Now hand over the key to the safe,

I'm guessing that's where we will find what we are looking for,' he added.

Harry passed him the key.

'Hmm. I was wrong. We will just have to turn the place upside down to find where you've hidden the stuff,' the detective said huffily.

The policemen then intensified their efforts tipping clothes and equipment over the floor as they did so. When this failed to produce anything, they started to lift the rugs and pull the sofa and armchairs apart. After an hour of fruitless searching, Craddock said he was going outside to the police car to contact the officers at the other search locations.

He returned a few minutes later and announced: 'Apparently, they've drawn a blank at the other places as well. Although they did find some "interesting" bondage gear at the Notting Hill flat. According to my men there, seems your dolly bird isn't too happy with you either. Bit of a double whammy eh?

'Now listen to me you piece of scum. You've been under surveillance for the past few weeks since the tart Keeler told us you'd been at Stephen Ward's flat. That information, together with one of Ward's letters was how we knew about the job you did for him. MI5 and some very powerful people are shitting bricks. They have decreed that those films should never see the light of day. For your own sake, it would be best for you if you told us where the films are.'

'I repeat, I don't know what you are talking about,' Harry responded calmly.

'Ok, have it your own way. But believe me, MI5 are not the sort of people to mess with. They will make your life a misery until you relent.'

Craddock instructed his men to box up the rolls of undeveloped film they had found and ordered them out. All three left the studio, slamming the door behind them.

Harry pulled the sofa upright, poured himself a large scotch, sat down and surveyed the disarray around him. Shortly after, the phone began to ring. It was Sarah Jane.

'You fucking idiot Harry. The police have ripped my place apart. They've confiscated all the filming props and equipment out of the garage. Not only that, but Special Branch officers have also interviewed my parents and friends. Were you shagging Christine Keeler and Mandy Rice Davies as well as me? I just hope they've not given you a dose because that would mean you've passed it on to me. In case you have not realised it, this is goodbye and good riddance.'

Harry tried to answer but the receiver banged down at Sarah Jane's end. He attempted to call back but there was no reply. She obviously knew it was down to him and he would try to use his schmooze tactics on her with another pack of lies. He shook his head and picked up the bottle of whisky.

Harry had just begun to get the studio back into some semblance of order the following week when he received a call from the solicitor in Manchester. It was to pre warn him that a letter had been sent to him that contained some disturbing news. Harry's Great Aunt Naomi's will was being contested by some of her relatives. They had discovered another will at her house that was dated later than the one held by the solicitor. Contrary to previous assumptions, it appeared that she did have living relatives and had changed her mind about who her fortune should be left to. Harry was not named as a benefactor in the newer version.

The solicitors consoling words did nothing to control Harry's angry response. How could such a situation have happened he demanded to know. And why had this document only just come to the surface, months after his great aunt's death? He went on to explain to the solicitor that he had taken out loans for business projects based on the information provided by the solicitors. Indeed, as they were aware, his bank had been in contact with them to verify the validity of his loan request.

The solicitor replied that although it was

extremely rare, such cases did arise from time to time. He suggested that Harry could contact the relatives in question, after all, they were also his kin, albeit distant. Perhaps they would be willing to come to an amicable agreement to share the inheritance. The solicitor offered to act as a go-between but pointed out this would incur further fees in addition to what Harry owed to date for their work on the case.

On hearing this, Harry became even more infuriated. The fact that he had debts outstanding to his bank and Freddie Mills were a direct result of the information supplied by the solicitors. But as the solicitor advised, they had told Harry that probate could take some considerable time to resolve. And that the decision to take out loans was taken by Harry. Therefore, the firm could not be held responsible for the consequences.

In a state of shock, Harry retorted that he would need to think things through and get back to the solicitor. If only Trisha was still around, he thought, she would be sure to have a solution to this latest disaster. Burying his head in the sand and hoping the problem would go away was not an option. Instead, Harry decided the best way to approach the matter would be to consult both parties he was indebted to and get their reaction. The bank manager and Freddie Mills were sympathetic but concluded that Harry should do everything possible to ingratiate himself with his distant relatives. At least by doing so, he might be able to extract some money to pay back what he had loaned.

Taking this advice onboard, Harry contacted the solicitor and asked him to arrange a meeting with his relatives and their lawyer. A date was agreed, and Harry travelled up to Manchester. The atmosphere in the conference room was acrimonious from the outset. Despite Harry's best efforts to smooth talk his kinsfolk, they treated him as though he was something they had stepped in en route to the gathering. Clearly, they had read about Harry's films and publications and considered him to be persona non gratis in family terms. They accused Harry of in some way influencing their wealthy relative to bequeath him her estate. Of course, he denied this emphatically. But they remained resolute that in a court of law, their claim based on the most recent will would be upheld. They were simply not prepared to grant Harry any monies.

After the meeting ended, Harry stayed on to consult his solicitor. He asked what chance his claim on his great aunt's estate, or even part of it, would stand in court. Using legal parlance, the solicitor prevaricated stating that there were so many factors to consider, it was impossible to make an accurate prediction. However, he said that similar cases in the past had generally gone in favour of the holder of the most recent will. He added that such cases could be very time-consuming and therefore, expensive in respect of legal fees. Also, that if Harry lost the case, he would have to pay the overall costs which could be substantial.

Unlike his last return journey from Manchester, Harry was totally despondent and travelled second class on the train. Mindful of what DI Craddock had said, he was sure that he was being followed. There always seemed to be a man in a dark suit and a trilby hat reading a newspaper wherever he went. It was always a different man but too much of a coincidence as far as he was concerned.

Back in London, reluctantly, Harry went to see Brian Statham. Like Freddie Mills and the bank manager, he was sorry to learn of Harry's plight but made it clear that he would not proceed with a third issue of "Spank" without being paid upfront.

Thinking things could not get any worse, Harry was sitting in The French House pub having a drink with Sidney when DI Craddock walked in with a uniformed PC. He approached Harry who looked up and said:

'Bloody hell, not you, again. Mr Bad Penny.'

The detective smiled and replied in a booming

voice so everyone in the pub could hear:

'Harry Levi, this is to notify you that you are being charged with supplying a minor with obscene material.'

Then under his breath:

'I told you MI5 are like a dog with a bonc. Suggest you get a good brief sharpish.'

The policemen then left the pub which had fallen silent.

'Shit Harry, that's serious,' Sidney said. "If you are found guilty, it could mean a prison sentence. Someone's really got it in for you, haven't they?'

'Thanks for that observation, Sidney. Got any more gems to cheer me up?'

'Sorry. Perhaps Freddie Mills can suggest a top-flight lawyer. He's had to deal with quite a few legal hurdles getting his club up and running.'

'Now that is good thinking Sid. I'll pop round and see him later.'

Genial as always, Mills was keen to assist. He had contracted a hot-shot barrister to help with his planning applications. In his opinion, the man was a genius. His name was James Burridge, and he was based at chambers in Lincoln's Inn in Holborn.

'Thanks Freddie, that's great but I assume this guy does not come cheap?'

'Too right. But if you want the best, it will cost.'

Harry hesitated, then awkwardly said: 'The thing is, I'm strapped for cash right now. The inheritance I was promised looks as if it will fall through.'

Seeing Harry's embarrassment, before he could continue, Mills interjected: 'Don't worry about that son. I will fund the costs and you can add it to what you owe me. This is important. We don't want you to end up in the slammer with a load of crims, do we?'

The relief on hearing this was palpable on Harry's face. He leapt up and hugged Mills: 'A million thanks, I'll pay back every penny.'

'Steady on mate. People might get the wrong idea about us,' Mills laughed.

Walking across Lincoln's Inn Fields carrying the letter he had received from the Director of Public Prosecutions; Harry was early for his appointment with James Burridge. It was a sunny day and office workers were sitting on the grass eating their sandwich lunches. They were mainly young girls wearing short skirts that looked very much like the ones he had seen when doing the "BIBA" shoots. Harry noticed a vacant bench and told himself he needed to get his mind off the girls' legs. He had to concentrate and gather his thoughts before going into the barrister's chambers on the far side of the large square.

Losing out on the inheritance had come as

a massive blow. So too had the departure of Trisha and Sarah Jane from his life. Then to further compound his problems, this legal matter had arisen that threatened imprisonment. It was vital that he should stay positive during the meeting he was about to attend.

James Burridge's office was exactly how Harry had envisaged it would be. An antique desk, leather chairs, plush thick carpet, wood panelling and shelves straining under the weight of leather-bound legal tomes. The barrister was in his late fifties, tanned, tall and fit. He had receding brown hair, bushy eyebrows and piercing green-blue eyes. He wore a black pinstriped double-breasted suit, white shirt and an RAF tie. Giving some background on himself, he informed Harry that he had been educated at Oxford, was called to the bar in 1932, and hoped to be appointed Queen's Counsel very soon. During the war he had served as a squadron leader in the RAF, and he was interested to hear Harry's account of his time in the air force.

Once the pleasantries were done with, the two men started to discuss the business at hand. Harry handed over the letter he had received from the Director of Public Prosecutions outlining the charges that were being brought against him. He also passed him the issue of

"Spank" and the short film mentioned in the letter. Burridge read the contents of the missive slowly, making notes on his pad as he did so. He then quickly flicked through the magazine and viewed the frames of the film by unwinding it from its spool and holding it up to the light. Having completed these tasks, he thought for a few minutes before addressing Harry:

'How did this 13-year-old boy from Newcastle come to receive a copy of "Spank" magazine and the film?'

'It was an error by the mailing house I use. It's a large concern in Park Royal. They print and mail out publications for many different companies. One of those organisations is Eagle Comics. It appears that instead of receiving the latest episode of Dan Dare's adventures, the lad opened the envelope and found a copy of "Spank," and the short film.'

'In other words, this is a genuine mistake made by the mailing house. Presumably, they have written to the boy's parents and apologised.?'

'Indeed, they have. But the lad's father is a vicar and was so disgusted that he went to the local police who referred the matter to their colleagues in the Met.'

'Even so, it's all a bit extreme, isn't it? Being charged by the DPP for a trial to be heard at the Old Bailey. It appears to me that somebody, or bodies, with influential friends, has it in for you Mr Levi.'

'That's most perceptive of you. No more than I would have expected in your position though,' Harry observed.

He then provided chapter and verse on the events leading up to the charges being made. This included details of the assignment he had carried out for Stephen Ward and the incriminating films in the Selfridges safe deposit box. When he finished, it was as though a huge burden had been lifted from his shoulders, as Burridge was the first person, he had related this information to.

'An intriguing story. You say this woman Keeler reported to the police that she saw you at Ward's flat?'

'That's what the detective said when they searched my studio, and the other locations.'

'I have to ask the question, what purpose do you have for keeping hold of the films?'

'Like Stephen Ward, I intended to retain them as a bargaining chip should the situation arise where the authorities tried to make me a scapegoat for the whole debacle.'

'I understand your thinking, but do you not feel that point has now been reached? Let's face it, Profumo has confessed, and the Russian has returned to Moscow.'

'Yes and no. Don't forget, Christine Keeler is

still under investigation. Besides, the press would pay me an absolute fortune for the films, and I am in real need of money to cover some outstanding debts. But don't worry, Freddie Mills has assured me that he will pay your legal fees on my behalf.'

'I admire your candour Mr Levi. Nevertheless, I would suggest that the police, MI5, and whoever else is involved in this affair will not cease making life difficult for you whilst you continue to refuse to release the evidence that they so desperately want.'

'Ok, so what do you recommend.'

'Well, firstly, I do not believe their case will stand up in court. We should defend the charges vigorously. Once the trial is underway, we shall approach the DPP out of court. We will advise them that we know the true reason for the charges being brought are to force you to give up the films without any publicity. We will offer to do this provided written assurances are made that you will not be hounded further by the police. Additionally, we will ask for a substantial amount to be paid to you off the record. What say you to my proposal?'

'Sounds fine but what do you call a substantial amount?'

'Well, how much do your debts total?'

'Between the bank, the printer, the Manchester solicitor and Mr Mills, around £20,000.'

'That is certainly a considerable sum. Let's see what we can do.'

The two men shook hands and Harry departed. James Burridge placed the magazine and film in the drawer of his desk and locked it. He didn't want his secretary to see the items. The barrister then stood and watched Harry from his window as he crossed Lincoln's Inn Fields. He noted that his client was ogling the young women sitting on the grass.

There followed three more sessions at Burridge's chambers during which he gave Harry detailed coaching on every aspect of his appearance in court. The briefings included the way Harry should answer questions from both the prosecuting and defence counsels, and what he should wear. He emphasised that he should remain calm throughout the proceedings even under provocation. The barrister insisted that his client take notes during these meetings and should continuously refer to them in the run-up to the trial.

Harry was feeling nervous as he approached the Old Bailey with James Burridge. Looking up at the dome of the building, Harry could see the sun shining on the bronze statue of Lady Justice holding a sword in her right hand, and the scales of justice in her left. The notes he had memorised in preparation for the trial were going round in his head. He just hoped he would be able to deliver them in an effective manner when under questioning.

The inside of the building was imposing. During the Second World War, the Old Bailey was bombed and severely damaged, but reconstruction work restored most of it in the early 1950s. The restored interior of the Great Hall was decorated with paintings commemorating the Blitz, as well as historical scenes of nearby St Pauls Cathedral. Running around the entire hall was a series of biblical references. They read:

"The law of the wise is a fountain of life"
"The welfare of the people is supreme"
"Right lives by law and law subsists by power"
"Poise the cause in justice's equal scales"
"Moses gave unto the people the laws of God"
"London shall have all its ancient rights"

Harry was transfixed with his surroundings but was brought back to reality when approached by two uniformed court officials. Burridge shook his client's hand and wished him good luck. Harry was then led downstairs by the officers and directed into a holding room below the courts. The barred gate was locked behind him. The room was occupied by four prisoners. One was standing, the others sat on a wooden bench. All were unshaven and dishevelled. They eyed Harry who was smartly dressed in a dark navy-blue suit, white shirt and black tie, with disdain.

'What ya up for, dressing like a poof?' The standing man enquired. He was very muscular with breath like a dog's after eating offal.

Before Harry could reply, one of the policemen waiting outside the gate shouted at the man:

'Shut it Johnson. You'll have plenty of opportunity to mouth off when you're taken up into the court room.'

'Cunt,' the man muttered. But, to Harry's relief, he obeyed the policeman's order.

Harry stood thinking that if this is what prison was like, he wanted no part of it. He was silently praying that his barrister's plan would be successful.

After what seemed ages trying to avoid the stares of the room's occupants, he heard the words: 'Mr Harry Levi. Court Number One,' called out. A policeman opened the gate and took Harry's by the arm while another locked the gate behind them. The police officer pointed Harry to a narrow wooden staircase that creaked under foot. Reaching the top, he walked into the dock escorted by the policeman. To his left sat the jury of 12 men. On a raised platform directly in front was the judge's vacant ornate throne-like wooden crested chair. Immediately below the dock was where the lawyers sat at a long table wearing silver-grey wigs and black robes. Beyond them were separate desks for the court bailiff and stenographer. Above these areas and behind the dock was public seating. Harry looked around and saw that these public seats were all occupied. He spotted Sidney, and on the other side, much to his consternation, Trisha. Presumably she had come in the hope of seeing him receive a long prison sentence.

James Burridge glanced up at Harry and gave him a thumbs up sign. The bailiff then stood and bellowed: 'All rise, the court is now in session, the Right Honourable Judge Dawkins presiding.' The judge called the court to order. He was a short rotund man with a chubby face. He wore gold half-rimmed glasses, a silver-grey wig and red gold braided robes.

When called upon, after the charges were read out, Harry reiterated his plea of not guilty that was made at a previous hearing. The counsel for the prosecution then put forward its case that focused on two key elements. The first related to providing obscene literature to a minor, whilst the second alluded to Levi Photography producing obscene magazines and films for public viewing. The father of the boy who had received the offending magazine and film was called as witness. As a vicar, he spoke eloquently, highlighting his disgust that his son had received the unsolicited material. The trouble was that his comments turned into a long-winded rant on the evils of pornography. And both the judge and jury were becoming visibly bored at being on the end of his sermon. The judge finally stopped the vicar, thanked him for his submission and asked him to stand down.

The prosecution then called Detective Inspector Craddock as its next witness. The policeman, like the vicar spent too much time providing unnecessary details, constantly referring to his notebook. Once again, the members of the jury and the judge showed signs of restlessness. The judge then called a recess. Harry was taken back down to the holding room. On arrival, he was pleased to see that he was the sole occupant.

When the proceedings reconvened, James Burridge gave a short but to the point resume of why the charges against his client were preposterous and should be dismissed. He called Brian Statham as a witness for the defence. In answer to Burridge's questions, the printer confirmed that the mailing to the 13-year-old-boy was an unfortunate error. He had written to the boy's father and apologised profusely for his company's mistake. Furthermore, as a gesture of goodwill, he had arranged for the lad to have two years free subscriptions to all of the children's publications his firm handled.

Harry was then called as a witness and answered his barrister's questions without showing that they had been well-rehearsed many times. In the prosecution's cross-examination, Harry responded to the questions positively and despite the counsel's repeated attempts to catch him out, failed to do so. The only time he strayed away from his coaching was when he stated that he was providing a public service by keeping the men of Britain entertained with his publications. This prompted a barrage of laughter from the jury and the public galleries, until the judge had to bang his gavel and restore order in the courtroom. But the defence's trump card was to call Freddie Mills as a character witness for Harry. The jury were clearly in awe of the former world boxing champion as he regaled them with Harry's numerous attributes. Especially the work he did for the local Soho charity and community.

The judge then called a recess for lunch.

Immediately following the recess, the judge instructed the clerk to clear the court of the public. During the break, a projector and screen had been set-up in the centre of the courtroom. The short film that had mistakenly been sent to the Newcastle address was shown to the jury twice. They were then each handed a copy of

"Spank" magazine, and the judge asked them to take their time examining the publication. He advised that he would do likewise. The members of the jury approached this task with obvious enthusiasm.

As if sensing the jury's need for refreshments to cool them down, the judge called a short recess. On everyone's return, James Burridge looked up at Harry in the dock, winked, smiled, and nodded. It was the pre-arranged signal to indicate that his proposals to the prosecution counsel and the police had been accepted.

In an annoyed tone, the judge announced that he had been approached by the prosecution lawyers and senior Metropolitan Police officers during the break. Having seen the film and magazine, on reflection, they had decided that neither contravened the Obscene Publications Act, and as such, Mr Levi and Levi Photography had no case to answer. They also accepted that the mailing of the material to a minor was a genuine mistake. Summing up, he continued to admonish the authorities by saying that he could not understand why they had brought the case in the first place in a court normally reserved for trials of a much more serious nature.

Judge Dawkins finally banged his gavel and declared: 'Case dismissed. Mr Levi, you are free to leave.' He then left the courtroom. The jury filed out. Most forgot to hand back their copy of "Spank."

Harry stepped down from the dock and shook James Burridge's hand showering him with thanks. They were joined by Sidney, Brian Statham and Freddie Mills who added their congratulations to the barrister. Mills insisted that they all catch a cab back to his club and celebrate with champagne. Statham declined the invitation as he had urgent work to complete at his factory.

As the group emerged from the Old Bailey, there were a few photographers and journalists waiting. Pack like, they pounced on Harry and started to fire questions. James Burridge took control and made a brief statement to the effect that his client was delighted with the outcome of the trial. He added that as Mr Levi had been totally exonerated by the court, he was now unfettered and could continue with the day-to-day running of his business. After posing for a photo with the barrister and Freddie Mills, who was holding up Harry's arm as though he had just won a fight, they hailed a taxi which sped off to the West End.

The celebrations went on until the early hours at The Freddie Mills Nite Spot with large quantities of fizz consumed. The only dampener on the evening was when, at one point, Harry noted a heated discussion going on at a separate table between Mills and the Kray Twins.

CHAPTER 36 – KNOCK OUT LOAN

Harry was woken later that morning by the phone ringing. He was lying on top of his bed fully clothed. The amount of bubbly he had drunk earlier had obviously taken its toll when he arrived back at the studio. He vaguely remembered staggering back from the nightclub, but little else.

'Hello,' Harry just managed to say in a dry throaty voice.

'Good morning, Harry. James Burridge here. Sounds like taking my leave early from Freddie's last night was the right decision.'

'It certainly was,' Harry croaked.

'You need to pull yourself together quickly. Get some coffee down pronto. Things are moving fast. As the police and men in grey suits kept to their part of the bargain yesterday, they want the goods today.'

'Can't it wait until tomorrow?'

'No, they want to take delivery this afternoon. You need to telephone Selfridges and advise that you want to reserve a private room in the safe depository at 4pm. In addition to yourself, tell them that you will be accompanied by me, Detective Inspector Craddock of the Metropolitan Police, and a uniformed police officer. Everyone attending will bring identification.'

'Ok, will do. But what about the written assurances and the money?'

'I have already given them the assurance letter which you have seen. They will bring it to the meeting duly signed by the Chief Superintendent of the Met. It will be handed to us with £20,000 in cash. You can then place both items in your safe deposit box. In return, you will give them the films.'

'Alright, I'll see you just before four o' clock at Selfridges.'

'One more thing Harry, no cheap shots at Craddock's expense. This is a business transaction. Let's keep it that way.'

The meeting went smoothly. The only slight deviation from the plan was that Craddock tabled an additional letter that Harry, after Burridge's agreement, signed. It stated that Harry swore that the items he was handing over were the originals and no copies had been made. If this was proved subsequently to be untrue, the assurance letter would be deemed null and void, and Harry would have to repay the cash.

On departing, Harry asked Burridge to join him for the hair of the dog at the Lamb & Flag pub round the corner in St Christopher's Place. He explained to the barrister that it was one of his haunts from years back. James Burridge politely declined the invitation saying he had an appointment at his chambers.

As he sat sipping his second double scotch in the pub, Harry flicked through the newspapers he had bought. Each one carried the story about Harry's acquittal at the Old Bailey. All referred to him as the King of the Camera, and how his celebrity status had been restored. He thought that once again his guardian angel had rescued him from a perilous situation. His euphoric mood lasted just one week.

The receipt of James Burridge's invoice came as a shock. Although the barrister's fees of £2,000 were more than Harry had anticipated, they were acceptable. Freddie Mills had agreed to pay the invoice, but Harry would have to reimburse him at some point. However, what he had not expected was that he would have to pay the costs of the trial, £2,000, Surely, this should be beholden on the police he thought. Naturally, he queried the charge, but Burridge confirmed that it was correct. A quick calculation of his finances highlighted that after he had paid off the bank and Brian Statham, he would only be able to pay Mills a small amount of the money loaned. Of course, there was still income from sales of the second issue of "Spank" and the short film, but this arrived in dribs and drabs and ultimately, would not clear the outstanding debt. He was totally stymied as he was not in a position to raise more funds to produce the third edition of the magazine or another film.

As much as he hated parting with the money, he decided to settle the bank and printer's outstanding bills. Both parties were overjoyed to receive the payments as they had started to have concerns that Harry would welch on their deals. This left the debt owed to Freddie Mills. Harry had not seen him since their post-trial celebration and made up his mind to call on his friend the following day to discuss the matter. After all, Mills had been sympathetic to Harry's plight in the past. Hopefully he would give him more time to pay which Harry would propose to do in monthly instalments.

'I feel for you Harry, but to tell you the truth, things have gone a bit pear-shaped here at the club recently,' Freddie Mills explained to Harry. 'My original plan was to make this gaff a family venue. That didn't work though so I was forced to go down the path of a members only place with gambling and girls.'

'Well, looking around, that seems to have worked Freddie,' Harry said.

'Looks can be deceptive. My partner, Andy and I had to sell off our entire property portfolio to get the club open. Problem was, it still fell short of what was needed, and I had to borrow from other sources. And I don't mean banks.'

Harry expression became darkened on hearing this. Suddenly, the memory of the heated exchange between Mills and the Krays he had witnessed came into his mind.

'What about those regular private functions you hold here like the theatre agency club that all the celebs come to. They must bring in a fair amount of gelt?' Harry asked.

'Yes, you're right, they are successful, but they don't generate enough income to cover the running costs of the club. I'm sorry Harry but I really do need to have the dosh I loaned you back sooner rather than later. The other sources I mentioned are pressing me for their money and I'm scared of what will happen if I don't come good.'

Harry left the meeting thoroughly dejected. He assured his friend that he would make an appointment to see his bank manager despite thinking to himself it would prove a complete waste of time.

The following morning there was a loud rapping at the studio door. 'Open up Harry, open up,' Sidney called out.

'Where's the fire?' Harry enquired as he opened the door dripping wet with a towel round himself having just got out of the shower.

'Haven't you heard about Freddie?'

Harry looked perplexed. 'Heard what?'

'He's dead. Topped himself in Goslett Yard behind the club last night. They rushed him to the Middlesex where he was pronounced dead.'

'How did you find out?'

One of the waiters who works at the club popped into my shop first thing and told me.'

'Why would he do such a thing? I knew he had money problems, but he wasn't the sort to commit suicide. He'd never do that to his missus and daughters. Sounds very dodgy to me,' Harry remarked.

'I agree with you,' Sidney said, 'but the police are treating it as suicide. They found a rifle next to him in his car. That's where they say he shot himself in the head.'

Harry's mind began racing with questions. Of course, he was deeply saddened by his friend's death, but where did this leave him in respect of the debts he owed to Freddie? For example, had the former boxer paid James Burridge's invoice for handling Harry's case? If not, the barrister would require payment from Harry. Would the Krays or some other criminal gang take ownership of the loans Freddie Mills had made? It was rumoured that the Krays were responsible for Peter Cook closing the Establishment Club a few weeks earlier. Apparently, Cook was not prepared to pay the increased protection monies the Krays were demanding. A couple of days previous, Harry had thought he had ridden out the immediate problems as regards his debts. It now appeared that he was right back in the eye of the storm.

The answer to one of these questions arrived in the post the following day. It was a letter from James Burridge stating that because of the sudden death of Freddie Mills, the amounts outstanding for his services and the court costs would now have to be met by Harry. The letter outlined that there was nothing in writing from either Mills or Harry regarding the payment arrangement, it was purely verbal. Consequently, Harry would have to settle.

Harry telephoned the barrister in the hope of finding a way to get the invoice for £4,000 redirected to somebody else.

'Surely James, as Freddie advised us both he would cover the costs of the case, the invoice should be registered against his estate?' Harry pleaded.

'I am sorry Harry, but that is not an option. Freddie had run up huge debts. He assigned a large proportion of the shares in the ownership of the club to other parties. As the property was the only asset with any value he had left, Freddie's share will be sold, and a few creditors will be paid a small percentage of what they are owed. The banks will be first in the queue, after them, it's unlikely that there will be anything remaining for others, including my chambers.'

'So, you mean that even as a lawyer, you could not make a case that Freddie Mills had advised you verbally that he would pay for my case?'

The barrister's tone became decidedly frosty at this juncture.

'Look Harry, I understand how you feel about this, but you are not the only one who's landed in the shit. My firm is a business like any other. Freddie owed us thousands for work we have undertaken for him in the past year. Despite continued efforts to secure payment, we were repeatedly fobbed off with excuses. Similar to all workplaces, the legal bar is a hive of gossip. My personal reputation has taken a dent for accepting your case when Freddie still owed us considerable sums. Jokes such as, "Burridge didn't box clever with that one," and, "Mills delivered a knockout blow to Burridge," are circulating. As you can imagine, I'm not happy about it.'

'But James, you know my financial position. I wouldn't have asked for Freddie's help if I had had the cash available to fund my case. Besides, Freddie had agreed to let me pay him back in monthly instalments,' Harry replied slightly distorting the truth.

'Very well Harry. I will instruct our accounts people to draw up a payments schedule for your written agreement. But let's be clear, any deviation in relation to the repayments will result in us prosecuting you rather than defending you. And we will require a reasonable sized initial payment.'

'That can certainly be fixed but I will need your help. Don't worry, it will only require you to telephone DI Craddock. Ask him to give orders for the return of the equipment and films his men confiscated from Sarah Jane North's flat and my studio. I can then sell the stuff and that will cover the initial repayment.'

'Happy to do that at no charge,' the barrister said in a business-like manner.

Harry knew that all he had done was to buy himself some time. It was true that the sale of the equipment and films would be just enough for a down payment. The problem was then how would he be able to meet the monthly instalments thereafter. A midnight flit like he had done in the past to escape trouble was not possible. Burridge's company had all the resources such as hiring private detectives to track people down.

'There's only one thing for it,' Sidney Solomon said in his capacity of Harry's personal agony aunt. 'You'll have to get some well-paid assignments PDQ. Especially if the Krays come knocking for their share of the non-legal fees you owed Freddie.'

The two friends were sitting in the studio drinking coffee. Harry had searched for scotch but found only empty bottles in the cupboard. Since Trisha's departure the place resembled a refuse tip.

The mention of the Krays made Harry shudder. 'I know it's a long shot, but I'm praying that Freddie had not written anything down about that money. So far, they have not been in contact. Let's hope it stays that way. I've heard they are fully occupied at the moment with a Chinese Triad gang that has muscled in on what the Krays consider to be their turf. The Chinks have rapidly established vice, gambling and extortion rackets amongst the Chinese restaurants and shops that have opened in and around Gerrard Street. If, as is predicted, a war breaks out, the Twins might be casualties and that could be beneficial to my cause.'

'Who else do you think might know about Freddie's loans to you?' Sidney asked.

'I really haven't a clue. Maybe his wife, his business partner that Andy fella, or his accountant. Who knows. It could be anyone of them or nobody at all.'

'I suppose all you can do is sit tight and keep *schtum*,' Sidney added. 'If it comes to it, and there's no written proof, you can just deny it.'

With a worried look on his face, Harry responded: 'All very well, but as the newspapers regularly inform us, the Krays have ways of making people talk. You will not be surprised to hear that I don't want to have electrodes attached to my balls and an electric current run through them.'

'That would be shocking,' Sidney quipped.

Like Queen Victoria, Harry was not amused.

Harry was in two minds whether to attend Freddie Mill's funeral. Although he had only met his friend's wife Chrissie once, and that was very briefly at the club, she had sent an invitation to the event taking place at St Giles Church in Camberwell. He had an early morning meeting scheduled at the Daily Express in Fleet Street on Friday 30th July 1965 to discuss a potential assignment. Still undecided as to whether he would go over to Camberwell after, Harry wore a dark suit and black tie in case. The meeting at the newspaper ended quicker than expected. It was a warm but overcast day and on the spur of the moment, Harry turned left out of the Express building and walked down to Ludgate Circus. There he caught a number 40 bus to Camberwell Green. On alighting, he was astounded to see hundreds of people lining the street as he approached the church. His timing could not have been better. The cortege comprising several big limousines festooned in floral tributes was just arriving. Harry's name was checked against a guest list by a heavy-set man at the entrance to the church and he was directed to one of the rows towards the back.

Looking around, it was like a who's who of the entertainment and boxing worlds. From the former sector were celebrities such as Frankie Vaughan, Tommy Trinder, Alfred Marks, Sid James, Bob Monkhouse, Anne Shelton, and Norman Wisdom. Those representing the boxing fraternity included the promoter, Harry Levene, and fighters such as Terry Downs, Dick Richardson, John Williams, and Len Harvey. Alarmingly, he also spotted Reggie and Ronnie Kray, and the detective Len "Nipper" Read, who had been unsuccessful in his attempts to arrest the Twins on numerous counts.

As the organ struck up, the congregation stood, and the coffin was borne into the church. The pallbearers included the comedian, Bruce Forsyth, the boxer Henry Cooper, Teddy Waltham, Secretary of the British Boxing Board of Control, and the promoter, Jack Solomons. The coffin was adorned with a wreath in the shape of a boxing glove. It was followed by Freddie Mills wife and daughters.

Bruce Forsyth delivered a moving eulogy stating how Freddie had become the British public's favourite sportsman. He made references to the boxer's working-class roots and tough upbringing in Bournemouth. Mills military service was highlighted and how he had overcome numerous obstacles during his career. The service ended on a fitting note with the singing of the hymn, "Fight the Good Fight."

As the attendees filed out, they were greeted and thanked by a tearful Chrissie Mills, her daughters, Bruce Forsyth, and the vicar of St Giles. Once outside, Harry lit a cigar and was chatting to two of his former acquaintances, Tommy Trinder and Norman Wisdom, when he received a tap on the shoulder.

''Allo 'arry Boy,' Reggie Kray said with his brother, Ronnie next to him. 'Need a word. We'll give you a lift back up West. We can talk on the way.' His words were more of an instruction than an invitation.

Trinder and Wisdom acknowledged the Twins with a nod and moved away swiftly leaving Harry alone with the gangsters. Desperately trying not to show any fear, Harry stubbed out his cigar and replied: 'Good to see you again. Although I would have preferred it to be in different circumstances. A lift would be great. Thanks.'

The Kray's big black Ford Zodiac car was parked in a nearby side street. On seeing the brothers approaching, the driver flicked his cigarette into the gutter and opened the back passenger door. Reggie slid in first and Harry was eased in next to him by Ronnie who, decidedly more rotund than his brother, squeezed in beside their passenger. This gave Harry the feeling of being like the meat in a sandwich. The car moved slowly along Camberwell New Road where the crowds were waiting behind barriers for a last glimpse of Freddie Mills coffin as it passed.

'Shame about The Establishment Club closing,' Reggie said. 'That tosser Cook couldn't come up with the readies he owed us, so he had no alternative but to call it a day.'

Harry thought it best not to say anything unless he was directly asked a question.

'Despite the rumours, we had nothing to do with Freddie's demise. We loved the geezer. Ain't that right Ron?'

His brother didn't respond but merely grunted.

'As far as we can find out, he was into the Chinky Triads big time. Huge amounts of dosh apparently. I guess they thought a warning was needed to be sent to other non-payers. Hence poor old Millsy ending up as chop suey.'

On hearing this, Ronnie Kray smiled.

'Still, we have plans for those slit-eyed bastards with an emphasis on the word slit,' Reggie explained.

Ronnie nodded in agreement.

'But that's not why we've asked you for a chat,'

Reggie continued.

Fearing the worst was about to be unveiled, Harry stared resolutely ahead as the car traversed the Elephant & Castle roundabout. His heartbeat accelerated as Ronnie Kray grabbed Harry's knee firmly as if he was expecting him to try to get out of the vehicle.

'Fing is "arry, we've got a little job for you. All above board of course. The Sunday Times Magazine wants to run an article on us. It would be a sort of tour of our favourite haunts around our manor in the East End. They've nominated a journalist and a snapper for the job. We're ok with the journo, but we've told 'em, we want you to do the photos. Tell the truth, the snooty wot nots aren't keen on the idea. Sounds like you had a run-in with them in the past. However, we've insisted. It's our mate 'arry Levi, or the answer's a no, no so, they've come back and agreed. They will pay your going rate but don't over do it. Keep it sensible.'

Having expected more of a diatribe from Reggie regarding loans, Harry somehow kept his composure and replied: 'Bloody brilliant Reggie. That's so good of you to think of me. I'd be honoured to do the work. And naturally, I will not be daft with my charges.'

'That's settled then. I'll get the Sunday Times to call you.'

As Reggie said this, Ronnie released his grip on

Harry's knee and patted it.

The car pulled to a halt on the corner of Wardour Street. Harry thanked the Twins again and got out. He closed the door and with a forced smile, waved them off. He then made for the nearby Round House pub where he ordered a large scotch to calm his nerves.

To Harry's surprise, the shoots on the Kray's tour of the East End were relatively uneventful. The Twins were not too keen on the journalist, Hugh Waddesdon, who had obviously drawn the short straw at the Sunday Times to write the article. Throughout the four days of the tour, they continuously ribbed him regarding his posh accent and as they put it, "poncy weirdo outfits." The brothers' standard attire was a sharp dark navy tailored mohair suit, white shirt, narrow black silk tie and highly polished black shoes.

Locations on the tour included the house where the Krays were brought up in Bethnal Green, Repton Boys Club the venue at which the Twins learnt their boxing skills, Pellicci's a greasy spoon café, Manze Pie and Mash Shop, Wilton's Music Hall, and The Blind Beggar and The Carpenter's Arms, both pubs. On arrival at each place, the brothers were treated like royalty. It was only at one place that things turned a bit nasty. On arrival at The Carpenter's Arms, Harry was setting up his Rolleiflex camera on a tripod when a Geordie customer, clearly the worse for drink, staggered out from the toilets. He collided with the tripod sending the equipment crashing to the pub's floor. Shouting and cursing, he went to throw a punch at Harry when he was lifted from behind by his collar by Ronnie Kray and dragged outside. There he was joined by Reggie, and they pounded the man unconscious.

On the twins return, they adjusted their cuffs in unison and Reggie said:

'Northern bastard. Why don't they speak fuckin' English?'

Addressing Hugh Waddesdon, Ronnie added: 'Mr Scribbler, that does not go in the article.'

As the remaining months of 1965 went by, Harry was relieved that he received no communications regarding the money he had owed Freddie Mills. Thanks to recommendations from the Krays, he picked up jobs from their contacts. Mercifully, all were legitimate assignments for which he was paid. These monies helped him to keep afloat and meet the monthly repayments to James Burridge's chambers.

CHAPTER 37 – THE RAKE

The dawning of the New Year brought a degree of optimism for Harry as financially, things continued on an even keel. Once again, it was the Kray Twins who were mainly responsible for this positive situation.

Harry had always been a jazz fan, and as such, was a regular at a club in the basement of 39 Gerrard Street in Soho since its opening in 1959. The club was owned by two musicians, Ronnie Scott and Pete King. Harry was friendly with Scott whose real name was Ronald Schatt. He was from an East End Jewish family and shared the same sense of humour as Harry. Although Harry was on good terms with King, he felt he was somewhat brusque. Indeed, it was King who handled business matters for the club, with Scott in the role of entertaining host.

Scott and King were keen to attract big bands to their London venue, but the Gerrard Street club was too small. Hence, at the end of 1965 they took out a lease on a bigger premises in nearby Frith Street. The Krays were instrumental in facilitating this move by ensuring that other local gangsters did not demand protection money from the owners of the new establishment that was named Ronnie Scott's Jazz Club. As part of this arrangement, Reggie

Kray suggested that Harry should be retained as the club's house photographer. Everybody involved was delighted with this development, especially Harry as not only would he be able to meet and listen to some jazz legends, but he would also be paid for the privilege.

The Krays were indirectly the reason that Harry landed another assignment just a stone's throw away from Ronnie Scott's. For some years, the upstairs private dining room at Wheeler's Seafood & Oyster Bar in Old Compton Street, had been the venue for The Thursday Club. Membership comprised high profile bon vivants such as Prince Philip, The Duke of Edinburgh, his uncle, Lord Louis Mountbatten, and the Prince's cousin, the Marquis of Milford Haven. Other notable attendees included the poet John Betjeman, the harmonica player, Larry Adler, and the actors Peter Ustinov and David Niven. Surprisingly, Ronnie and Reggie Kray, who loved rubbing shoulders with as they called them, the "toffs," regularly participated in the drink-fuelled sessions that went on until late.

It was on one such occasion that the Twins put forward the idea that a photographer should be appointed to record the gatherings. Prince Philip pointed out that the royal photographer, Cecil Beaton, sometimes attended the lunches. However, on reflection, he thought that Beaton was probably not the best choice as he would require time-consuming set-ups. It therefore looked as if Harry was about to be awarded the job when the members decided that the society photographer, Baron Nahum, would be a better option owing to his reputation for discreetness.

Harry was sitting downstairs at Wheeler's waiting for the Krays to emerge from upstairs and advise the outcome of their proposal. He had opted for a soft drink rather than a scotch in case he was called upon to take some shots. Whilst waiting he struck up conversation with a group of local artists and writers that he knew from the Colony Room and the French House pub.

Commanding centre stage in the group at the dining table was the artist, Francis Bacon who said to Harry: 'I think you know these other layabouts. Lucian Freud, Timothy Behrens, Frank Auerbach, and Michael Andrews.'

The others acknowledged Harry's presence by raising their glasses of wine towards him. Of course, Harry had interviewed Freud's grandfather many years ago when working for the Jewish Chronicle. But he chose not to mention this encounter.

Bacon was a short chubby faced character who had gained a reputation as a maverick producing work that was often described as unsettling. He was a homosexual and a key figure in the "School of London" a group comprising Bohemian Soho based artists.

Harry explained that he was hoping to be summoned to take some shots of the Thursday Club Lunch taking place upstairs.

'Fucking upper crust toss pots. Most of them are shirt-lifters. Down here is where the real world is Harry,' Bacon exclaimed which attracted a glare from two heavy-set suited men at the foot of the staircase.

'Whoops. Better mind my language,' Bacon added. 'Don't want to upset the pistol- packing royal bodyguards over there.'

His companions laughed out loud on hearing this comment.

'Pull up a chair and join us.'

Just as Harry did so, Reggie Kray came over to the table.

'Hello boys and girls,' he said addressing the group.

'Hiya Reg,' Bacon replied. "Where's Ronnie?'

'He's up with the toffee-nosed brigade.'

'Right. Well give him our best.'

'Will do. Harry, a quick word.'

Harry got up and followed Reggie over to a corner of the restaurant.'

'Sorry mate. We tried but they prefer some

prick called Baron. Have you 'eard of 'im?'

'I have and I get it Reggie. Unlike me, he's a bloke who moves in their circles, so they obviously trust him more than me. But thanks for trying. Much appreciated.'

'Ok, no problem, Harry. But a tip. Don't bend down to pick your serviette up with that lot.' Kray said pointing at the table of artists. 'You might get a tip and it won't be the kind a waiter expects,' he laughed, patted Harry on the back and went upstairs.

As Harry returned to the table Francis Bacon looked at Harry's face and said: 'I take it that the answer is, no?'

'Yep. That's about the size of it.'

'Don't fret dear boy. Sit yourself down and have some lunch. It's on me. I can assure you it will be a lot more fun with us than with that bunch of brown nosers up there. But before we all get too pissed, do me a favour and take a picture of us.'

Harry reached for his camera and was only too happy to comply with Bacon's request. He then ordered a Dover sole with chips and spinach. Throughout the lunch that followed, Harry's glass was continuously topped up with Chablis. Three hours later, the group, including Harry, left Wheeler's, and headed round to the French and thereafter, the Colony.

The chance meeting with Bacon and his cohorts would prove to be a catalyst in what was to follow. A deep friendship developed between Bacon and Harry. Although not sexual, as they came from opposite ends of that spectrum, it was intense. Both men were teetering on the brink of alcoholism. Having gained fame and fortune from his work during the fifties, Bacon was now focusing on subjects for his paintings drawn from friends and local Soho residents. Harry, who of course had equally experienced public notoriety from his magazines and films, was more in a state of limbo work wise. However, a vast disparity existed between the men's respective earnings. Bacon was extremely wealthy whilst the only real income of an ongoing nature for Harry was the sessions at Ronnie Scott's, and the odd job via the Krays.

Francis Bacon painted a series of works of Harry in a variety of different Soho haunts. But he did not carry out the work on site. He had developed a new way of working by getting Harry to arrange photos of himself in these places, using the timed exposure device on his camera. Inevitably, some of the locations included pubs and clubs. But there were also shots of Harry looking in shop windows, talking to prostitutes, chatting to stall holders in Berwick Street Market, and posing behind the counter in Sidney's shop.

The artist was pleased with the results, so he enlisted Harry's help in securing other subjects to enable him to work from the images the photographer supplied. This proved easy for Harry who, over the years living in the area, had established friendships with a large cross section of Soho residents. Perhaps the most notable of these portraits was of Henriette Moraes. Like Bacon and Harry, she was a regular at the Colony Room and other drinking holes in Soho. An artist's model, she had been married three times and had numerous love affairs, including one with Bacon's artist friend and rival, Lucien Freud. Moraes was a renowned foul-mouthed hedonist whose appetite for drink and drugs was legendary. The sixties had seen her enter a hippie phase. An amphetamine fuelled psychotic episode saw her arrested for a failed burglary and receive a sentence in Holloway Prison. Sensing her decline, Bacon asked Harry to photograph Moraes nude on a bed pretending to inject herself with a syringe filled with heroin.

Henrietta was for a change relatively sober when she arrived at Harry's studio for the shoot. At the age of 35, she was an attractive woman. Her flowing black hair, matching colour eyes, high cheek bones, long neck, and ample bosom, obviously proved key attributes for the many men she had shared a bed with. Surprisingly, she was a little shy undressing in front of the photographer.

Eventually, she came round to following Harry's directions for the various poses he required. Lying on the bed, she held the syringe in place on her arm and moved her body into different positions as the camera shutters snapped continuously. It was only when Harry instructed her to open her legs wide that she baulked.

'Nobody said anything about close-ups of my fanny,' she complained.

'Francis specifically requested that I get a few shots with your lady garden in full view,' Harry responded.

'I'm not going to end up in one of your porno mags for pervs to ogle at, am I?'

'Don't be daft,' Harry said. 'Regrettably, I don't have such a thing anymore. Besides, I don't know what you are griping about. Let's face it, hundreds of blokes have seen your welcome mat in the flesh before!'

Moraes laughed at this and shouted: 'Bastard, but it's true I suppose.'

Thumbing through the contact sheets with Harry as he rolled up some Gold Leaf tobacco in a Rizla cigarette paper, Bacon was generally happy with the outcome of the shoot.

‘My, my, once little Hen has certainly put on a few pounds of late. All that booze, I guess. Her tits, belly, and arse are magnificent. It certainly gives me plenty to work with,’ the artist quipped. ‘Not sure about the vag patch ones though. But for what I have in mind, it doesn’t matter.

‘I’m loving all the other photos you’ve taken of Sohoites. The thing is I will only be able to use a fraction of them, so I’ve had an idea. Why don’t I talk to my friends at the Mount Gallery regarding putting on an exhibition of your images? You have said they did it before with your stuff back in the fifties. Why not again?’

Harry liked the notion of regaining the celebrity status he had once enjoyed but was nevertheless, somewhat apprehensive: ‘I parted on good terms with the owners, so no problems in that respect. It’s just that things have moved on since then, and I’m not sure that they would be keen on shots of London’s low life. Don’t forget the gallery is the province of the ruling classes.’

‘Utter bollocks. For one thing, the ownership has changed and they’re much more open to running exhibitions that will appeal to all sectors of the public. I mean, your last one there was all tits and bums, and from what I understand, was a great success. At least let me try Harry. You could include some of the shots you've taken at Ronnie Scott's too,' Bacon pointed out.

Harry finally agreed and thanked the artist. They then toasted the decision with a couple of bottles of wine before heading out on their usual circuit of pubs and clubs. Conversations amongst their Bohemian counterparts ranged from politics in the form of Britain's Prime Minister, Harold Wilson, travelling to Moscow to initiate peace talks to end the war in Vietnam; to England beating West Germany 4-2 in the football World Cup. More localised topics included the opening of the 34-storey Centre Point building close by opposite the Dominion Theatre, and worryingly for Harry, the news that the police were questioning the Krays regarding the murder of George Cornell, a member of the rival Richardson's criminal gang, in The Blind Beggar pub in Whitechapel. It was widely speculated around the London pubs that Ronnie Kray had shot Cornell for calling him a "fat poof" at an altercation that took place at the Astor Club around Christmas 1965.

It was a fact that introductions from the Kray Twins had tailed off recently and Harry assumed that this was the reason. Clearly, they had other priorities than to feed their photographer pal with business leads.

Two major blows that shook Harry's

confidence followed in quick succession.

The first was a letter from Trisha's solicitor petitioning for divorce. He was already barely able to keep up the maintenance payments to his first wife, Marie. Another tranche of outlay monthly would prove a real struggle.

Francis Bacon tried to soften the impact of the second setback by treating Harry to dinner at Wheeler's. During the meal, he advised his friend that the Mount Gallery had rejected his suggestion of running an exhibition of Harry's photographs. He conceded that Harry had been correct in his assumption that the owners were only interested in more avant-garde exhibits. Frankly, they regarded Harry as yesterday's news.

Thankfully, Harry's work at Ronnie Scott's kept him busy most evenings. A particular performance of note was by the acclaimed American jazz musician, Roland Kirk. Harry took some great shots of the multi-instrumentalist during his act playing the tenor and soprano saxophones, the flute, and the penny whistle. But even this work that had provided a lifeline to Harry was in danger of ending.

Ronnie Scott had become a manic depressive. The worry of servicing the huge debt he and his partner, Pete King, had taken on to get the club open was beginning to take its toll.

In addition to his heavy drinking, Ronnie had, like so many other talented musicians, turned to drugs. On stage he was still the genial joker host introducing acts with one-liners such as: "This guy is the best trumpet player in the country. In the city, he's crap." However, out of the spotlight, he was struggling with his mental health. Together with Ronnie's wife Mary, Harry tried to help his friend. Sadly, their efforts were in vain. Ronnie became more distant from his friends and relatives. Consequently, Pete King had no alternative but to start cutting costs to keep the club open. Harry's contract was one of the first casualties.

By the beginning of 1967, Harry's financial position had become dire. Work projects had completely dried up. Most of his contacts on the picture desks of the newspapers and magazines had gone, replaced with a younger breed who were not interested in hiring what they considered a dinosaur from a previous era. To stave off the threats of eviction from his studio by the landlord for non-payment of rent, Harry rashly decided to sub-let the premises.

Bella and Branka were two prostitutes that Harry had known for some time. Indeed, they had featured in his ill-fated series of portraits of Soho residents for the exhibition that never materialised. The women were different from their competitors in that the services they provided were akin to a double act. In their mid-thirties, they were Serbian by birth, and supremely fit. Their modus operandi was to entertain clients with an acrobatic act clad in leather underwear, prior to administering mild punishment with whips to the client during sexual intercourse. As the lease had expired on their current flat further up Wardour Street, they were seeking a new base, and the large space that the studio afforded was ideal.

B&B, as Harry referred to the ladies, did not work under the control of a pimp. They were more than able to handle any client payment disputes themselves. Each of their sessions did not last longer than thirty minutes and were restricted to the hours between seven and eleven in the evening. This suited Harry as most nights, he would be out with Francis Bacon and his entourage at these times. His artist friend generously funded these binges, so Harry was not called upon to contribute.

A deal was reached by both parties and initially, things worked well. Harry received regular income from B&B which enabled him to cover the cost of the studio's rent. But after two months, an incident occurred that was problematic. During a session, a burly client had reacted badly to the whipping element and a fight broke out in the studio.

On hearing the rumpus, neighbours in the building who were already unhappy about the activities of Bella and Branka, called the police. The client insisted to the officers that he had been assaulted by B&B who were in the process of robbing him. The women denied this accusation and the man was led away. However, the policemen warned the prostitutes that if there was any reoccurrence of such trouble, they would be charged.

In the heat of the altercation, some of Harry's photographic equipment was damaged beyond repair. B&B apologised to Harry and assured him he would be reimbursed for the damage. But just a few days later when the women were entertaining another guest in the studio, four policemen and a policewoman burst in and arrested all three of them. Harry returned to the studio around two o' clock the following morning after a night drinking with Bacon and his friends. Two police officers were waiting and arrested him. They took him to Tottenham Court Road police station where he was charged with running a brothel and living off immoral earnings.

'Thanks for standing bail for me,' Harry said to Francis Bacon as they walked down the steps of the police station at lunchtime later that day. It was the end of January and sleet was falling through a murky overcast sky.

‘It was fucking freezing in that cell. The bastards wouldn’t even let me pick up my coat before they whisked me out of the studio.’

‘Let’s get you round to the Fitzroy Tavern for some grub and a few stiffeners. That should warm you up,’ Bacon suggested.

Once inside the pub, Harry attacked the bowl of tomato soup and crusty rolls he was served as though he hadn’t eaten for days. In between mouthfuls of food and scotch, he continued his outburst about the way he had been treated by the police.

‘They had no right to pounce on me like that. Anybody would think I’m a hardened criminal. I was totally set up. The neighbours obviously tipped off the law. And those shit bags have been waiting for the chance to get me since my previous run-ins with them. They’re trying to fit me up like they did Stephen Ward on the same charges.’

Bacon was trying his best to calm Harry down. ‘Don’t worry, I’ll pay for a good brief to get you off. That and a bit of palm greasing for senior officers at the nick should do the trick. I won’t let a mate go down, well not in that way,’ he laughed.

Harry was still fuming but nevertheless grateful that he had a friend with sway who could help him. Switching the focus of his rant, Harry asked his friend:

‘Have you seen that new film, “Blowup.” It stars David Hemmings and Vanessa Redgrave.’

‘Not yet,’ Bacon cautiously replied.

‘Well, Hemming’s role as the randy fashion photographer is based on me. No question about it. There are bits in the film that exactly mirror things that have happened to me. I should have been paid a fee or at least contracted as a consultant on the film. Do you think I could sue? I’m that desperate for readies.’

‘I think you’d have a difficult job proving your case. As far as I’m aware, the script is based on a book by some Italian author. The film’s lawyers would claim that there was never any conscious attempt to use your career as a template for the film. Besides, they would have mega bucks to back their case if it went to court,’ Bacon warned.

‘Point taken. I’m sorry to burden you with all my woes but it’s just that things seem to be getting out of control.’

After several more drinks, Harry thanked Bacon again and the two men parted outside the Fitzroy Tavern. Harry made his way back to the studio. It only took ten minutes to walk but by the time he arrived, he was soaked from the sleet that was still falling. On arrival he tried to open the door but found that his key would not fit. There was an envelope addressed to him sellotaped to the door. Harry opened it and read the letter from his landlord. It stated that Harry had contravened the terms of his lease by subletting and causing disturbances that were unacceptable to other residents. If he wished to retrieve the contents of the studio, he should contact the bailiff's office shown, and make an appointment. They would then open the studio and their staff would allow Harry to take any property that was rightfully his.

Grasping the letter, Harry lent his back against the door and slid down to the floor onto his bottom. He put his head in his hands and started to cry.

For the umpteenth time, Sidney Solomon came to the rescue by providing Harry with somewhere to stay. He also helped his friend to move his things out of the studio and store them in the basement of the shop. However, he made it clear to Harry that he could not lend him any money. As more competitors had opened around the Soho area, Sidney's profits from his shop had fallen sharply.

To Harry's great relief, Francis Bacon had somehow managed to carry out what he had promised over drinks in the Fitzroy Tavern. The police charges against Harry were dropped and he was issued with a caution. He learnt subsequently that Bella and Branka were not so lucky. They had been fined for soliciting but had paid and were once again plying their trade using a flat in Carlisle Street as their base.

In the months that followed, Harry's drinking became more acute. To fund this, he sold his remaining cameras and photographic equipment. And when the proceeds had evaporated, he began selling photographs of nude models including the shots of Henrietta Moraes undercarriage for ten shillings each in pubs around Soho. Any hopes he had of the Krays resuming their introductions for assignments were dashed on the news the Twins had been arrested for the murders of George Cornell and Jack McVitie. From the sale of his paintings, Francis Bacon acquired a house in Chelsea. And at the same time, he disowned most of his Soho drinking buddies including Harry.

For two more years, Harry lived off the generosity of his lifelong friend Sidney. Harry's drunken behaviour and failure to pay bar bills he had run up led to him being banned from most of his old haunts in Soho. He was taken to court by his former wives Marie and Trisha's solicitors for not making maintenance payments. But it was clear that he was effectively bankrupt with no assets and therefore, could not pay.

It was a clammy evening on 29th July 1969.

Harry was laying on the grass near the top of Hampstead Heath vaguely aware it was his fiftieth birthday. As dusk descended giving the sky a dull mushy complexion, he tightly gripped a half bottle of whisky with just the dregs remaining. The sounds of a Wurlitzer style organ floated up from the fairground rides in full swing at the foot of the Heath. Tilting his head sidewards, he caught sight of the block of flats where he had once lived in luxury. And he began to reflect on his life, likening it to Hogarth's series of paintings, "The Rake's Progress." He had seen them at the Sir John Soane's Museum in Lincoln's Inn Fields, a few doors away from the barrister's office he had dealings with in the past.

Harry knew he had originally come from a privileged background, albeit tainted with the criminality of his forefathers. Despite the death of his father when he was an infant, he had enjoyed a happy childhood. It was the loss of his beloved mother and his Uncle Lenny during his early adulthood that had really hit him hard. He wondered whether it was this that had led him to treat the women in his life so badly.

His fall from grace had not been spectacular. It was more of a gradual process spanning many years. How could he have frittered away fortunes on whims of impetuosity? In hindsight, he thought he would have loved to have had children. But his selfishness, unsuccessful relationships and drinking had put pay to this.

Despite a doctor's recent warning that unless he stopped drinking, the cirrhosis of the liver he was suffering from would lead to his imminent death, he had been unable to give it up. If anything, his consumption had increased. It had become clear to him that his guardian angel, for so long his saviour, had finally deserted him. It was this conclusion that caused a tear to trickle out from under his glasses down his cheek.

Feeling thoroughly dejected, he rolled over and fell into a deep sleep. He was awakened by a sharp prod in his buttocks. Looking up he saw a parkkeeper holding a walking stick. All at once his teenage years came flooding back to him. In particular, the time he was caught in flagrante with a girlfriend in some bushes not far from his present location.

'Dirty pisshead. Bugger off before I whistle for the police. There's plenty of 'em down there on duty at the fair,' the keeper shouted.

Harry smiled benignly, rose unsteadily to his feet, and staggered down the hill to the bus terminus to catch a number 24 back to the West End. As he passed the fairground, he saw excited young children tightly gripping transparent plastic bags filled with water containing a goldfish. Oh, to be a kid again he thought.

EPILOGUE

After delaying for what seemed like an eternity, he pressed the buzzer marked Jacks. From above came the sound of a creaking door hitting a latch. This was followed by a series of slow steps on stairs that squealed even under the pressure of her lightweight steps. The bottom stair was reached, and the door swung open outwards causing him to take a short step backwards. The King of the Camera and the Queen of Fitzrovia looked at one another for the first time in over two decades.

In total contrast to his appearance, despite seven years his senior, she looked good.

Without saying a word, as though they had been out of each other's company for just a few hours, she beckoned him to follow her up the two flights of stairs. He did as directed noting the location of the bathroom and toilet at the midway stage had not changed. Despite the recent installation of a handrail, there were dirty hand marks on the walls presumably made by other residents in the building to steady themselves following a heavy night out. The house had, since his last visit, obviously been converted into flats.

Once inside her flat, Marie Jacks pointed to a

chair at the kitchen table and Harry Levi sat. 'Cup of tea?' she asked. 'Got anything stronger?' was his subdued reply. 'Sorry, no, I don't do it much these days. Just the odd mini bottle of red wine from the off license,' she replied. 'Tea's fine thanks, two sugars,' Harry said.

Marie went over to the kettle, flicked the switch and grabbed a couple of mugs before opening the ancient fridge for the milk. Harry looked around. Amazingly, nothing much had changed since he was last here all those years ago. The table and chairs, Welsh dresser and kitchen cabinets were the same ones as before. The walls had been painted cream but needed another coat. The ceiling also was crying out for a refresh of white matt. The patterned carpet, whilst clean, was very old-fashioned and worn in places. A potential trip hazard he thought.

The kettle boiled and Marie poured the water onto two tea bags in the chipped brown tea pot. As they waited for the tea to draw, they viewed one another across the big round table, blue and white striped mugs at the ready with milk and sugars in each. Neither of them wanted to be the first to speak but when they did, they did so at the same time. Harry gestured for her to go first but she insisted that he should take the lead. After all she thought, it was he who had come a calling and she was intrigued to ascertain his motives, albeit that she had a shrewd idea what they were.

So began his tale of woe. He freely admitted that he had been an alcoholic for many years. His second wife had left six years ago, and he was living in the Salvation Army Hostel in Judd Street not far from St Pancras Station. Prior to this, his dear friend, Sidney Solomon, had been putting him up for some time, but the strain of Harry's drink problem had become too much for both parties. He had been declared bankrupt last year and was penniless, apart from his dole money, most of which went on Scotland's finest.

Almost reluctantly it seemed, within his preamble, he sewed in enquiries about Marie's mother, Esther, the Russian émigré, his fearsome one-time mother-in-law, who had been his nemesis in terms of how he treated her daughter. He also asked after her brothers, Rudi and Izzy, who had equally given him a hard time about the way he had ditched their little sister. 'All passed away, I light a candle for them every Friday night,' she stated without emotion.

Marie had already guessed where this was leading and therefore it was no surprise when the "tap" as she called it came. But what did surprise her was what accompanied it. In addition to a request for money, he asked if he could stay in her flat until he kicked the booze and got himself back on the straight and narrow. ‘All above board of course,’ he said. ‘I could sleep in the spare room.’ His facial expression had become pleading as though he was about to burst into tears.

Marie had always been a caring person. Indeed, that is why her voluntary work for Camden Council, had earned her the title in the local press as the Queen of Fitzrovia. But she was never what could be called a “soft touch.”

Marie waited for a few seconds to collect her thoughts before replying. ‘I can help you with some money to tide you over but staying here at the flat is a non-starter.’

This was more than he had expected, and he slowly said, ‘I fully understand, that’s really good of you, I’ll pay you back.’ She knew this was never going to happen but remained silent. She got up and went over to the stack of plates on the dresser and lifted half of them off putting them to one side. She counted out five crisp new twenty pounds notes. This was savings she had withdrawn from her Post Office account in Newman Street in recent weeks.

‘Here you go,’ she said, handing him the money. He took the notes and put them in his pocket. 'Don't drink it away in one go,' she said firmly. Whilst thanking her profusely, he bowed his head and mumbled unconvincingly he wouldn't and that the cash would help him tremendously. Sensing this was his cue to leave, he rose and gave her a gentle hug, promising that he would be in touch.

As the flat's door closed behind him and the door at the bottom of the stairs slammed closed, she sat down and knew that she would never see him alive again.

She was proved right. Just under a year later, Marie stood in the smallest chapel at Golders Green Crematorium in north London alongside her nephew who had driven her there. For June, the weather was pleasantly warm with blue skies and cotton wool clouds. The Crematorium was situated on a steep hill with commanding views over the surrounding area.

They had arrived well in advance of the scheduled service time as Marie had asked if her nephew would take her to the grave of his father, her elder brother, who was buried in the Spanish and Portuguese Jewish Cemetery directly opposite the Crem. She also wanted to see the plaque for his mother, her sister-in-law, and those of some of the famous stars Marie had met during her time with Harry, which were located around the Crematorium grounds.

On the path to the grave, they passed a plaque that her nephew had arranged to be placed in front of a vibrant yellow rose bush now in full bloom. The plaque bore the name of his father's close family relatives including that of Marie. At his father's graveside, he recited the Kaddish, the Jewish prayer for the dead as the date coincided with the anniversary of the death of his dad. Like his father, he was not a religious person and read out the words of the prayer in English as he did not speak Hebrew. Marie shed a tear as the memories of her childhood with her beloved brothers entered her mind. In line with Jewish tradition, they both placed a stone on the grave which symbolises the permanence of memory whereas flowers die after a short period of time.

Slowly, they made their way back to the grounds of the Crematorium. Having spent a short time in silent thought while at the plaque for his mother that was also adjacent to a blooming yellow rose bush, they moved barely a matter of yards before coming to the plaque for Peter Sellers, the star of radio and film. Marie reminisced about the time when, very early in his career, before the big time occurred, she had cornered him in the Grafton Arms pub near Victoria Station whilst he was drinking with his friend Harry Secombe who years later would become his co-star in the Goon Show. Marie convinced both to order 100 black and white photographs of themselves that they could sign and give out to fans. Before they had time to consider the proposition, Marie waved to Harry who was standing nearby camera at the ready and he quickly created an individual head and shoulders pose for each. The photographs were duly delivered to the pub for Sellers and Secombe's collection later that week. According to Marie, Secombe paid for the goods, but Sellers never did. 'That's stardom for you,' she snorted.

The time of the service was getting closer but further stops were made at the plaques for the "Carry On" films stars Sid James and Bernard Bresslaw, the harmonica player Larry Adler, jazz saxophonist and Soho club owner, Ronnie Scott and Bud Flanagan the music hall artiste and comedian who was one of Harry's heroes. Marie had met some of them all through her photo sales work with Harry.

Fortunately, her nephew knew the location of these plaques having escorted his aunt to them on previous visits to the grounds. Although the comments she uttered on such occasions were the same, he never bored of them and admired her powers of recollection of events that took place decades previously.

Finally, back at the chapel, they were surprised to see just thirteen people in attendance. No sign of the other ex-wife. A poor turnout for somebody who had led such an eventful life encountering literally hundreds of famous and infamous people. There was no printed order of service with photographs of the deceased which had become the norm at funerals in recent years. Strange, bearing in mind the man in the cheap coffin had made and lost fortunes for his photography.

Although he was born into the Jewish faith Harry had not been in any way religious. The short service therefore was devoid of biblical content. It was conducted by his life-long friend Sidney Solomon who in later years had suffered from a hip disorder but struggled to the lectern with the aid of a silver capped walking cane, a poignant prop from his days on the theatre circuit with Harry. Sidney's eulogy was heartfelt but sanitised in terms of Harry's days of associating with criminals, drinking, womanising and the pornographic photography and film work. No references were made to his less appealing character traits such as being impulsive, immodest, bossy, boastful, and egotistical. Summing up Sidney invited those present back to the nearby pub of music hall song fame, The Old Bull and Bush. He joked that Harry would have approved because of his deep love of the music hall but added he would have wanted everyone to pay for their own drinks.

Marie had earlier agreed with her nephew that they would not attend the wake. 'Too many *schnorrers*, too many memories,' she had said.

As Sidney finished the words of the committal, something happened that made everybody present burst out laughing. The coffin started to move slowly along the electric powered rollers towards the doors through which it would pass to its final destination. Suddenly, one of the rollers stuck causing the coffin to halt and bop up and down. Sidney quipped that it was typical of Harry to make a dramatic exit.

A chapel steward stepped forward and rectified the problem with the rollers and the coffin passed through the doors. As it did, Marie stared at it and whispered, 'Shalom Harry.'

◆ ◆ ◆

GLOSSARY

Alte kakers – Old people
Arrivederci – Goodbye
Bastardos - Bastards
Bubbleleh – Term of endearment
Fanculo – Fuck you
Feckin – Fucking
Fershers – Person wandering aimlessly
Fershtinkiner – A louse or stinker
Fershtinkiner chaser – Smelly pig
Fresser – Someone who eats too quickly
Gelt - Money
Grazie – Thank you
Gvir – Wealthy person
Haimisha cucumber – Pickled gherkin
Hanukah – Jewish religious festival
Hoyzn – Underwear
In piedi – Stand
Kaddish – Jewish prayer for the dead
Kriah – Jewish custom at funerals of tearing clothing
Mamma Mia – My goodness
Mamzer – Moaner
Mazeltov – Cheers!
Molto bene – Very well
Mosher – Mate
Mushuganahs – Mad people
Nonna – Grandmother

Numi – Sleep
Putain de merde – Holy shit
Putz – Male genitals
Schiemiels – Fools
Schmuter – Poor quality clothing
Schnorrer – Mean person
Schtum – Quiet
Shicker – Drunk
Shiksa – Non-Jewish female
Si – Yes
Spiel – Chat-up
Stupido – Stupid
Tachrichim – Traditional white burial clothing
Tahara – Cleansing of the body
Testicolis – Testicles
Tokhes – Arse

ACKNOWLEDGEMENTS

My heartfelt thanks to my brilliant editor Linda Moore. She has patiently aided me throughout the writing process, checking copy and suggesting changes. Thanks also to Kate Parker who created the eye-catching cover design.

ABOUT THE AUTHOR

Mike Bugsgang

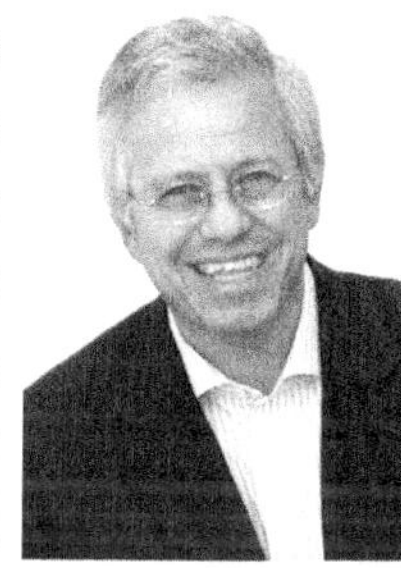

Mike Bugsgang was born and has lived in London his entire life. He has a deep love of the capital and has worked in it throughout his career. Prior to setting up his own marketing & PR consultancy, he held senior positions in the travel and tourism industry. These included Marketing Manager of the London Tourist Board and Public Relations Director of Hilton International Hotels. Mike is a Freeman of the City of London and a Liveryman of the Worshipful Company of Marketors.

Printed in Great Britain
by Amazon

50614446R00364